# Stoicism in Renaissance English Literature

# American University Studies

Series IV
English Language and Literature

Vol. 82

PETER LANG
New York • Bern • Frankfurt am Main • Paris

Audrey Chew

# Stoicism in Renaissance English Literature

## An Introduction

PETER LANG
New York • Bern • Frankfurt am Main • Paris

**Library of Congress Cataloging-in-Publication Data**

Chew, Audrey
  Stoicism in renaissance English literature.
    (American university studies. Series IV, English
language and literature; vol. 82)
    Bibliography: p.
    Includes index.
    1. English literature — Early modern, 1500-1700 — in
literature.  2. Stoics — Influence.  3. Ethics in
literature.  4. Philosophy in literature.  5. Renaissance
— Great Britain.  I. Title.  II. Series.
PR418.S74C48      1988        820'.9'384        88-866
ISBN 0-8204-0730-5
ISSN 0741-0700


**CIP-Titelaufnahme der Deutschen Bibliothek**

**Chew, Audrey:**
Stoicism in renaissance English literature : an
introd. / Audrey Chew. — New York; Bern;
Frankfurt am Main; Paris: Lang, 1988.
  (American University Studies: Ser. 4,
  English Language and Literature; Vol. 82)
  ISBN 0-8204-0730-5

NE: American University Studies / 04

Printed by Weihert-Druck GmbH, Darmstadt, West Germany

For B. B.

## ACKNOWLEDGMENTS

I should like to thank the staffs of the following libraries:  the Peabody Library in Baltimore, the Johns Hopkins University Library, the Library of Congress, the library of the
University of California at Berkeley, the Mills College library, and the Mesa Public Library in Los Alamos, N. M.
Material from Sir William Temple's Five Miscellaneous
Essays, ed. Samuel Holt Monk, is reprinted by permission of
the University of Michigan Press.  Material from Robert Burton's
The Anatomy of Melancholy, ed. Floyd Dell and Paul Jordan-Smith,
is reprinted by permission of Amiel Book Distributors Corpora-
tion.

## CONTENTS

# CONTENTS

# Chapter I.  Background

Those of us who have wandered through the usual courses
in the history of English literature have grown accustomed
to meeting here and there the fuzzy word "Stoic," and have
usually hurried past with a vague feeling that we have brushed
something slightly unpleasant.  In the beginning we may
obediently have jotted "stoic" with a small s beside an
Old English lyric or have written "Boethian Stoic" beside
a passage in Chaucer; but with the passing centuries a dim
sense of confusion was likely to surface as we discovered
that in the sixteenth and seventeenth centuries Stoicism
was sometimes associated with self-sacrificing patriotism,
at other times with rampant individualism, here with melancholy malcontents, there with contented happy men, while
in the eighteenth century it had links first with Deism
and later with the American and French revolutions.  In
the nineteenth century we found Shelley now and then toying
with Stoic physics and Matthew Arnold praising Marcus Aurelius.
In the twentieth century there are the Existentialists,
who are sometimes said to be only one more Stoic manifestation.
These few obvious examples indicate that a subject that
may at first seem thoroughly dead is not only very much
alive but also large.[1]  In its best-known, moral, branch
it embraces not only private morality but also law and
politics, while the areas of logic and physics are still
receiving attention from the experts.  In trying to follow
the tangled thread, therefore, we are forced to abandon
the idea that we can find one simple all-embracing definition;
for ideas that have power are ideas that can adapt themselves
to changing circumstances.  As Heraclitus, an important
ancestor of the Stoics, reportedly said, "You cannot step
twice into the same rivers; for fresh waters are ever flowing
in upon you."[2]  First of all, then, it is necessary to accept
the fact that Stoicism, which is sometimes described as
a philosophy, sometimes as a religion, and sometimes as
merely an attitude, has a variety of meanings, all of which
are continually changing color.  Next, we must remember
that an important characteristic of Stoicism, throughout
its history, has been its versatility as a good mixer, which
means that it is as difficult to find a pure Stoic as to
find pure water.  Where Stoicism in its legendary pure state
has been consistently ridiculed, Stoicism when combined
with other sets of ideas has had a pervasive influence
on Western culture.  Over the centuries the rational, emotionless Stoic, who soon reveals himself as an idealistic man
of faith, continues to pit himself against his doubting
opponent (sometimes a Skeptic, sometimes an Epicurean) as
he tries to defend his unshakable confidence that the soul
of the universe is both reasonable and benevolent, that
absolute moral truth actually exists, that truth is more
or less easily available through common sense, and that
obedience to the unwritten moral law provides the key to
the problem of how to live.  The Stoic faith in absolute

truth has led to the ambiguity that comes from ignoring
history and assuming that words have one clear meaning.
For the favorite Stoic words, "nature," "reason," "virtue,"
and "apathy," are all of them vague generalizations that
change their connotations with their environments.

As an eclectic philosophy, composed of ingredients
borrowed from other philosophies and religions, the Stoic
doctrine, which was not entirely homogeneous even in the
beginning, has undergone many modifications and combinations.
Not only did different early teachers emphasize different
aspects of the creed, but later teachers soon began the
long process of combining Stoic ideas with other sets of
ideas, such as, Aristotelianism, Epicureanism, Christianity,
and Neo-Platonism. As a consequence, the frequent practice
of dividing the history of Classical Stoicism into three
neat phases, early, middle, and late, is not always as helpful
as it might be. Some writers prefer to talk about the older
and younger Stoics or simply to distinguish between primitive
Stoicism (the tenets of the founding fathers) and historical
Stoicism--thus reminding us that there is always a difference
between the mathematical ideal and the historical fact.
Although primitive Stoicism, for instance, stressed moral
self-sufficiency, historical Stoicism has often interpreted
self-discipline primarily as social duty. Among those who
have talked about Stoicism or Neo-Stoicism in English literature of the sixteenth and seventeenth centuries there have
been some in recent years who have tended to over-emphasize
the private kind of Stoicism and consequently to ignore
the large branch that interests historians of law or political
science and that is just as evident in English literature
as the private kind. There is also a tendency to over-emphasize
the influence on literary men of such sixteenth-century
"Neo-Stoic" scholars as Justus Lipsius and to see the thinking
of such specialists behind any writer who subordinates Stoic
fate to Christian providence, although that accommodation
was an old one that a writer need not necessarily have learned
from Lipsius.

The familiar story of early or older or primitive Stoicism,
which begins in Athens around 300 B.C., during the Alexandrian
period, generally emphasizes individualism, since Stoicism
at that time offered one response to the disruption of familiar
values that accompanied the breakdown of the Greek city
state. Zeno of Citium, the father of Stoicism, who lived
between the fourth and third centuries, B.C., came to Athens
from Cyprus and after a period of study set himself up as
a teacher in the Stoa or porch from which Stoicism takes
its name. The doctrines that he and the other early Stoics
taught, which were mainly an outgrowth of the teachings
of such earlier Greek philosophers as Heraclitus, Socrates,
and the Cynics, may also include some ideas from the religions
of Persia and India. It is sometimes pointed out, for instance,
that there are similarities between some elements of early

Stoicism and some elements of Buddhism, while, later on,
we find historians referring to similarities between Roman
Stoicism and the Confucianism of China. Along with Zeno
there were a number of other teachers who contributed ideas,
but the early Stoics most frequently mentioned by literary
men are Zeno, Cleanthes, and Chrysippus, whose names occur
often in the essays of Cicero and Seneca. It happens that
most of the writings of these almost-legendary founding
fathers have been lost and that, except for a few fragments,
our knowledge depends on compilations made several centuries
later, sometimes by writers unsympathetic with the ideas
they were reporting. In the usual way, unkind criticism
has often been repeated as fact and has supplied the basis
for many a Stoic caricature in English literature.[3]
    Although Stoicism in English literature of the Middle
Ages and the Renaissance usually concentrates on Stoic answers
to the practical problems of how to live, with relatively
little interest in Stoic physics, as the story continues
into the nineteenth and twentieth centuries, Stoic physical
theories occasionally turn up. Whether or not Stoic physics
was originally simply a justification for Stoic morality,
the fact remains that Stoic morality is directly related
to Stoic physics and that a few rudimentary remarks about
physics are necessary. Stoic physical theory, which goes
back ultimately to the theories of Heraclitus (sixth-fifth
century, B.C.), considers everything in nature to be fated
because everything is part of an eternally repeating cyclic
process.[4] In Stoic theory all things are composed of the
four elements--fire, water, earth, and air--which elements
change in due process into one another. At the end of the
great cycle (sometimes called the Platonic year) all these
are consumed by the primary element, intellectual fire or
ether; and then everything starts all over again. As Shelley
says in Hellas, "The world's great age begins anew." We
are all familiar with such axioms as that Stoics are fatalists,
that Stoics believe in a universe governed by law, and that
a good Stoic accepts the fact of mutability without complaint.
What these ideas may mean in actual practice, however, is
what makes the story interesting. Although many Stoic ideas
were early acceptable to Christians, some were not. If
references to mutability and fate are literary commonplaces,
the idea of an ever-repeating, unending cycle of history
did not mesh easily with Christian teaching and had to wait
for a time when writers like Shelley and Yeats and Joyce
were free to toy with unorthodox ideas. Because everything
in history belongs to the great ever-repeating cycle, logically
Stoic physics excludes the notion of progress--possibly
one reason why some Stoics emphasize doing one's duty and
accepting the facts of life instead of trying to change
the world or win lasting fame. However, not all Stoics
accepted or remembered the theory of cycles; and, illogical
though it may seem, fatalism did not include the idea that

moral evil is part of the plan. It is no safer to assume
that all Stoics are what is known as "fatalists" in the
sense of defeatists than it is to assume that all Christians
interpret accepting the will of God as being placidly content
with the way things are.

The ambiguous Stoic concept of god has made it possible
to regard some Stoic writers as almost Christians, for although
it is customary for Christians to describe Stoics as atheists,
they have long made exceptions for favorite writers like
Seneca. Since the Stoics believed in an orderly universe
and since some Stoic writers used the word "god," it is
not surprising to find that the Stoic concept of god can
be adapted to other systems. During the centuries of Greek
and Roman Stoic history there were many ways of expressing
the principle that holds everything together: intellectual
fire, <u>pneuma</u>, reason, the will of god, god, fate, destiny,
providence, universal law, nature, reason of the world,
soul of the world, Jupiter, Zeus, ether, atmospheric current.[5]
We are all familiar with Wordsworth's description of "A
motion and a spirit, that impels / All thinking things,
all objects of all thought, / And rolls through all things"
and with Shelley's phrase, "the one spirit's plastic stress."
And though it is also customary to hear Stoics called pantheists
because they do not separate god from the universe, actually
some of them made a distinction between the ruler and the
ruled in the same way that man's reason was customarily
distinguished from his body. As Alexander Pope phrased it,
"All are but parts of one stupendous whole, / Whose body
nature is, and God the soul."[6] Since universal reason or
the law of nature are two synonyms for god, it is axiomatic
that the impersonal Stoic god does not act outside the law
and that the good Stoic does not expect special dispensations
to be made for him. As part of a universe where everything
operates according to law, the individual can only notice
how well everything fits together, how the four elements
are actually subdivisions of the primary element, intellectual
fire, and how the four virtues, justice, prudence, temperance,
and fortitude (which were originally Platonic virtues and
later became Christian virtues) are all subdivisions of
the one virtue, reason. Since we are all parts of the plan,
our job is simply to play our parts; for individual virtue
and happiness, on the one hand, and social virtue and happiness,
on the other, depend on cooperation with eternal law, which
is often referred to as the Stoic law of nature.[7]

Although the Stoics only acquired from their Greek
predecessors the notion that the universe is governed by
concealed laws, they were the ones who popularized it and
passed it on to the rest of us. How the Greeks first arrived
at the idea and where it originally came from are fascinating
questions that puzzle the experts.[8] Although the concept
that there are physical laws of nature is behind the development
of modern science, Stoic influence is primarily associated

with the idea that in addition to physical laws there are also
universal unwritten moral laws, an idea which appears in
Greek drama.  We think, for instance, of Antigone's refusal
to obey an edict of Creon that she regarded as contrary
to "the unwritten and unfailing statutes of heaven. . . .
[whose] life is not of today or yesterday but from all time."[9]
In addition the early Stoics derived this idea from Socrates'
statement that he had within himself an inner moral guide
that told him what not to do.[10]  In its Stoic form this
idea is behind much moral, legal, and political thinking.
We recall, in particular, the Roman legal tradition, which
propagated the powerful notion that the only just and binding
laws are the ones rooted in the laws of nature.  When we
try to find out what the laws of nature are, however, we
run into the difficulty that all along the line opinions
have differed; for if the laws are supposed to be universal
and readily available through common sense, so that the
individual can easily find them out for himself, in practice
it seems that only the hypothetical good man, who, according
to Seneca, is as rare as the phoenix, can really see them
clearly.  The rest of us need to rely on such approximations
as the consensus gentium and what our teachers tell us.[11]

      The early Stoics, who looked back to Socrates as a
saint, actually espoused a particular segment of Socratic
doctrine that came to them by way of Socrates' rigid disciples,
the Cynics, who taught that virtue is the one thing necessary
for the good life, that virtue means living according to
nature, and that living according to nature means living
so far as possible without the trappings of civilization,
sometimes, in fact, like savages or animals.  Anti-Stoic
caricatures are often based on the Cynic streak in Stoicism,
for the Cynics were extremists whose unconventional mode
of life shocked other members of society.  But the early
Stoics, although they were more extreme than the later ones,
were not quite so extreme as the Cynics.  When Zeno incorporated
Cynic doctrine into his own recipe for how to live, he widened
the definition of the key word "nature"[12] and softened some
of the less acceptable aspects of Cynic behavior.  While
agreeing that virtue goes with the simple life, the early
Stoics put less stress on living "naturally" in the sense
of living like an animal than on living "naturally" in the
sense of cooperating with the total cosmological system,
a vague idea that could be given many interpretations.[13]
By combining the physics of Heraclitus with Cynic advice
on how to live, the Stoics arrived at various formulas that
were more widely acceptable than the Cynic stress on total
unconventional personal integrity.  The Cynic aspect of
Stoicism, which has contributed to a lack of enthusiasm
for the development of technology and to a de-emphasis on
acquiring possessions, is familiar to us in such nineteenth-
century manifestations as Carlyle's admonition to lessen
our denominators or Emerson's complaint that "things are

in the saddle, and ride mankind." With the ideal of the
simple life the Cynics combined not only the Socratic belief
in an inner moral guide but also added a claim to be citizens
of the world--not merely Athenians or Corinthians--for they
argued that all men are basically alike and that local customs
and nationalities are merely artificial distinctions. This
important idea, another one that the Stoics acquired from
them, has received many different interpretations in the
course of its history and, like the other Cynic ideas, has
waxed and waned in popularity.[14] Finally, the Stoics borrowed
from the Cynics the idea of setting up heroes who would
typify their ideals. And much of our story revolves around
various literary manifestations of the Stoic hero or wise
man, whose changing form reflects changing interpretations
of the law of nature. Socrates himself early passed into
legend as one of these heroes or saints or sages, and so
did Diogenes the Cynic, whose continual debates with Alexander--
the symbol of everything the Cynics scorned--were so popular
in Medieval and Renaissance literature. Other heroes, some
mythical, some historical, some both, whom the Stoics adopted
for their calendar of saints are Hercules, Ulysses, Aeneas,
Cato, Brutus, and even--in later times--Adam, Moses, and
Solomon.[15] The Stoic hero or wise man, an ideal much talked
of, seldom seen, was often a godlike someone who had lived
long ago, though sometimes it was doubted whether he had
ever lived at all.[16] Supposed to be a perfect embodiment
of all the Stoic virtues, absolutely self-sufficient morally,
absolutely happy, this ideal man, though rare in life, has
a tendency to appear in fiction, where his attributes change
as definitions of virtue change. Sometimes he is human,
at other times a god or a demi-god. In fiction it is sometimes
his education or his overcoming of trials that provide the
plot. Sometimes he merely stands on the sidelines as an
ideal against which the imperfect struggling protagonist
can be measured. And, of course, he is often travestied
by anti-Stoics as an example of Stoic pride and exhibited
either as a figure of fun or as an emotionless monster.

The early Stoics, even though they were less extreme
in their behavior than the Cynics, still set up ideals of
behavior that were beyond the capacity of ordinary well-
intentioned human beings. They reportedly insisted, for
instance, that the wise man is absolutely perfect, that
the foolish man is absolutely perverse, and that all sins
are equally sinful. Refusing to consider individual differences, they argued that friendship is only possible between
virtuous men and that all virtuous men are automatically
friends--an absolutist position that makes friendship practically impossible and that has been frequently ridiculed
in literature. They also maintained that a nation populated
by good men would need no government, since men of integrity
would rule themselves by the laws of nature, an idea that
no nation has ever tried seriously but which has nevertheless

attracted such political idealists as Godwin and Shelley.[17]
In addition to despising wealth, the early or primitive
Stoics tried to argue that the wise man is without passion
and that pleasure is never a proper object of pursuit--doctrines
which in English literature earned them their title of sour
Stoics.[18] All these teachings, which come under the heading
of the mathematical ideal, were soon modified in actual
practice. As early as Chrysippus (third century, B.C.)
the number of things a Stoic might desire began to increase,
while the Roman Seneca, as we may remember, was a millionaire.[19]

The big dividing line between Stoics as self-sufficient
individualists and Stoics as self-sacrificing patriots comes
in the Roman period, which is sometimes divided into middle
and late Stoicism because some of the later Stoics like
Epictetus stood aside from the main stream and again stressed
individual self-sufficiency. Although from the point of
view of the English Renaissance the Roman period is the
important one, we need to distinguish between actual Stoic
ideas of the kind we associate with the Roman law tradition--
which may not always have come down to us with the Stoic
label still attached--and such things as anti-Stoicism--
generally based on a caricature of the early Stoics--and
Renaissance Senecanism--a blend of various elements, some
Stoic, some Epicurean, some neo-Platonic. In connection
with Renaissance Senecanism, we will do well to remember
the caution recently set down by Anthony Levi to the effect
that it can be seriously misleading to use the term "Neo-Stoic"
as if it clearly denoted the content of any one body of
moral doctrine.[20] Stoicism of the middle period is difficult
to date since it was the most generally accepted kind and
was never really superseded by what is known as late Stoicism.
Ludwig Edelstein, who reminds us that Roman Stoicism is
a major component of what we know as humanism, like other
commentators, calls attention to the general softening among
the Romans of the primitive Stoic harshness, a greater emphasis
on such virtues as brotherly love. He says, "Whereas the
Old Stoa considered wisdom, moderation, and courage to be
virtues in respect to the individual himself and summed
up his duties to others as justice, the younger Stoics emphasized the virtue of philanthropy, or humanitas, as the truly
altruistic virtue."[21]
With Roman Stoicism we particularly associate the name
of Cicero (106-43 B.C.), not because Cicero was himself
a professing Stoic but because he was a powerful disseminator
of Stoic ideas who was so effective in spreading what is
sometimes known as the middle-period brand of Stoicism that
the latter is often called simply humanism or Roman virtue
rather than Stoicism. Although aspects of Stoic morality
can be found in many of Cicero's works, the one most popular
in the Renaissance is his Of Duties (De Officiis, sometimes
called by the Elizabethans, "Tully's Offices"), which was

a free translation of a treatise by Panaetius of Rhodes
(185-109 B.C.), a work setting forth the ideal of the good
man as public servant.[22] Panaetius, often called the founder
of Roman Stoicism, was a pragmatist who combined Aristotelian
and Platonic ideas with the earlier Stoic mix in such a
way as to make the lonely self-sufficient ideal wise man
into a self-sacrificing, patriotic, member of the group--
whether soldier or civil servant. By combining the Stoic
idea "that an individual must play his part in the cosmic
drama and submit to his fate" with the Aristotelian ideas
that man is by nature a political creature and that the
whole is superior to the part, Stoic virtue was identified
with civilized patriotic cooperation instead of with rude
Cynic self-sufficiency.[23] Instead of the Cynic argument
that living according to nature meant living like a savage,
the argument now was that if man is by nature a rational
social animal, he can only be natural by behaving in a civilized manner. Not only was the civilized man preferred
to the savage, it was even argued that worldly possessions--
if properly used--could contribute to virtue. For Panaetius
laid particular stress on such social virtues as magnanimity
and benevolence that require one to be a man of property,
while he at the same time admired the active life more than
the studious or the contemplative. One of his influential
disciples was Scipio Africanus, the younger (185-129 B.C.),
who himself sometimes appears in English literature as a
symbol of a good Stoic.[24]

In addition to Panaetius, the other important philosopher
of Roman Stoicism was Posidonius (135-50 B.C.), who was
likewise much admired by Cicero. Where Panaetius might
loosely be described as a philosopher especially noted for
his concern with practical social problems, and one influential
Stoic who failed to accept the theory of cycles and the
idea of a periodic world conflagration, Posidonius continued
and expanded the earlier interest in physics; it was through
him that some of these ideas passed into the Christian tradition. Like Panaetius, however, Posidonius also contributed
to the process of transforming the lonely Stoic into a
cooperating member of the group; according to Hadas it was
he who interpreted the earlier doctrine that a wise man
is a citizen of the world in such a way as to identify world
citizenship with Roman patriotism.[25] In Roman Stoicism
the destiny of Rome tends to be seen as the law of nature
or the will of God. The result is that the history of Stoicism
has been able to include both the idea that the Stoic's
first allegiance is to his conscience, otherwise known as
the law of nature, and the idea that the Stoic's first duty
is to his country. Some Stoic-like characters in literature
are even to be found saying, "My country right or wrong,"
though stricter ones insist, "I am bound to lose my life
but not my conscience for my country." We must never forget

that any writer interested in miscellaneous Stoic ideas is free to adopt whichever ones he likes.[26]

Cicero, who was a contemporary and even a pupil of Posidonius, was a major prophet of the Stoic middle way; for Stoicism by now was so widely accepted that it had made the transition from esoteric philosophy to popular religion and had become the dominant upper-class Roman attitude, the habitual way of thinking of the Roman bureaucrat.  "Duty" is the word we associate with Roman Stoicism.  Playing out our role in the cosmic pattern, or accepting our fate, means doing our duty in such a way as to preserve the status quo.  Duty--so the theory goes--does not allow us to retire to the country in search of private peace of mind but requires an active life of public service, with peace of mind coming as a pleasant sense of satisfaction in a duty well done. Although Cicero did not claim to be a thorough-going Stoic, he was a great compiler of Stoic ideas to whose collections we owe much of what we know about the earlier Stoics.  More-over, the school of thought to which he did profess allegiance actually taught doctrines very similar to those of the diluted contemporary brand of Stoicism--especially on matters of practical conduct.  And Cicero was one of the world's masters of the art of communication.[27]

In addition to propagating Roman Stoic ideas about private morality, Cicero was also important in the history of politics and legal theory; for he accepted both the Stoic belief in a universal moral law and the teaching that all men are basically alike since all possess reason.[28]  Although the related teaching that all men are equal has been around a long time and has been repeated continuously, it has never been interpreted to everyone's satisfaction.  Even Cicero, though he accepted the idea in theory, deviated from it in practice.  In theory he exalted the supremacy of the law of nature while in practice he advised caution in inter-fering with local custom.  The distinction that Cicero accepted between man-made laws based on local custom and man-made laws based on the law of nature (or justice or truth) is one that has had a long history.  Although the laws based on custom are regarded as valid, for the time being, they are subject to change, while the eternally binding laws are the ones based on the laws of nature, which cannot be annulled.  Occasionally idealists go so far as to insist that statutory laws that oppose the law of nature need not be obeyed.  No matter how much skeptics may laugh, these ideas or ideals have been commonplaces of Western thinking; and one reason they have become commonplaces is that they were effectively spread by Cicero.[29]  When the Justinian compilation of Roman law was published in A.D. 533, it was based on philosophical ideas belonging to the Roman Stoic or Ciceronian tradition; and it has been a cliché of Western thinking that government should be exercised through law and that law should be based on morality--even though the

ways of interpreting these principles have been various.[30]
   Inside politics and outside politics, Cicero has been
influential in propagating the pervasive notion that whatever
is natural is good--another idea that has had many interpretations.  According to Lovejoy, "To the phraseology in which
nature is described as guide or model or standard Cicero
probably did more than any other Latin author to give currency
and sanctity."  Not only did he tell us that we ought to
obey the laws of nature, he also explained how to discover
them, choosing, as one might expect, a compromise position
between identifying truth with commonly received opinion
and relying too much on private intuition.  The problem
of how to read the laws of nature correctly is a perennial
one, for it is only in a stable homogeneous society that
it is easy to argue, as Stoics have often done, that the
important truths are self evident and convince us at once
merely by making a strong impression on us.  Although we
particularly associate with Cicero the idea that the laws
of nature are closely related to the consensus gentium, that
something believed by all people everywhere must be true,
nevertheless, says Lovejoy, he also furnished "the chief
classical text" for the idea that one can arrive at truth
through the light of nature alone.[31]  This idea, which goes
back to Plato but which has been much associated with the
Stoics, tends to surface when a poet sees himself as a self-
sufficient wise man with his own channel to moral truth.
To avoid the danger that what seems to be the consensus
gentium may only be the voice of the mob or that someone
else's intuition about the law of nature may only be subjective opinion, Cicero made the important reservation that
something accepted by all men everywhere must be true, "provided
the natural light of reason has not been corrupted in them."[32]
This useful proviso dealt handily with the recurring Stoic
difficulty of deciding when the truth is really the truth
and will turn up again and again during the Christian period
of Stoic history.  When majority opinion is acceptable to
a writer, he stresses the notion of consensus gentium; but
when he disagrees with customary thinking, he argues that
the basic insight of the people at large has been clouded
by luxurious living or corrupt institutions or other deviations
from the path of virtue. At such times, it is suggested,
the insight of a wise man--otherwise known as a poet-prophet--
is needed, a Milton or a Shelley perhaps, or a D. H. Lawrence.
   Over the centuries the three major Stoic ways of arriving
at the moral laws of nature--our own common sense, the original
insight of a wise man, and tradition--have fluctuated in
popularity.  Sometimes we are taught that the voice of the
people is the voice of God, sometimes that kings or poets
have superior insight, sometimes that we should study the
best that has been thought and said.  The Greek and Roman
Stoics, who tended to de-emphasize individual intuition
in favor of a proper education, derived from Socrates not

only the idea of an innate moral sense but also the idea
that virtue must be learnt.  Even Epictetus, for all his
emphasis on self-sufficiency, said that education is necessary "that we may learn so to adjust our preconceptions
of rational and irrational to particular conditions as to
be in harmony with nature."[33]  Again and again we discover
that everyone will agree to such vague generalizations
as that to be wise is the same thing as being virtuous,
that following nature means being ruled by reason, that
reality is not that which actually is but that which ought
to be, that the customs of any time and place may be based
on reality but may also be based on false appearances. The
trouble starts as soon as we try to get down to specifics.

     As a character in literature, Cicero himself occasionally
appears as a semi-mythical man of integrity who preferred
to be good rather than to be great, though he did not attain
quite so high a literary pedestal as his contemporary, Cato,
who committed suicide rather than give in to Ceasar.  Cato,
who himself wrote nothing of consequence, became through
his death a favorite symbol of the Stoic wise man and appears
as such more than once in English literature.[34]

     Another of the great differences between the Stoics
of the Roman period and the earlier ones was that with the
Romans the Aristotelian doctrine of the golden mean softened
earlier Stoic absolutism.  Instead of insisting that a good
man has to be absolutely perfect, the Roman Stoics introduced
a middle ground between absolute virtue and absolute sinfulness.
In Cicero's influential treatise on friendship, which combines
some Stoic ideas with Aristotelian ones, we learn that although
true friendship is only possible between men of virtue,
a virtuous man is now defined as one working as well as
he can toward the impossible goal of perfect virtue.[35]
This qualification is important for English literature,
for in general when a wise man is treated sympathetically
he belongs to the modified Roman type, someone who is good
but not perfect, while characters who pretend to be perfect
in the older sense usually turn out to be frauds.

     Before we make the transition from the Ciceronian type
of Stoicism to the Senecan type, we need to make a detour
in order to look at the Epicurean point of view.  Although
Stoics and Epicureans are traditional enemies, particularly
because they belong to the same family, they are in many
ways so much alike that in literature their doctrines have
become intertwined.  Writers like Horace, Virgil, and Seneca,
who had a great influence on English literature, freely
mixed Stoic ideas with Epicurean ones.  Both Stoicism and
Epicureanism arose during the Alexandrian period with their
own solutions to the same problems; both looked back to
the teachings of Socrates--though to different ones;[36] both
defined happiness as peace of mind; neither concerned itself

with life after death; and both were faced with the difficulty
that it is practically impossible to have peace of mind
in a world containing other people.  Where the Stoic is
technically a philosophical optimist and the Epicurean a
philosophical pessimist, the Stoic writer often impresses
us with his bad temper more than his equanimity.  Having
required of himself a high standard of moral integrity,
he is so annoyed at the low standards of other people and
so irritated by the discrepancy between the way things are
and the way things ought to be that his peace of mind is
completely destroyed, while in the meantime the skeptical
Epicurean, who never expected very much, is able to contemplate
the world with tranquillity.  The result is that those Stoics
who have truly wanted peace of mind more than anything else
have been likely to take lessons from the Epicureans.  For
although Epicureans and Stoics were continually attacking
one another, the ironical fact is that outsiders have often
had difficulty telling them apart and have commonly borrowed
from each whichever doctrines happened to appeal, since
people looking for practical advice about how to act are
seldom worried by the fine points of logical consistency.
Those attracted by Epicurean recipes for a happy life have
found no difficulty in substituting optimistic Stoic ideas
about a meaningful universe for pessimistic Epicurean godless-
ness and pointlessness.  Such basic Epicurean ideas as that
in the long run the universe seems to be run by accident
and that ultimately life has no meaning were easily ignored
in favor of concentrating on the argument that the best
way to deal with a bad world is to live as pleasantly as
possible, concentrating on harmless pleasures and frankly
admitting that the individual will be happier if he can
succeed in running away from society.  The consequence is
that although philosophical Epicureans, even more than the
Stoics, earned for themselves a reputation as atheists,
an innocuous literary blend of Stoic and Epicurean ideas
was soon accepted, even by Christians, and over the centuries
has provided one of the major channels through which Greek
and Roman ideas have been infiltrated into the barbaric
Western world.

A brief look at Epicureanism as a philosophy shows
that it remained more unified than Stoicism, that the great
Epicurean teachers--Epicurus (342-270 B.C.) and Lucretius
(c. 96-55 B.C.)--though widely separated in time, both taught
substantially the same lessons.  Epicurus lived and taught
in Athens at about the same time as Zeno, while the Roman
Lucretius was a contemporary of Cicero.  Where we associate
the Stoics with humanism and the Roman law tradition, we
associate the Epicureans with Machiavelli, with seventeenth-
century science, and with nineteenth-century Utilitarianism.
Where Stoic physics looks back to Heraclitus and the idea
that all nature is in a recurring state of flux, Epicurean
physics goes back to Democritus (b. ca. 460 B.C.), who

said that in the last analysis only atoms and void are real.[37]
Where the Stoics thought of everything as planned, the Epicureans emphasized accident--atoms accidentally coming together
to form matter.  Partly because they opposed the fatalism
of the Stoics, the Epicureans attempted to introduce free
will into the picture by adding to the atomic theory of
Democritus the idea that the individual falling atoms could
deliberately swerve.  From the literary point of view the
result is that where the Stoics are frequently caricatured
as tough fatalists, the Epicureans are depicted as scheming
manipulators of their chances.

The Stoics and Epicureans have in common the relatively
uncontroversial, and widely accepted, idea that the good
life is a state of mind.  The Epicureans, following Democritus,
once more, described the happy man as one possessed of a
pleasant state of inner calm and defined success in life
as tranquillity, an emotional state so similar to the Stoic
ideal of apathy that it is very difficult for any outsider
to tell them apart.  Such terms as "ataraxia," "apathy,"
"equanimity," "tranquillity," "imperturbability," "peace
of mind," "calm of mind," "content," though some are frankly
Stoic and others frankly Epicurean, actually refer much
of the time to the same ideal state of emotional balance.
Moreover, since Epicureans and Stoics are seldom found in
their pure state, we are accustomed to writers who combine
a certain amount of Stoic duty with a certain amount of
Epicurean tranquillity.  As William Temple in the seventeenth
century remarked in his essay "Upon the Gardens of Epicurus,"
to the Stoics happiness consisted in virtue and to the
Epicureans in pleasure, "yet the most reasonable of the
Stoics made the pleasure of virtue to be the greatest happiness,
and the best of the Epicureans made the greatest pleasure
to consist in virtue; and the difference between these two
seems not easily discovered."[38]  We may also be reminded of
John Stuart Mill, an idealistic nineteenth-century Epicurean,
who said that the greatest pleasure comes as an unexpected
by-product of the pursuit of virtue.

Both Stoics and Epicureans were rationalists who thought
it was possible to solve the eternal problem of how-to-live-
with-the-facts-of-life-without-going-out-of-our-minds by
the simple process of using our heads.  While the Stoics
argued optimistically that everything is for the best if
we take the cosmic view, the Epicureans, who were more pessimistic, comforted themselves by reflecting that there is
no such thing as fate and that nature is completely impersonal.
Hence they argued that by taking a sensible look at the
probabilities we can avoid some of the agony caused by such
prime disturbers of tranquillity as fear and hope.  Fear,
which comes in many forms--fear of the gods, fear of death,
fear of pain, fear of loss, fear of other people--comes
often from false notions about the nature of things.  If
we accept the idea that there is nobody and nothing in charge

of the universe, we will not torture ourselves by fear of
the gods; for although there are gods they are happy ones
who personify Epicureans ideals of tranquillity and who
do not worry about the world.  From them nothing is either
to be hoped or to be feared.

When the Epicureans start giving specific advice about
what to do about hope and fear, they often sound as tough
as the Stoics.  Death is not to be feared because it is
merely a dispersion of atoms; the important thing is not
how long we live but how well.  Pain is not to be feared
because if it lasts long it cannot be intense; and if it
is intense, it cannot last long.[39]  Fear of loss will not
trouble us if we learn to travel lightly, both materially
and emotionally.  Like the Stoics, the Epicureans considered
that the simple life is the one most conducive to happiness.
Both Stoics and Epicureans agreed that the more desires
we have, the less peace of mind--the more we get, the more
we want; the higher we climb, the farther we fall.  We have
to remember, of course, that both Stoics and Epicureans--
and especially the later ones--came from the educated classes
and that when they praised the simple life they did not
mean grinding poverty.  What they meant was that such emotions
as ambition, greed, and fear of loss will promote neither
virtue nor tranquillity. Moralizings on the perils of high
place and counsel to withdraw to the humble cottage in the
valley can come from either Stoics or Epicureans, and both
tend to look back nostalgically to a legendary idyllic pastoral
golden age when men were content with few possessions and
did not strive after the superfluities that only serve to
bolster self esteem.  The Epicureans, however, who were
not troubled as much as some of the later Stoics by a feeling
of duty to society, had fewer qualms about retiring to their
pastoral retreats.  If  they needed justification for their
lack of interest in public affairs, they could point to
the example of the unconcerned gods.  For them, the good
life was the retired country life, with a garden to enjoy
and friends to talk to.[40]  Staying away from the mob, they
conformed sufficiently to local custom to avoid attracting
unpleasant attention; and they always tried to remember
that the important things in life are the procurement of
pleasure and the avoidance of pain.

Although the Epicurean is frequently satirized as a
Circean hog who riots in fleshly pleasure, the serious followers
of Epicurus found that having the most pleasure with the
least pain required a thoughtful assessment of probabilities
and a careful balancing of extremes, with the result, again,
that by the time the Stoic had qualified what he meant by
virtue and the Epicurean had explained what he really meant
by pleasure, they were often rather close together.  If
we insist on thinking that "eat, drink, and be merry" is
the Epicurean motto, we must always remember that these
things can only be enjoyed with moderation, that the Aristo-

telian golden mean is essential to the Epicurean notion of
pleasure. The Epicurean, who wants pleasure without such
painful side effects as satiety, boredom, illness, prefers
tranquillity to constant excitement. The quiet enjoyment
of small pleasures that Lamb gives us in his essays is more
typically Epicurean than the perpetual itch for a being
more intense of Byron's "Childe Harold." And since the
utility of any course of action depends on its relation
to pleasure, it turns out that virtuous action is more conducive to pleasure than anti-social behavior. Epicurus,
who considered prudence to be the chief of the virtues,
said that "the virtues are by nature bound up with the pleasant
life," and Lucretius said, "The life of fools at length
becomes a hell here on earth." Even if we do not have a
Stoic conscience that tells us when we misbehave that we
are going against the laws of nature, we can still torture
ourselves with an Epicurean fear of being found out and
punished. Since either way we lose peace of mind, virtue
is the best policy. Epicurean virtue, however, which belongs
to what later became the tradition of Machiavelli and Hobbes--
and, still later, of the Utilitarians--is not an absolute
in the way virtue is with the Stoics, not something obvious
to all men, written into the total plan and binding on all
people at all times. Rather it is frankly relative to time
and place and may be tied to what the nineteenth-century
Utilitarians called the greatest happiness of the greatest
number. Where the Stoics insisted that there is such a thing
as universal justice, the Epicureans said that ideas of
justice can be extended only to those people and those nations
that agree to those ideas. Instead of insisting that a
true law is one that is based on the laws of nature, the
Epicureans say that whenever a law no longer suits the circumstances, it becomes obsolete.[41] As is obvious, of course,
a Stoic in practice can be as relative as an Epicurean,
since he has only to say that a law that no longer suits
the circumstances is not truly based on the law of nature.

In theory, neither Stoics nor Epicureans considered
study of the physical world to be important for its own
sake, the Stoics considering that the proper study of mankind
is man and the Epicureans measuring the worth of knowledge
by its relation to pleasure. In practice, however, the
Epicureans found it useful to study external nature because
such study helps free us from superstition and hence from
pointless fear. At the same time, the study of our instincts
helps us control them and keep them in their proper place.
For the Epicureans, even if they rejected the idea of an
overall plan, still thought of the ordinary processes of
nature as following certain discernible patterns, and, as
we shall see later on, they too talked about the laws of
nature, meaning something different from what the Stoics
meant, something closer to a description of the way things
look to the experimental observor. Since the aim of all

Epicurean activity, however, is to procure "the health of
the body and the soul's freedom from disturbance,"[42]  even
intellectual pleasures, which are among the least harmful,
must be pursued with moderation, the ideal being the gentleman's
generalized knowledge rather than the curious lore of the
pedant.  Since greed and ambition of any kind are only likely
to disrupt our tranquillity, it is as useless to climb on
the intellectual dung hill as on any other.

Both Stoics and Epicureans were suspicious of the passions.
Though the Stoics in their early days tried to argue that
the wise man, whose happiness comes from conformity with
the laws of nature, is totally without passion, the Roman
Stoics took a midway position and made distinctions between
good emotions and bad emotions.  While condemning anger
and putting aside pity, they praised kindness, sympathy,
and benevolence.  Seneca says in De Clementia, "The wise
man, therefore, will not pity, but will succour, will benefit,
and since he is born to be of help to all and to serve the
common good, he will give to each his share thereof" (II.vi.3).
The evil passions of the Stoics are often, in fact, similar
to the deadly sins of the Christians, such things as anger
and greed.  While the Epicureans put pleasure rather than
virtue at the top of their list and did not specifically
exclude emotion, they were about as wary of passion as the
Stoics, since peace of mind is easier to obtain if we avoid
hope and fear and stay out of the storm.

Though both Stoics and Epicureans started out as extreme
individualists, with the Stoics insisting on the self-sufficiency
of the individual conscience and the Epicureans insisting
that the important thing is selfish personal pleasure, both
soon found themselves making compromises, the Stoics in
time becoming patriotic civil servants while the Epicureans
forgot selfish individualism in love for their friends.
Though Epicurus tried to put friendship on a frankly utilitarian basis, arguing that friends are useful as a potential
source of pleasure, he soon abandoned restraint and idealized
friendship as the highest earthly good, saying, "Of all
the things which wisdom acquires to produce the blessedness
of the complete life, far the greatest is the possession
of friendship."  In Roman literature the Epicurean praise
of friendship is found not only among frankly Epicurean
writers but also among some who are frequently classified
as Stoic.[43]

If we return now to some of the Roman writers who were
influential in communicating Stoic attitudes to English
writers we find, as we might expect, that men of letters
like Cicero and Seneca, who were not technically philosophers
in the modern sense, are the ones whose names are familiar;
we seldom hear mention of such teachers as Panaetius or
Posidonius.  Though it is a commonplace to call Cicero an
eclectic, Seneca is generally classified as a Stoic, partly

because he himself made much of his Stoic leanings. But
Seneca's Stoicism, though it may not have been exactly the
same as Cicero's, was still an adulterated kind that included
many Epicurean ideas. The years between Cicero and Seneca
had produced the influential poets Virgil (70-19 B.C.) and
Horace (65-8 B.C.), both of whom illustrate the kind of
Stoic-Epicurean literary compromise that has had a long
popularity. Although on the one hand both writers give us
Epicurean pictures of the idyllic virtuous retired simple
life, on the other they hold up for admiration the patriotic
Stoic hero--Ciceronian style--or perhaps one should say,
Augustan style. As Maurice Bowra points out, Augustus (63
B.C.-A.D. 14), for obvious administrative reasons, encouraged
the ideal of the "quiet, self-denying, self-sacrificing
citizen who was prepared to do what he was told."[44] Virgil's
_Aeneid_ gives us the education of a Stoic hero, Roman style,
a model citizen who, somewhat like the earlier Stoicized
Hercules, develops moral strength by undergoing various
ordeals that teach him to temper his passions and to accept
his fate, which last is bound up with the fate of Rome.
In this poem, where God and fate are the same, Jupiter,
who personifies universal law, does not act arbitrarily.
Aeneas, whose virtue is of the modified Roman variety, does
not lack feeling; and though he learns to temper his passions,
he shows pity and righteous anger without losing his status
as a Stoic hero.[45] Horace, whose philosophic mixture is
slightly more Epicurean than Stoic, is sometimes described
as Stoic, sometimes as Epicurean. While the illustrations
of Roman virtue contained in his patriotic odes--together
with isolated sentiments found here and there throughout
his poetry and generally quoted out of context--give him
a Stoic flavor, the pictures of quiet rural content for
which he is also famous are variously called Stoic or Epicurean.[46]

Though Seneca, along with Epictetus and Marcus Aurelius,
belongs to the group sometimes classified as late Stoic,
he also has much in common with the Epicurean-Stoic Horace;
and like Horace he was long popular as a source of edifying
quotations conveying Stoic or semi-Stoic morals. Seneca,
whose continuous popularity during the Middle Ages and the
Renaissance also often went hand in hand with that of Cicero,
lived a hundred years later than Cicero (c. 5 B.C.-A.D.
65). Though he, like Cicero, tried to combine activity in
the world of affairs with ideals of moral self-sufficiency,
and though his influence as tutor and minister to Nero is
said to have been on the whole beneficial--even if not sufficiently effective--he did much of his writing during his
disillusioned later years when he had retired to the country;
and his name is often associated with the idea that Stoicism
is primarily a private rather than a political philosophy.
He, like Horace, often talked about the vicissitudes of

fortune and offered recipes for maintaining peace of mind
that have long been acceptable to Christians.

While Cicero's name has come to be associated with
positive patriotic responsibility and Seneca's with negative
resignation and cowardly retirement from the world of affairs,
both merely illustrate that Stoic ideas can be packaged
in various combinations. Though Seneca did write, on occasion,
of the duty of engaging in public life, he wrote more often
that the wise man will not go out of his way to mix in politics. His non-dramatic writings, which often tend to be
a consolation for the miseries of life instead of a recipe
for action, contain, like the writings of Virgil and Horace,
an admixture of Epicureanism, which is only labeled Stoicism
because it comes from the pen of Seneca.[47]

Leaving discussion of Seneca's tragedies for a later
chapter, I shall concentrate here on some generalizations
based on his prose writings; and since there has perhaps
been a too-great tendency to classify Seneca, as Erasmus's
Folly did, as a "double-strength" Stoic, I shall probably
go too far in the other direction, over-emphasizing his
kinship with an eclectic like Horace. It is important to
remember, however, that he was a man of letters rather than
a philosopher and that one of his favorite forms was the
personal letter, addressed to a friend, inspired by a particular occasion, centered around a specific topic. For like
Cicero and Horace, he had a high regard for friendship and
spoke warmly of the fellowship of kindred minds.[48] Unlike
Horace, who seldom forgot that he himself was as ridiculous
as the rest of us, Seneca took himself seriously and easily
fell into a moralizing or sermonizing tone of voice. His
high seriousness, however, did not lessen his popularity
with serious-minded Christians; and for centuries Seneca
with his catchy, epigrammatic, easily quotable style and
his sermonlike advice on practical, everyday problems was
a standard classic. In fact, his tone and content were
so appealing to Christians that in the fourth century a
correspondence was fabricated between him and St. Paul,
a correspondence which was considered authentic not only
by such early writers as Jerome and Augustine but even in
Elizabethan times. By Christians Seneca was classified
as one of those pagans who, through the light of nature,
had managed to glimpse a number of important truths.[49]
Although Seneca disagreed with the basic Epicurean doctrine
that the important thing is the procurement of pleasure
and the avoidance of pain, preferring instead the Stoic
emphasis on virtue, he did not object to pleasure in its
proper place and made no pretence that he himself was an
ideal Stoic prodigy, completely immune to pleasure and pain.
Though even among the strict early Stoics there were differences of opinion about whether all pleasures had to be
rejected, some pleasures being classified as natural and
desirable,[50] the later Stoics like Seneca made a convenient

distinction between things essential to virtue and things indifferent.  Moderate pleasure was one of those indifferent
things--like life, health, wealth, family, and fame--which
it was all right to enjoy while they lasted but which, because
they were vulnerable to fortune, the wise man must always
be prepared to lose without losing emotional balance.   The
one essential thing was moral integrity.[51]

    With a nostalgia that could be either Stoic or Epicurean,
Seneca looked back to the mythical good old days, praising
the rugged simple life as Lucretius and Virgil had done.
Possibly he inclined somewhat to the Stoic side in that
he stressed the superior virtue of such a life more than
its superior pleasure; and according to Lovejoy his "Epistulae
morales and tragedies were probably the most important classical sources of hard primitivism in the sixteenth and seventeenth centuries."  Popular Senecan morals that have been
echoed down the centuries have connected luxurious living
with moral depravity and have suggested that simple diet
goes with good health.[52]

    Although Seneca talks much about virtue and duty, we
associate him less with the striving kind of Stoic who has
Herculean obstacles to overcome than with the resigned Stoic
who is primarily interested in equanimity; and it is here
that his frame of mind comes closest to that of the Epicureans.
In two of his areas of special expertise--consolations in
adversity and remedies for fortune--Seneca's arguments are
quite as likely to sound like Lucretius as like Zeno.   Stoic
patience or fortitude--two of the many names for peace of
mind--is a quality possessed by those who are able to accept
without surprise whatever may come. Whatever happens--death,
exile, servitude, loss of friends, loss of wealth, loss
of reputation--the Stoic had expected it, and so had the
Epicurean.  While the Stoic is trying to keep a stiff upper
lip and go about his duty, the Epicurean is telling himself
to rejoice that he at least has a few pleasant days to remember.  While the Stoic commonly accepts his fate on the assumption that there is a purpose behind everything that happens,
the Epicurean makes the most of every accidental good moment.

    That Seneca was not always careful to remember which
side of the fence he was on is indicated partly by his fondness for the word "fortune" and partly by his melancholy
tone; for, technically, a Stoic should emphasize benevolent
fate or providence rather than irresponsible fortune and
should be cheerful rather than melancholy about the way
things are going.  However, Seneca, who was not actually
expecting himself or anyone else to reach a perfect state
of wisdom, concentrated less on how to be perfect than on
how to avoid unnecessary suffering.  As a rich man he praised
the virtuous frugal life of the early Romans without himself
trying to imitate it.  As a man who was fond of his family
and his friends, he knew about the pain of loss and offered
various remedies for grief, such as, not letting it last

too long, softening it ahead of time by expecting the worst,
remembering that some supposed evils, like death, are not
really evils; for life is a heavy and earthly prison, and
nature is generous in making death inevitable. In fact,
when there is no other remedy, suicide is always available
as a way to freedom.[53]

Like other Roman Stoics, Seneca distinguished between
good emotions and bad emotions, calling anger the most hideous
and frenzied of all the passions, continually attacking
greed, but classifying mercy and benevolence as good emotions.[54]
One reason for Seneca's long popularity was that he gave
specific advice on how to be virtuous though human; and
although he was well aware that the ideal Stoic wise man
is practically non-existent, he was fond of listing the
attributes of this mythical creature, descriptions which
may have helped provide stuffing for some characters in
fiction. The mythical wise man is the only one really above
the vicissitudes of fortune, the only one who fully realizes
that fortune can harm only indifferent things and that real
evil, such as sin, cannot befall the good man. The following
quotation describes the ideal Stoic happy life.

> The happy life is not that which conforms to
> pleasure, but that which conforms to Nature,
> when he has fallen deeply in love with virtue
> as man's sole good and has avoided baseness
> as man's sole evil, and when he knows that
> all other things--riches, office, health,
> strength, dominion--fall in between and are
> not to be reckoned either among goods or among
> evils, then he will not need a monitor for
> every separate action to say to him: 'Walk thus
> and so; eat thus and so. This is the proper
> conduct for a man and that for a woman; this
> for a married man and that for a bachelor.'[55]

This impossible ideal, with its vague definitions of virtue
and baseness, is often ridiculed in English literature,
where we frequently meet examples of the proud Stoic who
is only a fraud. But occasionally, also, the ideal is transferred to superhuman characters or to saints or near saints.

Although Seneca's name is often singled out as that
of the great disseminator, especially to the sixteenth and
seventeenth centuries, of the Stoic word, there were actually
many Roman and Greek writers from whom English writers could
acquire Stoic morals. A few of them are Persius (A.D. 34-
61), whose satires interested Donne and Dryden; Seneca's
nephew, Lucan (b. ca. A.D. 39), whose <u>Pharsalia</u> provided
one of the literary sources for the treatment of Cato as
a Stoic hero; and Plutarch (A.D. 46?-?120) and Juvenal (ca.
A.D. 60-after 127), who communicated a number of Stoic moral
attitudes without themselves being practising Stoics.[56]

Of the Roman Stoics whose names are still familiar to us, Epictetus (c. A.D. 55-135) was the one who put the heaviest emphasis on primitive Cynic-Stoic self-sufficiency. Unlike Cicero and Seneca, who lived among the rich and powerful, and Marcus Aurelius, who was an emperor, Epictetus was a former slave who spent his life not only preaching the simple life but also living it. What we know of his teachings comes to us from a pupil, Arrian, who recorded them in Greek. Where upper-class Roman Stoics discussed such problems as the proper use of riches and how to equate one's duty as a citizen with the will of god, Epictetus concentrated on such things as learning to make perfect one's will and learning to understand which things are under our control and which not. His particular heroes were Socrates and Diogenes, and it is partly through his remote influence that these two often appear in late Medieval and Renaissance literature as examples of Stoic self-sufficiency.[57]

The Epictetan kind of Stoicism is more muscular than that of Seneca, with fewer offers of consolation and more admonitions to stop complaining. Like other Stoics he used the words "fool" and "sinner" synonymously--since a fool is one who sins against the laws of nature--and he believed that most men were fools. Like the early Stoics, he restricted friendship to the fellowship of virtuous men (<u>Discourses</u>, II.xxii), and if he did not go so far as to say men could live without society, his stress was on how to be free in spite of social pressure. The ubiquitous Stoic moral that only the good man is free is particularly associated with Epictetus, who emphasized that freedom is a state of mind, that we are always free if our will is under our control, if we willingly accept our assigned role in the cosmic order. We should think of our lives as a game in which we have been assigned certain pieces, which it is our duty to play as well as we can, remembering that it is not important whether our life be long or short, tragic or happy. Difficulties give us a chance to show our character; and when we are tired of the game, we can always leave. Suicide is the way out. Except for the approval of suicide, the Elizabethans echoed such ideas when they compared the world to a stage; and Yeats took them up when he said, "Hamlet and Lear are gay."[58]

A short digression on the Stoic insistence on the compatibility of fate and free will is in order here. Though for Stoics it is axiomatic that everything in the universe operates according to plan, nevertheless even the early Stoics refused to regard moral evil as part of the plan and separated the virtuous men from the fools. When a literary villain blames his villainy on fate, the author may be intending to travesty the Stoics; but the Stoics themselves never exempted the individual from responsibility for his own behavior. For the irony is that although the

Stoic law of nature is supposed to be universal, it seems
to be susceptible to a great many different interpretations;
and although it is supposed to be absolute, sinners are
able to break it. The classic early example of this paradox
comes in Cleanthes' famous "Hymn to Zeus," which, while glori-
fying nature or Zeus and saying that all nature is good,
nevertheless excepts, "whatsoever deeds wicked men do in
their foolishness."[59] Wicked men or fools, who are left
temporarily free to disobey the laws of nature, provide
the stuff from which much Stoic literature is made. The
harm that they do, though it may be temporary from the point
of view of geological time, nevertheless brings misfortune
on many an innocent victim like Boethius. The wise man,
who is not necessarily physically stronger than the foolish
man, frequently has to be content with the remote consolation that although justice will ultimately prevail, he,
in the meantime, can only assert his freedom by choosing
to perish rather than go against his conscience. Since
suicide is always available, the good man is always free.
Cleanthes' hymn illustrates the slippery quality of much
Stoic language as it equates "nature" on the one hand with
the physical world (the way things are) and on the other
hand with the human moral ideal (the way things ought to
be). Wicked or foolish men, even though they may be conforming to the statistical average, doing what everybody
else is doing, are nevertheless "unnatural."

Epictetus, more than Seneca, makes us think of the
legendary Stoic who banishes emotion and equates being natural
with being superhumanly reasonable. Complaining that most
men seem to prefer their kinship with the animals to their
kinship with god--or reason, or virtue--he says that being
natural means striving to imitate god, an aspect of the
Epictetan creed of self-sufficiency that crops up periodi-
cally in later times. But what it means in actual practice
depends on the particular definition of god being used.
The Epictetan kind of Stoicism, though we find it occasionally
in literature, has never been so widely popular as the less
rigorous, more social minded, Ciceronian kind. Though Epictetus tells us that we must accept the part we have been
assigned, thus implying that we should cooperate with the existing social framework, he nevertheless, like Socrates and
the later Seneca, advises staying out of public affairs.[60]
However, as someone primarily concerned with monitoring
his own behavior, he is not a potential threat to a corrupt
government--in the way a Panaetian-Ciceronian type of Stoic
may be--but instead represents the kind of solution to the
problem of how to live that appeals to those who have no
faith in their own ability to affect the social framework
and no belief that any change would be for the better.
Like Seneca, and also, to a certain extent, like Marcus
Aurelius, he is the gloomy type of Stoic whom we associate
particularly with the later empire and who appears periodi-

cally in English literature when a writer is feeling out of sympathy with the life of the times.

The emperor Marcus Aurelius (A.D. 121-180), who is generally considered to be the last of the Roman Stoics, was torn between his desire for peace of mind and his duty as a public servant; for though he had studied Epictetus on self-sufficiency, he was a soldier, not a teacher. Unlike some of Shakespeare's escapist kings, he went on doing the duty that had been assigned him by fate while at the same time making private jottings, frequently entitled Meditations, in an attempt to make himself sit still. Though he kept reminding himself of cosmic benevolence and the need to accept whatever happens, he was well aware of the evils that men do. Instead of a confident belief in the destiny of Rome, his dominant mood seems to have been one of resignation; and his thoughts have an emotional tone foreign to what is usually considered Stoic. He reminded himself that "to be vexed at anything which happens is a separation of ourselves from nature" that "nothing is evil which is according to nature," that death is no evil, merely "a dissolution of the elements of which every living being is compounded."[61]

His emphasis on doing his social duty and faintly trusting in cosmic justice made him appeal particularly to writers of the eighteenth and nineteenth centuries, and his thoughts are echoed by such writers as Carlyle, Emerson, and Matthew Arnold. Zeller says that the Stoic teaching that all mankind are one, which imposed "the practice of the most extended and unreserved charity, of beneficence, gentleness, meekness, of an unlimited benevolence, and a readiness to forgive in all cases in which forgiveness is possible" appears in all the later Stoics, but especially in Marcus Aurelius (p. 297).

After Marcus Aurelius the history of Stoicism merges with that of Christianity; and as Stoicism in all its ambiguity goes marching on, the Stoic law of nature, which had earlier been identified with the destiny of Rome, now becomes identified with the destiny of Christendom, while the Stoic wise man merges with the Christian hero. As we have already seen, Stoic fate and Stoic virtue are versatile and adaptable concepts. And as we shall continue to see, those who find themselves in harmony with the dominant powers and thus able to identify the established system with the law of nature, feel virtuous when they are doing what they are told, while others, who think the ruling powers have left the true path and that they themselves have been endowed with a superior insight into the real truth, can only feel virtuous if they fight the good fight and use their pens in an effort to make reason and the will of God prevail. Still others, however, though they continue to maintain their faith in the existence of a just universe, can only conclude that the workings of fate are inscrutable. These, like

Boethius, try to content themselves with Job's comfort,
concentrating on doing the duty nearest them and leaving
the workings of cosmic law to take care of themselves.
In English literature, where these fluctuations are common,
Shakespeare--some of the time--advises cooperation with
a relatively tidy universe, while Milton fights the good
fight against the corrupt system; Pope admonishes us, "Presume
not God to scan"; and Adam Smith warns us to leave things
alone.

Since one combination of Stoic ideas need not permanently supersede another combination, the following rudimentary survey of some of the more familiar ways in which
Jewish and Christian thinkers have combined Stoic ideas
with their own systems of thought will see-saw back and
forth between those who tied virtue to a private conscience
and those who tied it to a social conscience, though, of
course, there is nothing to prevent the same person from
holding now one point of view, now the other.  Since it
is the Stoic thesis that peace of mind, or happiness, comes
to the virtuous, or wise, man who obeys the laws of nature,
our task is to notice some of the varying definitions given
those terms.

The law of nature concept, which takes us into such
untidy areas as the Stoic concept of god, Stoic fate, and
Stoic self-sufficiency, was early combined with Jewish and
Christian ideas; for it was only to be expected that thinkers
who were products of the Roman world and who were in the
habit of thinking along generalized Stoic lines would amal-
gamate ideas that were not in obvious conflict.  George
Boas reminds us that the Stoic concept of god was always
somewhat obscure, particularly in Rome, that the idea of
an impersonal yet rational, virtuous, and benevolent cosmic
law, which was sometimes called Zeus or god, was difficult
to keep in focus and that Virgil and Seneca, who left their
meanings of the word "god" slightly vague, were easily adapted
to Christianity.  We can see how Seneca's talk about the
fatherhood of god, his emphasis on duty, his melancholy
welcoming of death as an end of troubles, all made it easy
to regard him as a Christian sympathizer, while even with
Epictetus and Marcus Aurelius the distinction between god
as the spirit that rolls through all things and god as the
creator outside his creation had become unclear.  The benevolent fate of Marcus Aurelius, which organizes everything
ultimately for the best, is easy to identify with the Christian
providence.[62]

Long before Marcus Aurelius and long before Rome was
officially Christianized, however, the process of harmonizing
Stoic ideas with Jewish and Christian ideas had been going
on, one famous contributor in this area being the Jewish
theologian Philo of Alexandria (d. ca. 40 A.D.), who was
fond of Plato and the Stoics and whose commentaries on the
Old Testament showed how the truths of Greek philosophy

could be illustrated from Old Testament history.  E. V.
Arnold tells us that Philo had so completely absorbed the
Stoic system that "where other authorities fail us, we may
often trust to his expositions for a knowledge of details"
and says it was Philo who transmitted the doctrine of the
Logos--the moral law of nature that precedes man-made laws
and binds all men alike--from the Stoic tradition to the
Judaeo-Christian tradition.[63]  St. Paul, whose education
like Philo's had been Jewish, Greek, and Roman, described
the good Christian as having--like the good Stoic--moral
ideas engraved on his heart.[64]  Other early propagators
of this idea were Justin Martyr (100?-?165) and Tertullian
(160?-?230).[65]  St. Ambrose (340?-397), who had much to
do with the conversion of St. Augustine and who had been
a lawyer and an administrator before he found himself Bishop
of Milan, is described by E. K. Rand as having been greatly
influenced by both Philo and Cicero.  Not only did he give
a series of sermons based on Cicero's De Officiis, he also
wrote a manual of ethics for young men who were preparing
to enter the Church which he entitled De Officiis Ministrorum.
　　While Paul, who belongs to the time when Christians
were non-conformists in the Roman world, sometimes reminds
us of Seneca, with whom he was thought to have carried on
a correspondence, Ambrose, who lived when Christianity was
becoming a world power, has more affinities with Cicero.
According to one historian of political science, the Church
got its organization from Rome, "bishops being mitred prefects"
and its systematic moral theory from the Stoics, which theory
"reached expression in St. Ambrose of Milan."  And according
to another, "The fathers of the Church, in respect to natural
law, human equality, and the necessity of justice in the
state, were substantially in agreement with Cicero and Seneca."[66]
Like Cicero and the Roman law tradition, Ambrose put emphasis
on such things as a law of nature which precedes written
law and on the oneness of all mankind, with its correlaries
that charity toward all is a prime duty and that the wise
man is everywhere at home.[67]
　　With Augustine (354-430), who accepted, like others,
the idea that moral laws are universal and innate,[68] we
encounter a major point of difference between Stoics and
Christians, one which continually troubled theologians but
which did not always vex mere literary men, namely, the
exact relationship between God, fate, fortune, and free
will.  Although we know that a specific semi-Stoic like
Seneca did not always make it entirely clear what he meant
when he used the word "god," we also know that Stoic natural
law or god or fate is supposed to be something completely
impersonal and unchangeable, something entirely distinct
from fortune--which is another name for luck or chance or
accident.  Whatever these concepts, when reduced to mathematical purity, may mean when discussed by experts, they tend

to become thoroughly confused in everyday usage. The words
"fate" and "fortune" are used interchangeably; people try
to learn their fate by reading the stars and then assume
that by proper action they can affect their fortune. Even
though everything is fated, fate is not held responsible
for our evil deeds.[69] Even if we agree with Job that the
ways of God, though meaningful to Him, are confusing to
us, or insist with Marcus Aurelius that everything that
happens, happens justly, we may still go on behaving as
if we know where we want to go and as if accidents are both
possible and avoidable.

Augustine, who disliked the word "fate" because it
suggested the popular belief in astrology, which he had
repudiated, did not identify God with the law of nature.
The law of nature was merely the will of God, otherwise
known as providence. Though he rejected both Epicurean
and Stoic physics, he did not, however, reject everything
written by individual Stoics. He quoted Seneca as an example
of one who was wise enough to equate fate with "the will
of the supreme father,"[70] and on the question of free will
he sometimes agreed with the Stoic doctrine that the good
man is free because he wills what God wills, that "if a
wicked man rule, he is a slave," that the evils imposed
on the good by the bad are not so much a punishment as a
test of virtue. In fact, on the apparent contradiction
between God's foreknowledge and man's free will he quar-
relled with his beloved Cicero, who had disliked Stoic fate
because it seemed to him that it left no room for free will
and personal integrity. "The God-fearing mind," says Augustine, "chooses both." "Against these rash assertions, blasphemous and irreligious as they are, we Christians declare
both that God knows all things before they happen, and that
it is by our free will that we act, whenever we feel and
know that a thing is done by us of our own volition" (IV.3;
V.9). Even though Augustine disliked the word "fate," he
nevertheless emphasized God's foreknowledge; and in popular
usage, the word "fate" has persisted, just as the popularity
of astrology has persisted. In fact, in popular literature
it often happens that fate works as some sort of malignant
free agent while at the same time the good characters are
the ones who believe in fate; it is the bad ones who assert
free will.

If Augustine's explanation of God's foreknowledge is
somewhat reminiscent of Stoic fate, his City of God has
some similarities with the old Stoic dream of a cosmopolis,
one world, in which all men will be brothers, all free and
equal. The big difference, of course, is that Augustine
removed this dream from our world to the next, where he
populated it with saints, who are the Christian version
of the Stoic wise man.[71] And like the Romans, who had preached
the supremacy of natural law while being wary of substituting

individual insight for established custom, Augustine drew
a distinction between the verities of natural law as they
might have appeared to the unclouded insight of Adam before
the Fall and the actualities of the world as we now know
it.  Not only has sin deprived us of the ability to distinguish
truth clearly, but the world as it is must be accepted as
part of our punishment.  Instead of hoping to reproduce
heaven on earth, we must carry out the will of God by accepting our assigned roles and playing our parts to the best
of our ability.  For example, though slavery, as the Stoics
had said, was not a part of the original order of nature,
yet, says Augustine, it is now a part of the order of things
and should not be disturbed.  In the world as it is now,
the proper social order, modeled on the family, is hierarchical, though with Augustine the gradations of the system
are not so complex as they were to become some centuries
later.  In this society, virtue tends to be defined in terms
of relationships.  Virtue for a slave means being a good
slave.  "Those who are concerned for others give commands,
the husband to his wife, the parents to their children,
the masters to their servants; while those who are objects
of concern obey; for example, the women obey their husbands,
the children their parents, the servants their masters.
But in the home of the just man who lives by faith and who
is still a pilgrim in exile from the celestial city, even
those who give commands serve those whom they seem to command.  For they command not through lust for rule but through
dutiful concern for others" (XIX.14, 15).[72]  This doctrine,
that everyone is part of the pattern, that those who apparently command are themselves servants to duty, remains standard
Christian-Stoic doctrine for centuries and appears everywhere
in Elizabethan literature.

Augustine, who died in 430, just as the Vandals were
entering his city of Hippo, still belonged to the Roman
world, while Boethius (c. 480-524) has been called the last
of the Romans and the first of the scholastics, mainly because
of his rationalistic desire to confirm faith through reason
but also in part because he was a child of Roman civilization
who had to try to adjust to an Ostrogothic world.[73]  His
enormous popularity, both during the Middle Ages and during
the Renaissance, makes him an obvious source for many of
the so-called Stoic platitudes that are always appearing
in English literature.  His readers, who were not troubled
by the fact that his Consolation of Philosophy offered philosophical rather than religious help, regarded him as a Christian martyr and accepted his teachings as dogma.  Since
Boethius, like other Roman intellectuals, was an eclectic,
Stoic arguments were not the only ones he used.  In his
system, which has been described as Platonic, modified by
Aristotelianism, with a strong dash of Stoicism tingeing
the whole, the influence has been seen of such various writers
as not only Plato and Aristotle but also Cicero, Seneca,

Virgil, Horace, the Neoplatonists, Origen, and Augustine.[74]
Because Boethius had to write without a library, he could
not make the Consolation a mass of pretentious quotations
like Chaucer's "Tale of Melibee." What he produced was
a well-digested whole, written under stress in answer to
a problem that was vital to him and that has also seemed
vital to many a later reader.

Since the Consolation was written while Boethius was
in prison, shortly to die, he was less concerned with tying
virtue to good citizenship than with holding on to his sanity.
Peace of mind was the one thing that now mattered. In order
to attain peace of mind he had to convince himself that
in spite of the unjust treatment he had himself received,
there actually was justice in the universe.

He might have taken for his motto Marcus Aurelius'
admonition, "Consider that everything which happens, happens
justly, and if thou observest carefully, thou wilt find
it to be so" (IV.10); for like the Stoics, and unlike Augustine, Boethius refused to argue that we are simply living
in a bad world. He neither said that he himself was being
punished for sin, nor believed that a good God could make
a bad world. Arguing from a philosophical rather than a
Christian point of view, he concluded that evil is only
an illusion, or, in Alexander Pope's phrase, "All partial
evil universal good."

If the universe is just, how can one justify the apparently pointless fall of a virtuous great man from his high
place through no fault of his own? The solution is to place
such things as fate and fortune in their proper perspective,
to remember that no misfortune can befall the good man as
long as he still has his integrity. Lady Philosophy, as
she lectured the complaining Boethius into a better frame
of mind, gradually reminded him that he had been confusing
good fortune with happiness and that he had failed to remember that only the good man can be happy, since only the
good man can enjoy peace of mind. Along with the Stoics,
she pointed out that fortune or chance does not really exist,
since the universe is ruled by God or providence. The eternal
plan, which is in God's mind, is carried out by fate or
destiny, while the apparent accidents, or vicissitudes of
fortune, arbitrary though they may seem, are really only
part of the general pattern. Boethius did not suggest that
providence was likely to depart from its overall plan for
the sake of any individual or that it would interfere with
the laws of nature. Although he identified providence with
God and fate with the will of God, which meant that his
terminology was slightly different from Augustine's, it
is unlikely that the average reader paid much attention
to the difference.[75] Like Augustine, he said that God has
perfect foreknowledge of the way things will turn out, while
at the same time he insisted, as Augustine had done and
as the Stoics had done, that men's acts are free. Although

the universe is controlled by destiny and even though there is
no such thing as chance, man is still morally responsible
for his own behavior.

Boethius, whose influence is mainly on the side of
individual self-sufficiency, is nevertheless not the kind
of Stoic who endangers the system. Like Augustine before
him and Aquinas afterwards, he can be seen as a supporter
of the status quo. Augustine was not interested in changing
the social framework because he defined obeying the will
of God as, among other things, accepting as part of our
punishment the world as it is. Our duty is merely to play
our assigned part. Boethius, intent on convincing himself
that all fortune, rightly understood, is good fortune, was
only trying to change his own state of mind, not to reform
society. His arguments, therefore, would have been attractive
not only to other victims of the system but also to main-
tainers of the system; for although his troubles were largely
man made and though he asked plaintively why good men seem
to receive the small end of the stick while evil men get
away with their evil, still he accepted the fact that the
evil men in his case had power on their side, and he did
not pretend to himself that God would suddenly strike them
down with a thunderbolt. Nor did he encourage other men
to strike them down for him. What he said was that only
the good man can be happy, that happiness is the only thing
really worth having, and that the wicked man, who can never
have peace of mind, is a psychological punishment to himself.
No one could object to such sentiments.

The enormous popularity of the Consolation of Philosophy
is something we have continually to keep in mind when talking
about so-called Renaissance Neo-Stoicism, for Boethian self-
sufficiency, or Boethian Senecanism, had long been an uncontroversial aspect of everyday thinking, and many of the
Senecan clichés in popular writing are not really so new
as they look. As everyone knows, the Consolation was translated over and over again, with each translator modifying
the thought slightly to bring it into line with contemporary
thinking. "No other book, except the Bible," says Highet,
"was so much translated in the Middle Ages." There are
translations in Old English, Provençal, Old High German,
Anglo-Norman, Old French, Middle English, and modern English,
the most famous English translations being those of King
Alfred (about 900), Chaucer (1380), and Elizabeth I (1593);
but in addition to translations, numerous copies were made.
These are listed in university catalogs all over Western
Europe, with approximately four hundred manuscripts still
in existence.[76]

In the time of Thomas Aquinas (c.1225-1274), many centuries later than Boethius, the Consolation was still an
influential work and one of the many with which Aquinas
himself was familiar. In some ways we think of Aquinas

as symbolizing, during the late Middle Ages and the Renaissance, the Panaetian or Ciceronian kind of Stoicism that emphasized social responsibility, while Boethius symbolizes the Stoicism that concentrates on individual peace of mind.  Though it is customary to stress Aquinas' debt to Aristotle and to associate him with the doctrine that man is by nature a social animal, we should, as usual, remember that Aquinas added his new infusions of Aristotle to the old Roman-Christian mixture handed him by his predecessors and that this mixture included many of the modified Stoic ideas accepted by writers like Cicero, Seneca, St. Paul, St. Ambrose, St. Augustine, and Boethius.  If Aquinas adapted Aristotle and others for Christian uses, he was only doing something similar to what Panaetius had done long before when he adapted Aristotle and Plato for Stoic uses.  Another possible source that has been suggested for Stoic ideas in Aquinas is the revived twelfth-century Italian interest in Roman law.[77]  Whatever the source of his ideas, he was powerful in spreading them, for he, like Cicero, was both a gifted writer and a skilled mediator, one who explained how to feel as self-sufficient as Socrates (within Christian limits) and yet be a well integrated member of society, how to keep one's eyes on heaven and earth at the same time.  The solution was to have a properly ordered system of values.

In determining the order of priorities, the conventions of the hierarchical system were a great help, for by the time of Aquinas it was accepted as an unquestioned law of nature that everything in the universe, including good and evil, was arranged in a graded series;[78] and the really influential Stoic ideas were the ones that could adjust themselves to such basic assumptions as that different people are born with different positions in the hierarchy, that the degree of our sinfulness is related to our social position, and that each station in the social framework has its own particular virtues.  As we have already seen, the foundations of some of these notions had already been laid by the Roman Stoics, who had rejected such early Stoic teachings as that all sins are equally bad and all virtues equally good and had emphasized the importance of doing one's duty as a citizen, which last included a moral responsibility toward work, the doctrine of doing a good job for its own sake.  The idea, which we can find in Cicero, Epictetus, and others, that everyone has been assigned a part to play in life, which it is his duty to play as well as he can, was one that adapted itself well to a hierarchical conception of society.[79]  We have already seen that Augustine stressed such ideas when he compared the social system to a family, with some having the duty to rule and others having the duty to obey.  During the Middle Ages notions of one's place in life become much more stratified, much more complex, and much more fixed than they had been, with the consequence that moralists are forever trying to persuade unruly human

beings that virtue means performing well the particular
duties that belong to the particular niche into which they
happened to be born.  If we keep in mind these unquestioned
assumptions, we can see that the Stoic doctrine that virtue
means living in accordance with the laws of nature was interpreted in such a way as to identify virtue with team work.
Echoing down the centuries go variations on the Stoic moral
that it does not matter whether we win but how we play the
game.  It is against this background that Aquinas teaches
such basic Stoic doctrines as that happiness results from
virtue, that virtue means action in accordance with reason
and the laws of nature, that we all possess by nature an
inborn aptitude for virtue, and that this aptitude needs
to be developed by training--a qualification which, as usual,
makes all the difference.  For it is obvious that those
who train us or educate us will indoctrinate us with their
own system of values, which values they, of course, will
identify with the laws of nature.  Aquinas admitted that
virtue as an absolute exists only in the mind of God, that
in life it varies with different times and different men.[80]

During the Middle Ages, complex definitions of virtue
based on an elaborate network of social relationships were
preached not only from the popular pulpit and by popular
writers like Langland and Gower but also were written into
the legal system, with the result that the laws were appropriately different for people of different classes.[81]  Although
at birth and death all men might be equal, in between they
had different roles to play, with the emphasis always on
duties, not on rights.  A favorite theme for preachers and
writers was the failure of members of various classes to
live up to ideal class standards.  A poor workman, for instance,
was chastised for sinning both against his employer and
against the laws of nature.  The same went for disobedient
wives and children.

In terms of the hierarchy, God, of course, comes at
the top.  God's will and the law of nature are one and the
same, though God is at the same time theoretically above
the law and could have willed otherwise had he so desired.
Evil is sometimes explained in the optimistic Stoic way
as something necessary to promote the greater good and sometimes as an aspect of man's freedom.  Though God's power
is infinite, he does not legislate every minute detail but
instead leaves man free to make his own mistakes and to
suffer the consequences.[82]  We are all familiar with the
favorite plot of Elizabethan dramatists that shows foolish
men succeeding temporarily, but only temporarily, in going
against the laws of nature.

The hierarchical system permits a certain relativity
in the definition of truth, for although virtue means obeying
the truth, God is the only one who absolutely knows what
the truth is.  Since, in the world of approximations in
which we live, happiness for the state means justice, or
the proper relationship of the parts to the whole, it depends

on our social position what virtue means for us.  For example,
it may be that in an absolute sense the contemplative life
is more excellent than the active, but in a particular instance
the active life may be more virtuous "on account of the
needs of the present life" and because man is by nature a
social or political animal. A king, who has been assigned
the duty of ruling, is required to choose the active life--
no matter how much he personally may prefer the contemplative.[83]

Again, the individual's ability to read the general
principles of natural law, which are written on his heart, is
related to his place on the social scale; for inequality
is part of the law of nature, and some of us are born wiser
than others.  Theoretically, those who are born to sit in
high places and make the laws are higher on the scale of
moral insight than the rest of us, which means that rulers
are presumed to be more virtuous than those whom they govern,
to have a clearer perception of moral law.[84]

Although the individual is, of course, responsible
for disciplining himself, self-discipline generally means
cooperating with the rules made by those in authority.
Obeying the laws of nature means obeying the established
rules.  For although Aquinas recognizes that an occasional
saint will be born who is so completely in tune with eternal
law that the coercion of human laws is unnecessary, in general
Aquinas recommends conforming to custom.  If we all have
some rudimentary insight into the large principles óf natural
law, we have different abilities when it comes to interpreting
the practical applications and need experts to explain the
laws to us. Also, since reason in any individual may have
been perverted "by passion, or evil habit, or an evil disposition of nature," we need specific laws to guide us "on account
of the uncertainty of human judgment, especially on contingent
and particular matters."  Although in theory "every human
law has just as much of the character of law as it is derived
from the law of nature; but if in any point it differs from
the law of nature it is no longer a law but a corruption
of law," nevertheless in practice, when it is a question
of knowing when a human law is contrary to the law of nature
and therefore in need of change, Aquinas is wary.  He considers
that in the long run custom may be a safer guide than individual intuition, since man's reason is "changeable and imperfect,"
while custom may have roots in divine reason.[85]  So, although
Aquinas distinguishes theoretically between the law of nature
and custom, his influence is on the side of leaving things
alone, with the result that he reinforces the recurring
human tendency to identify the law of nature (that which
ought to be) with custom (the way things are).  Just as
Alexander Pope recognizes that for poetic geniuses there
is such a thing as the grace beyond the reach of art, so
Aquinas recognizes that an occasional saint may approach

the Socratic ideal of the self-sufficient just man.  For most
of us, however, virtue comes from obeying the rules.

The process of endowing various saints and Biblical
figures with the characteristics of the legendary Stoic
wise man has a long history; for although most Christian
anti-Stoicism centers on the concept of the ideal Stoic
sage, who is supposed to be immune to sin and pain, nevertheless the characteristics of the perfect Stoic may appropriately be ascribed to Adam before the Fall or to God and
the angels.  Moreover, the Roman sort of Stoic hero, who
was not considered to be absolutely perfect but only doing
his best with the lot he had received, was easily Christianized.  A mythical hero like the Stoicized Hercules,
who endured great hardships for the benefit of mankind,
was also acceptable to Christians.  According to Boas, Philo
depicted the young Moses as "half Stoic-Sage and half Philosopher King" and made Adam a citizen of the world.  Paul
described the good Christian as avoiding the love of money
(I Timothy, vi.10; II Cor. vi.10), as morally free, even
when physically a slave (I Cor. vi.12, vii,21, ix.19), as
believing evil was sent to help strengthen the spiritual
muscles (Heb. xii.6-7), as despising vain learning (I Cor.
i.17-21, iv.10; Gal. v.16-24, vi.1).[86]  From Cicero, Ambrose
borrowed, and Christianized, the four so-called Stoic virtues
of justice, prudence, temperance, and fortitude.[87]  Lactantius
(c. 260-c.340), who was later to influence Milton, was among
those who taught that evil is sent as a test of virtue,
that virtue has to be acquired and is not the same as untried
innocence.  As Epictetus had said, "Difficulties are what
show men's character.  Therefore when a difficult crisis
meets you, remember that you are as the raw youth with whom
God the trainer is wrestling" (Disc., I.24).  Basil (330?-
?379), Gregory of Nyssa (331?-396), and Augustine were three
who endowed Adam before the fall with the classic qualities
of the wise man who is in direct contact with the laws of
nature.  Basil used Hercules to exemplify Christian ideals
of simple living.[88]  Although Augustine had no patience
with legendary Stoic claims to self-sufficiency, he did
describe the saintly inhabitants of his City of God as living
together as brothers in happy coordination with the laws
of nature, and he did describe a good Christian, a pilgrim
on the way to the heavenly city, in terms reminiscent of
the Roman ideal of the virtuous but imperfect citizen doing
his duty to the best of his ability.[89]
    If Augustine and Aquinas rejected the Stoic claim that
all we need to make us happy is to be virtuous, pointing
out that no one is without sin and that there is no such
thing as perfect happiness on earth, Macrobius and Boethius
both argued that virtue is sufficient for happiness.[90]
Though Macrobius (c.400-430), like Boethius, may not have
been a Christian, his commentary on the Somnium Scipionis

(from Book VI of Cicero's _De Republica_) was another popular
channel through which Stoic ideas passed to the Middle Ages
and the Renaissance. Boethius, who was thought to be a
Christian, strongly promoted the ideal of moral self-sufficiency,
maintaining that no misfortune can befall the good man.
The virtuous Boethian man, though tossed by the storms of
fortune, can remain imperturbable as he reminds himself
that only his baggage can be hurt (I. Pr 3), that one who
neither hopes nor fears is safe both from the violence of
nature and from the anger of tyrants (I. M 4). Happiness,
which is the supreme good, is defined as the state of mind
belonging to him who can bear all calmly, to the person
who is master of himself (II. Pr 4). Riches--usually considered
a benefit--may actually cause harm by promoting covetousness
(II. Pr 5), and fortune, in general, is not necessarily
good, since she is not always associated with good men and
since she does not make good those with whom she is joined
(II. Pr 6). But virtue is sufficient for happiness, since
a good man is both happy and godlike, while wicked men are
punished by losing their nature as men and becoming beasts.
The wicked cease, in fact, to exist (III. Pr 10, IV. Pr 3).
Paradoxically, then, apparent bad fortune may actually be
good fortune; for if good fortune can turn men into beasts,
bad fortune gives the wise man a chance to strengthen his
wisdom (IV. Pr 7). In typical Stoic allegorical fashion
Boethius summarizes the adventures of Hercules, showing
that Hercules' reward for enduring his trials was to be
made a god (IV. Pr 7).

Aquinas, who reserved perfect virtue for God and the
angels[91] and considered that only a saint could safely let
his inner voice speak louder than tradition and authority,
nevertheless described the limited virtue that an imperfect
human being might hope to acquire. This virtue, which was
tied to one's place in the hierarchy, placed different requirements on different people. But since kings came at the
top of the ladder and were supposedly endowed with better
insight into natural law than the rest of us, they were
also supposed, in theory, to meet higher standards of virtue.
The effect of this doctrine on literature, where it was
easier than in life to produce kings to specification, was
that good kings often bear a marked resemblance to the Stoic
wise man. As Erasmus said in _The Education of a Christian
Prince_, "A good, wise, and upright prince is nothing else
than a sort of living law" (p. 221).

The argument that virtue is sufficient for happiness
is another one that has a number of ramifications. Sometimes,
as in the case of Boethius, a sufferer is consoled with
the argument that since he is virtuous he must, by definition,
be happy. At other times we are given a picture of virtuous
Stoic-Epicurean content, as, for instance, the poor widow
at the opening of Chaucer's "Nun's Priest's Tale."

This Classic theme, which began to spread again during the
Renaissance and which we associate especially with English
literature of the eighteenth century, had not been entirely
eradicated even in the Middle Ages. The contented Christian
who lives simply, accepts his lot without complaint, and
tries as well as he can to obey the will of God has many
similarities with the tranquil Stoic-Epicurean country mouse.
Strictly speaking, from the theological point of view, perhaps,
a Christian should never expect to enjoy the content that
comes from being pleased with his own performance; but,
as we have already seen on the subject of fate and the
stars, the teachings of theologians often change color when
they appear in the work of popular writers. And even theologians made use of peace-of-mind terminology when they
were trying to describe the condition of mankind before
the Fall, or of saints in heaven, or of God and the angels.
Augustine said that before the Fall Adam and Eve enjoyed
peace of mind, that God and the angels have peace of mind,
and that saints will ultimately be rewarded with peace of
mind. Adam and Eve, in their sinless state, lived like
good Stoics, loving virtue for its own sake, not from fear
of punishment, and were as yet undisturbed by desire for
forbidden fruit; for, as Augustine said, it "is surely sin,
to desire the things that the law of God prohibits and to
abstain from them through fear of punishment and not through
love of righteousness." If there had been no Fall, the
whole human race would have lived "as fortunate, therefore,
as were the first human beings, who were neither troubled
by any agitations of mind nor distressed by any ailments
of body." Similarly the angels, as they carry out the will
of God--punishing the wicked, relieving the miserable, aiding
those in danger--are undisturbed by such human emotions
as anger, sympathy, or fear. But when Augustine was talking
about ordinary sinful human beings, he considered the Stoic ideal
of emotionless apathy to be vicious and said the Stoic hope
of living free from fear and pain is unattainable on this
earth, "if we would live in the right way, that is, according
to God." However, just as he transferred the Stoic dream
of an ideal commonwealth to the next world, so he transferred
to heaven the Stoic ideal of tranquillity. For he said
that we may hope to enjoy this kind of peace "in that happy
life which we are promised will be everlasting."[92] Likewise,
Aquinas, who said that perfect happiness or perfect pleasure
is another name for blessedness, the joy of the saints in
God, reserved true bliss for heaven and said that perfect
equanimity and perfect freedom from passion, like perfect
virtue, are not attainable by imperfect human beings (see
n. 91).

The fact is, however, that imperfect human beings have
a way of wanting to be happy on earth; and just as the Stoics
admitted that their wise man was only a far-off ideal, so

the Christians borrowed Stoic and Epicurean recipes for
limited earthly peace of mind.  In this art, one of their
favorite teachers was Boethius, who, as we have seen, had
argued in the Classical manner, that the virtuous man is
rewarded psychologically with emotional tranquillity and
that the evil man is punished with emotional perturbation.
In addition to recommending the pursuit of abstract virtue
as the avenue to peace, Boethius, like Horace and Seneca,
also gave specific advice on how to soften the jolts of
fortune.  For even though he argued that in an absolute
sense fortune does not really exist, he admitted that from
our limited human point of view we all seem to be affected
by the ups and downs of chance.  The advice that he offered
echoes down the pages of English literature.  He tells us
to stay away from high places, to live small, to avoid the
ladder of ambition: "He that would build on a lasting rest-
ing-place . . . must leave the lofty mountain's top. . . .
Let him be mindful to set his house surely upon the lowly
rock."  Lady Philosophy, like Seneca, Virgil, Ovid, et al,
sings of the rugged simple life of the happy former age
before men began digging up gold and pursuing other luxuries.
She reminds us that those whose pockets are empty need not
fear robbers.  Boethius, who was generally accepted as a
Christian, was for centuries a source for Greek and Roman
ideas about the dignity of the good man and the sufficiency
of virtue for the happy life.[93]  Though he was not the only
writer responsible for the recurrence in English literature
of the democratic theme that true happiness and true nobility
are based on virtue, he was long a favorite teacher.

Meanwhile the objections of Christians like Augustine
and Aquinas to the Stoic argument that virtue is sufficient
for happiness have also become embedded in literature as
part of the long Christian attack on Stoic pride; for even
though Augustine and Aquinas numbered many Stoic and Epicurean writers of the Roman period among their favorite authors,
they generally used the word "Stoic" with a bad connotation.
Augustine, who pointed out that Stoics and Epicureans were
simply ignoring the facts when they tried to convince themselves they could be happy during this one short, unpleasant
life, asked why anyone would need the virtues of prudence,
temperance, justice, and, especially, fortitude if the world
were not full of evil.  Moreover, if the ills of life are
not real ills, how illogical for the wise man to commit
suicide.  Augustine suggested that it was not fortitude
but weakness that prompted Cato to kill himself.  The Stoic
ideal of self-sufficiency, of living virtuously through
one's own efforts, is merely pride; and the argument that
virtue is the one true good and that all the external and
bodily advantages valued by most people are really of no
consequence, is only verbal quibbling.  We do have to admit

the justice of Augustine's argument; for even Boethius, who was steeped in philosophy, had to wait until he was thrown into prison to remind himself that the gifts of fortune are only cheats. If we look closely at a Stoic, Augustine strongly implies, we are likely to find a hypocrite. Illustrating his argument with a story from Aulus Gellius that belongs to a type frequent in English literature, he describes a smug Stoic who is tested and found wanting. Under stress, in this case a storm at sea, the boastful Stoic becomes so agitated that he is unable to match the unpretentious fortitude of the other, non-Stoic, passengers. From Fielding's Parson Adams to Conrad's Lord Jim the type is familiar. The Stoic in Augustine's illustration was described as reading from "a work of the Stoic Epictetus, which contained doctrines that agreed with the pronouncements of Zeno and Chrysippus, who were, as we know, the founders of the Stoic school."[94] Since virtue, says Augustine, requires a proper response to a situation, a Christian must be angry when necessary, must be able to fear and desire, to grieve and rejoice. Augustine devotes several chapters to his disagreement with the Stoics on the question of self control, a quarrel that undoubtedly had much to do with the later custom of deriding Stoicism as merely emotionless passivity. For, like many a writer after him, Augustine associated Stoicism with the early Stoic condemnation of all feeling, particularly accusing Stoics of rejecting compassion[95]-- which may be one reason why ambitious but pitiless villains in Elizabethan literature are sometimes described as Stoics.

Aquinas, in similar vein, said that the Stoics were wrong to say that no evil can happen to a wise man, pointing out that perfect peace of mind on earth is not possible, partly because the body, even if it is not the supreme good, is nevertheless a valuable possession that can be hurt and partly because the happiness that comes from being completely pleased with one's own virtuous performance is simply not possible for sinful human beings. In fact, moderate sorrow is a mark of virtue. Although the perfect virtue of God and the angels is without passion, nevertheless the passions are in themselves neither good nor evil. If disordered passion is bad, moderated passion is good.[96] This relative position, emphasizing the golden mean--which is the one generally accepted in popular writing--though it takes issue with the absolutist position of the earlier Stoics--is actually similar to the position of moderate writers like Cicero and Horace and Seneca.

When we turn at last in the direction of English literature and look to see what Stoic ideas, if any, have appealed to the ages of _Beowulf_ and Chaucer, we find, as we might expect, that although by the time of Chaucer many of the Stoic commonplaces of Elizabethan literature are clearly evident, the Old English picture is more obscure.

Although it is customary to speak of the stoic mood of Old
English poetry, this generalized stoicism, which we may
spell with a small s, has only tenuous connections with
the Classical types. Some elements of Old English literature that we loosely call stoic are the melancholy tone
and the emphasis on mutability, which may remind us of Seneca
or Marcus Aurelius; the omnipresence of Wyrd, which makes
us think of Stoic fate; and the fortitude either of heroes
fighting against impossible odds or of sufferers forced
to endure incurable misfortunes.

Since here, as in much literature, a coating of Classical
and Christian ideas has often been applied to attitudes
that belong to other traditions, it is not easy to make
generalizations. Does the melancholy mood mask an underlying
cheerfulness about the ultimate benevolence of the world
ruler, or are we to concentrate on the many evidences that
things seem to be falling apart? In a number of the short
poems that have been called lyrics, a speaker, who seems
to have reached the bottom of woe, seeks emotional relief
by loudly complaining about his misery. There is no evidence
that he or she is seeking peace of mind through the consolation of philosophy, or even that the speaker has much faith
in a just universe. The various speakers who are outcasts
from society never console themselves with the thought that
they can still be citizens of the world, for the worst thing
that can happen is to be driven out of the tribe as Beowulf's
cowardly retainers were. In general a remedy for misfortune
is pictured in material rather than in psychological terms.
Good luck rather than equanimity is the goal. Although
the unhappy, masterless speaker in the "Wanderer" derives
some comfort from reflecting that since mutability is everywhere those on top may soon be as miserable as he, he is
not really interested in peace of mind. Motivated partly
by prudence, partly by aristocratic pride, he considers
it good policy to keep his thoughts to himself and to maintain the pose of outer calm that is frequently described
as stoic. If he tells himself that help might come from
God, it is help in reversing fortune that he wants, not
help in learning to accept the will of God. In a poem like
the "Wife's Lament" the speaker, presumably a wife who has
been turned out, concentrates on her woe without offering
any moral. In "The Ruined City" the poet emphasizes the
universality of mutability as he mourns the remains of what
was once a magnificent city. But even if the speakers in
most of these Old English complaints manifest little interest
in philosophical comfort and need not have derived their
themes from classical sources, there is still a possibility
that they are echoing earlier writers from Greece and, particularly, Rome. A number of scholars have called attention
to the possible relationship between the Old English lyric
and the classical complaint and to the popularity in both
genres of the theme of mutability.[97] Many a lyric is built

around the old and ever popular theme that, as Boethius said,
"The memory of happier things is of memories most miserable"
(II. Pr 4), a theme most familiar to us in Dante's later
version (Inf. V.121).[98]  But where the Stoic is forever
reminding us that bad fortune will afflict us less if we
remember that good fortune is one of those indifferent things
that we must always be prepared to surrender, the usual
speaker in an Old English lyric concentrates on regret for
what has been lost.  A possible exception is the poem "Deor,"
where the speaker, perhaps a homeless scop, tries to teach
himself patience by calling to mind the tales of various
legendary sufferers.  As he recalls their woes, he tells
himself again and again, "That now is gone; this too will
go,"[99] emphasizing the eternal flux as a potential source
of comfort; for bad fortune may pass as well as good fortune.
As he tells himself, in a reflective passage (lines 28-34),
neither well nor woe is the constant; all these ups and
downs of fortune reflect the will of wise God who gives
to some honor, fame, and fortune; to others, woe.  Although
this unhappy speaker, like the speakers in the other lyrics,
obviously wishes he were one of the lucky ones, there is
a faint echo here of the moral, whether Christian or Stoic,
that all fortune must be accepted as the will of God.

Although the cause of much of the woe in Old English
poetry is inscrutable Wyrd, the meaning of Wyrd is as difficult to decipher as the meaning of fortune or fate in later
poetry;[100] for Wyrd behaves sometimes like fate, sometimes
like fortune, sometimes like a good providence, and sometimes
like a malignant demon.  The Beowulf poet who, like many
another narrative poet, was not primarily concerned with
expounding complex philosophical ideas, gives the word "Wyrd"
different meanings in different contexts.  Sometimes Wyrd
seems to act as the instrument of an arbitrary god who saves
or slays at his pleasure (lines 696-702); and in general
Wyrd is associated with the idea that we are all under sentence
of death, though with an indefinite reprieve.  Unlike Stoic
fate, Wyrd is not completely impersonal. "Wyrd oft saveth /
an earl not doomed, if he dauntless prove" (lines 572-73).[101]
This idea appears not only in Beowulf but also in other
Old English works.  In the "Andreas," a religious poem about
saints Matthew and Andrew, Andrew heartens his followers
by telling them that God will never desert a man whose courage
avails; and we are subsequently shown the saints, who have
patiently endured suffering and torture for the glory of
God, receiving earthly rewards.[102]  In Alfred's translation
of Boethius' Consolation one of the interpolated non-Boethian
passages defends free will and insists that although men
may not escape death, "they can keep him back with good
deeds, so that he comes later" (Ch. XLI).[103]  There is little
evidence that death is welcomed as a release from troubles.
Even when Saint Guthlac is carried to heaven by angels,
his friends mourn instead of rejoicing, telling themselves

that "endurance is best in the blows of affliction, / When
the hour woven by Wyrd is come."[104]  When Beowulf dies,
he dies against his will (lines 2586-90).  Although the
optimistic Boethian doctrine that all fortune must be accepted
as good fortune makes little appearance, we do find in Beowulf
the more generalized idea that we are forced to accept the
facts of life.  We are told early in the poem that Wyrd
goes as it must ("swa hio scel") (line 455) and are reminded
later that death is not easy for any man to escape (lines
1002-1008).  At the end of the dragon fight we are told
that every man must give up this transitory life (lines
2590-91).  Beowulf loses because Wyrd has not decreed that
he should win (lines 2574-75).  The total poem impresses
on us the vanity of human wishes and the dominance of mutability.  For we are shown that a nation or a family or a
man may flourish for a while, but only for a while and that
ideal kings like Hrothgar and Beowulf are helpless to prevent
the destruction of their people.  Instead of the benevolent
providence of the Elizabethan dramatists, we have here only
an inscrutable Wyrd.  Every good intention of Hrothgar seems
to go wrong.  If he plans to spend his old age enjoying
his mead hall, out of the mere comes Grendel; if he tries
to promote peace by marrying his daughter to an enemy, he
only brings on more war; and his attempts to provide powerful
Geatish friends for his son are frustrated.  Even Beowulf,
the flawless hero, has no greater success with his long-
term efforts, since he sacrifices his life only to hasten
the destruction of his people.  Though it is possible that
the Beowulf poet inserted here and there a Boethian thought,[105]
just as he may have introduced some Augustinian thoughts,
we miss the general optimistic Boethian message that apparent
evil is only part of the universal benevolent and rational
plan.  Missing likewise is the finally optimistic message
of a poem like the Aeneid.  For where Aeneas in carrying
out his assigned lot was also carrying out the will of God
and fulfilling the destiny of Rome, Beowulf and his people
were destroyed by Wyrd.

But even if Wyrd has only tenuous connections with Boethian
providence, Beowulf himself may still display some characteristics of the Stoic hero, especially a hero of the Hercules
type who overcomes dangers for the sake of mankind.  Since
so little is known about the circumstances under which the
few surviving Old English works were composed, there has
been room for speculation that some or all of the writers
were influenced by the Roman ways of thinking to which both
the Germanic peoples and the British had long been exposed.
Prominent among these ideas were Roman notions of patriotic
duty, the idea of playing one's allotted part.[106]  Among
the commentators who believe that Beowulf was composed by
a cleric, there are some who see evidences not only that
the poet had been reading Augustine or Boethius but also
that he had been reading Virgil.  They point out that Beowulf,

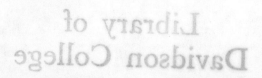

who demonstrates in youth the qualities of the ideal Germanic
thane and in old age those of the ideal Germanic king, has,
in addition--when compared with some other Germanic heroes
who can be glimpsed fleetingly in the surviving fragments
of other heroic poems--a wider conscience than these others,
a less purely tribal loyalty, a more selfless devotion to
the welfare of his people, a less exclusive concern with
revenge or fame or gold.[107] It has even been proposed that
the poem may have been composed as a manual for princes,
presumably in the tradition of Cicero's De Officiis or Virgil's
Aeneid.[108] Klaeber, who has compared Beowulf to Hercules,
to Aeneas, even to Christ, calls him "a perfect hero, without
fear and without reproach,--the strongest of his generation,
valorous, resolute, great-hearted and noble of soul, wise
and steadfast, kind, courteous, and unselfish, a truly 'happy
warrior.'" Chambers says that "here we have the character
of the Christian hero, the medieval knight, emerging from
the turmoil of the Germanic Heroic Age." Brodeur, in describing Beowulf's death, says, "The good man can only face
his responsibility and accept his destiny."[109] Klaeber,
who emphasizes the Christian elements in Beowulf, thinks
some of the classical ideas came by way of Augustine and
goes along, also, with the idea that the Beowulf poet may
have been familiar with the Aeneid, which could have given
him lessons not only about epic poetry but also the recipe
for a selfless hero.[110] Other scholars remind us that Roman
civilization could have affected the Angles even before
they came to England, since literary influences are not
the only ones. R. C. Sutherland argues that the idea of
eorlscipe in Beowulf has overtones of the Roman ideal of
discharging one's office.[111]

If we accept these suggestions, we must nevertheless
keep our emphasis on overtones without trying to push the
resemblance too far. The same caution applies when we are
considering the fortitude displayed by Beowulf and by other
Germanic heroes. Their courage is of a generalized sort
that does not tell us much about the underlying philosophical
attitude of the protagonist.[112] There are many possible
motives for bearing pain or distress without noise. A hero
may be conforming to the standards of his tribe or his class
or refusing to give pleasure to his enemies or to the malignant powers that rule the universe, for the desire to make
a dignified exit is not restricted to those who believe
that God's in his heaven and all's right with the world.
Byrhtwold in "Maldon" (ca. 991) demonstrates the generalized
fortitude that we loosely call stoic. As he and his followers
go on fighting in a lost cause, their courage the keener
as their might grows less (lines 312-13), they illustrate
the popular maxim that it is less important whether we win
than how we play the game. Similarly Beowulf, who dies
against his will, nevertheless wins not only because he
kills the dragon but also because he dies with his integrity

intact. King Alfred's famous statement of the ideal occurs
as another of the interpolated passages in his translation
of the Consolation. "My will was to live worthily as long
as I lived, and after my life to leave to them that should
come after, my memory in good works" (Ch. XVII). We meet
here a difference from the strict Stoic contempt for worldly
opinion, to which Milton glancingly referred when he spoke
of that last infirmity of noble mind, namely, the frequently
expressed Old English hope that good deeds will be rewarded
with earthly fame. Ironically, Alfred's hope that his memory
will endure has been inserted just before the long Boethian-
Stoic demonstration of the emptiness of fame (Chs. XVIII-
XIX). Beowulf is frankly motivated both by a desire for
gold and a desire for fame. He himself considers earthly
reputation to be the only worthwhile attainment (lines 1386-
89), while the last words of the poem praise his great desire
for fame. In the "Seafarer" the unhappy wanderer, who sees
nothing certain but mutability, tells us that praise is
the thing to work for, heavenly as well as earthly.

The obvious place to hunt for Old English Stoic ideas
is, of course, in King Alfred's translation of Boethius'
Consolation (ca. 900).[113] Since Alfred (849-901) included
the Consolation among the half dozen essential Christian
works he translated or had translated, it suggests that
he regarded Boethius as a Christian. At the same time,
however, of all the books that were Englished under his
name, this was the one that was altered most.[114] And even
a cursory glance at some of the ideas that were accepted
or rejected will indicate which aspects of Stoicism (and
Epicureanism) could be fitted into the contemporary creed.
For instance, the Stoic insistence on the self-sufficiency
of the good man has to be carefully qualified before it
can be accepted. Alfred therefore inserts a statement to
the effect that "God only is without need, not man; God,
being self-sufficing, needeth nothing besides what He hath
in Himself" (Ch. XXIV). However, Alfred seems to accept
the Stoic argument that virtue is sufficient for happiness
because "one man can injure another only in the body, or
at least in those worldly possessions that ye call happiness.
But no man can harm the discerning mind, nor make it other
than it is" (Ch. XVI). And, as we might expect, he accepts
the four Platonic-Stoic-Christian virtues of prudence, temperance, fortitude, and justice, here said to be contained
in the highest virtue, wisdom (Ch. XXVII). In addition
to the above assertion that virtue is sufficient for happiness,
he also accepts some aspects of the Stoic-Epicurean dream
of earthly tranquillity. He includes, for instance, the
well-known primitivistic passage praising the simple life
of the golden age (Boethius, II, M 5) with its conclusion,
"Alas, what was the first avaricious man, who first began
to dig the earth after gold, and after gems, and found the
dangerous treasure, which before was hid and covered with the

earth!"(Alfred, Ch. XV).[115]  Even in <u>Beowulf</u> there may have
been an echo of this passage when after Beowulf's death
the mourning Geats unexpectedly buried along with him the
dragon's gold that he himself had plainly regarded as such
a good thing that he wanted a last look at it before he
died.  The idea of returning the gold to the ground where
it belongs, though a commonplace of Cynic, Stoic, Epicurean,
and Christian writing, is, as Klaeber notes (p. 230), not
Germanic.  It may be that we have here an instance of an
isolated Boethian thought that has found its way into the
Beowulf story.  At any rate, this passage, which in Alfred's
version is embellished slightly by the addition of a few
lines underscoring a similarity between the fires of hell
and the fires of covetousness, was also to become a commonplace of English literature.

Other Boethian passages that remain unchallenged in
Alfred's version are classical recipes for achieving earthly
content through cutting down desire, warnings that wealth
and success do not give happiness--since there is always
something more to be wished for or something possessed but
not wanted (Chs. VII, XI, XXVI)--and reminders that all
fortune is good fortune, since nothing happens by chance
and God has a reason for the way he distributes good and
bad fortune (Ch. XL).  But a mention of the Epicurean opinion
that pleasure is the highest good is accompanied by the
usual Christian anti-Epicurean remark about sensuality (Ch.
XXIV).

Divorced from its Epicurean label, however, the idea
that happiness on earth is possible for those who choose
the simple life is a Classical dream that came to be accepted
by a great many Christian writers.  Though it makes little
appearance in Old English poetry, it is plainly evident
by the time of Chaucer.  The spread of its popularity doubtless owes much to the popularity of Boethius, for if at
the time of Alfred, Boethius was still the property of the
intellectuals in the monasteries, by the time of Chaucer,
Boethian ideas had become commonplaces.

As we enter the time of Chaucer we need to remind ourselves of one commonplace that is so obvious it is easy
to overlook, namely, that the ideas in scholarly treatises
take a long time to make their way into popular writing
and that when writers do pick up these ideas they are quite
likely to acquire them from some second-hand source.  Among
influential second-hand sources for Stoic ideas about the
law of nature, for instance, there was the Medieval legal
system, which carried on the Roman teaching that man-made
laws should be a reflection of the universal unwritten
laws.[116]  (Although the OED's first English reference to
Stoics comes from Wyclif in 1382, it cites English allusions
to the distinction between natural law and positive law

from the Cursor Mundi [c. 1300].)  Second, there were the
popular preachers, who hammered home in diluted form for
everyday use, what was actually meant, in terms of currently
accepted doctrine, by living in conformity with the laws
of nature.  And lastly, of course, there were the works
of other literary men.  A bookish writer like Chaucer, for
instance, could have found Stoic ideas not only in Boethius
but also in such other writers from whom he borrowed as
Alain de Lille, Jean de Meun, Dante, Petrarch, and Boccaccio.[117]  Seneca's name is often mentioned by medieval writers,
and there is even an occasional reference to Epictetus.
Proverbs, allegedly quoted from Seneca, the quasi-Christian
moralist, fill us with advice on how to adjust to our fate
or fortune.  Sometimes, also, there are references to the
Stoicized Socrates or Diogenes, both favorite heroes of
Seneca and Epictetus, from whom we learn that fortune cannot
harm the man of reason.[118]

Again and again throughout this study I shall be returning to the three recurring Stoic themes on which I am concentrating:  peace of mind, the law of nature, and the ideal
wise man, with emphasis constantly on the various ways in
which succeeding literary generations managed to re-adapt
these basic themes to changing times.  In Chaucer's writings
the peace-of-mind tradition, often associated in later periods
with Horace and Seneca, has a distinctly Boethian flavor
and puts heavy stress on remedies for fortune.  We may note
in passing, however, that not all Chaucerian references
to fortune are Boethian.  In "The Book of the Duchess,"
where the mood is reminiscent of that in an Old English
complaint, no effective consolation is offered against the
meaningless blow of fortune that has struck down the Knight
in Black.  Even if the Dreamer-narrator half-heartedly tells
the Knight to remember Socrates, who cared not three straws
for anything fortune could do, his argument is silenced
when he is finally made to realize what an unparalleled
treasure the Knight has lost.  And in "The Monk's Tale,"
fortune is the ambiguous creature who appears in much litera-
ture--sometimes merely capricious and heartless, delighting
in the harm she causes; sometimes self-righteously punishing
the proud and wicked.[119]  For example, where Boethius had
treated Hercules as the Stoic hero who endured his trials
so well that after death he became a god, Chaucer emphasized
only the tragedy of a great man overthrown by fortune.
Where Boethius had used Nero to illustrate his argument
that good fortune is not the same as happiness--since Nero,
in spite of his worldly prosperity, is neither happy himself
nor able to make others happy--Chaucer shows righteous fortune
overthrowing Nero as a punishment for his wickedness.  Incidentally, Chaucer's story about Nero illustrates the usual
Medieval attitude toward Seneca, described here as the wise
teacher, the flower of morality, who had succeeded for a
time in keeping his young master from vice (line 2495) but

who was forced in the end to bleed in his bath because his moral lessons had irked his pupil. Seneca here plays the role not of a sour Stoic but of a quasi-Christian moralist.[120]

In marked contrast to these other works is Chaucer's treatment of fortune in "The Knight's Tale" and "Troilus and Cressida," both of them probably written shortly after he made his translation of Boethius' Consolation of Philosophy (c. 1380).[121] Although Chaucer's translation is adulterated Boethius, much as Alfred's translation had been--interlarded with explanatory Christian asides and based not only on the Latin original but also on a French version ascribed to Jean de Meun and a Latin commentary by Nicholas Trivet--nevertheless Boethian lessons for a time tint Chaucer's poetry.[122] Not all Boethian ideas are Stoic, of course; nor is Boethius the only possible source of Stoic ideas in Chaucer. Another treasure trove of miscellaneous Classical lore, which likewise contained ideas from Boethius, was Jean de Meun's continuation of the Roman de la Rose.

The Boethian theme that appears heavily in both "The Knight's Tale" and "Troilus" is the doctrine that fortune does not really exist, that fate and fortune are really the same thing, both instruments of providence. Consequently the wise man accepts all fortune as good fortune, realizing that happiness is peace of mind. Since nothing happens by chance, Chaucer gaily explains the various improbable coincidences in his plots as all part of the divine plan, taking advantage, in the process, of popular ideas about astrology. For in spite of the objections of Augustine and Aquinas to the recurring fondness for seeing a relationship between human activities and the motions of the planets, the Roman fascination with astrology went marching on. Astrology has some ties with the Stoic tradition, even if it was not accepted by all Roman Stoics.[123]

Although fortune does not exist and although everything is fated, nevertheless the good man is free. This paradox, whether Christian or Stoic, interprets freedom, or peace of mind, as an inner thing. It is the emotional reward, otherwise known as happiness, that comes from making virtue of necessity, of gladly accepting the will of God. This peace, which Troilus achieves only after death, is possessed by the wise King Theseus in "The Knight's Tale," as well as by his father, Aegeus. These ideal characters stand on the sidelines while the stories themselves are concerned with the sufferings of the passion-driven young lovers who wrongly assume that happiness means winning the lady of their choice. Since few of us can expect to achieve the serenity of Theseus, we easily identify with the comical-tragical woes of Palamon, Arcite, and Troilus. An ironical undercurrent in the story of Palamon and Arcite is the habit these two have of quoting Boethius while at the same time paying no attention to the meaning of the words they are quoting. When Palamon in prison first cries out in pain

at the distant vision of Emily, Arcite lectures him in the
manner used by sham Stoics throughout the pages of literature. Pompously he tells Palamon that since their present
adversity has been decreed by the stars at the time of their
birth, there is nothing to do but "taak al in pacience. . . .
We moste endure it; this is the short and playn" (1084).
But a moment later, when he too glimpses Emily, he switches
his argument into an attempt to twist another passage from
Boethius so that it will support the idea that love knows
no law (1164). Chaucer was well aware of the joke here
since the lines come from his own gloss to Boethius' account
of the way the slave-to-passion Orpheus impatiently spoiled
his chance for happiness (II.m.12).[124] Later, when Arcite
is released from prison but banished from Athens, he complains
about his bad luck while at the same time moralizing in
the Boethian manner that men ought not to complain against
fortune, since the ways of providence are inscrutable (1251)
and we may be well off when we think we are worst off.[125]
Arcite, who speaks better than he knows, bemoans his fate
because he has been removed from the chance of glimpsing
Emily. Meanwhile Palamon, left behind in prison, also frets,
complaining as Boethius himself had done before Lady Philosophy
came to lecture him into a better frame of mind (I.m.5).
Palamon insists there is no justice in the universe if good
men like himself can be locked up in prison while thieves
and other evil creatures may go where they like (1304).
But Arcite, who is technically free, is no happier than
Palamon in prison since he is actually a slave to passion.
And when the god Mercury tells him to go back to Athens
where an end to his woe has been worked out, he mistakenly
thinks the god means he will win Emily, not perceiving that
the god is talking about real peace of mind; for the end
to woe is death.

Since nothing happens by chance, coincidences are not
real coincidences. Through chance or destiny Palamon escapes
from prison; fortune brings it about that he and Arcite
meet and start a fight, which is accidentally interrupted
by Theseus (1490, 1506, 1515, 1524), all of which Chaucer
justifies in his well-known Boethian or Augustinian passage
on "the destinee, ministre general, / That executeth in
the world over al / The Purveiaunce that God hath seyn biforn"
(1663). In fact, Chaucer here emphasizes fate so much that
he leaves little room for individual responsibility, Christian
or Stoic, actually saying that our appetites, whether for
war or peace or hate or love, are all ruled from above (1670);
for in this part of the poem he is concentrating on showing
the way the young people are forced to work out their destinies.
Even though they pray to the gods for help and receive riddling
promises of appropriate consideration, they are caught in
the master plan. Arcite must die. Although Palamon eventually
receives the girl--for reasons of Athenian-Theban foreign
policy--we are left with the riddling question: Which young

man do we consider the more fortunate? For Arcite dies glori-
ously before his fame has had time to tarnish while Palamon,
who is ostensibly the lucky one, merely dwindles into a
husband.

If the young people seem to be driven completely by
fate, Theseus and his father, Aegeus, teach us that nevertheless the good man is free. The wise man accommodates himself
to fate and to the fact that mutability is a constant law
of nature. As Aegeus says after Arcite's death, "Joye after
wo, and wo after gladnesse" is the nature of life (2837).
Although we are given the Christian message that in an absolute
sense happiness is not for this world, we also receive from
Theseus some classical or Boethian advice on how to make
the best of our present lot. His parting counsel to Palamon
and Emily is to learn to accept their fate, to make virtue
of necessity (3041). In his long speech (2987), much of
it drawn from Boethius, he offers them the consolation of
philosophy, echoing in his own words the message of Marcus
Aurelius that "to be vexed at anything which happens is
a separation of ourselves from nature." As Theseus puts
it, "Whoso gruccheth ought, he dooth folye, / And rebel
is to hym that al may gye" (3045).

In "Troilus and Cressida" the theme is similar, although--
with the possible exception of Cassandra--there is no wise
raisonneur to serve as a contrast to the passion-driven
lovers; for Pandarus, in spite of being wily in the ways
of the world, is far from being wise in the Stoic sense.
Chaucer (or the narrator) makes the point clear, however,
through numerous authorial asides and by having Troilus,
after his death, pause for a moment in the eighth sphere
to look back and contrast the difference between "the pleyn
felicite / That is in heavene above" and the perturbation
he has confused with happiness while pursuing Cressida.
Troilus and Cressida are truly a pair of star-crossed lovers,
their personal woes only a part of Trojan history, as they
carry out a destiny no more comprehensible to them than
the ways of the gods had been to Palamon and Arcite.[126]
Chaucer, while recording Cressida's half-hearted attempts
to resist Troilus (III.617), playfully repeats the moral
from Boethius (IV.pr.vi) that fortune merely executes the
decrees of fate and that it is not for us lowly creatures
to understand the hidden causes. Though Pandarus can read
the stars well enough to make use of a foreordained thunder-
storm, everything he does is part of the overall plan.
The Trojan people, when they insist on exchanging Cressida
for Antenor, show how difficult it is for blind human beings
to know how to make the right choice (IV.197), as Chaucer
points out in his reference to Juvenal (Sat X.9) and to
the vanity of wishing--since it is impossible to know how
to wish wisely. He might, of course, have found the same
ideas in Boethius.

The Stoic-Epicurean advice, that one should train

oneself to stop wishing and learn to accept serenely whatever
comes, was not at all Troilus' notion of how to live.   Until
he died he was always complaining about fortune and battling
against fate and the facts of life.   His story is the story
of one who is never content, forever either hoping or fearing.
First he tortures himself by wishing for something he does
not have; then he attains his desire and tortures himself
with fear that he will lose his prize; then he does lose
Cressida and, instead of accepting the facts, tortures himself with hope that she will return.   Throughout the story
we hear him complaining about fortune and fate and generally
refusing to accept his lot.   In the beginning he foolishly
pretends to be immune to Cupid; but, as Chaucer says, no
man may "fordon the lawe of kynde" (I.238).   Troilus here
is behaving like a sham Stoic, while Chaucer is using "nature"
to mean the physical facts of life that no one may escape.
For his pride Troilus is stricken with an unusually painful
infatuation; since, as Chaucer remarks, the stick "is bet
that bowen wole and wynde / Than that that brest" (I.257).
This popular maxim--best known in La Fontaine's fable of
the proud oak tree and the humble reed--is one way of saying
that the wise man is not the one who boasts of his own self-
sufficiency but the one who bows to the laws of nature--or
the facts of life, or the will of God.   The moral is one
of those adaptable ones that can appear Stoic or Epicurean
or Christian depending on the context.

Troilus suffers for his refusal to accept the fact
that it is the nature of fortune to be changeable (I.846;
IV.1); and he suffers because he is unable to control his
passions; (when Pandarus at one point tries to calm his
misery by offering miscellaneous bits of conventional Senecan-
Boethian consolation, Troilus gives the customary anti-Stoic
answer, accusing his friend of wanting to turn him into
a stone [IV.463]).   Although he keeps saying that everything
is run by fate, that his own destiny was shaped before his
first clothes were made (III.715), he does not really believe
it and prays to every god he can think of--including the
fatal sisters--for help in winning Cressida.   Later, when
he realizes he is likely to lose his briefly won prize,
he lashes out at fortune as if she were a free agent, saying
he has always honored her above all the other gods (IV.260);
later still he tries to obtain emotional relief by blaming
everything on fate, drawing much of his argument from Boethius
(V.pr.2-3).[127]   "Thus to ben lorn, it is my destinee" (IV.959).
Having convinced himself that everything is fated and having
given up the attempt to understand Boethius' argument for
the coexistence of fate and free will, he again begins acting
as if things can be changed for him, praying to almighty
Jove either to kill him soon or to rescue him and Cressida.
He does not pray that he may learn to accept the will of
Jove.[128]   Even when the gods try to explain the facts by
sending him a dream, he refuses to heed his sister Cassandra's

obvious explanation.  So, since he will not accept his fate,
since he cannot learn "to take it for the beste" (V.1750),
he has to be dragged along kicking.

Pandarus and Cressida, like Palamon and Arcite, are
both adept at echoing Boethius' words while generally ignoring Boethius' point.  Early in the story Pandarus inverts
the Consolation by arguing that since peace of mind is the
important thing, Troilus ought not to resist his passion
for Cressida (I.891).  Later, during Troilus' brief period
of happiness, he warns him to be circumspect and not spoil
his good fortune because the worst kind of misery is to
remember happier days (III.1625), borrowing, in this instance,
Boethius' argument for staying off the wheel of fortune
as a justification for using one's wits in an effort to
stay on top.  And still later he argues, like Arcite, that
love knows no law (IV.618).

Though Cressida resists fate less than Troilus, and
suffers less than he, and though Chaucer pointedly refuses
to be severe with her, yet he does not pretend that her
behavior is entirely blameless.  He simply avoids the vexing
conflict between accepting one's fate and maintaining one's
integrity.  More complex than Troilus, Cressida debates
the pros and cons of letting herself fall in love (II.763),
seeing clearly that yielding to passion will mean loss of
freedom and tranquillity.  And at the high point of her
affair with Troilus she responds to teasing from Pandarus
by sliding into a long Boethian soliloquy on the impossibility
of expecting true joy from the gifts of fortune (III.813)
(see Jefferson, p. 130).  As her thoughts go back and forth
between Troilus and Boethius, she, like Palamon complains
about cosmic injustice, asking why an innocent person like
herself should have to suffer while the guilty go free (III.
1016).  And finally, when she is leaving Troy and Troilus,
she offers her lover some useless Stoic advice--to be patient
and make virtue of necessity because fortune has no power
over one who is not afraid of her (IV.1586).  Here, though
she sounds like Theseus, she is scarcely speaking with the
same moral authority as he, and she is speaking to one who
is unable to listen.  The plight of Troilus and Cressida
is only the plight of most of us, and Chaucer's use of an
ironic Boethian backdrop for his little tragedy hardly deprives
his comic-tragic human beings of sympathy or suggests that
mere mortals are likely to be able to achieve Boethian serenity.
His habit of playing with several ideas at the same time
always keeps him from being an entirely satisfactory propagandist
for any system.

Though Chaucer's fascination with the idea that since
everything is fated there is nothing to do but "take it
for the beste" is most evident in "The Knight's Tale" and
"Troilus," there are occasional reminders in the other tales
of the dangers of trying to go against fate.  Two familiar

examples are Chanticleer, who nearly pays dearly for failing
to heed the warnings he receives in a dream, and Dorigen
in "The Franklin's Tale," who, although she says she is
quite familiar with the optimistic philosophical argument
that "al is for the beste" since a wise and perfect God
creates nothing without a reason (865), nevertheless forgets that wishing to change the balance of nature may have
unexpected consequences.  In other poems than "The Knight's
Tale" and "Troilus," also, there are evidences of the doctrine
that earthly happiness, or at least content, is possible
for those who have learned to stay off the wheel of fortune,
to live simply, and to make virtue of necessity.  We think
of "The Former Age" with its description of the happy time
in the mythical past when all men lived the virtuous simple
life.  Here there is, appropriately, a reference to Diogenes
the Cynic; and though the poem obviously echoes Boethius
(II.M.5), other possible sources for this popular idea have
been pointed out, and no doubt many more could be found.[129]
In "The Wife of Bath's Tale" (line 1183) the loathly lady
alludes to Seneca and Juvenal as she gives the reluctant
knight the old argument that the less one has the less vulnerable one is, not only to fortune but also to sin, telling
him that the poor man who gladly accepts his poverty is
actually rich because he is free from fear and free from
desire.  In the beginning of "The Nun's Priest's Tale" there
is the poor widow, one of those rare characters who has
actually found the Stoic-Epicurean good life on earth.
Contented poverty and simple diet reward her with good health
and peace of mind. She is happy because she accepts all
fortune as good fortune.  Although all of these recipes
for earthly felicity contain a faint Epicurean strain, Chaucer,
like others, kept his public references to Epicurus and
Epicureans safely uncomplimentary.[130]

Chaucer's most famous recipe for the good life comes
in the ballade "Truth," which again contains a combination
of classical and Christian ideas.  The poem begins with
the classical recipe for heaven on earth, familiar in such
writers as Horace and Seneca and Boethius, that tells us
to run away from the corrupt world, to be content with what
we have, to stay off the ladder of ambition, and to rule
ourselves (i.e., make perfect our wills).  Although the
advice to dwell with truth sounds Christian, it is not necessarily more Christian than Stoic or Cynic or Socratic, since
truth is a vague word and since both Stoics and Christians
expect virtue to make them free, to give them peace of mind--
the Stoic here, the Christian hereafter.  It was a favorite
Boethian idea that those who follow reason are free while
those who give way to passion become slaves or beasts, lose
humanity.[131]

The law-of-nature tradition, to which we now turn,
aims at the same final result from a different angle.  Although
the need to make virtue of necessity--or to accept all fortune

as good fortune--remains unchanged, the emphasis is more
on active cooperation than on passive acquiescence. Accepting our lot in life means doing our duty to the best of
our ability in our ordained social station. Where we associate
Seneca and Boethius with the tradition of patient resignation,
we associate Cicero and Aquinas with the active performance
of duty. One humanist of earlier times who had set down
for Englishmen the ever-popular Ciceronian ideals was John
of Salisbury (c. 1120-1180), whose Latin Policraticus
(Statesman's Book), which belongs to the long line of works
modeled on Cicero's Of Duties, describes the functions of
the ideal state and the ideal prince in terms of the doctrine
that virtue means playing our allotted parts.[132]  Chaucer's
friend John Gower (c. 1330-1408) is described by John Fisher
as having written all three of his long major works (Mirour
de l'Homme, Vox Clamantis, and Confessio Amantis) on "the
theme of universal harmony based upon individual virtue
and social law and order" (p. 217). To indicate how closely
Gower reflected contemporary thinking, Fisher points out
the similarity between his arguments about law and those
of Aquinas, though he says Gower never mentions Aquinas.
G. R. Owst, in his study of the relations between Literature
and Pulpit in Medieval England, emphasizes the similarity
between Gower's many pictures of social deviation and the
attacks on those deviations contained in popular sermons.
As an idealist, Gower was ever hopeful that men could be
reasoned or shamed into living up to the cooperative dream
of selfless dedication to an assigned part in a particular
class. Interestingly, when Gower looked back to idealize
a golden former age, it was not the primitive simple life
described by Boethius that attracted him but rather the
well-run commonwealth of his dreams.[133]

Since the idealized hierarchical system, known in
Gower's time and Shakespeare's as the law of nature or reason
was not supposed to be susceptible to different interpretations, writers always assumed that the interpretation that
seemed obvious to them was the true one. Fisher says that
Gower, in addition to satirizing delinquent members of all
social classes, complained--as later humanists were to do--
that the Church bureaucracy was multiplying positive laws
that had no relation to the laws of nature. Baugh reports
that John Wycliffe (c. 1320-84) argued "that all temporal
lordship is under the overlordship of God, that the condition
on which it may be exercised is righteousness, and that
if this condition is violated the unrighteous may be deprived
of their property" (p. 269), the presumption here being
that Wycliffe thought everyone agreed with his definition
of righteous property holding.

The righteous person, the one who directs all his actions
in accordance with the laws of nature, is the happy or wise
man. Although rare in the flesh, he often appears, under
various guises, in didactic literature. One of the many

ways to read the Prologue to Chaucer's Canterbury Tales
is to regard the knight, the parson, and the plowman as
ideal representatives of their respective classes, while
most of the other characters stand for deviations from the
ideal, even though treated less harshly than analogous characters in Gower or Langland. Similarly in the tales themselves there are occasional examples of characters who have
achieved happiness through virtue. At one end of the social
scale there is Theseus in "The Knight's Tale" who combines
Boethian peace of mind with excellence as a wise Ciceronian
ruler.[134] At the other end of the scale there is the poor
widow of "The Nun's Priest's Tale" who makes the best of
her assigned lot. Incidentally, the theme of glad poverty,
which Chaucer touches on here and in "The Wife of Bath's
Tale," is one that appears a number of times in the fifteenth
century. Chaucer's poor widow belongs to the same class
of characters as the wise hero of Langland's Piers Plowman.
Piers, who stands in sharp contrast to all the unideal types
with whom his world is peopled, is the only one who is properly playing his assigned part, the only one who realizes
that for him the way to truth consists in patiently ploughing
his half acre.[135] Another Chaucerian example of ideal wisdom
is Griselda in "The Clerk's Tale." For although Griselda
may be intended primarily as an example of Christian fortitude,
she also exemplifies the ideal wife in terms of the hierarchical system. At the end of the tale the Clerk tells us plainly
that the moral is "that every wight, in his degree, / Sholde
be constant in adversitee"(line 1145). Since Griselda's
degree is that of wife, her first duty is obedience to her
husband, which here seems to imply that she must accept
without question anything he requires, even if she is asked
to acquiesce in the murder of her children. Although in
her case obedience to the will of God (namely, her husband)
would seem to conflict with common sense, nevertheless she
is not the only female character in English literature for
whom virtue is defined as unquestioning obedience. She
is no Antigone.[136]

A brief look at Chaucer's friend John Gower will show
similar examples of wisdom. Gower describes the ideal king,
who rules over the ideal state and guides himself by the
eternal laws of nature. Because this king has learned to
rule himself before he tries to rule others and because
he has a true sense of justice he is able to supervise the
administration of the state in such a way as to maintain
everywhere a proper balance and to promote the common welfare.
But in contrast to this perfect king, Gower points to Richard
II, who failed to rule himself and who in consequence was
punished by God.[137] Among the stories in Gower's Confessio
Amantis there is one concerned with the ever-popular debate
between Diogenes the Cynic and Alexander the Great. Gower,
like Seneca, uses Alexander as an example of a king who
could not govern his own will, while Diogenes represents

true reason. Diogenes, to illustrate the Socratic-Stoic
moral that only the good man is free, calls Alexander a
slave. According to the well-worn Stoic paradox, Diogenes
is free because he is ruled by reason and keeps passion
(or will) as his servant, while Alexander, on the other
hand, is a slave to will (or Greed) "for to ben a conquerour
of worldes good" (III.1265). In another story Diogenes,
who was historically a disciple of Socrates and a precursor
of the Stoics, argues with his traditional opponent, Aristippus, another disciple of Socrates, who was the precursor
of the Epicureans. Aristippus here has been given the usual
unsympathetic treatment accorded Epicureans and is presented
as an unhappy, ambitious, and greedy flatterer of princes.
Diogenes, the virtuous upholder of the simple life, who
is free from desire and has cut his needs to the minimum,
urges Aristippus to reform and live the life of reason (VII.
2300). In other stories Gower echoes fashionable pseudo-
Stoic commonplaces or uses Seneca's name to give weight
to snippets of practical morality on such subjects as avoiding envy and being content with one's income (II.3095, V.7735).
Though Gower frequently talks about fortune--sometimes to
remind us of mutability, sometimes as another name for fate,
sometimes to illustrate the idea that fortune favors the
virtuous--he does not follow Boethius in denying fortune's
existence.[138]

   In the fifteenth century some of the same Stoic ideas
that interested Chaucer and Gower can be found in the poems
of Lydgate, Hoccleve, Henryson, and Dunbar, although it
must be admitted that most fifteenth-century writers of
lyrics, ballads, plays, and romances preferred other themes
than Stoic ones and that even if Boethius continued to be
regarded as a classic, with yet another translation appearing in 1410, the poets who liked to drop his name seldom
showed more than a superficial acquaintance with his ideas.
Most story tellers, then as always, continued to identify
success with good fortune, as, for instance, James I of
Scotland (1394-1437) did in the Kingis Quair. For although
he began his dream vision by putting himself to sleep over
a copy of Boethius and although he included one pseudo-
Boethian discussion of the difference between fortune and
fate, he ended the poem with the emphasis on happiness as
good luck. Similarly, Robert Henryson (1429?-1508) in his
sequel to "Troilus and Cressida" ("The Testament of Cresseid")
meted out poetic justice to Cressida instead of punishing
her psychologically in the Stoic way as Chaucer had done.[139]
   Stoic ideas, predictably, are most apparent in the
work of writers who were influenced not only by Chaucer
but also by literary trends on the continent, where the
Renaissance was farther advanced than it was in England.
For instance, the long Fall of Princes of John Lydgate (1370-
1452) is a second-hand translation (from the French) of

Boccaccio's popular <u>De</u> <u>Casibus</u> <u>Virorum</u> <u>Illustrium</u>[140] which
contains many of the same remedies for fortune to be found
in Boethius or Chaucer. Sometimes the remedies lean in
the Christian direction, telling us, for instance, that
we can escape from fortune by despising earthly rewards,
since, "in worldly worshepe may be no surete" (I.56). We
learn that fortune has no power in heaven, no power over
the holy martyrs, no power even over virtuous Christians
(V.239-301). Sometimes the remedies are more frankly of
the Stoic-Epicurean type that we associate with Horace and
Seneca. We can decrease our vulnerability by retiring from
the world to cultivate our gardens, for it is the people
of high estate who have the tragedies. Those of low degree
are protected from some of the agonies of the great because
they have had long exposure to hardship and have built up
a resistance against the blows of fortune. We learn again
that great men only increase their woe by remembering past
joy and that the restless itch for fame and wealth and power
can never be satisfied.[141] The basic remedy for fortune,
whether Stoic or Epicurean, is somehow to learn to stop
coveting. One of Lydgate's attacks on covetousness includes
again the old story, found in Boethius, Juvenal, Seneca,
<u>et</u> <u>al</u>, about the way covetousness first caused men to dig
treasure from the ground where it belonged and to engage,
as a consequence, in war, robbery, murder, extortion, violence,
rebellion, and subversion. Covetousness keeps men in a
constant state of fear, while poverty, when borne with contentment, brings good health and security (i.e., peace of
mind) (III.447). A story, which Farnham (pp. 87-88) says
is the key to Boccaccio's handling of fortune, describes
a disputation between fortune and glad poverty that ends
in a hand-to-hand fight between the two. The struggle is
easily won by poverty because fortune, who can overthrow
everything else in the world, cannot throw poverty to the
ground. The moral of this story emphasizes free will, whether
Stoic or Christian: "How God aboue put vnder mannys cure /
Fre chois off good, his resoun to assure" (III.664). Psychologically we are free if we gladly accept our lot. The
theme of glad poverty echoes through the poem. Again and
again we are told that content goes with the simple life:
"In litel good to hauen suffisance" (I.904); "Who climbeth
hiest, his fal is lowest doun; / A mene estat is best" (I.3435).
Solomon at one time, Seneca and Diogenes at others, all
teach the same lesson: We should accept all fortune as
good fortune, neither rejoice at abundance nor take offence
at poverty (I.3443); "Glad Poverty is the richest of all
things, content in joy and adversity, nurse of study, mother
of sciences."[142] A life of contented retirement, away from
the storm, "with suffisaunce," is the life that gives "in
this erthe grettist felicite" (IV.673). The Solomon, incidentally, who adds his authority to that of the Roman writers
is the golden mean Solomon of Proverbs 30.9 with its prayer:

"Give me neither poverty nor wealth, / provide me only with
the good I need. If I have too much, I shall deny thee /
and say, "Who is the Lord?" / If I am reduced to poverty,
I shall steal and blacken the name of my God."
      Similarly Thomas Hoccleve (1370-1450) refers to Solo-
mon's proverb in defense of the mean and sure estate:

> Salamon yaf conseil, men sulden preye
> Two thynges vn-to god, in soothfastenesse:
> Now herkne, sone, he bad men thus to seye:
> 'Enhance thou me, lord, to no richesse,
> Ne by miserie me so sore oppresse,
>   That neede for to begge me compelle:'
> In his prouerbes thus, lo! can he telle.[144]

Hoccleve, however, is less inclined to idealize glad poverty
as a remedy for fortune than to emphasize the necessity
of learning to accept all fortune as good fortune. Unlike
Lydgate, who was a monk, he was a pleasure-loving city man,
a civil servant who was seldom free from money worries;[145]
and unlike Lydgate and Henryson he does not idealize the
retired life of Horace's country mouse. In his best-known
poem, The Regement of Princes, which is a long discursive
collection of miscellaneous ruminations supposedly intended
as advice for Prince Henry (later Henry V), he emphasizes
again and again that change is the nature of life[146] and
that those in high places are especially vulnerable. At
one point he remembers the fall of Richard II (stanza 4);
at another he meditates, as Shakespeare's Henry IV does
later, that uneasy lies the head that wears a crown (stanzas
311-12). He reminds us of the lesson that Shakespeare's
Edgar was to learn, that no matter how badly off we may
be, we can always be worse (stanzas 5, 6). Those of us
seemingly stuck at the bottom of the wheel can console ourselves with the thought that the worst misery is that which
follows prosperity (stanza 8) and should learn to practice
patience, while those at the top should remember mutability
"And releeue hem that myscheef hath doun throwe" (stanza
131). Hence he admonishes us: "Make of necessite, read
I, vertu" (stanza 179) and gives us the Boethian advice:
"The iugementz of god been to vs hid; / Take al in gree"
(Stanza 192). The phrase, "Take al in gree," which can
be loosely translated as advice to accept all fortune as
good fortune, is one of Hoccleve's favorite remedies. Patience,
Christian or Stoic, is the best way to meet adversity, since
complaining only makes things worse. Though poverty is
not to be wished for, it has the advantage that the poor
man can sleep without fear of thieves. Ideally one should
gladly accept whatever comes--whether prosperity or adversity (stanzas 152, 153, 157, 158).
      Hoccleve was not alone, of course, in underscoring
this idea. Chaucer had said in "Truth," "That thee is sent

56

receyve in buxomnesse" Lydgate had said, "Atwen ioie and
smert / Thanke God off all, and auer be glad off hert" (I.
3450); and Robert Henryson (1429?-1508?) said in his much
admired "Tale of the Uponlandis Mous, and the Burges Mous"[147]
"'Under the hevin their can not better be, / Then ay be
blyith and leif in honestie'" (line 212).  This tale, which
after all included Horace among its early tellers, is another
one that praises the mean and sure estate and refers to
the golden-mean proverb ascribed to Solomon (line 221).
As Henryson says, "The sweitest lyfe, thairfoir in this
cuntrie / Is sickernes, with small possessioun" (line 218).

The word "blyith" in Henryson's poem, as well as in
the poem "Best to be Blyth" by William Dunbar (c. 1460-1522)
probably means cheerful or well-pleased, something similar
to "content."  It is one of the many ways of expressing
the idea of happiness as peace of mind or tranquillity.
Dunbar in his poem repeats once again the Stoic-Epicurean-
Christian teaching that we should cheerfully accept whatever fate or fortune or providence may bring--including
death.  As he says,

> How evir this warld do change and vary
> Let us in hairt never moir be sary,
> Bot evir be reddy and addrest
> To pas out of this frawdfull fary;
> For to be blyth me think it best.[148]

Dunbar, a Scottish poet who had very likely studied in France,
is here expressing the same idea that the next century will
repeat over and over again, that there is no evil for him
who considers death no evil.  Similarly Dunbar's poem "Of
Content" expresses the uncontroversial Stoic-Epicurean thought
that has had a long literary popularity.  It starts out:
"Wuho thinkis that he hes sufficence, / Off guidis hes no
indigence" and ends with the refrain, "he hes anewch that
is content" (p. 144).  Ideas like these, in addition to
Dunbar's craftsmanship possibly contribute to C. S. Lewis's
feeling that there is a certain affinity between Dunbar
and Horace.[149]

The remedies for fortune from the tradition of Boethius,
Seneca, and Horace that attract our attention in the writings
of these four fifteenth-century poets should not obscure
the many lessons from the tradition of Cicero and Aquinas
that are also evident, particularly in Lydgate's long narrative
poem.  Most of Lydgate's tragedies result from the failure
of those climbing on the wheel of fortune to remember that
virtue means obeying the rules of the hierarchical system.
And if Lydgate-Boccaccio, like a chorus in a Senecan play,
sometimes tells us in passing that fortune has little power
over glad poverty and that the mean and sure estate is the
safest one, nevertheless most of the space is devoted to

the misfortunes either of princes who for one reason or another
have tumbled off the wheel or of ambitious rascals of low
degree who have been punished for trying to rise out of
their ordained social places. When Lydgate in this mood
remarks that "fortune hath no domynacioun / Where noble
pryncis be gouerned be reasoun" (I.809, 4971-84; II.43-56,
575-81), he does not have a Boethian interpretation in mind
but rather the practical moral that reason and virtue are
the best policy. Princes who obey the rules will be able
to maintain their position on the wheel. The sins against
virtue and reason that have brought notable people tumbling
down began with the pride and disobedience of Adam and Eve,
who were the first ones to forget their places (I.570, 687).[150]
Sins especially common to those princes who have put their
personal desires ahead of duty have been greed, ambition,
and vicious living. Greed and ambition, which tend to upset
due order, are particularly reprehensible. Though Lydgate
is willing to admit in theory that virtue is not inherited
and that men should be judged by their actions rather than
their births, such an admission does not mean that he con-
dones interference with the way things are. Virtue does
not include the right to change one's social place. A beggar
who has risen to high estate makes the most vicious tyrant.
Churlish blood, he says, is seldom gentle by nature. Harmony
in the state, with everyone playing his assigned part, is
contrasted with the discord that goes with individualism.
One of his several pictures of the golden age resembles
Gower's--a rather civilized time with everyone doing his
duty. For him the fickle mob has a marked resemblance to
fickle fortune; for if on occasion the mob acts as an instrument of God's vengeance against tyrants, more often the
mob is merely unpredictable. Princes who trust fortune
or trust the mob sin against reason and may expect disaster.[151]

Although Lydgate's interpretation of the law of nature
is the orthodox one that will remain dominant for several
more centuries, it is interesting to note that scholars,
as opposed to story tellers, might, even in Lydgate's time,
acquire potentially subversive ideas by putting an unconven-
tionally heavy emphasis on individual reason. Bishop Reginald
Pecock (1390?-1461?), whose orientation was actually more
scholastic than humanistic, became enthusiastic over the
old argument that through the strength of natural reason
men could arrive at the laws of nature. When he imprudently
took to setting down in English some unconventional thoughts
that might have been overlooked if he had only written them
in Latin for other theological specialists, he was punished
by having his books burned and by being banished to bookless
retirement. Another unorthodox thinker of the same period
was Pecock's legal contemporary John Fortescue (c. 1394-
c.1476) who discussed the nature of monarchy and the conduct
of princes in terms of the laws of nature. Arthur B. Ferguson says that Fortescue "in response to the challenge of

a changing political order, likewise adapted old tools to
new uses."[152] Although the writings of Pecock and Fortescue
may have had little immediate influence on the common reader
or the popular writer, their very existence serves to remind
us that the ambiguous law-of-nature concept, which is often
invoked in support of the established system, is forever
undergoing reinterpretation and is quite as likely to be
used to undermine tradition as to support it.

And so, as the sixteenth century approaches, it is
plain that although there is much to be said for the common
assumption that Stoic ideas did not strike English literature
with full force until the official arrival of humanism,
we should also remember that these ideas could be transmitted
in a variety of ways and that Stoic doctrine could assume
a variety of forms, in short, that many of the Stoic commonplaces of Elizabethan literature had become commonplaces
long before. The work of poets like Lydgate and Hoccleve
contains not only continuations of ideas apparent in Gower
and Chaucer but also foreshadowings of ideas to be met in
Skelton and the _Mirror_ _for_ _Magistrates_ and Tottel's _Miscel-_
_lany_. Lydgate's translation of Boccaccio offers an illustration of the continuing process by which Senecan-Stoic adages
became English literary adages. For whether or not Lydgate
himself had first-hand acquaintance with Seneca, his translation contains frequent references to the latter, including
many moral sentiments drawn from the plays. In addition,
of course, there is also the fact that during the fifteenth
century the rate at which humanistic ideas from the continent
were entering England was accelerating. Even before Caxton
and other printers at the end of the century began making
translations of such popular classics as Boethius and Cicero,
easily available, literary patrons like Humphrey, Duke of
Gloucester (1391-1447) had been building up libraries of
classical manuscripts. For even if popular writers continued to borrow their adages from other popular writers,
scholars were exploring more and more of the writings of
the Greeks and Romans and were gradually adding to the future
supply of acceptable Stoicisms.

Chapter I.   Notes

[1]Sonnenschein in his short article, "Stoicism in English
Literature," calls attention to such writers as Milton,
Wordsworth, and Emerson and says, "I believe Stoicism to
have been one of the great agencies by which British character has been moulded" (p. 365).

[2]Burnet, trans., Early Greek Philosophy, fragments
41, 42.

[3]For some discussions of early Stoicism see Zeller,
Stoics, Epicureans, and Sceptics; Arnold, Roman Stoicism;
Lovejoy and Boas, Primitivism in Antiquity; Sabine, History
of Political Theory; Mates, Stoic Logic; Boas, Rationalism;
Hadas, Essential Works of Stoicism; Long, Hellenistic Philos-
ophy

[4]On Stoic physics see Diogenes Laertius (third century,
A.D.) "Life of Zeno," Essential Works of Stoicism, ed. Hadas,
pp. 38-47; Cicero, De Natura Deorum, II.15, 51 ff; De Re
Publica, VI.24 ff; Seneca, "De Consolatione ad Marciam,"
Moral Essays, II, XXVI.6; Zeller, pp. 130-67, 371; Murray,
Stoic Philosophy, pp. 18-19; Hicks, "Stoics"; de Santillana,
Origins of Scientific Thought, pp. 293-300; Boas, Rational-
ism, pp. 250-51; Long, pp. 147-78.

[5]One list of Stoic names for god occurs in Cicero's
De Natura Deorum, I.37 ff; see also Seneca, "De Consolatione
ad Helviam," Moral Essays, II, VIII. 2-3.

[6]See, e.g., Cleanthes, "Hymn to Zeus," trans. James
Adam, ed. Oates, Stoic and Epicurean Philosophers, p. 591;
Cicero, De Finibus, II.19.64; Marcus Aurelius says, "Con-
stantly regard the universe as one living being having one
substance and one soul" ("Meditations," IV.40, trans. G.
Long, ed. Oates).  On the other hand, according to Edelstein,
Posidonius was one who did not identify God with nature
and fate ("The Philosophical System of Posidonius," p. 293).

[7]On the four virtues, see Cicero, De Officiis, I.v.15;
XLIII.152 ff; on virtue as playing one's part, Cicero says,
"Just as an actor or dancer has assigned to him not any
but a certain particular part or dance, so life has to be
conducted in a certain fixed way, and not in any way we
like" (De Finibus, III.24; see also 21, 22, and Epictetus,
"Manual," II.10; trans. P. E. Matheson, ed. Oates).  On
the joy of the wise man as he contemplates the divine plan,
see Cicero, Tusculan Disputations, V.xxiv.68-71; see also
Seneca, "De Otio," Moral Essays, II, V. 5-8.

[8]For some discussions see Whitehead, Science and the
Modern World, pp. 14-16; Lovejoy and Boas, Primitivism,
pp. 11-12, 108, 451-52; Sabine, pp. 163-73; W. C. Greene,
Moira; Brinton, History of Western Morals, pp. 129-30; de
Santillana, p. 47; Boas, Rationalism, pp. 65-68, 119; Hoopes,
Right Reason, p. 18; McNeill, Rise of the West, p. 215;
Horowitz, "Stoic Synthesis of the Idea of Natural Law in
Man."

[9]Trans., Jebb, _Complete_ _Greek_ _Drama_, ed. Oates and O'Neill, I, 434.

[10]"Apology," _Works_ _of_ _Plato_, trans. Jowett, III, 121; mentioned by Cicero, _De_ _Divinatione_, I.liii.122.
[11]_Epistulae_ _Morales_, XIII.1; Cicero says, "It oftener happens that a mule brings forth a colt than that nature produces a sage" (_De_ _Divinatione_, II.xxviii.61); for Cicero's identification of the law of nature with the _consensus_ _gentium_, see _Tusculan_ _Disputations_, I.xiii.30; _De_ _Natura_ _Deorum_, I.44.
[12]For a discussion of the many meanings of this word, see Lovejoy and Boas, _Primitivism_, Appendix and pp. 115-23; Boas, _Rationalism_, pp. 108-11.
[13]Diogenes Laertius' "Life of Zeno" contains one oft-repeated summarizing statement of the idea: "Zeno was the first writer who said in his _On_ _the_ _Nature_ _of_ _Man_, that the chief good is life according to nature, which is life according to virtue. . . . Our individual natures are all parts of universal nature: hence the chief good is to live according to nature, that is, according to one's own and to universal nature, doing nothing which the common law of mankind forbids. That common law is identical with the right reason which pervades all things, identical with Zeus, who is the regulator and director of all things. This is the virtue of the happy man" (trans. C. D. Yonge, ed. Hadas, pp. 25-26). See also Cicero, _De_ _Officiis_, III.13.
[14]See, e.g., Epictetus, "Discourses," I.ix: "If these statements of the philosophers are true, that God and man are akin, there is but one course open to men, to do as Socrates did: never to reply to one who asks his country, 'I am an Athenian', or 'I am a Corinthian', but 'I am a citizen of the universe'" (trans. Matheson, ed. Oates). Cf. Cicero, _De_ _Officiis_, III.vi.28; Seneca, "Ad Helviam," XI.7; "De Otio," IV.1.
[15]See, e.g., "Manual," 15, where Epictetus compares Diogenes and Heraclitus to gods. In "Manual," 33, he suggests basing our conduct on what "Socrates or Zeno would have done." In "Discourses," I.xix, he asks, "Who pays regard to you as a man? Show me. Who wishes to become like you? Who regards you as one like Socrates to admire and follow?" See also Seneca, "De Tranquillitate Animi," VIII.9 (_Moral_ _Essays_, Vol. II), for praise of Diogenes, and "De Beneficiis," I.xiii.2-3, II.xvi.i, V.iv.4, V.vi.1 (_Moral_ _Essays_, Vol. III), for disparaging remarks about Alexander and comparisons of Alexander to his discredit with Hercules and Diogenes. See also Arnold, pp. 15-17, 31, 42, 48, 296-98; Bussell, _Marcus_ _Aurelius_, pp. 38-39; W. C. Greene, _Moira_, p. 243; Boas, _Rationalism_, pp. 80-81, 100, 287, 376-77, 400.
[16]"But who is a wise man or ever has been even they themselves do not usually say" (Cicero, _Academica_, II.145).
[17]See Diogenes Laertius, "Life of Zeno," ed. Hadas,

pp. 35-37; Cicero, <u>Tusculan</u> <u>Disputations</u>, II.xiv.33. Zeller, p. 301; Hicks, "Stoics"; Ferguson, <u>Moral</u> <u>Values</u> <u>in</u> <u>the</u> <u>Ancient</u> <u>World</u>, pp. 68-69.

[18]See Diogenes Laertius, ed Hadas, pp. 32-34; Zeller, pp. 221-24, 228-38, 273-74, 297.

[19]See Cicero, <u>De</u> <u>Officiis</u>, III.42; Zeller, pp. 268-69; Lovejoy and Boas, <u>Primitivism</u>, pp. 261-63.

[20]<u>French</u> <u>Moralists</u>, pp. 331-32; in general, the point made by A. H. Armstrong about the diverse forms taken by Platonism over the centuries applies equally well to Stoicism (see "Platonism and Its Influence").

[21]<u>Meaning</u> <u>of</u> <u>Stoicism</u>, p. 90. See also Hadas, ed., <u>Stoic</u> <u>Philosophy</u> <u>of</u> <u>Seneca</u> (introduction). See Cicero, <u>De</u> <u>Officiis</u>, I.22, III.28; <u>De</u> <u>Finibus</u>, V.65.

[22]For Cicero's way of interpreting the Stoic equation of virtue with following nature, see <u>De</u> <u>Officiis</u>, III.13, 21, 22. For praise of Panaetius as mellower in doctrine and more lucid in style than the earlier Stoics, see <u>De</u> <u>Finibus</u>, IV.79.

[23]Boas, <u>Rationalism</u>, p. 218. See, e.g., Aristotle, "Ethica Nicomachea," trans. Ross, <u>Works</u>, IX, 1097b, 11; 1162a, 17; 1169b, 18; "Politica," trans. Jowett, <u>Works</u>, X, 1253a, 7; 1337a, 28; 1253a, 15; 1255b, 10; 1288a, 26; Cicero, <u>De</u> <u>Officiis</u>, I.22, 153; III.64, 70; <u>De</u> <u>Finibus</u>, V.65; Marcus Aurelius, IV.4, V.30, VIII.59, IX.23.

[24]On the proper use of riches, see Cicero, <u>De</u> <u>Officiis</u>, I.92; II.15, 52-64; on the active life, see <u>De</u> <u>Officiis</u>, I. 19, 28, 71, 73, 153, 155; <u>De</u> <u>Finibus</u>, III.68; on the Scipios, see <u>De</u> <u>Officiis</u>, II.76; III.15. On Panaetius, see Arnold, pp. 101-103; Sidgwick, <u>Outlines</u> <u>of</u> <u>the</u> <u>History</u> <u>of</u> <u>Ethics</u>, pp. xviii, 93-95; Lovejoy and Boas, <u>Primitivism</u>, p. 83; Sabine, pp. 152-53; Hadas, <u>Seneca</u>, pp. 25-26.

[25]On Posidonius, see Cicero, <u>De</u> <u>Natura</u> <u>Deorum</u>, I.6, 123; II.88; <u>De</u> <u>Officiis</u>, I.159; III.8, 10; <u>De</u> <u>Finibus</u>, I.6; <u>Tusculan</u> <u>Disputations</u>, II.61; Arnold, pp. 102-105; Boas, <u>Rationalism</u>, pp. 217-18; Edelstein, <u>Meaning</u> <u>of</u> <u>Stoicism</u>, pp. 45-70; Grant, <u>World</u> <u>of</u> <u>Rome</u>, pp. 193-94; Hadas, <u>Seneca</u>, pp. 25-26; Hoopes, p. 25.

[26]For some of Cicero's discussions of social duty and his argument that there is no real conflict between the useful and the good, see <u>De</u> <u>Officiis</u>, I.22, 153; III.7, 33, 47, 70, 110; <u>De</u> <u>Finibus</u>, III, 64, 68; V. 65.

[27]See Arnold, pp. 108-10; Lovejoy and Boas, <u>Primitivism</u>, p. 243; Grant, <u>Roman</u> <u>Literature</u>, pp. 65-66, <u>Roman</u> <u>Readings</u>, pp. 30-31, 35; Brinton, pp. 119-20; Muller, <u>Freedom</u> <u>in</u> <u>the</u> <u>Ancient</u> <u>World</u>, pp. x-xii.

[28]See Cicero, <u>Laws</u>, I.30; <u>De</u> <u>Officiis</u>, I.107.

[29]See Cicero, <u>De</u> <u>Officiis</u>, III.70; <u>Laws</u>, II.13; Sidgwick, pp. 97-98; Wenley, <u>Stoicism</u>, pp. 27, 34-35; Sabine, pp. 163-73; Catlin, <u>Story</u> <u>of</u> <u>the</u> <u>Political</u> <u>Philosophers</u>, p. 120; Brinton, p. 212; Edelstein, <u>Meaning</u> <u>of</u> <u>Stoicism</u>, pp. 82-87.

[30]Sabine, pp. 167-68.

[31]On self-evident truths see, e.g., De Officiis, I.5-6.

[32]Lovejoy and Boas, Primitivism, pp. 252-59; Cicero, Tusculan Disputations, I.30; De Natura Deorum, I.44.

[33]Epictetus, Discourses, I.ii; see also Plato, Republic, passim; Diogenes Laertius, p. 26; Cicero, De Officiis, II.5-6; Seneca, Ep., XCIV.25; Zeller, pp. 58, 76-88; Lovejoy and Boas, Primitivism, p. 264; Boas, Rationalism, pp. 267, 359, 371, 372.

[34]For praise of Cato, "the living image of all the virtues," see Seneca, "De Tranquillitate," Moral Essays, II, XVII.1-4; "De Constantia," Moral Essays, I, I.ii.1-2, vii.1.

[35]De Amicitia, V.18-19. Similarly in De Officiis (III.16) he distinguishes between the virtue he is discussing and the kind of virtue that is the peculiar property of the hypothetical Stoic wise man. When men like the two Scipios or Marcus Cato are described as "brave men" it is not because they were perfect models but because through "their constant observance of 'mean' duties they bore a certain semblance and likeness to wise men." Even Seneca says of the wise man, "Where will you find him whom we have been seeking for so many centuries?" and advises, "In place of the best man take the one least bad" ("De Tranquillitate," VII.4). See Zeller, pp. 221-24, 254, 274-78, 301; Arnold, pp. 94-95; Ferguson, pp. 65-69.

[36]See Arnold, p. 51.

[37]Boas, Rationalism, pp. 53-54; Oates, pp. xvii-xviii; "Epicurus to Herodotus"; Lucretius, II.966-1019, ed. Oates. Quotations are from this edition.

[38]Five Miscellaneous Essays by Sir William Temple, ed. Monk, p. 6.

[39]Zeller, p. 449; Ferguson, p. 149; "Epicurus to Menoeceus"; Lucretius, II.607-660, VI.44-91.

[40]Lovejoy and Boas, Primitivism, pp. 241-42; Epicurus, "Principal Doctrines, XIV, XXVII."

[41]Zeller, p. 463; Epicurus, "Principal Doctrines, XVII, XXXI-XXXVIII," "To Menoeceus"; Lucretius, III.966-1068.

[42]Zeller, pp. 298-99; Epicurus, "Letter to Herodotus, paragraphs 28-31," "Letter to Menoeceus, paragraph 10," "Principal Doctrines, X-XIII."

[43]Zeller, pp. 465-69; Epicurus, "Principal Doctrines, XXVII"; Ferguson, p. 72; Grant, Roman Readings, p. 199; Highet, Juvenal, p.123.

[44]Bowra, From Virgil to Milton, p. 59; W. C. Greene, pp. 366, 424-25; for Virgil's well known praise of the contented retired life of the husbandman, see the end of the second Georgic.

[45]Zeller, pp. 296-97; Arnold, p. 391; Bowra, pp. 33-85; Grant, Roman Literature, pp. 183-86.

[46]Arnold, p. 389; Bowra, p. 58; Fraenkel, Horace, pp. 254-56; Grant, Roman Literature, pp. 197-98. Horace expressed his ambivalence in Ep. I.i.13 ff, when he said

he was sometimes the Stoical Man involved in life but at
other times retired "to fit the world to myself, not me
to it." In Ep. I.4.15-16 jokingly called himself "one of
Epicurus' sleek, well-cared-for swine" (Satires and Epistles, trans. Bovie).

[47]See, e.g., Seneca, Ep., LXVIII; "De Otio," II.1 ff,
III.1, V.1; "De Tranquillitate," III.1, 7; XV.2, Moral Essays,
Vol. II; Arnold, p. 116; Hicks, "Seneca"; Grant, World of
Rome, pp. 195-98.

[48]Ferguson, p. 69. "Nothing, however, gives the mind
so much pleasure as fond and faithful friendship" ("De Tranquillitate," VII.3); see also, Ep., IX.6, 8; XXXV.1; CIX.

[49]Bussell, pp. 40-41; Hicks, "Seneca"; Boas, Primitivism in the Middle Ages, pp. 105-108; Grant, Roman Literature, pp. 67-68, Roman Readings, pp. 288-89; Hadas, Seneca,
p. 26; D. C. Allen, Mysteriously Meant, pp. 47-51.

[50]See Seneca, "Ad Helviam," V.2, "De Vita Beata," XVII.
3-4, Moral Essays, Vol. II; Zeller, pp. 221-24.

[51]See "De Vita Beata," XVI.3, XXI.1-2.

[52]Seneca, Ep., XC.5 ff; XCV; XCVII, CIV.34, CVIII.16;
"Ad Helviam," X.7; Zeller, p. 301; Lovejoy and Boas, Primitivism, pp. 260, 264, 274-79.

[53]Seneca, Ep., LXXVI, LXXXVII, XCI.4, XCIV.7, XCVIII,
CI.15, CII.21, CIV.34, CVIII.16, CXXIV.2 ff; "Ad Marciam,"
II.xix.4-5, xxiv.4, xxv.1; "De Constantia," XIX; "De Tran-
quillitate," XI.1, XIII.3; Arnold, p. 269.

[54]Ep. CXVI; "De Ira"; "De Clementia," II.vi.3; Zeller,
p. 297; Hicks, "Seneca"; Sabine, p. 177; Edelstein, Meaning
of Stoicism, pp. 58-59.

[55]Ep. XCIV.8; see also LXXVI, CXXIV; "De Constantia,"
I.v.4, VII.1; VIII.2; "De Providentia"; on the rarity of
the good man, see Ep. XLII.1.

[56]Arnold, p. 402; Wenley, p. 52; Highet, Juvenal, p.93;
Classical Tradition, p. 303; Grant, Roman Literature, p. 223
ff. Plutarch, for instance, though openly antagonistic
to both Stoics and Epicureans nevertheless borrowed many
ideas from both. See discussions, Moralia, trans. Frank C.
Babbitt, et al, Loeb, I, xiv-xv. Thomas Wyatt translated
Plutarch's "On Tranquillity of Mind." Christopher Marlowe
translated a portion of Lucan's Pharsalia. Juvenal's Tenth
Satire had a long popularity, Dryden being one of the more
familiar translators.

[57]Epictetus, "Discourses," II.xxii, IV.xi, "Manual,"
33; Arnold, p. 131; Boas, Rationalism, pp. 361-65, 377-81;
Grant, World of Rome, pp. 199-202; Ferguson, pp. 69-70.

[58]"Discourses," I.i; xxiv; II.v; IV.vii; "Manual,"
15, 17.

[59]Copies of the text, trans. Adam, may be found in
Oates and also in Hadas, Essential Works of Stoicism. For
comment on this point see Zeller, p. 233; Hicks, "Stoicism";
Murray, p. 30; Boas, Rationalism, p. 286.

[60]Epictetus, "Discourses," I.iii; Boas, Rationalism,

pp. 285, 373-4; Hadas, _Seneca_, p. 23; Hoopes, p. 25.

[61]Marcus Aurelius, "Meditations," II.17, IV.10, ed. Oates; Arnold, p. 127; Murray, pp. 30-31; Grant, _World of Rome_, pp. 202-207; Boas, _Rationalism_, pp. 371, 382-92.

[62]See Seneca, _Ep._, XLI.1-2; "De Providentia"; "De Beneficiis," IV.vii; "Questiones Naturales," II.xlv; Cicero, _De Natura Deorum_, II.xxix-lxvii; Boas, _Primitivism in the Middle Ages_, pp. 105-106; _Rationalism_, pp. 361-72.

[63]_Roman Stoicism_, pp. 23, 105; see also Boas, _Primitivism in the Middle Ages_, pp. 1, 4, 7-8, _Rationalism_, p. 28; Gilson, _Christian Philosophy in the Middle Ages_, p. 29; Ferguson, p. 153.

[64]Romans, 2.15; Arnold, pp. 24, 408-36; Wenley, pp. 114, 123; Rand, _Founders of the Middle Ages_, pp. 34-35; Adler, _Idea of Freedom_, pp. 84-85.

[65]See Boas, _Primitivism in the Middle Ages_, pp. 20-21, 28, 31, 37-39, 112-13; Gilson, pp. 13, 31-32; Zanta, _Renaissance du Stoicisme_, pp. 99-122; Lovejoy, "'Nature' as Norm in Tertullian," pp. 308, 336-37.

[66]Catlin, p. 135; see also Rand, p. 79 ff; Sabine, pp. 180-81; Muller, _Freedom in the Ancient World_, p. 307.

[67]Rand, pp. 69-101; Boas, _Primitivism in the Middle Ages_, pp. 43, 95.

[68]Boas, _Primitivism in the Middle Ages_, pp. 99-103.

[69]For some general discussions of these topics, see Patch, _Goddess Fortuna in Mediaeval Literature_; W.C. Greene, _Moira_, p. 366 ff; Grant, _World of Rome_, pp. 129-53; S.C. Chew, _Pilgrimage of Life_.

[70]_City of God_, trans. McCracken, IV.12, 13, 33; V.1, 8.

[71]_City of God_, V.1, XIV.9, XIX.13; Rand, pp. 19-20, 275-77; Grant, _Roman Readings_, p. 444.

[72]Cf. Cicero, _De Re Publica_, III.37; Erasmus, _Education of a Christian Prince_, trans. Born, pp. 91-92. See Deane, _Political and Social Ideas of St. Augustine_, pp. 85-87; Mommsen, "St. Augustine and the Christian Idea of Progress," pp. 265-98.

[73]Rand, pp. 155-56; Wenley, p. 135.

[74]Stewart, _Boethius_, pp. 53, 78-89, 100. See also Boethius, _Consolation_, trans. Cooper, ed. Edman, p. xv; Gilson, pp. 102, 603; Boethius, _Consolation_, trans. Green, p. xv ff; Highet, _Classical Tradition_, pp. 42-45; Rand, pp. 155-80.

[75]See _Consolation_, IV.pr.5, m.5, pr.6; V.pr.1; Stewart, pp. 88, 90-91. Cf. Seneca, "De Providentia," I.1-2, 5; ii.1, 4, 6, 9; iii.1, 4; iv.1, 7, 16; v.18; vi.1.

[76]Highet, _Classical Tradition_, p. 571; Patch, _Tradition of Boethius_, pp. 27-32, 76-82; Stewart, pp. 160-240.

[77]See "Ethics," _Ency. Brit._ (11th ed.).

[78]See Lovejoy, _Great Chain_, Chs. 2-3; Boas, _Rationalism_, p. 437 ff; Huizinga, _Waning of the Middle Ages_, pp. 46-55.

[79]A frequently mentioned idea from Cicero is that "we are invested by Nature with two characters, as it were: one

of these is universal, arising from the fact of our being all
alike endowed with reason. . . . The other character is
the one that is assigned to individuals in particular. . . .
We must so act as not to oppose the universal laws of human
nature, but, while safeguarding those, to follow the bent
of our own particular nature" (De Officiis, I.107-10, 112,
114, 126). Depending on the interpretation given this passage,
it can be used to support either the notion of playing one's
assigned social role or the idea of expressing one's unique
individuality.

[80]Summa Theologica, II, i.q. 63, a.1; q. 66, a.1.

[81]Aquinas, Summa, II, i.q. 97, a.4; Owst, Literature
and Pulpit, p. 548 ff; Schoeck, "Recent Scholarship in the
History of Law," pp. 279-91.

[82]I, q. 19, a.3-4, 9; q. 23, a.1-2; q. 103, a.1-2;
q. 105, a.6; q. 116, a.1-4; II, i, q. 93, a.4, 6. For a
discussion of contradictions see Lovejoy, Great Chain, p. 74.

[83]II, i, q. 61, a.5; q. 90, a.2; q. 91, a.5; q. 94,
a.3. On the relationship between Erasmus' ideal prince and
the ideas on kingship of Aquinas, see Christian Prince,
pp. 114-17.

[84]I, q. 47, a.2; II, i, q. 91, a.5; q. 92, a.1; q.96,
a.5; Lovejoy, Great Chain, Ch. 3.

[85]II, i, q. 91, a.4; q. 94, a.4; q. 95, a.2; q. 97,
a.1-3. For a discussion of the Thomistic distinction between
natural law and positive law see Carlyle, History of Medieval
Political Theory, V, 38-39.

[86]See Primitivism in the Middle Ages, pp. 1, 4, 7-8,
105-108.

[87]Rand, p. 81; Ferguson, pp. 48-50.

[88]Boas, Primitivism in the Middle Ages, pp. 28, 31,
37-39, 99-103, 112-13.

[89]City of God, V.1, XIV.9, XIX.13; Grant, Roman Readings,
p. 444.

[90]On Macrobius, see Patch, Tradition of Boethius, p. 32;
Wenley, p. 134.

[91]II, i, q. 34, a.1-3; q. 59, a.1-3; q. 5, a.3; q. 61,
a.3-5; ii, q. 182, a.1.

[92]City of God, IX.5, XIV.9, 10, 26; Boas, Primitivism
in the Middle Ages, p. 48.

[93]II.m 4-5, pr. 5, trans. Cooper; Boas, Primitivism
in the Middle Ages, pp. 64-65; Stewart, pp. 78-79; Gilson,
107-108; Greene, pp. 388-91; Patch, Tradition of Boethius,
pp. 43-44.

[94]City of God, IX.4, XIX.4; Rand, p. 276; Adler, pp. 91-
92.

[95]City of God, IX.5, XIV.8, 9.

[96]Summa, II,i, q. 5, a.3, 5, 7; q. 34, a.1-2; q. 59,
a.1-5; q. 66, a.1.

[97]See, e.g., Cross, "On the Genre of the Wanderer";
W. C. Greene, pp. 241-2, 332, 336, 368, 388-91; Greenfield,

Critical History of Old English Literature, p. 218; Malone,
"Old English Period," p. 91; Williams, ed., Gnomic Poetry,
p. 47.

[98]W. C. Greene, pp. 388-91; Rand, p. 168.

[99]Trans. Malone, Ten Old English Poems, pp. 48-49.
See also his edition of Deor.

[100]For some discussions of the meanings of "Wyrd" see
Brodeur, Art of Beowulf, pp. 224-27, 243-44; Jackson, Literature of the Middle Ages, p. 177; Klaeber, ed., Beowulf,
p. xlix; Patch, Goddess Fortuna, p. 29, Tradition of Boethius,
p. 51; Roper, "Boethius and the Three Fates of Beowulf";
Whallon, "Idea of God in Beowulf"; Williams, pp. 37-38,
65-66.

[101]"Wyrd oft nereth / unfaegne eorl, thonne his ellen
deah!" (ed. Klaeber). Translation from Spaeth, Old English
Poetry.

[102]"The Legend of St. Andrew," Poetry of the Codex
Vercellensis, trans. Kemble. Many of the saints' lives
have the popular folk-tale moral that good deeds will be
rewarded with good fortune.

[103]King Alfred's Version of the Consolations, trans.
Sedgefield. Quotations are from this edition. Alfred,
incidentally, had abandoned Boethius' elaborate demonstration of the compatibility between God's foreknowledge and
man's free will.

[104]Lines, 1315-16, "Saint Guthlac," Old English Poetry,
trans. Spaeth.

[105]For some discussions of the question of whether there
are hints of Boethian fate behind the Wyrd of Beowulf, see
Stewart, p. 167; Brodeur, pp. 196, 218, 245; Roper, pp. 386-
400.

[106]See Brodeur, p. 69, n. 9; Chambers, "Beowulf and
the 'Heroic Age,'" Man's Unconquerable Mind, pp. 55-57;
Klaeber, pp. lxviii, cxviii, cxx.

[107]See Brodeur, pp. 73, 80, 86, 105, 185; Chambers,
p. 67; Klaeber, pp. li, lxi, lxii; R. C. Sutherland, "Meaning
of Eorlscipe."

[108]See Brodeur, p. 183; Klaeber, pp. cxxi, clviii.

[109]Klaeber, lxi-lxii, cxxi (the Wordsworthian phrase
"happy warrior" has, of course, a Stoic sound); Chambers,
p. 67; Brodeur, p. 105; see also p. 185.

[110]clviii, see also Kaske, "Sapientia et Fortitudo
as the Controlling theme of Beowulf" and "The Sigemund-
Heremod and Hama-Hygelac Passages in Beowulf." Kaske says
that in Beowulf wisdom is a practical virtue, prudence to
protect one's fame; fortitude is courage used wisely.

[111]Klaeber, cxviii-cxx; Brodeur, p. 69, n. 9; Chambers,
p. 57; R. C. Sutherland, pp. 1141-42.

[112]On fortitude see Jackson, p. 177; Muller, p. 43.

[113]G. F. Browne, King Alfred's Books; Sedgefield's introduction to King Alfred's Version of the Consolations.

[114]See Stewart, pp. 170-78 and Patch, Tradition of Boethius,

p. 51.

[115]See discussion by Boas, <u>Primitivism</u> <u>in</u> <u>the</u> <u>Middle</u> <u>Ages</u>, p. 64.

[116]McNeill says, the canon law of the Church was "closely modeled upon the Roman code" (p. 553). Tierney emphasizes that the study of Roman and Canon law was basic in the education of "thousands of influential men" during the Middle Ages and the Renaissance (rev. of <u>Les</u> <u>Juristes</u> <u>Suisses</u>); see also his "Natura id est Deus" and Schoeck, "Recent Scholarship in the History of Law." John Fisher discusses the possibility that Gower may have been trained as a lawyer, in addition to having ties of friendship with churchmen (<u>John</u> <u>Gower</u>, p. 55 ff).

[117]See Owst, pp. 548-93; Patch, <u>Tradition</u> <u>of</u> <u>Boethius</u>; Farnham, <u>Medieval</u> <u>Heritage</u>, pp. 30-68; on Alain de Lille's defense of the simple life and the golden mean see Boas, <u>Primitivism</u> <u>in</u> <u>the</u> <u>Middle</u> <u>Ages</u>, pp. 117-18, and Lovejoy, <u>Great</u> <u>Chain</u>, Chs. 2 and 3.

[118]For one mention of Epictetus, see Schofield, <u>English</u> <u>Literature</u> <u>from</u> <u>the</u> <u>Norman</u> <u>Conquest</u> <u>to</u> <u>Chaucer</u>, pp. 423-25. For a discussion of allusions to Seneca and Cicero by Medieval scholars, see Palmer, Seneca's <u>De</u> <u>Remediis</u> <u>Fortuitorum</u>, pp. 7-15. For a discussion of the use of Seneca's tragedies in the fourteenth and fifteenth centuries as sources of moral adages, see Manlio Pastore-Stocchi, "Un Chapitre D'Histoire Littéraire."

[119]See Patch, <u>Goddess</u> <u>Fortuna</u>, pp. 31, 75-79.

[120]"The Tale of Melibee," so long and boring to the modern reader, looks more Stoic than it is. Although the names of Cicero and Seneca clutter every page and Melibeus has a lecturing wife called Prudence, the message is strictly practical. The wrathful Melibeus learns reluctantly that controlling one's passions and forgiving one's enemies is the best policy for survival, both in this world and the next. The form vaguely resembles that of Boethius' <u>Consolation</u>. Cicero and Seneca, often credited with thoughts not their own, are merely used to embellish a rambling discussion.

[121]The ballade "Fortune" is also a poem that has Boethian as well as Christian components, with the speaker boasting to Lady Fortune that he, like Socrates, is free from her power because he is self-sufficient while she not only agrees with his argument but also reminds him that she herself is only an instrument of providence and that her power extends only to this world (see Jefferson, <u>Chaucer</u> <u>and</u> <u>the</u> <u>Consolation</u>, pp. 57-60; Patch, <u>Goddess</u> <u>Fortuna</u>, p. 31).

[122]See Jefferson, pp. 1-15, 120-32; Patch, <u>Tradition</u> <u>of</u> <u>Boethius</u>, p. 43; Robinson, pp. 319 ff and 797.

[123]It was supported, for instance, by Posidonius. See Curry, <u>Chaucer</u> <u>and</u> <u>the</u> <u>Mediaeval</u> <u>Sciences</u>; Farnham, p. 110. Of the Romans, Grant says that "an enormous majority of the population of the Roman empire" believed in the stars, that "this belief was so predominant and indeed universal that it

must be thought of as the religion par excellence, at this time, of the Mediterranean world" (World of Rome, p. 135).

[124]A sermon treatment of the Orpheus-Argus story recorded by Owst shows that Orpheus was also sometimes allegorized as a symbol of lust (pp. 186-87). Quotations are from Works, ed. Robinson.

[125]Consolation, III.pr.2 ff.

[126]See Curry, "Destiny in Chaucer's Troilus."

[127]See Jefferson, p. 123.

[128]See Jefferson, pp. 71-80; Robinson's note to lines 953 ff.

[129]Jefferson, pp. 90-93, suggest the Roman de la Rose, Ovid, Virgil, St. Jerome, John of Salisbury. For the prevalence of the idea see Lovejoy and Boas, Primitivism.

[130]See Prologue, 336; "The Merchant's Tale," 2021; Boece, III. pr.2, 78.

[131]Consolation, IV. pr. 3; see Robinson, p. 535.

[132]See, e.g., Erasmus, Christian Prince, pp. 110-14; Zanta, p. 127; Atkins, English Literary Criticism: Medieval Phase, p. 60 ff; Baugh, Literary History, pp. 144-45.

[133]Confessio Amantis, Prologue, 92-118 (Gower's English Works, ed. Macaulay).

[134]Fisher, pp. 204-302, argues that Chaucer's interest in social problems may have been influenced by Gower. On Theseus see Muscatine, "Form, Texture, and Meaning in Chaucer's Knight's Tale," and Chaucer and the French Tradition.

[135]See Baugh, p. 243; Owst, pp. 548-93.

[136]Constance in "The Man of Law's Tale" is the other major Chaucerian example of Christian patience. Like Griselda she makes no complaint against seemingly unjust suffering and having stood the test is rewarded on earth, as frequently happens in folk tales, even though neither Stoic nor Christian doctrine promises any such reward.

[137]See Fisher, pp. 105, 160, 199, 201.

[138]Prologue.549, VI.150, VIII.1736, 2009.

[139]Jefferson says "Lydgate probably thought that the Consolation of Philosophy was one huge outcry against Fortune" (pp. 53-54). See also Patch, Tradition of Boethius, pp. 87-113.

[140]See Bennett, Chaucer and the Fifteenth Century, p. 140; Lydgate, Fall of Princes, ed. Bergen, pp. xviii-xxi.

[141]I.715, 4796; III.729, 3718; IV.2192. See also "The Churl and the Bird," Neilson and Webster, pp. 310-11.

[142]I.6126, Bergen's summary. See also "Lydgate's Dietary," Secular Lyrics of the XIVth and XVth Centuries, ed. Robbins, no. 78.

[143]Quoted from New English Bible.

[144]Regement of Princes, ed. Furnivall, stanza 172.

[145]See Bennett, pp. 146-50.

[146]Stanzas 3, 10, 194, 196-98. See also "The Complaint," Neilson and Webster, p. 205.

[147]Poems and Fables, ed. Wood, pp. 8-16.

[148]Poems, ed. Mackenzie, p. 143.

[149]English Literature in the Sixteenth Century, pp. 96-97.

[150]See also I.5524, 6252; II.43-56; III.127-61; V.2333-40.

[151]III.2157, 2192; V.2333; see Fisher, pp. 104-105, for Gower's expression of similar ideas about the mob as an instrument of vengeance.

[152]See Bennett, p. 190 ff; Ferguson, "Reginald Pecock and the Renaissance Sense of History."

# Chapter II.  Massive Doses of Humanism

Although no one is going to prick up his ears to learn
that English literature of the sixteenth and seventeenth
centuries is well saturated with Roman ideas or that the
conglomerate called "humanism" contains a large mixture of
that other conglomerate called "Stoicism," yet commentators
frequently use the word "Stoic" as if it had a tidy meaning
immediately comprehensible to the innocent reader.  Some of
them also assume that hard-working sixteenth-century popular writers quickly assimilated contemporary scholarly up-
datings of Stoicism as soon as they appeared in print, even
though we know that twentieth-century popular writers pay
little attention to what the scholars are saying.  Although
we recognize that writers were likely to have absorbed Stoic
ideas unconsciously from a multiplicity of sources, including their favorite Roman popular writers--many of whom subscribed to a moderate or diluted Stoic philosophy of life--
yet we continue to stumble over undefined references to
"Stoicism," "Christian-Stoicism," "Neo-Stoicism," "Revived
Neo-Stoicism," "Ciceronianism," and "Senecanism."  If scholars
would pause to explain which particular shade of meaning they
have in mind, things would be easier for students.  The term
"Neo-Stoicism," for instance, merely warns us that the
Stoicism under discussion is some variation on the real
thing, without telling us which variation.  Since the real
thing began to be contaminated almost from the moment of
birth, we have a wide variety of possible choices of meaning:
Platonic Stoicism, Aristotelian Stoicism, Epicurean Stoicism,
Boethian Stoicism, Augustinian Stoicism, Thomistic Stoicism,
Calvinistic Stoicism, and so ad infinitum.
Some writers use the terms "Christian Stoic" and "Neo-
Stoic" interchangeably.  Others confine the term "Christian
Stoicism" to the early Christian centuries and call later
infusions "Neo-Stoicism."  Some call the later infusions
"Revived Neo-Stoicism."  Some writers remember that Cicero
was a prime transmitter of Stoic ideas.  Others concentrate
on Seneca to the exclusion of Cicero.  Sometimes Neo-Stoicism
suggests ruthless individualism.  At other times it is associated with the cultivation of patience and equanimity or
with the Horatian life of contented, though virtuous, retirement.  And to add to the confusion, the term "Neo-Stoic" may
also be used to refer to the sixteenth- and seventeenth-
century reaction against Ciceronian style in favor of Senecan
style.[1]  Side by side with the various meanings of Neo-
Stoicism are the variations played on Seneca's name.  We hear
of Senecan style and Senecan tragedy, neither of which has
any necessary connection with Stoicism.  Though a Senecan
hero-villain should not be confused with a Stoic hero, he
sometimes is.  Occasionally we also hear about Senecal drama
and wonder whether that has any connection with the Senecal
man who turns up in Jacobean drama.

Although I cannot hope to talk about Stoicism without
falling into the same confusions that have trapped others,
my aim in this chapter and the next is to try to sort out
in a general way some of the various meanings attached to
Stoicism and Epicureanism during the sixteenth and seventeenth centuries. After that will come a series of chapters
devoted to subdivisions of the main topic that will illustrate
the ways various writers made use of Stoic and Epicurean
recipes for the happy life on earth, the life of social
duty, and the ideal man. In the present chapter the first
problem is to review briefly some of the many sources from
which the ideas were coming. After that will come attempts
to distinguish between Ciceronian Stoicism and Senecan Stoicism, followed by a look at Seneca's tragedies.

An easy way to picture the infiltration of Stoic ideas
into English literature is to think of the way Latin words
entered the English vocabulary. Although we know that there
was a great influx of Latin words during the sixteenth century, we also know that some Latin words came in with the
first Roman invaders and that the Norman French introduced
some more. Similarly, when we are emphasizing the sixteenth-
century humanistic enthusiasm for things Latin, we should
not forget the quantity of Stoic ideas that were early Christianized by such respectable authorities as Paul, Augustine,
and Aquinas. We should remember that the perennial popularity
of Boethius continued marching through the sixteenth and
seventeenth centuries, with several new translations coming
out, including one by Queen Elizabeth.[2] Because Boethius,
like other intermediaries, was larded with ideas from writers
like Virgil, Horace, and Seneca, there is no easy way to tell
whether an Elizabethan who used those same ideas got them
from the original source or from someone like Boethius who
was paraphrasing. Not only did poets like Dante, Petrarch,
and Boccaccio hand on Stoic ideas, but also, among the recent
continental humanists, there were scholars whose enthusiastic
search for universal truth was tempting them to yoke together
all sorts of heterogeneous ideas, including Stoic ones.[3] Some
scholars like the prolific Erasmus (1469?-1536) published collections of pithy sayings (many of them Stoic), with which
less well-read men might decorate their works.[4] The essays
of Montaigne (1533-1592) served as a useful storehouse from
which others might borrow quotations from Seneca, Horace,
Lucretius, Epicurus, Cicero, etc. In addition to these secondary sources, there was a long stream of editions and translations of Cicero, Horace, Virgil, Seneca, Plutarch, Epictetus,
and Marcus Aurelius. Those who could read Latin did not need
to wait for English translations. For example, the Greek of
Plutarch and Epictetus was available in Latin translation long
before English versions came out.[5] In connection with such
influential writers as Plutarch and Montaigne it may be well
to remember that although neither can be classified as a pure
follower of Stoic philosophy, both were tinged with Stoic ways

of thinking and communicated Stoic attitudes as well as quotable lines. Plutarch's <u>Lives</u> and his <u>Morals</u> taught many a
Stoic lesson, such as, that it is unwise to put trust in the
gifts of fortune, that giving way to passion is dangerous,
that only the good man is free. His popular "On Tranquillity
of Mind," which was translated by Thomas Wyatt in 1528, contains such Platonic or Stoic morals as that we must learn to
make the best of whatever our lot may be, accepting apparent
misfortunes as opportunities to grow in wisdom. We can
lighten our pains by observing that others have endured similar evils cheerfully; by calling to mind the pleasant things
still remaining to us; by comparing ourselves with those who
are worse off instead of with those who are more fortunate;
by contenting ourselves with the calling for which nature has
fitted us; by realizing that the store rooms of tranquillity
are within our soul, not outside; by saying, while still
alive, "'I will not lie nor play the villain nor defraud nor
scheme.' For this is in our power."[6] The following sentiment from Montaigne's essay on death was so popular that it
soon became a cliché. Paraphrases of it turn up in plays,
essays, poems, and novels: "There is no evill in life, for
him that hath well conceived, how the privation of life is
no evill. To know how to die, doth free us from all subjection and constraint."[7] Although the sentiment is usually
classified as Stoic because Montaigne borrowed it from Seneca, Seneca himself might easily have acquired it from Lucretius. It is one of those borderline ideas at home equally
with Stoics, Epicureans, and Christians.

Among the scholars whose writings contributed to the
so-called Neo-Stoic movement of the late sixteenth and early
seventeenth centuries, one who is frequently mentioned is
Justus Lipsius (1547-1606), a Belgian caught, somewhat as
Erasmus had been, in the intellectual battle between con-
tending Protestants and Catholics. A voluminous and popular writer, he is known especially for his editions of Seneca and Tacitus and for his <u>De Constantia</u> (1584) with its long
discussion of the compatibility between fate and free will.
Jason Lewis Saunders, like others, credits him with being the
first of his time "to make a systematic re-evaluation and comparison of the doctrines of Stoicism with those of Christianity" (p. 219).[8] <u>De Constantia</u> was translated into English
in 1594-5 by Sir John Stradling as <u>Two Bookes of Constancie</u>.[9]
Because Lipsius was involved, as Erasmus and Montaigne were,
in the continental turmoil that was disrupting old alleg-
iances, he found Stoic universalism appealing--the old dream
of universal brotherhood, citizenship of the world.[10] "His
real 'message' in this work," says Saunders,"was his firm
conviction that man must renounce his selfish interests and
think of his fellow man as his brother, whose best interests
were also his own" (p. 59). Saunders also points out that
unlike most popular writers, Lipsius was able to distinguish

between the ideal wise man (not found in nature) and the actual wise man of the Roman writers "who is in a state of progress toward wisdom" (pp. 69, 84-85). As a theologian he set down the standard Christian opposition to the ultimate Stoic freedom of suicide (pp. 112-13). Since many of Lipsius' doctrines, such as that living according to nature means living according to virtue or reason, can also be found in such writers as Boethius or Cicero, it is not easy to tell how much influence his ideas had on popular writers. A scholarly reader like Robert Burton, was, of course, aware of him, mentions him as Seneca's "chief propugner," and may, like others, have used his edition of Seneca. Joseph Hall, sometimes called "our English Seneca," may also have read Seneca in Lipsius' edition but was certainly not interested in substituting universal brotherhood for national patriotism.[11] Although it is possible that a churchman like Hall with a taste for Seneca got some new Christian-Stoic ideas from a fellow theologian like Justus Lipsius, the argument would be hard to prove, especially since Hall was a conservative thinker who avoided controversial ideas and preached a form of Stoicism that would hardly have offended Thomas Elyot or Richard Hooker. The point here is that there were quantities of Stoic ideas floating around, that most of them had been accepted for a long time, and that it is difficult to say with certainty that a specific writer like Lipsius made any immediate change in well-established habits of thought.

When we are considering the various meanings of the word "Stoicism," we have to bear in mind not only that it has different meanings to different modern commentators but also that the attitude of sixteenth- and seventeenth-century writers was, to say the least, ambivalent. The very same writers who quoted Cicero and Seneca endlessly were likely to sneer when they used the word "Stoic."[12] They thought of a Stoic as an atheist afflicted with pride in his own moral self-sufficiency and, above all, pride in his emotional imperturbability. As caricatured, the Stoic is a stonelike stock immune to all emotion, not only the violent passions of ambition, envy, greed, and anger but also the gentler emotions of pity and sympathy. He is, of course, completely fearless. Sometimes he is a dangerous villain, at other times only a ridiculous hypocrite. The villain will show no pity to his enemies and will himself accept death without emotion. In the popular view, Stoic fortitude means pride in one's own ability to take what comes, while Christian patience is meekly coupled with humility. A popular literary device is to show Stoic pride turning into hypocrisy when the sanctimonious Stoic gives edifying advice to other people that he fails to take himself or when his self-sufficiency crumbles under stress. Sometimes his courage fails; sometimes he loses his temper or gives way to some other passion, such as lust. The stereotype of the Stoic as a fraud goes back at least to Roman times and is not necessarily derived from any direct acquaintance with Stoic writing.

When the names of specific Stoics are used instead of the general words "Stoic" or "philosopher," they are likely to be those of Zeno or Cleanthes or Chrysippus from among the earlier Stoics and Seneca or Epictetus from the later. As whipping boys the earlier ones were more convenient than the later, since they were known mainly by report--which was often unsympathetic. What Cicero or Plutarch or Diogenes Laertius or Augustine had set down about them was repeated as gospel. However, at the same time that hardly anyone had a kind word for a Stoic, certain aspects of Stoic doctrine were everywhere accepted without question.

To cite some random examples, we can start with Erasmus, who had Folly at one point in The Praise of Folly reflect the average person's contemptuous attitude toward Stoics when she said Stoics considered themselves next-door neighbors to gods. Erasmus himself, however, filled his Adages with Stoic morals, annotated an edition of Cicero's De Officiis, edited Seneca, and included Cicero, Seneca, and Plutarch among his favorite writers.[13] Roger Ascham at one point in The Schoolmaster (Bk. II) lumped Stoics with Anabaptists as haters of pleasure and at another listed them along with Anabaptists, friars, Epicures, libertines and monks as writers who combined foolish opinions with a rude and barbarous style. While he was exulting that "Stoickes and Epicures" had been "first contemned of wise men and after forgotten of all men" he was apparently unaware that his beloved Cicero was a prime transmitter of Stoic ideas and that Seneca, Virgil, and Horace, whom he classed among the best authors, were exposing him to Stoic and Epicurean contamination.[14] Shakespeare, who had absorbed his share of Stoic thinking, liked to rouse an occasional laugh at the expense of the Stoics. A well-known example from Much Ado has Leonato responding with childish irritation to his brother's soothing platitudes. "There was never yet philosopher," says Leonato, "that could endure the toothache patiently" (V.i.35).[15] At the same time, it is obvious from the context that the real joke is on Leonato, who is only increasing his misery by giving way to passion and who would be wiser if he could heed some of the popular Boethian or Senecan commonplaces at which he is sneering. It was a favorite device of Shakespeare's to show both sides of the picture. On one side there is the good Stoic advice on how to keep cool and not make things worse by responding irrationally while on the other we are shown the fallible human being, completely incapable of listening to reason. Even Joseph Hall, "our English Seneca," said "I will not be a Stoic, to have no passions . . . but a Christian, to order those I have."[16] Hall, like most people referring to Stoics, was obviously thinking of the uncompromising early Stoics, not of the average Roman Stoic, who preferred the golden mean. Milton had the same sort of thing in mind when in the Christian Doctrine he described "stoical apathy," i.e., insensibility to pain, as being contrary to true patience (CM.XVII,253). William Temple, well known for his love of Horace and Seneca, scoffed at the claim of "rigid Stoics" to be without any sense of pain or pleasure and called it a principle "against common nature and common sense."[17]

With very few exceptions, the standard literary attitude toward "the old paynim philosophers" was the one set forth by Thomas More in A Dialogue of Comfort against Tribulation. This attitude is the long-accepted one that can be found in Augustine or Aquinas and that appears later in Joseph Hall or Jeremy Taylor. It tells us that as long as we remember that the comfort against tribulation offered by the ancients is insufficient, partly because it is self-sufficient and partly because it does not include the aim of pleasing God or the hope of future reward, it can still be helpful. Although these old writers were not licensed to act as physicians, says More, they had some good drugs in their shops and could still be useful as apothecaries.[18] In the Utopia it was reported of Raphael Hythloday that he thought there was nothing to any purpose extant in Latin "saving a few of Seneca's and Cicero's doings" (p. 15).

As a prologue to our examination of Seneca's and Cicero's doings, we need to remember that neither of these men was in technical modern terms a philosopher. Each was an eclectic man of letters. We need to remember that primitive Stoicism was as rare in Roman times as primitive Christianity was in Elizabethan times and that the Stoicism that the Elizabethans borrowed was already well diluted with ideas from Aristotle or Epicurus--to name only two. Moreover, with one or two exceptions, it was rare for a literary man of the sixteenth or early seventeenth century to be interested in Stoic physics or Stoic logic.[19] At this period, Stoicism practically always means Stoic recipes for how to live.

In the introduction to his Seneca's De Remediis Fortuitorum and the Elizabethans, Ralph Graham Palmer warns, "One should be careful to distinguish between (1) earlier Stoic thought as presented by Cicero and (2) Stoic thought in the Silver Age of Latin literature, of which Seneca is an important representative" (p. 19). What we have to remember about Cicero, in simplified terms, is that he gathered information about early Stoic teaching, which he passed on without giving it an unqualified vote of approval. He also, in such a work as his highly influential De Officiis ("Of Duties," Tully's "Offices") set forth the Panaetian brand of Stoicism that he did espouse. This kind of Stoicism, which was well mixed with Aristotle, early became part of the Christian tradition. Since Christian doctrine, however, is seldom the same as Christian practice, the Ciceronian ideal of selfless patriotic responsibility has continually to be preached anew. And so we have

Erasmus writing his <u>Education</u> <u>of</u> <u>a</u> <u>Christian</u> <u>Prince</u> and Thomas
Elyot writing <u>The</u> <u>Book</u> <u>Named</u> <u>the</u> <u>Governour</u>. It was this form
of Stoicism, with its heavy emphasis on social duty, that was
the most influential. Instead of being superseded by the fad
for Seneca it continued to exist side by side with it, much as
it had done all through the Middle Ages. What is heralded as
Senecan Stoicism during the late sixteenth and early seventeenth centuries is often difficult to distinguish from what
earlier writers borrowed from Boethius.

When we think of Cicero's ideal man, we tend to visualize
the good leader, the man who is part of the public scene,
while we think of Seneca as concentrating on retired private
virtue. However, we might just as well see them as both part
of the same picture. Both were experienced public servants
who did much of their writing during the period of enforced
retirement at the end of their lives. While Cicero often continued to write from the point of view of the public man, Seneca turned to advice on ways of achieving personal equanimity.
We can find both points of view reflected in a work like
Joseph Hall's <u>Characters</u> <u>of</u> <u>Virtues</u>. And if Shakespeare's
Henry V uses the language of a responsible Ciceronian leader,
his Richard II--out of power--consoles himself with Senecan
platitudes.[20]

If Cicero's Stoicism is well mixed with Aristotle, Seneca's advice on how to make the best of a bad world often
sounds like Lucretius. It is, in other words, as misleading
to overemphasize the pure Stoicism of Seneca as to under-
emphasize the Stoic streak in Cicero. The eclectic Horace
was one of Seneca's favorite writers, and the pleasant country life that Horace describes as prelude to his fable of the
town mouse and the country mouse (II Satire VI) is the same
good life later idealized in Seneca's prose. Retiring from
the hurly-burly to a simple life of rural content, the Senecan Stoic hardens himself to endure the unavoidable blows
of fortune but meanwhile enjoys the tranquil pleasures that
come to those who are satisfied with themselves--even if they
cannot say much for the rest of mankind. Like Horace, Seneca
stresses the Aristotelian-Epicurean golden mean rather than
the absolute perfectionism of the early Stoics. The person
for whom his advice is intended is not expected to reach absolute virtue, only to do the best he can. Though Seneca's virtuous man does not consider wealth essential to happiness, if
he has it he uses it wisely instead of scorning it. Though
not a slave to destructive passion, he is by no means without feeling and, in fact, shares the high Epicurean regard
for friendship. The early Stoics--as well as such later ones
as Epictetus--had made friendship practically non-existent by
saying it was only possible among their mythically perfect
wise men. As Erasmus's Folly says, "Among the god-like Stoics,
of course, either friendship does not spring up at all, or
there exists a certain austere and cold variety of it, and

even this in but few cases" (p. 26). Much of Seneca's literary composition, however, like that of Horace and Cicero, was
grounded on the idea that he was composing a letter to a
friend. Before he could start composing, he needed a human
being at the other end of the line. Like Horace, too, Seneca in much of his writing was ambiguous about fate, using
the words "fate" and "fortune" interchangeably.[21] His melancholy advice to expect the worst and not to be surprised at
anything that happens is quite as much in accord with Epicurean and Christian teaching as it is with Stoicism. If some
sixteenth- and seventeenth-century writers got, or pretended
to get, their Seneca from the master himself rather than from
some secondary source, the ideas that appealed to them were
not much different from those that had appealed to Boethius or
Boccaccio. Most of the time it was not the Seneca whom Folly
calls a "double-strength Stoic" (p. 39), but Seneca the
quasi-Christian moralist and alleged friend of St. Paul that
they found.[22]

One popular collection of Senecan fragments on how to
withstand the blows of fortune was the De Remediis Fortuitorum, which had long been available in various Latin editions and which was translated into English in 1547.[23] Its
miscellaneous remedies are similar to those found in Boethius' Consolation or Chaucer's "Tale of Melibee." They are
the uncontroversial inhabitants of a Stoic-Epicurean-Christian
no-man's land and aim to promote our peace of mind by freeing
us from fear. The idea is that if we will only be reasonable
we can acquire immunity to the dread of such things as death,
illness, slander, banishment, poverty, or injustice. Here
once again are the ever-popular Stoic-Epicurean commonplaces
that go on being repeated by writer after writer. Death is
not to be feared: it is part of the nature of things; this
life is only a pilgrimage; it is folly to dread what we cannot avoid. Sickness is not to be feared: "Either I will
forsake sickness or sickness me." Slander or banishment cannot hurt the man who is sure of his own integrity, who carries
his peace of mind within him. Poverty is only a state of mind:
very little is needed to support life. "You may have to suffer wrong but should be merry because you can do none." The
happy man is not the one who looks happy to others but the
one who feels happy within himself. Although there may be
some heretical notions lurking between the lines, they are
not clear enough to bother anyone. We hop quickly from an
Epicurean suggestion that accidents are bound to happen to
a Stoic reassurance that everything is governed by universal
law, which law we automatically assume is controlled by
Christian providence. A hint of Stoic self-sufficiency can
easily be converted into Christian patience. The snippets
are only snippets, adaptable to a variety of uses. And, anyway, few Christians recognize a heretical notion when they
see one.

Although it is undoubtedly true that learned readers

like Francis Bacon or Joseph Hall or Robert Burton were likely
to have been acquainted with Seneca's prose in the original
and that Thomas Lodge made available an English translation
of "The Workes both Morrall and Naturall of . . . Seneca"
(1614), still, the ideas most readers of the prose found in
the original were the familiar remedies for discontent, more
consolation in adversity. Francis Bacon, who was probably
less interested in Stoic ideas than many of his contemporaries,
spoke of the Stoics as a class in the usual contemptuous way,
saying, for example, in "Of Anger," "To seek to extinguish
anger utterly is but a bravery of the Stoics." Although in
his essays he often made use of snippets from Seneca,[24] he
was usually more interested in advice on how to stay on the
wheel of fortune than on how to get off. Joseph Hall, who
imitated Seneca by writing essay-like epistles, emphasized,
like the proper clergyman he was, that although true happiness or tranquillity can be expected only in heaven, it is
possible to have a certain amount of equanimity by following Seneca's advice. As Christians we must accept whatever
happens, including misfortune, as the will of God, remembering that although evils are sent us as a test of virtue, if
we stand the test we can look forward to a future reward.
From the Stoics we can learn that freedom is an inner thing,
that no man who is a slave to his passions is free, but "see
how free the good man is; he doth what he will; for he wills
what God wills, and what God would have him will" (Works, V,
397, 404). As remedies for fortune Hall advises us to be
emotionally prepared for the worst, remembering that high
places are more vulnerable than low places. Those of us
who are poor should consider that the simple life leads to
content, that we are only poor if we think we are, that the
more we have the more we want, that a poor man can sleep
with his doors open. As a conservative Englishman--rather
than a self-sufficient citizen of the world--Hall also
taught conformity to the way things are. We must remember
that everyone has a duty to society as well as to himself,
that diversity is part of God's plan, and that it is our duty
to play our assigned part in the social scheme. Though he
approved of the simple life, he did not approve of retirement, which he associated with monks and nuns. Hall's careful qualification of how far a Christian might go in following Seneca was not greatly different from the position taken
by Thomas More in A Dialogue of Comfort or that briefly suggested when John Donne lamented in "Satire III," that blind
philosophers, "whose merit / Of Strict life may be imputed
faith" might get to heaven sooner than worldly Christians.
Robert Burton, another clergyman who read the ancients dar-
ingly, was always careful to protect himself against charges
of atheism. On the one hand, he often referred to "that
divine Seneca," "that superintendent of wit, learning, judgment, learned to a marvel, the best of Greek and Latin

writers in Plutarch's opinion:  that renowned corrector of
vice as Fabius terms him, and painful omniscious philosopher
that writ so excellently and admirably well."[25]  "When I
read Seneca," he said, foreshadowing Keats on his peak in
Darien, "methinks I am beyond all human fortunes, on the
top of an hill above mortality" (p. 460).  Yet, he goes on,
"If this comfort may be got by Philosophy, what shall be
had from Divinity?" (p. 460).  And at the end he includes
Seneca among such philosophers as Socrates, Plato, Plotinus,
Pythagoras, Trismegistus, and Epictetus as one of those who
"went as far as they could by the light of Nature; writ many
things well of the nature of God, but they had but a confused
light, a glimpse" (p. 889).  A point worth noting here--to
be discussed further in later chapters--is that neither Anglican clergymen like Hall, Donne, and Burton nor skeptical lawyers like Bacon and John Selden were ready to follow the optimistic Stoic thesis that by the light of reason alone man can
learn the rules of good conduct.

     Before turning to Seneca's plays, I need to say a word
or two about the much discussed stylistic battle between
Ciceronians and Senecans, which, although it has no necessary connection with the presence or absence of Stoic ideas,
is sometimes spoken of as if it had.  Francis Bacon, who, as
a philosopher, was skeptical about the Stoic law of nature,
finds himself lumped together with a traditional thinker like
Joseph Hall because both sometimes used the pithy aphoristic
style known as Senecan.[26]  Imitators of Seneca's style claimed
to like his way of expressing himself because it was unadorned
and reached the point quickly.  For a time terseness was the
fashion, and was favored or disfavored by writers of all shades
of opinion.  Bacon praised Seneca for giving "an excellent
check to eloquence."[27]  Burton said, "I call a spade a spade,
I write for minds, not ears . . . seeking with Seneca rather
what than how to write" (p. 25).  John Earle described "A
Pretender to Learning" as having "sentences for company, some
scatterings of Seneca and Tacitus, which are good upon all
occasions."[28]  Owen Felltham said in "Of Preaching" that he
agreed with Seneca's opinion that "fit words are better
than fine ones,"[29] but Abraham Cowley made unkind reference
to "the dry chips of short-lung'd Seneca" ("Of Wit," st. 7).[30]
     Even if we could easily see a connection between style
and doctrine, we would still become tangled in the fact that
both Cicero and Seneca were propagators of Stoic doctrine.
However, to cut the Gordian knot, we can simply note in passing
that when some commentators use the term "Neo-Stoic" they mean
the late sixteenth- early seventeenth-century fashion for imi-
tating Seneca's prose style, whether the style is imitated from
collections of elegant extracts or modeled on the work of some
intermediary like Justus Lipsius or based on a direct study of
Seneca's prose itself.  Sometimes imitations of the style of
other writers, like Tacitus and Tertullian, also come

under the heading "Neo-Stoic." However, Neo-Stoic prose style obviously does not include imitations of such familiar transmitters of Stoic ideas as Epictetus or Marcus Aurelius or Plutarch, all of whom had to be translated from the Greek; or of Horace and Virgil, who wrote poetry; or of Cicero, whose style was Ciceronian. A twentieth-century irony is that people trained in philosophy rather than literature sometimes omit Seneca almost entirely when discussing the history of Stoicism, though they may include Cicero as well as Epictetus and Marcus Aurelius.

Another tough knot to untie is the relation between Senecan tragedy and Stoic doctrine.[31] By 1581 all ten of the plays ascribed to Seneca had been translated into English. The fact that all may not actually have been his makes little difference in a discussion of what may or may not be Stoic about them. But in order to recognize Stoicism when we see it in action, we need to avoid such easy sources of confusion as looking up a definition of Stoicism based on the teachings of the early Stoics and then trying to find those doctrines exemplified in these plays. Another way to go wrong is to identify anything that happens in the plays with Stoic doctrine. If Seneca the essayist was only Stoic some of the time, Seneca the playwright was equally eclectic. In an attempt to separate a few strands at a time, I shall divide the subject into four main areas: miscellaneous Stoic-Epicurean moralizing, peace of mind, fate, and the hero-villain.

Beginning with the moralizing, we notice that the plays are filled with what have been termed "philosophic tags" or "brilliant commonplaces."[32] These tags are the familiar Stoic-Epicurean remedies for fortune that appealed to Boethius and Chaucer and Lydgate and that turn up in Erasmus's Adages or the collection known as the De Remediis Fortuitorum. Frequently recited by the chorus, these commonplaces cover such topics as that high places are dangerous (uneasy lies the head that wears a crown); that misfortune is often only a state of mind; and that the retired life in the lowly cottage has greater chances of tranquillity than life on the mountain top.[33]

Aside from these easily extractable, highly quotable morals, many of the plays taught the overall message that those who become slaves to passion lose their peace of mind. Ludwig Edelstein, who traces Seneca's conception of poetry back to Posidonius, sees Seneca's drama as the analysis of emotions. He says, "In his philosophical writings Seneca in agreement with Posidonius asks that the physician of the soul examine the disease and draw it to the light of day, for only then will he be able to heal. . . . While in classical tragedy the conflict is that between man and objective fate, in Seneca it is the conflict within our souls that predominates."[34] Once again it is obvious that this message, though Stoic, is not exclusively Stoic. There is nothing particu-

larly controversial about the thesis that people who lose
their sense of proportion and allow themselves to be dom-
inated by such passions as ambition, revenge, anger, or desire, will end up miserable. As Roy Battenhouse points out,
in Seneca's plays the punishment for doing evil does not
come from outside. The only punishment meted out to Medea,
to Hercules (in _Hercules Furens_), to Atreus (in _Thyestes_),
to Phaedra, or to Deianira (in _Hercules on Oeta_) is that
they have "opened their breasts to the furies."[35] Over and
over we are told that the only kind of power that really matters is power over oneself.[36] Most of the plays give us
negative examples, show us how not to act, instead of representing heroes whom we can admire. In only one case, the
Hercules of _Hercules Oetaeus_, are we shown a hero who
achieves the success of equanimity. In this play, as Hercules dies, the chorus describes him as a free man because
he has accepted all fortune, including death, as good fortune
(line 104 ff). He dies like a god and becomes a god.[37]

Although the dying Hercules here resembles the traditional Stoic wise man, the wild Hercules of _Hercules Furens_,
who has opened his breast to the furies, is an angry man who
has gone over the edge into temporary madness. Nevertheless,
because such characters as the Hercules of this play and the
villainous Atreus of _Thyestes_ are central characters, they are
often called heroes, sometimes tragic heroes, sometimes Senecan heroes, sometimes Stoic heroes. When they are called
"Stoic" heroes, a certain ambiguity enters the picture. The
commentator, forgetting that the ideal wise man is sometimes
called a Stoic hero, may only have in mind that since Seneca
was a Stoic, all his heroes are Stoic heroes, or the commentator may have the vague idea that since the Stoics emphasized self-sufficiency, anyone with the courage to follow his
own will and accept the consequences without complaint can
qualify as a Stoic hero. The tendency to see a connection
between a contemporary Renaissance strong man, a Senecan
villain, and a Stoic hero comes under this category.

Perhaps the commentator is thinking that since the
Stoics are known to be fatalists, they must think that character traits are set by fate and that a Stoic can only
accept himself as he is, proceed to do what his nature directs, and heroically face the tragic consequences. Battenhouse speaks of the prominence of the theme of hereditary
sin in Seneca's dramas (p. 204). Cunliffe says, "In addition to the large stock of brilliant commonplaces, there is
in the tragedies a considerable body of thought which is
part of Seneca's philosophic faith. The leading doctrine is
that of fatalism . . . the absolute, hopeless fatalism of
the Stoic school, which includes the gods themselves in its
universal sway" (pp. 25-26). Pierre Grimal sees Seneca's
characters as condemned persons acting out their fates (pp. 8-
10). The difficulty here is that although fatalism is indeed
an important element in Stoic thinking, the word "fatalism"

has many meanings.[38]  Hopeless fatalism is actually more characteristic of Greek tragedy than of Senecan tragedy.  I have
already referred to Edelstein's comment that it is classical
tragedy that emphasizes the conflict between man and objective fate while Senecan tragedy concentrates on the conflict
within our souls.  Moses Hadas says of the Roman Stoics that
"the most important change [from the Classical Greek] has to
do with a new concept of the world which so far as belief in
a ruling providence and in external sanctions for conduct are
concerned, is virtually Christian."[39]  Seneca's passion-driven
characters are not entirely fate driven.  By refusing to listen to reason, they bring much of their suffering on themselves.

     Although Stoic fate--whose overall purpose was supposed
to be benevolent--was easier to reconcile with Christian providence than the harsh fate in Greek tragedy, we can never be
sure that an individual playwright, whether Stoic or Christian,
is at all times thinking like a Stoic philosopher or a Christian theologian.  Often in a play--whether by Seneca or by an
Elizabethan--fate is as ambiguous as Wyrd in Beowulf, seeming
to operate capriciously, to be deliberately mischievous, and
to be hardly distinguishable from the goddess Fortuna.[40]
Seneca, hovering between Epicureans and Stoics, tends both in
his plays and in his other writings to use the words "fate"
and "fortune" interchangeably.  Both Stoics and Epicureans
emphasized that psychologically we will weather the storm
better if we can train ourselves to accept what comes without
surprise.  Whether our misfortune comes from accident or from
fate, we can make it better or worse by the way we meet it.
A frequent choral theme with Seneca is the inevitability of
change and the necessity of bearing whatever fate or fortune
brings.  We are told to be happy while fate permits, not to
make our troubles worse by complaining, to endure adversity
with dignity, to accept what we cannot alter.[41]  Although we
associate this melancholy mood with Seneca, as well as with
Marcus Aurelius, we need also to remember that in spite of
the fact that it is distinctively Senecan it is not necessarily distinctively Stoic.  In fact, we frequently hear
Stoicism criticized not because it is pessimistic but rather
because it is superficially optimistic--with its belief that
everything if for the best in this best of all possible
worlds and its failure to explain effectively the problem of
evil.

     Side by side with Stoic belief in fate goes Stoic insis-
tence on free will. As Emerson said, a foolish consistency is
the hobgoblin of little minds.  Through reason, argues the
Stoic, man can learn to understand the moral laws that govern
the universe and can learn to live virtuously.  The kind of
Stoic hero who is largely missing from Seneca's plays (since
Seneca was not writing plays about heroes) is the one who
asserts that only the good man is free and that death is preferable to loss of integrity.  A good man is free because he

cooperates willingly with virtuous eternal law; a bad man is one who tries to set up his own will as law and has to be dragged along kicking at the heels of fate. If the good man can find no other way to avoid doing evil, he can always commit suicide. He is always free. Integrity is the most important thing. Since most of Seneca's main characters are people who have lost their inner freedom, they are not heroes in the Stoic sense. However, it is easy to see how the idea that Stoics are hopeless fatalists can lead to the argument that a slave to passion is fated to be the way he is and therefore is as perfect as he ought.

Fate is a difficult topic to discuss in connection with any work of literature that has a plot, since any plot-driven character can be considered to be fate driven. Though no one thinks of Chaucer as a hopeless fatalist, he made the most of fate as a motivating force in "The Knight's Tale" and "Troilus." The Elizabethans loved the metaphor that all the world's a stage. Yet they did not excuse villains for having been assigned the roles of villains.

If we run the chance of ambiguity when we call Seneca's leading characters Stoic heroes, we run the same chance if we call them Stoic villains. Once again we are speaking from the point of view of the anti-Stoic caricaturist who is thinking of a Stoic as a hypocrite or an emotionless monster or a proud atheistic self-sufficient egotist. From this point of view, to be sure, a villain like Seneca's Atreus might be considered a Stoic--by someone other than Seneca. Such a character might even be blamed for fathering that two-headed monster, the "Stoic Machiavel," who would hardly have been claimed as an offspring by Machiavelli. Such villains may find themselves called Stoic because they claim to be godlike in their self-sufficiency and because they are immune to such kindly feelings as pity, sympathy, or remorse--though they may be as angry, revengeful, greedy, or ambitious as they like. The Machiavel half of this monster is a self-serving immoral villain who will engage in any sort of machination in order to advance his own interest. Oddly enough, though these devious villains are often self-proclaimed Epicureans, we seldom see the term "Epicurean-Machiavel."[42]

As contrasted with the "Stoic Machiavel," that other ambiguous hybrid, the "Stoic malcontent" is not necessarily evil. Presumably he is an idealist, like Marston's Malcontent or Molière's Misanthrope, embittered by the discrepancy between the way things are and the way things ought to be. Though he may be classed as a Stoic for a number of reasons, he is Senecan less because he is modeled on a Senecan character than because he sometimes talks like a Senecan chorus. Our sympathy towards him depends on his creator's sympathy. Marston, for instance, obviously approves the Ciceronian moral standard against which he has Malevole measure the corrupt court. Molière, on the other hand, finds Alceste's moral extremism somewhat excessive. Sometimes, too, the term "Stoic malcontent" is applied to a character like Marston's Feliche, an unworldly happy man who laughs at the unhappy ambitious people at the corrupt court. He may be contrasted with Joseph Hall's Character of the Malcontent who, though no Stoic, since he is always making himself miserable by yearning for something he does not have, might solve his psychological ills if he could only learn the Stoic device of accepting all fortune as good fortune.

Seneca's characters, whether seen as heroes or as villains, often have another quality commonly characterized as Stoic, namely fortitude. Someone who is a Stoic in no other way may still be described as dying like a Stoic. Cunliffe, emphasizing "the invincible resolution" of Seneca's characters in the face of death, goes on to talk of the desperate fortitude with which Shakespeare's villains die and "the Stoical fortitude of the heroines of Elizabethan tragedy."[43]

The so-called "Senecan" plays written for the Elizabethan and Jacobean stage may or may not contain Stoic messages. The popular plays written by Kyd and Marlowe are less Stoic than the ones written by Chapman and Marston, though all may borrow the same theatrical devices. It is customary to make a distinction between the well-known "Senecan" plays written for the popular theatre and the little-known "Senecal" plays written for a select clique.[44] "Senecal" plays, influenced by contemporary French fashions in Senecanism, conformed more closely than did the popular plays to such things as Seneca's style and form and sometimes included long moralizing choruses on the ever-popular themes of mutability, the dangers of high place, the security of life in the valley, etc. Most of the writers or translators of these plays belonged to a group centered around Sidney's sister, the Countess of Pembroke. In addition to the Countess herself, the writers in the group included Thomas Kyd; Samuel Daniel; Fulke Greville, Lord Brooke; and William Alexander, Earl of Stirling. As examples, we have Fulke Greville's two closet dramas, Mustapha and Alaham, which have some structural resemblances to Seneca's plays and include one or two characters with a few Stoic traits, along with one or two slaves to passion. These plays are less concerned with individuals and with analysis of the passions or remedies for fortune, however, than with Greville's thoughts on statecraft.

The well-known "Senecan" plays are divided by F. L. Lucas into two types: the revenge play (e.g., The Spanish Tragedy) and the conqueror play (Tamburlaine). A few obvious examples will suggest the way Stoic ideas might be included in varying amounts: The Spanish Tragedy has little Stoicism; Hamlet has more; Chapman's The Revenge of Bussy d'Ambois has so much it almost forgets the revenge; and Marston's Antonio's Revenge exposes a sham Stoic who turns into a revenger. Similarly, Marlowe's Tamburlaine concentrates more on the strong man's

success story than on the emptiness of power, while <u>Macbeth</u>
shows us a criminally ambitious hero-villain being immediately
punished by loss of peace of mind.

To illustrate the point further, we can look at a few
plays by George Chapman and John Marston, two writers often
cited as having a more than average interest in Stoicism.
(Longer discussions are to be found in later chapters.)  John
W. Wieler says Chapman's "knowledge of Stoicism transcends
the conventional patterns of the age, [that he] displays a
familiarity with the distinguishing concepts of the philosophy,
and . . . follows the thinking of Epictetus, for example, not
merely as a mental exercise but as a philosophy of life."[45]
Of Marston, Cunliffe says, "Of all the Elizabethan dramatists, Marston owed the most to Seneca, and was the readiest
to acknowledge his indebtedness" (p. 98 ff).[46]  Travis Bogard
says Marston combines the Machiavellian revenger and the
"tragic stoic" with "the stoicism of the satirist" to produce
"the earliest example in English drama of tragic satire."[47]
Chapman's early play, <u>Bussy d'Ambois</u>, combines such familiar
components of "Senecan" tragedy as ghosts, bloody murders, and
an atmosphere of horror, with a hero who sometimes makes fine
Stoic speeches, sometimes seems too self-sufficient, sometimes
seems to be a slave to passion, sometimes blames fate for driv-
ing him to sin, and who dies at the end insisting that he can
accept either life or death with equanimity--even though he
also hopes, unstoically, that his fame will live on.  The
quasi-Senecan, quasi-Stoical <u>Bussy d'Ambois</u> has provided many
an interesting argument for the critics while its less ambiguous sequel, <u>The Revenge of Bussy</u>, has generally been considered a bore.  By the time he wrote that play Chapman was less
fascinated by the popular claptrap of the "Senecan" play than
with the Stoic ideas he was expounding.  It is in this play
that we meet what is known as the "Senecal man," a phrase used
by Chapman to describe Bussy's brother Clermont but picked up
by modern critics as a way of describing various virtuous semi-
Stoics who appear in Jacobean plays.  Chapman says, "this Senecal man" is one "to whom the day and fortune equal are," who
"fix'd in himself, . . . still is one to all" (IV.iv.42).  He
is, in other words, a sympathetic picture of the self-
sufficient Stoic wise man (discussed at length in Chapter VI)
who has learned to accept all fortune as good fortune.  Ironically, though Chapman chose to call him "Senecal," he might
have borrowed his portrait from Horace or Virgil or Epictetus
quite as well as from Seneca.

Marston's early pair of "Senecan" plays, <u>Antonio and
Mellida</u> and <u>Antonio's Revenge</u>, though even more confusing than
Chapman's <u>Bussy D'Ambois</u>, are less successful as plays.  To
add to the confusion, the first is a comedy, the second a tragedy, somewhat as though <u>Hamlet</u> had been written as a sequel to
<u>As You Like It</u>.  In these plays we are given a "Machiavellian"
villain who resembles Seneca's Atreus and a victim who resem-

bles Thyestes as well as the usual murder and blood and
ghosts.  In addition, there are passages of Stoic moralizing drawn from Seneca's plays, from the De Remediis Fortuitorum, and from some of Seneca's prose writings, combined
with several characters who represent variations on the wise
man ideal.  Antonio and Mellida contains the good Feliche
and Andrugio.  Feliche, who might have come out of Horace, is
the happy man who, like Chaucer's Povre Widwe, is content
with his lot and able therefore to laugh at the rest of society.  Andrugio, more of a Ciceronian, is the ideal Christian
prince--unfortunately now out of office and therefore sometimes inclined to cheer himself with Senecan platitudes.
Antonio's Revenge brings in Feliche's father, Pandulpho, who
talks like Chapman's "Senecal" man but whose imperturbability crumbles under stress.  Early in the play, when we find
him weeping, we suspect that his Stoic facade is a sham (II.
ii).  Later Marston shows the usual Christian distaste for
Stoic pretenses to self-sufficiency.  He has Pandulpho join
the revenge plot saying, "Man will breake out, despight Philosophie. . . . I spake more then a god; yet am lesse then a
man" (IV.v).[48]  Other conventional jabs at Seneca and at
Stoic pride occur when Antonio, the hero, comes on stage
(II.iii) reading a passage from Seneca that advises us to
remain calm under the blows of fortune.  Disgusted, he
throws the book away. In The Malcontent (III.i) the ineffec-
tual usurping Duke Pietro has a similar reaction when the
silly, sycophantic Bilioso recommends Seneca's remedies for
fortune.  He scorns Seneca as one who "writ of Temperance and
Fortitude, yet lived like a voluptuous Epicure, and died like
an effeminate coward."  Although both Antonio and Pietro are
emotional characters like Shakespeare's Leonato, who can
hardly be expected to listen to Seneca, the episodes look as
though they were introduced to arouse an approving laugh from
the audience.
     Marston's seeming ambivalence toward Stoicism is actu-
ally only a result of the fact that as a thoughtful Christian
he was careful to pick and choose among acceptable and unacceptable doctrines.  Feliche's contented poverty is acceptable.  So is the Ciceronian social conscience exemplified by
Andrugio, by Malevole (in The Malcontent), and by several
characters in Sophonisba.  Also in Sophonisba we learn that it
is preferable to die rather than to sin against the moral law.
At the same time we notice that villains or frauds are the
ones who claim to be without passion, to be godlike in their
self-sufficiency, or to be able to manipulate fortune.  (For
more discussion see Chapters IV-VI.)
     In all this talk of Cicero and Seneca, it may seem that
Epictetus and Marcus Aurelius are being completely forgotten,
which is almost true. Although a scholar like Erasmus was
aware of them both, their day of general popularity came later
than that of Cicero and Seneca.  In fact, we tend to associate

the popularity of Marcus Aurelius with the eighteenth and
nineteenth centuries.  The name of Epictetus, however, begins
to occur fairly often during the seventeenth century and
seems by Dryden's time to have been something of a symbol for
a "double-strength Stoic."  Erasmus in his Adages had quoted
Epictetus' admonition to sustain and abstain, a lesson which
was often repeated by sixteenth- and seventeenth-century
writers.  Some of the more erudite, like George Chapman, John
Marston, Robert Burton, and John Milton, mention Epictetus'
name approvingly.  Dryden in his essay on "The Original and
Progress of Satire" couples him as a moralist with Aristotle
and sounds as though his own definition of Stoicism is derived from a reading of Epictetus.  And William Congreve opens
Love for Love with a scene in which the hero, Valentine, and
his servant, Jeremy, updating Falstaff's cynical remarks on
honor, make merry at the expense of Epictetus' notions of mind
over matter.  Valentine tells Jeremy:  "Go you to Breakfast--
There's a Page doubled down in Epictetus that is a Feast for
an Emperour."

Jeremy asks, "Was Epictetus a real Cook, or did he only
write Receipts?"

"Read, read, Sirrah," says Valentine, "and refine your
Appetite, learn to live upon Instruction; feast your Mind, and
mortifie your Flesh; Read, and take your Nourishment in at
your Eyes; shut up your Mouth, and chew the Cud of Understanding.  So Epictetus advises."

"O Lord!" says Jeremy, "I have heard much of him, when
I waited upon a gentleman at Cambridge.  Pray what was that
Epictetus?"

"A very rich Man--Not worth a Groat."

"Humph, and so he has made a very fine Feast, where there
is nothing to be eaten?"

"Yes."

"Sir, you're a Gentleman, and probably understand this
fine Feeding:  but if you please, I had rather be at Board-
Wages.  Does your Epictetus, or your Seneca here, or any of
these poor rich Rogues, teach you how to pay your Debts with-
out money?  Will they shut up the Mouths of your Creditors?
Will Plato be Bail for you?  Or Diogenes, because he under-
stands Confinement, and liv'd in a Tub, go to Prison for you?
'Slife, Sir what do you mean, to mew your self up here with
Three or Four musty Books, in commendation of Starving and
Poverty?"[49]

# Chapter II. Notes

[1]For some examples of different uses of the term "Neo-Stoic" see: Zanta, p. 333; Baker, Dignity of Man, pp. 301-309; Higgins, "Development of the Senecal Man"; Haydn, Counter-Renaissance, passim; Palmer, Seneca's De Remediis Fortuitorum, p. 19; Saunders, Justus Lipsius, p. 19; Rostvig, Happy Man, passim; Henderson, "Neo-Stoic Influence." On prose style see Palmer, p. 19; Croll; Williamson. Recent studies that help to disentangle some confusions are Miner, "Patterns of Stoicism," and Vickers, Francis Bacon and Renaissance Prose.

[2]In addition to Zanta's longer study, brief surveys of the infiltration of Stoic ideas can be found in Baker, Wars of Truth, pp. 110-16; Dignity of Man, p. 299; Wenley, pp. 140-44; Hoopes, pp. 132-33. On Boethius see Patch, Tradition of Boethius, p. 76 ff.

[3]The key word, as a number of scholars have pointed out, is not Stoicism or Platonism or Aristotelianism or Ciceronianism or Senecanism, but syncretism. See, e.g., Zanta, pp. 72, 88; Schoell, Etudes sur L'Humanisme, p. 105; Haydn, pp. 55, 329; Kristeller, "Platonic Academy of Florence"; Levi. Levi shows in detail how such conventional critical categories as "Neostoic," "Augustinian," "skeptic," "Platonist," and "Epicurean" were blurred and mixed in actual usage. Although he is discussing French thinkers rather than English popular writers and is confining himself to one topic, theories of the passions, his conclusions are equally applicable when applied to the mixture of Stoic and other ideas in English popular writing.
Some continental writers who wrote treatises incorporating especially large quantities of Stoic morality into their own recipes for how to live were: Justus Lipsius (1547-1606); Philippe de Mornay (1549-1625); and Guillaume du Vair (1555-1621). (Incidentally, John Calvin's first book [1532] was a commentary on Seneca's De Clementia.) For some discussions of the above writers see Zanta, Croll, Baker, Dignity of Man, pp. 306-307; Hoopes, pp. 133-34; Levi, pp. 40-95; Kirk, ed., Lipsius, Two Bookes of Constancie, pp. 13-23, and Du Vair, Moral Philosophie of the Stoicks; Kristeller, Classics and Renaissance Thought, p. 22.

[4]Of the Adages of Erasmus, Starnes says, "By 1550, more than ninety editions, including selections and epitomes, had been printed; and by 1599, at least one hundred thirty" (Proverbs or Adages, p. 51); Schoell says that Chapman, like most educated men of his time, was steeped in the adages of Erasmus and suggests that the only reason Chapman did not versify any Erasmian passage of any length is that the Adages were too well known, and he preferred to make a parade of erudite

knowledge (p. 61).  Of Erasmus' Oration on Peace and Discord
Against the Seditious (ca. 1490) Adams says, it "is saturated
with ideas either echoed or reworked from Lucretius and Seneca, intended apparently to illuminate the contemporary scene"
(Better Part of Valor, p. 26).  See also introduction to Erasmus, Christian Prince, ed. Born.  Another collection of adages
was Baldwin's, Sayings of the Wise (1555).  For extensive information about commonplace collections see Ong, "Tudor Writings on Rhetoric."  On the Stoic ideas of Erasmus' friend
Vives (1492-1540) and his influence on later scholars, see
Norena, Juan Luis Vives, pp. 289-90.

5For information on editions and translations see Zanta;
Schoell, pp. 67-81, 105-106, 131; Lathrop, Translations from
the Classics; Bolgar, Classical Heritage; Palmer; Baker,
Dignity of Man, pp. 305-306; Hoopes, p. 133 ff; Wieler, George
Chapman, p. 3 ff.

6Trans. Helbold, Moralia, Loeb, VI, 181-85, 191, 197, 215,
221, 235.

7Essayes, I.19, trans. Florio, Everyman, 440.

8See Zanta, pp. 167-240; Levi, p. 69.

9See Kirk's edition.

10See Zanta, p. 183.

11On Joseph Hall's ambivalence toward Lipsius, see Croll,
p. 8.  Hinman (Abraham Cowley) sees the influence of some of
Lipsius' ideas on Cowley; see especially pp. 75-76.

12See OED and Sams, "Anti-Stoicism."

13Praise of Folly, trans. Hudson, pp. 14, 39-40.  See
Adams, pp. 29, 46-47; Mason, Humanism and Poetry.

14Ed. Ryan, p. 116.

15Quotations are from Works, ed. Kittredge.

16Works, ed. Wynter, VIII, 547.

17"Upon the Gardens of Epicurus," Five Miscellaneous Essays,
ed. Monk, p. 6; see also Early Essays and Romances, ed. Smith,
p. 140.

18Utopia, ed. Warrington, Everyman, 461, pp. 149-50.

19Though Lipsius, especially in his later works (see Zanta,
pp. 225-40), explores some aspects of Stoic physics, his early
De Constantia concentrates on the sort of lessons in fortitude
that were already well accepted.

20Zanta's discussion of Lipsius and Du Vair points up the
difference in the Neo-Stoicism of the two men.  Lipsius admired
Seneca, chose the retired life, concentrated on private peace
of mind, and exalted world citizenship above patriotic duty.
Du Vair always put duty to country above personal tranquillity

and was a disciple of Cicero and the Roman law tradition as
well as of Epictetus and Seneca (see pp. 300-302, 309-11, 321).

[21]See Mendell, Our Seneca, pp. 152-55.  Zanta points out
that although Lipsius went to great pains to reconcile Stoic
fate and Christian providence, Du Vair followed the contemporary practice of failing to discriminate among the terms,
"providence," "destiny," "nature," and "fortune" (p. 315).

[22]Baldwin's Sayings of the Wise is one of the many books
that reports in good faith the story that Seneca was influenced by and was a friend of St. Paul (p. 76).

[23]Quotations are from Palmer.  See also discussion by
Farnham, Medieval Heritage, p. 56, and Zanta's discussion of
sixteenth-century humanistic pedagogical books (pp. 75-94).

[24]See, e.g., "Of Adversity" and "Of Death."  Quotations
are from Everyman, 10.

[25]Anatomy of Melancholy, ed. Dell and Jordan-Smith, pp. 16,
23.

[26]On Hall see H. Fisch, "The Limits of Hall's Senecanism,"
and A. Chew, "Joseph Hall and Neo-Stoicism."  On Senecan style
see Croll and Williamson.

[27]Advancement of Learning, ed. Kitchin, Everyman, II.xx.2.

[28]Microcosmography, ed. Osborne.

[29]Resolves, No. 20.

[30]Poems, ed. Waller, p. 16.

[31]The large contribution of Seneca's tragedies to the
form of Elizabethan tragedy is not the question here.  For
some discussions of Seneca and Elizabethan tragedy, see Cunliffe, Influence of Seneca; Lucas, Seneca and Elizabethan
Tragedy; T. S. Eliot, "Seneca in Elizabethan Translation,"
Selected Essays; Bowers, Elizabethan Revenge Tragedy; Jacquot
and Oddon, eds., Les Tragédies de Sénèque.

[32]See Cunliffe, pp. 25-26; Lucas, p. 71; Eliot, p. 72,
Grimal, "Les Tragédies de Sénèque," p. 4.

[33]Agamemnon, lines 57-62; Oedipus, 6 ff, 882 ff; Troades,
1 ff; Hercules on Oeta, 636 ff; Troades, 1010 ff; Phaedra,
480 ff, 1120 ff; Hercules Furens, 161 ff; Thyestes, 450 ff.
References are to The Complete Roman Drama, ed. Duckworth,
Vol. II.  The Pseudo-Senecan Octavia introduces Seneca himself as a chorus character moralizing on how much happier he
was as an exile in his Corsican retreat than he was after the
goddess Fortuna rescued him, only in due course to cast him
down again.  This theme, which appears often in Elizabethan
literature, is coupled here with one that rarely appears there,
though it was taken up at a later date by such writers as
Shelley, Yeats, and Joyce.  It is the idea from Stoic physics

that time goes round in a circle. In _Octavia_ the character
Seneca speculates that the corruptness of the present age
must be a sign that a cycle is about to end; soon time will
start over once more with the golden age of Saturn (lines
376 ff). Although the notion that the world had now reached
the stage of senility was common enough in Elizabethan literature, the cyclic view that history would repeat itself was not
yet in fashion. For discussion of this passage, see Lovejoy
and Boas, _Primitivism_, pp. 58-59.

[34]_Meaning of Stoicism_, pp. 58-59. See also, Lapp, "Racine, est-il Sénèquien?"

[35]_Marlowe's Tamburlaine_, p. 98 ff.

[36]Especially popular with English poets of the sixteenth
and seventeenth centuries was the choral ode from _Thyestes_,
lines 338 ff. I quote Thomas Wyatt's version:

Stond who so list vpon the Slipper toppe
    Of courtes estate, and lett me heare reioyce;
And vse me quyet without lett or stoppe.
    Vnknowen in courte, that hath such brackishe ioyes:
    In hidden place, so lett my dayes forthe passe,
That when my yeares be done, withouten noyse,
    I maye dye aged after the common trace,
For hym death greep'the right hard by the croppe
    That is moche knowen of other; and of him self alas,
    Doth dye vnknowen, dazed with dreadfull face.

(Quoted from _Collected Poems_, ed. Muir, No. 176). For other
expressions of the idea, see _Hercules Oetaeus_, lines 104 ff,
and _Troades_, lines 257 ff.

[37]For discussion of Hercules as a Stoic hero see Waith,
_Herculean Hero_; Morel, "'Hercule sur l'OEta.'"

[38]See, e.g., W. C. Greene, _Moira_; Arnold, p. 199 ff; Boas,
_Rationalism_, p. 295 ff. On the distinction between Stoic fate
and Calvinistic predestination, see Zanta, pp. 62-63, 65, and
Haydn, pp. 109-10.

[39]_Stoic Philosophy of Seneca_, pp. 3-4.

[40]Craig in "The Shackling of Accidents," argues that "with
Seneca the very nature of things was disastrous" (p. 13) and
says the Stoics stressed "the totally evil nature of all
things" (p. 14). He says that "in Jacobean drama Neo-Stoicism
perhaps tended to express itself in terms of titanism" (p. 17)
and interprets Chapman's Bussy as a Titan, a proponent of passion against reason.

[41]See Greene, p. 368; _Hercules Furens_, 179 ff; _Oedipus_,
80 ff, 978 ff; _Thyestes_, 929 ff.

[42]Aside from stage caricatures of the "Stoic-Machiavel"
there were also writers who seriously combined Stoic and
Machiavellian ideas. If we take note of the continuing ten-

dency of politicians to justify a divorce between political
morality and private morality, we can easily see that someone might base his private conduct on certain Stoic morals
and his political theory on Machiavelli. It has been said of
Justus Lipsius, for instance, that he "owed his political and
military theory to Machiavelli and his moral philosophy to
Seneca" (Wood, "Some Common Aspects of the Thought of Seneca
and Machiavelli," p. 22). Daiches says of Fulke Greville,
Lord Brooke (1554-1628) that "in practical political affairs
he was Machiavellian; in personal ethical matters he was a
Stoic; in religious thought he was a Calvinist" (Critical
History, I, 202). Something along the same lines might be
said of Walter Ralegh. A gentlemanly essayist with a taste
for Stoic platitudes like William Cornwallis (1579?-1614) had
no objection to combining a line from a Senecan play with a
Machiavellian moral (see Essayes, ed. Allen).

[43]Pp. 29-30. See also T. S. Eliot, p. 72.

[44]For discussions of "Senecal" plays see the introduction
by Kastner and Charlton, eds., to Poetical Works of Sir William
Alexander, Vol. I; Lucas, p. 112; T. S. Eliot; Ellis-Fermor,
Jacobean Drama, p. 21; Farnham, p. 394; Bullough, "Sénèque,
Greville et le Jeune Shakespeare."

[45]George Chapman, pp. 3-4.

[46]See also Lucas, p. 123; Eliot, p. 129; Palmer, p. 22.

[47]Tragic Satire of John Webster, p. 92. Caputi, John
Marston, Satirist, emphasizes the influence of Epictetus on
Marston's thinking. Ure, "John Marston's Sophonisba," dis-
cusses Sophonisba as an exposition of Marston's Stoic ideas.

[48]See Ornstein, Moral Vision, pp. 156-58, and Finkelpearl,
John Marston, pp. 145-59. Quotations are from Chapman, Plays
and Poems, ed. Parrott, and Marston, Plays, ed. Wood.

[49]Quotations are from Complete Plays of William Congreve,
ed. Davis.

# Chapter III.  Epicureanism

Philip Sidney's attack on atheistical Epicureans in the
_Arcadia_ stands out not only because Sidney obviously had gone
into the subject more deeply than most such attackers but also
because he rejected more Epicureanism than most.  In Chapter
10 of Book 3, the virtuous Pamela, who has fallen into the hands
of her wicked aunt Cecropia, receives a long Lucretian lecture
intended to persuade her to deviate from the path of truth.  Cecropia argues that this world is all there is, that the gods
are no more interested in the doings of men than men are interested in the relative capabilities of dancing flies, that
thunder and lightning do not come from an angry god but rather
have natural causes, that man is the only thing that forsakes
the course of his own nature and "while by the pregnancie of
his imagination he strives to things supernaturall, meane-
while he looseth his owne naturall felicitie."  Cecropia's
advice is, "Be wise, and that wisedome shalbe a God unto thee;
be contented, and that is thy heaven."[1]  Cecropia shocks Pamela by denying that virtue should have such supernatural moti-
vations as hope of reward or fear of punishment and by not
believing that there is a providence looking out for the individual.  Wickedly she suggests that Pamela should use her own
reason as a guide and should learn to be contented with her
present lot, gaining, in that way, all the heaven there is to
have.  Pamela's long rebuttal, which concentrates on refuting
the Epicurean argument that the universe functions without the
help of providence, lets pass the suggestion that a contented
heart will bring her heaven on earth.

Whatever Pamela may have thought, however, Sidney, by
the very fact that he put into the wicked Cecropia's mouth the
admonition, "Be contented, and that is thy heaven," indicated
that he--unlike many of his more lenient contemporaries--ad-
hered to the purist Christian teaching which deferred true
happiness until the next life.  In so doing, he took issue not
only with Lucretius but also with all the moderate followers
of Horace who had long been managing to combine Stoic, Epicurean, and Christian lessons into a recipe for the pleasant life
on earth.  That large topic, which is the subject of the next
chapter, is the main reason for interposing here a short review
of the fortunes of Epicureanism in the literature of the sixteenth and seventeenth centuries.  Because the history of Epicureanism is intertwined with that of Stoicism, it is difficult to talk about the one without talking about the other.
The same language is applied to both, with different meanings
intended.  Both were termed atheistical, even though Epicureanism was considered worse. Both encouraged in their followers the sin of pride, the classic examples being the Stoic with
his head bloody but unbowed and the Epicurean denying the influence of the stars.  Though both talked about the necessity
of following nature, they had entirely different interpreta-

tions in mind.   (See Chapter V.)

Over the centuries, while the Stoics were being called emotionless stones, the Epicureans were represented as gross sensualists.   Where the Stoics were supposed to have too much self control, the Epicureans were accused of having too little. John Davies alluded briefly in _Orchestra_ (1596) to the erroneous opinions of those who say that atoms "concur by chaunce" (st. 20) and in _Nosce Teipsum_ (1599) referred to the arguments of those who say that since the soul dies with the body we should therefore "eate and drinke."   According to Davies "no heretikes desire to spread / Their light opinions, like these _Epicures_."[2] Later the popular distaste for Epicureans was expressed by Goneril when she complained that the "Epicurism and lust" of Lear's knights were turning her palace into a tavern or a brothel (I.iv.265-267).   The villainous Edmund of the same play exemplified the stage Epicurean when he denied that he was ruled by fate, insisting instead that his wickedness was his own fault (I.ii.129-145).   It was the Epicurean Cassius, not the Stoic Brutus, who said, "The fault, dear Brutus, is not in our stars. . . ."   Ben Jonson in _Catiline_ had the wicked Catiline's followers make such blasphemous statements as "A valiant man is his owne fate, and fortune" (IV.568-572). Sejanus (in _Sejanus_) was accused of slighting or denying the power of the gods (V.x).   And just as the stage Stoic claimed to be master of his fate--whatever that might mean--so the stage Epicure pooh-poohed the stars.   Stage villains, who frequently numbered pride first among their deadly sins, tended, whether they belonged to the Stoic or the Epicurean persuasion, to have an overweening confidence in their own powers.   Virtuous characters, on the other hand, bowed to fate, even though, if cornered, they would have insisted that what they really had in mind was providence--meaning by that something vague that might range anywhere from pure accident at the one extreme to pure determinism at the other--as long as it was outside themselves.[3]

In addition to denying fate, the Epicureans allegedly subscribed to an atheistical definition of what was "natural." Where the Stoics, like other idealists, identified what is natural with what ought to be, considering that a man was being natural only when he was using his Godlike faculty, reason, to guide himself toward his God-given duty, the Epicureans were popularly supposed to identify being natural with relaxing all restraints--acting like non-rational animals, letting the senses or the passions take over, imposing no unselfish controls on personal desires.   Mingled with the elements of caricature there were also some grains of an actual important difference between Epicureans and Stoics, namely, that the Epicureans were more relativistic in their attitude toward moral standards than the Stoics were.   The Stoics, who claimed to believe in objective truth--in innate ideas that could be known through common sense--saw no excuse for shilly-shallying

about the difference between right and wrong--whether they
were talking about morality or politics or aesthetics or
whatever.  The Epicureans, more like the later physical scien-
tists, claimed to arrive at general principles through empiri-
cal observation, an attitude which had its appeal for skeptical thinkers like Machiavelli, Montaigne, Bacon, and Hobbes.
Although the Epicurean identification of "nature" with the
observed facts, instead of with the hypothetical ideal, was
to become more and more acceptable with the passing of time,
it was not standard doctrine on the Elizabethan stage.  Edmund
in _Lear_ only marked himself a villainous Epicure when he said,
"Thou, Nature, art my goddess," going on to argue that nothing
but foolish custom labels a bastard inferior to a legitimate
child (I.ii.1-6).[4]  Although from the point of view of empiri-
cal observation he was doubtless right, from the context of
the play it is clear that he was wrong.  What he was labeling
as custom, other people accepted as the law of nature; and the
proof that the popular conception was supposed to be correct
is that Edmund at once proceeded to act like a stage bastard.

When we turn from the Epicurean as he was caricatured on
the stage to the actual aspects of Epicureanism that seeped
into English literature, again we notice the parallels with
Stoicism.  Although it was customary whenever one mentioned
an Epicurean to pause for some disparaging remarks about atheists, it was also popular to decorate one's compositions with
quotations from Lucretius.  Even if there were no English translations of Lucretius until the late seventeenth century, there
were plenty of Latin editions available.  Michael Grant says,
"The Renaissance rejected Lucretius' philosophy but revered
his poetry.  Montaigne quotes him 149 times--once more even,
tnan Horace, and most of all ancient poets."[5]  Bacon in "Of
Truth" called Lucretius, "the poet that beautified the sect
that was otherwise inferior to the rest," whlle he ridiculed
Epicureans in the Advancement of Learning (II.xiv.9) as
contributors to the anthropomorphic view of the gods.  In
the essay "Of Unity in Religion" he said Lucretius would have
been "seven times more epicure and atheist than he was" if he
could have seen some of the things now done in the name of religion, such as "the massacre in France, or the powder treason
of England."  Robert Burton, possibly to cover up his own Epicurean leanings, noisily identified Epicureanism with worldly
greed, saying Epicureans loved nothing but money, compared
Epicureans to vultures, accused them of vanity, said that as
atheists they undermined the commonwealth, and that they were
lascivious.  He said, "There be those that apologize for Epicurus; but all in vain, Lucian scoffs at all, Epicurus he
denies all, and Lucretius his Scholar defends him in it."[6]
Thomas Browne, in a letter to his son Edward (Feb. 25 [1676?])
expressed a typical seventeenth-century attitude: "My neibour
Mr. Bickerdike going towards London to morrowe I would not

deny him a letter, and I have sent by him Lucretius his six
bookes de rerum natura, because you lately sent mee a quotation out of that Author, that you might have one by you to
find out quotations wch shall considerably offer themselves
at any time; otherwise I do not much recommend the reading
or studying of it, there being divers impieties in it, and
tis no credit to bee punctually versed in it; it containeth
the epicurean naturall philosophie."[7] Thomas Mayo describes
Milton's attitude toward Epicureanism as "consistently contemptuous, in spite of his obvious familiarity with the poem
of Lucretius, whom he likewise lists among the poets whom
his ideal schoolboys ought to read" (p. 31). Even at the end
of the century, during the libertine Restoration Period, John
Dryden, who translated into pleasant verse a few sections of
Lucretius, felt it necessary to remark that the latter "was
so much an atheist, that he forgot sometimes to be a poet."[8]

A favorite Lucretian passage for quotation or allusion
was the one from the opening of Book II about the advantages
of being removed from the center of things--able to get a
proper perspective on a storm or a battle by watching from
a safe distance. Bacon was one who adapted the passage for
his own purposes in the well-known section from "Of Truth"
which starts, "It is a pleasure to stand upon the shore, and
to see ships tossed upon the sea." This Lucretian passage
may well be compared with the equally popular Senecan lines
from the end of Act II of Thyestes on how much happier it is
to live far from the court, learning to know one's own heart,
instead of living among men and worrying continually about
the effect one is making on others. Another favorite Lucretian passage was the section from the end of Book III (830 ff)
against the fear of death. Bacon started his "Of Death" with
an echo of Lucretius: "Men fear death, as children fear to
go in the dark; and as that natural fear in children is
increased with tales, so is the other." Dryden, who was particularly pleased with his translation of the end of Book III,
said in his preface to translations from Theocritus, Lucretius,
and Horace that although he rejected as absurd Lucretius'
"opinions concerning the mortality of the soul," he found helpful Lucretius' arguments against the fear of death and his
antidotes against love.[9]

Robert Burton, when he was looking for antidotes against
melancholy, likewise found Epicurean recipes helpful, saying,
"A quiet mind is that pleasure, or highest good, of Epicurus;
not to grieve, but to want cares, and have a quiet soul, is
the only pleasure of the World, as Seneca truly recites his
opinion, not that of eating and drinking, which injurious
Aristotle (possibly a slip for Athenaeus) maliciously puts
upon him, and for which he is still mistaken, slandered without a cause, and lashed by all posterity" (p. 467). Burton's
own idea of the good life was presumably the one he described
at length as lived by Democritus--from whom Epicurus borrowed
many of his ideas. Without having to use the offensive word

"Epicurean," Burton told how Democritus amused himself in his
garden, letting the busy world go on its way as he carried on
scientific experiments into the causes of madness and melancholy.  Because he laughed at the worldly things considered
important by most people, he himself was thought to be out
of his mind.  Like Erasmus' Christian fools he had other values
than the usual ones of getting and spending and laughed "at the
vanity and fopperies of the time, to see men so empty of all
virtuous actions, to hunt so far after gold, having no end of
ambition; to take such infinite pains for a little glory"
(p. 38 ff).

The custom of combining certain Epicurean assessments
of the gloomy nature of life with Christian recommendations
to think of the next world or with Stoic-Epicurean advice on
how to make the best of this one, goes back a long way.  Earlier we saw Lydgate borrowing such ideas from Boccaccio.  Erasmus' The Praise of Folly and More's Utopia give us more examples.  These ideas, to be discussed further in the next chapter, come under the heading of safe Epicureanism and are generally the ones that keep turning up in literature.  Although
they increase in quantity during the course of the seventeenth
century and are thus possibly an indication of increasing sec-
ularism, they seldom make a deliberate break with Christian
teaching.  In English literature it is difficult to find anything even so mildly daring as La Fontaine's mocking laughter
at astrologers for pretending to be able to read the stars
while neglecting to notice the pit they are about to fall into
or his Lucretian ridicule of human beings for fearing death
and clinging to life long after all the pleasure has gone.[10]

In spite of the popular attitude that Epicureanism should
be touched only with a long pole, scholars--mainly on the con-
tinent--had long been poking into forbidden areas.[11]  Beginning
in the fifteenth century, various Epicurean ideas began moving
gradually from Italy to France to England, combining themselves
with acceptable ideas as they went and taking every advantage
of ambiguous words like "nature."  As we look back from where
we are now, we can see that the physical sciences were to make
use of Epicurean atomic theory and that in the eighteenth and
nineteenth centuries such other fields as psychology, aesthetics, economics, and politics were to be affected by Epicurean
attitudes.  Over the centuries the battle goes on between Stoic
belief in absolute truth and Epicurean tentativeness.  Where
the Stoic tries to insist that the moral law, as he sees it, is
universal truth, the Epicurean confines himself to saying that
this is the way things look from where he happens to be sitting.  Where a good Stoic will try to make his personal behavior conform to alleged universal standards, an Epicurean will
try to decide which course of action will be most conducive
to his own happiness.  Though his decision--otherwise known as
enlightened self-interest--may result in action as altruistic
as that of the Stoic, his basic motive is frankly selfish.

Among the thinkers tinged with Epicurean modes of thought we
call to mind such men as Machiavelli and Hobbes, whose ideas
in due course found their way into popular literature. However, in sixteenth- and seventeenth-century popular writing
what is sometimes known as the Epicurean revival tends only to
mean a defense of the pleasant life.

Since heretical thinking was dangerous, even when written
in Latin, thinkers who were attracted to Epicurean ideas often
went to great pains to amend their Epicureanism so as to make
it conform, more or less, to Christian doctrine. Just as the
fashion for Seneca was stronger in France than in England, so
Epicureanism was more widespread among French writers than
among English. In spite of the late seventeenth-century popularity of things French, the English were cautious about how
much French Epicureanism they borrowed. Mayo says that the De
Vita et Moribus Epicuri (1647) of Pierre Gassendi and the Dis-
cours de Morale sur Epicure (1645 or 1646) of Jean François
Sarasin were "the only French works which exerted any considerable amount of direct influence on the Epicurean revival
in England" (p. 10). Both these writers, arguing that the
ideas of Epicurus really supported Christianity, added a few
Stoic ingredients to their Epicurean mix so as to make it more
acceptable. Gassendi who, like Bacon, was useful in helping
the natural philosophers find a justification for prying into
the secrets of physical nature, stressed, like the Epicureans,
the importance of the experimental attitude while, as a circumspect churchman, he was careful not to follow Epicurean
physics in asserting chance rather than providence as the
ruler of things. In fact, he even included in his system
proof of the existence of the Christian God, along with such
un-Epicurean ideas as foreknowledge and particular providence.

Among the various clever but naughty young men who
belonged to the world of Charles II, one who stands out as a
typical pleasure-worshipping libertine and Epicure is John
Wilmot, Earl of Rochester. Though in his personal life he was
more libertine than Epicurean, being--for one thing--no prudent disciple of the golden mean (see Mayo, p. 174), in the
area of intellectual speculation his skeptical attitude toward
conventional clichés inclined him toward an Epicurean or a
natural philosopher's definition of nature as something based
on observed facts. His skepticism, also, led him for a time
to entertain forbidden ideas about death and the gods, though
he ended--as skeptics often do--by arbitrarily accepting on
faith that which he could neither prove nor disprove through
reason. In his "A Satyr against Reason and Mankind" he amused
himself by giving to the prestigious Stoic-Christian term
"right reason" an Epicurean meaning (lines 100-101). Instead
of identifying right reason with an intuitive method of reaching absolute truth, he, like Sidney's Cecropia, called it
"That reason which distinguishes by sense / And gives us rules
of good and ill from thence." Although he might have acquired
the notion from Hobbes, he might also have got it from

Lucretius, or from Gassendi or Montaigne, among others. The experimental attitude was the coming thing.[12]

Rochester's tendency to skepticism was something that often went with a taste for Epicureanism. Although an Epicurean is not necessarily a skeptic and although it is also possible to mix Stoicism with skepticism, it is true that the Epicureans do not give quite so strong an impression as the Stoics that they know all the answers. It is easy to draw up a list of writers with a skeptical streak who had likewise a taste for Lucretius. We need only call to mind such familiar names as those of Montaigne, Bacon, Burton, and Dryden. We realize also, however, that all of these men used their skepticism about reason's ability to arrive at final answers as a justification for accepting on faith traditional Christian doctrines. Bacon, whose skeptical attitude toward popularly accepted Stoic doctrines of natural law inclined him to choose authoritarian answers not only in religion but also in politics and legal theory, actually used Epicurean ideas to support his contention that the universe needed an authoritarian ruler. In his essay "Of Atheism" he said that the Epicurean atomic theory, in spite of itself, really proved the existence of God. If the universe was formed of all those chaotic atoms whirling through the void, it would have even more need of a divine marshal to govern it than under the other system of "four mutable elements and one immutable fifth essence," which, being less complicated, might more easily get along without constant supervision. Similarly Dryden, at the beginning of "Religio Laici," classed Stoics and Epicureans along with all the other ancient madmen who had vainly tried to reach truth through reason, saying of Aristotle that "Epicurus guess'd as well as he."[13]

There is no profit in trying to make philosophers out of literary men, especially when the purpose of this study is to illustrate some of the various ways Stoic and Epicurean ideas were combined in miscellaneous literary salads. The skeptical tendency that may lead some writers to choose unquestioning fideism may cause others to leave ultimate questions hanging in the air while for practical reasons they elect to conform to local custom. In "The Character of a Trimmer" George Savile, Marquis of Halifax (1633-1695)--sometimes classed as a Machiavellian thinker--said religion "is as necessary to our Living Happy in this World as it is to our being Sav'd in the next." The pious sister of William Temple (1628-1699) defended her brother--another free-thinking statesman who was fond of Montaigne--by insisting, "His Religion was y$^t$ of the church of England he was borne & bred in, & thought nobody ought to change since it must require more time & pains then ones life can furnish to make a true judgement of that wch interest & folly were commonly the motives too."[14]

Halifax and Temple, both of whom devoted much of their lives to the public service and neither of whom can be classified as a Restoration rake, belonged to the fairly large group of literate men who were attracted by certain well-tried Epicurean recipes for how to live. Another member of this group was the sober garden-loving John Evelyn (1620-1706) who, though he may have modeled his private life on the recipes of Epicurus, was careful what he said in print. His translation of the first book of Lucretius, according to Mayo, "devotes thirty-three pages to translating Lucretius into mediocre verse, one hundred and five to proving that most of the ideas thus translated are fallacious, and twelve to apologizing for translating him at all."[15] Evelyn's friend and fellow garden lover, Abraham Cowley, whose essays idealized the Horatian golden mean, occasionally in his verses made fun of sour Stoics and pretended to espouse eat-drink-and-be-merry hedonism. A poem entitled "Another" from a group of "Anacreontiques, or some copies of verses translated paraphrastically out of Anacreon," concludes, "Let me alive my pleasures have / All are Stoicks in the grave"; and a second verse praises "The Grashopper" for being "Voluptuous, and wise withall, / Epicurean animal!"[16] If the originals from which Cowley translated actually used the words "Stoic" and "Epicurean," they only prove that the verses were not by Anacreon, who lived long before Zeno or Epicurus. Although Cowley's poems, as exercises in translation, need not express his own opinion, they go along with his general sympathy for the pleasure theory of life.

The irresponsible pursuit of pleasure that we associate with some Restoration verse and some Restoration plays, however, is typical neither of men like Cowley nor of Epicureanism. The flippant sort of hedonistic chatter to be found in such a play as George Etherege's The Man of Mode turns out, on closer examination, to be merely old-fashioned Elizabethan anti-Epicureanism turned upside down. The completely selfish, pleasure-loving Epicure, who appeared on the Elizabethan stage as a villain, is now transformed into a semi-sympathetic hero. Although the reversal of roles may be a sign of changing times, it is not necessarily a sign of serious interest in Epicureanism.[17] The serious Epicureans generally belonged to the old, unexciting, tranquillity school. Of such a man as William Temple, for instance, Mayo says, "Like Epicurus he set ethics far above all other departments of thought. His contribution to the Epicurean revival was not like Creech's Lucretius or the remarks in Spence's Miscellanea--half glorification and half refutation of the philosopher. It was written genuinely in the spirit of Epicurus" (p. 92). As we shall see in the next chapter, the important thing about the insidious desire for earthly happiness was not so much that it was new as that it was rapidly becoming a literary commonplace.

Chapter III.  Notes

[1]*Works*, ed. Feuillerat, I, 406-407.  For discussion, see Greenlaw, "Captivity Episode."  In addition to this section in the *Arcadia*, there are also unkind remarks about Epicures in the Preface to *Of the Trewnes of the Christian Religion* by Philip Mornay "Begunne to be translated into English by Sir Philip Sidney Knight, and at his request finished by Arthur Golding," *Works*, III, p. 250.  Fulke Greville, in similar vein, has the Chorus Tartarorum in *Mustapha* argue, like Cecropia, that if only men had not been corrupted by the false teachings of religion they could easily follow "the laws of beneficent nature" (see discussion by Rebholz, *Life of Fulke Greville*, p. 106).

[2]Quotations are from *Poems*, ed. Howard, p. 167, st. 3, 4. Buckley discusses translations from the French of Pierre Viret, Pierre de la Primaudaye, and Philip Mornay that attack Epicures and probably supplied writers like Sidney and Davies with material for their own attacks (*Atheism in the English Renaissance*, pp. 97-101).  For other discussions of some of the many identifications of Epicures with atheists, see Battenhouse, *Marlowe's Tamburlaine*, pp. 88-91; Strathmann, *Sir Walter Ralegh*, pp. 61-97; Reese, *Cease of Majesty*, p. 9.

[3]The popular identification of a belief in astrology with Christian doctrine was not necessarily shared by scholars. Buckley says, for instance, that Roger Hutchinson in his *Image of God or Layman's Book* (1550) was one of those who pointed out the conflict between the popular belief in the stars and Christian belief in "God's direct providence over his creatures" (p. 65).  See also Elton, *'King Lear' and the Gods*, p. 149 ff. However, the fact that both Augustine and Aquinas had attacked astrology had as little effect on Elizabethan popular writers as it had had on Chaucer.  See D. C. Allen, *Star Crossed Renaissance*.  Chang, "'Of Mighty Opposites,'" discusses the way in which both Stoicism and Epicureanism put the individual above fortune's power.  For more discussion of Elizabethan treatments of fate see Chapter V.

[4]For comment on this passage in connection with the opposing Stoic and Epicurean meanings of "nature" as understood by the Renaissance, see Bredvold, "Naturalism of Donne"; Crane, *Collection of English Poems*, pp. 1179-80; Bald, "'Thou Nature art my goddess'"; Ornstein, "Donne, Montaigne and Natural Law." Another Epicurean atheist who identifies following nature with forsaking all morality is D'Amville in *The Atheist's Tragedy* of Cyril Tourneur.  See discussions by Bradbrook, *Themes and Conventions*, p. 175; Ornstein, *Moral Vision*, pp. 121-22, and "Atheist's Tragedy"; Ribner, *Jacobean Tragedy*, p. 87, and ed., Cyril Tourneur, *Atheist's Tragedy*, pp. xxxvii-lvii; D. C. Allen, *Doubt's Boundless Sea*, p. 19.

[5]_Roman Readings_, p. 63.

[6]Quotations are from _Essayes_, Everyman, 10, and Burton, _Anatomy of Melancholy_, ed. Dell and Jordan-Smith, pp. 45, 51, 66, 271, 278, 932.

[7]_Letters_, ed. Keynes, p. 65. For a discussion of Thomas Browne's "sprinkling of allusions to the Philosophy of the Garden," see Mayo, _Epicurus in England_.

[8]"Translations from Theocritus, Lucretius, and Horace: Preface to the Second Miscellany," _Poetical Works_ (London, 1867), p. 197.

[9]P. 197; see Mayo, p. 78 ff, for a discussion of Dryden's translations from Lucretius; he says, "The appearance of [Dryden's] translations must have convinced many a reader that Epicureanism in 1685 had at least the respectability of success" (p. 81).

[10]See "L'Astrologue qui se Laisse Tomber dans un Puits" and "La Mort et le Mourant."

[11]See Wenley, p. 142; Buckley, p. 10; Elton, p. 46; D. C. Allen, "Rehabilitation of Epicurus," says that defenses of Epicurus like the one in Burton belong to a tradition three hundred years old.

[12]Quotations are from _Complete Poems_, ed. Vieth. For a discussion of Rochester's intellectual struggles and Christian death, see D. C. Allen, _Doubt's Boundless Sea_, p. 201 ff. One of Rochester's most Epicurean-sounding passages, incidentally, comes from Seneca, the lines beginning, "After death nothing is, and nothing, death:" which are from "A Translation from Seneca's 'Troades,' Act II, Chorus." Sixteenth-century Senecans had avoided these lines as atheistical (see Lebègue).

[13]As eclectics, both Dryden and Bacon, incidentally, expressed the customary preference for Stoic virtue over Epicurean pleasure when it was a question of personal conduct. Dryden said, "The wiser Madmen did for Vertue toyl" ("Religio Laici," 31 [quoted from _Poems and Fables_, ed. Kinsley]); and Bacon ended his essay on atheism by quoting Cicero the practical politician in support of his own argument that man's nobler qualities, and especially his qualities as a good citizen, are fostered through a belief in God and an attempt to imitate Him.

[14]Quotations are from _Complete Works_, ed. Raleigh, p. 67, and "The Character of Sir William Temple," _Early Essays and Romances_, ed. Moore Smith, p. 31.

[15]Pp. 43-44. The important Lucretian translation described by Mayo was that of Thomas Creech, 1682, which excluded what Dryden called the "luscious" passages and devoted its notes to refuting Lucretius.

[16]*Essays, Plays and Sundry Verses*, ed. Waller, pp. 56-57.

[17]For a helpful discussion of the libertine tradition, see Underwood, *Etherege*, pp. 10-40 and 74, n. 5.

Chapter IV.   Heaven on Earth

The desire to have one's cake and eat it too, to have
heaven on earth as well as in heaven, though scarcely a wish
invented by Christian humanists, was a dream that became
increasingly acceptable during the sixteenth and seventeenth
centuries.  Unexciting Stoic-Epicurean recipes for tranquil
happiness, though not of interest to all writers, enjoyed a
certain modest and continuous popularity, coexisting with the
sterner aspects of Stoicism that emphasized social responsibility.  Leaving aside, for the most part, the question of the
individual's duty as part of the social clockwork, this chapter will focus on the selfish desire for private happiness, or
at least, peace of mind.  Whatever the differences of Christians, Stoics, and Epicureans about the ultimate nature of the
universe, they often found it possible to meet on the question of how to make the best of a bad world.  This is the
aspect of Stoicism that in earlier centuries was associated
with Boethius but which writers of the sixteenth and seventeenth centuries often liked to get directly from Virgil or
Horace or Seneca--or Lucretius.  The happiness to be discussed
here should not be confused with good fortune.  Whether it is
called Christian patience, Stoic resignation, or Epicurean content, it means wanting what we get--not getting what we want.
Since, in Hamlet's words, "There is nothing either good or bad
but thinking makes it so," the state of mind known as happiness has to be deliberately nurtured, first, by a careful
assessment of the nature of things and, second, by disciplin-
ing--so far as possible--that primary source of misery, the
emotions.
    Assessing the nature of things meant, above all, coming
to terms with the omnipresent wheel of fortune which, in its
widest sense, stood simply for mutability, or change, or
chance.  The individual had to learn to live with the fact that
the wheel went round and round and that nobody was going to
give him an entirely satisfying clue to how it operated.  When
it came to the details of everyday life, the Stoic or the Christian who believed that the universe was operated on just--
though incomprehensible--principles was no better off than the
Epicurean who believed that chance was in control.  Although
some Christians used the fact of mutability as an argument for
concentrating entirely on the joys of heaven and completely
divorcing the affections from worldly things, others saw no
objection to borrowing Stoic-Epicurean suggestions for making
the best of a bad lot--especially since Christians who complained about their lot on earth were not likely to receive a
better one in heaven.
    At the beginning of the sixteenth century John Skelton
(1460?-1529) moralizes in the familiar medieval way about
earthly mutability and "Fortune's double cast," telling us
to put first things first, to fix our eyes on heaven.[1]  The
same emphasis on earthly woe turns up again and again in the

lengthy, many-authored <u>Mirror</u> <u>for</u> <u>Magistrates</u> that continued to
appear in new versions between 1559 and the end of the century.
In the "Induction" to the <u>Mirror</u> Sorrow comes on stage to
preach the message that life is a "maze of misery, / Of
wretched chance. . . . [where] no earthly joy may dure."  Later
in the poem "Morall Senec" is apostraphized as one who moralized well on the universal power of fortune.[2]  Senecan emphasis
on the vagaries of fortune fits in easily with Christian teaching, since neither point of view encourages us to think that
life on earth will grow permanently better.  Take, for example
the choral song at the end of Act III from Thomas Kyd's "Senecal" play <u>Cornelia</u>, that concludes, "From chaunce is nothing
franchized: / And till the time that they are dead, / Is no
man blest: / He onely, that no death doth dread, / Doth liue
at rest."[3]  This idea, which might equally well be Christian,
or Stoic, or Epicurean, is best known in Montaigne's Senecan
version:  "There is no evill in life, for him that hath well
conceived, how the privation of life is no evill."[4]

Montaigne's emphasis on death as a release from the vicissitudes of life, leans slightly in the Epicurean direction;
while Edmund Spenser's advice to comfort oneself by contemplat-
ing the total picture, inclines slightly to the Stoic side.  In
his mutability cantos (FQ, VII) Spenser links himself with the
optimistic Christian-Stoic tradition, which had attracted such
other poets as Boethius, Dante, and Chaucer ("Balade of Fortune") and which offers the remote comfort that in the ultimate sense mutability does not really exist--since no matter
how confusing the ways of the world may look to those of us
with limited vision, everything that happens is part of an
eternal plan.

This sort of comfort, which leaps over specifics to concentrate on the world view, is difficult to keep in focus for
long.  Although such orthodox clergymen as Joseph Hall (1574-
1656) and Robert Burton (1577-1640) would doubtless have agreed
with Spenser, they were also interested in collecting from the
ancients whatever specific advice they could find about maintaining equanimity in the face of changing fortune.  Having
conceded that this life is always a series of ups and downs
and that true peace comes only in the next, they then suggested that one step on the road to equanimity was to learn
to gaze steadily at the flux without blinking.  Hall optimistically entitled one of his better-known works, <u>Heaven</u> <u>Upon</u>
<u>Earth</u>, while Burton, who preferred not to oversell his product,
called his book, <u>The</u> <u>Anatomy</u> <u>of</u> <u>Melancholy</u>.  Burton actually
went into the subject more deeply than Hall, partly because he
spent all his life as a retired scholar, continually poking
away at his problem, trying his recipes out on his own melancholy, borrowing good ideas wherever he found them.  Hall,
who mixed writing with administrative work, progressed up the
ladder until he became a bishop, and was not entirely pleased
when fortune, aided by the civil war, flung him out of office
in his old age.  Burton, who liked to call himself Democritus

Junior, evidently believed like Montaigne that if we try to
face the probabilities without deceiving ourselves, we will
reduce the unnecessary torture. Failure to accept change as
a constant brings on a "labyrinth of cares, woes, miseries."
That man is not fit to live who is not armed to endure the
fact that in this world "with a reciprocal tie pleasure &
pain are still united, and succeed one another in a ring."
Even the greatest happiness is a short-lived thing; content
or security are not to be found in any particular profession;
"we must not think, the happiest of us all, to escape here
without some misfortunes." "Whatsoever is under the Moon is
subject to corruption, alteration; and, so long as thou
livest upon the earth, look not for other." John Keats, a
lover of Burton, was fond of expressing the same ideas.

Since change is inevitable, the first remedy is to be
prepared. Like Seneca, Burton considered it prudent to be
emotionally ever ready for disaster, saying, "The Commonwealth
of Venice in their Armoury have this inscription, Happy is that
city which in time of peace thinks of war; a fit Motto for
every man's private house, happy is the man that provides for
a future assault."[5] This theme was likewise a favorite with
Hall, who said, "Before sorrow come, I will prepare for it;
when it is come, I will welcome it; when it goes, I will take
but half a farewell of it, as still expecting its return."
He tells us that small afflictions help us prepare for greater
ones, since we cannot expect to live in perpetual sunshine,
that since sorrows "come on horseback and go away on foot," and
since pleasures "come like oxen, slow and heavily, and go away
like post-horses, upon the spur, he is his own best friend that
makes the least of both of them." Although these bits of advice
have the grim sound commonly associated with the Stoics, the
following maxim leans faintly in the Epicurean direction. Less
gaily, perhaps, than Horace, Hall nevertheless tells us not to
live in hope of better days but to make the most of the present
more or less smiling hour, reminding us that "oft times those
things which have been sweet in opinion have proved bitter in
experience. . . . Whereas the custom of the world is to hate
things present, to desire future, and magnify what is past; I
will contrarily, esteem that which is present best."[6]

The Stoic-Epicurean ideal is to learn to be surprised
at nothing, to accept the fact that the seasons go round and
round, that what is here today is likely to be gone tomorrow,
that bad fortune today may be good fortune tomorrow, all of
which requires an exceedingly well disciplined set of emotions.
Burton says, at one point, "A wise man's mind, as Seneca holds,
is like the state of the world above the Moon, ever serene.
Come then what can come, befall what may befall, meet it with
an unbroken and unconquerable courage . . . What can't be
cured must be endured" (p. 527). Wistful efforts to persuade
the passions to listen to reason go echoing down the pages of
literature. Epictetus lectures away on the necessity of learn-

ing to make perfect one's will; Marcus Aurelius writes meditations telling himself to accept all fortune as good fortune;
Ben Jonson translates from Horace, "Remember, when blinde
Fortune knits her brow, / Thy minde be not deiected over lowe";[7]
and T. S. Eliot prays, "Teach us to sit still" ("Ash Wednesday,"
VI). Although Stoics and Epicureans agreed in general that a
settled state of calm would be a good thing if we could get it,
individual writers seldom expected to achieve it themselves,
and Christians thought it was something to be hoped for only in
heaven. The line from Dante that T. S. Eliot was fond of
quoting, "In his will is our peace" (Paradiso, III.85), was
spoken by the tranquil spirits revolving in paradise. As
John Davies asks in his Nosce Teipsum (1599), "Who did euer
yet, in honor, wealth, / Or pleasure of the sense contentment
find?"[8] However, in spite of the strict Christian position
that relegated perfect tranquillity to the next world, some
Christians, among whom were moderate humanists like Hall and
Burton, saw no harm in striving for whatever small amount of
earthly peace of mind might be attainable, since, as Burton
said, "We are torn in pieces by our passions, as [by] so many
wild horses, one in disposition, another in habit; one is
melancholy, another mad; and which of us all seeks for help,
doth acknowledge his error, or knows he is sick?" (p. 57).

After they had made the required derogatory remarks about
Stoic apathy or Stoical dullness, they freely borrowed lessons
from their favorite Stoic and Epicurean sources, avoiding
offensive words like apathy and choosing instead words with
pleasant connotations like patience, tranquillity, and content;
for when castigating Stoics, sixteenth- and seventeenth-century
writers were as apt as we to forget the difference between the
ideals of unadulterated primitive Stoicism and the practice of
actual historical Stoics.[9] Their attitude toward Seneca, who
wrote essays or epistles on various topics--some of them more
acceptable to Christians than others--is a prime example.
Although they willingly borrowed his remedies for fortune, they
were fond of deprecating him as a Stoic, forgetting that on the
subject of passion he adhered most of the time to the mild
middle way that we tend to call the Aristotelian golden mean.[10]
Seneca did, of course, describe on occasion (e.g., Ep. LXXV)
the state of ideal imperturbable wisdom, the mathematical
abstraction never actually to be reached but only to be striven
for as a distant goal. But if the rare bird who finally
reached this hypothetical absolute might expect to be free from
all perturbation, even those very near perfection would still be
troubled by the passions. Most of the time, when Seneca was
writing epistles to his friends he was only giving advice to
fallible human beings on how to moderate the passions so as
to reduce the pointless agony. Unlike Epictetus, who did make
an effort to return to the absolute doctrine of the early
Stoics, such popular moderates as Seneca, Horace, and Cicero
generally taught a mixed doctrine. Since precise facts seldom
bother any of us when we are engaged in generalizing, we simply

have to recognize that it was the fashion for Christian writers to insist that a Stoic had no passions.  A classic
description is given us by Folly in Erasmus' The Praise of
Folly, as she repeats the standard Christian objection to
Stoic apathy:

> We distinguish a wise man from a fool by this, that reason governs
> the one, and passion the other.  Thus the Stoics take away from
> the wise man all perturbations of the soul, as so many diseases.
> Yet these passions not only discharge the office of mentor and
> guide to such as are pressing toward the gate of wisdom, but they
> also assist in every exercise of virtue as spurs and goads--
> persuaders, as it were--to well doing.  Although that double-
> strength Stoic, Seneca, sternly denies this, subtracting from the
> wise man any and every emotion, yet in doing so he leaves him no
> man at all but rather a new kind of god, or demiurgos, who never
> existed and will never emerge.  Nay, to speak more plainly, he
> creates a marble simulacrum of a man, a senseless block, com-
> pletely alien to every human feeling.[11]

Similarly Burton, at one point, says, "Seneca & the rest of the
Stoicks are of opinion, that, where is any the least perturbation, wisdom may not be found" (p. 61).  Like other Christians,
Burton rejects this ideal, believing that "all affections and
perturbations arise out of these two fountains [concupiscible
and irascible], which although the Stoics make light of, we
hold natural, and not to be resisted" (p. 141).  In like manner,
Hall says, "I will not be a Stoic, to have no passions; for
that were to overthrow this inward government God hath erected
in me; but a Christian, to order those I have" (VII, 547).  The
ideal as he described it was "an even disposition of the heart,
wherein the scales of the mind neither rise up towards the beam
through their own lightness or the overweening opinion of prosperity, nor are too much depressed with any load of sorrow; but,
hanging equal and unmoved betwixt both give a man liberty
in all occurrences to enjoy himself" (VI, 4).

Whether we consider it immoral to pretend to have no passions or simply impossible, the final effect is the same.  Long
before Shakespeare began making jokes about sham philosophers
who could not bear the toothache patiently, Horace had joked
that the wise man "is only surpassed by Jove. . . .if a cold
doesn't keep him in bed."[12]  Although for most writers the
golden mean was the ideal, with total immunity from passion
not to be expected, Stoic remedies for perturbation were often
borrowed as a means to promoting the happy life.  The following
discussion will concentrate on those passions that caused the
most difficulty and received the major share of literary attention, namely, anger, grief, and desire.

Although English writers seldom agree with the Stoic
absolute condemnation of all anger, they often echo Stoic
phrases when they are condemning excessive anger.  The ideal
Aristotelian middle position is set forth by Milton when he
says in his Christian Doctrine, "In Anger, we are to consider

the motive for the passion, its degree, and duration."[13]   And
Joseph Hall is among those who point out that righteous indig-
nation is sometimes a necessary Christian virtue:   "The great
doctor of the Gentiles, when he says, <u>Be Angry</u>, <u>and</u> <u>sin</u> <u>not</u>
(Eph. IV.26) shows that there may be a sinless anger. . . .
If a man can be so cool, as without any inward commotion, to
suffer God's honour to be trod in the dust, he shall find God
justly angry with him for his want of anger" (VI, 437).   Or,
as Owen Felltham (1604?-68) says, "A continued patience I commend not 'tis different from what is goodness.   For though God
bears much, yet he will not bear always."   Yet a few lines
earlier in this same essay, "Of Apprehension in Wrongs," Felltham had quoted approvingly from Seneca's essay "On Anger"
(II.xxxii.2) and had related the incident (to which Seneca also
referred in "De Constantia," I.xiv.3) in which, in Felltham's
words, "A fool struck Cato in the bath and when he was sorry
for it, Cato had forgot it," since he considered it wiser to
ignore the incident than to resent it.   In other words, the
golden mean lay somewhere between the dull passivity of the
legendary Stoic and the insane fury that becomes excited over
trifles and imaginary wrongs.[14]
     The mythical imperturbable Stoic was ridiculed from var-
ious points of view.   John Donne, using the word "Stoic" as a
synonym for superhuman apathy, suggests an extremity of irritation by asking:   "Would it not anger a Stoicke?" ("Satire,"
V.64).   Molière, whose sympathies lay somewhat in the Epicurean direction, shows the hypocritical stage philosopher dis-
pensing lofty advice on the need for remaining calm but immediately losing his temper when attacked himself.[15]   And Bacon,
the pragmatist, weighing the possibility of continuous serenity against the physical probabilities, observes that "to seek
to extinguish anger utterly is but a bravery [boast] of the
Stoics" ("Of Anger").
     On the other hand, it was equally commonplace to condemn
excessive anger or rage and when doing so to allude to Horace's
description of anger as a short madness (Ep. i.2, 62; see also
Seneca, Ep. CXVI and "De Ira," I.i.1-2).   In "The Defence of
Poesie" (<u>Works</u>, III, 14), Sidney, to exemplify the superiority
of poetry to philosophy as a moral teacher, points out that
the generalization, "Anger the <u>Stoikes</u> said, was a short mad-
nesse," is less effective than Sophocles' dramatization of the
insane anger of Ajax.   The moral itself is of course accepted
without question.   Hall and Burton refer to it also.   Hall says,
"There is no difference betwixt anger and madness, but continuance; for raging anger is a short madness" (VII, 541); Burton
says,"They [the angry] are void of reason, inexorable, blind,
like beasts & monsters for the time, say and do they know not
what, curse, swear, rail, fight, and what not?   How can a mad
man do more?" (p. 234).   Spenser, using both example and pre-
cept, illustrates in Book II of <u>The</u> <u>Faerie</u> <u>Queene</u> (Canto iv)
the destructive effects of fury that has progressed into mad-
ness.[16]   Lear's sudden fury at Cordelia is somewhat reminiscent

of Seneca's description of Alexander "who in the midst of a feast with his own hand stabbed Clitus, his dearest friend, with whom he had grown up, because he withheld his flattery and was reluctant to transform himself from a Macedonian and a free man into a Persian slave" (De Ira, III.xvii.1). And Thomas Heywood in A Woman Killed with Kindness shows Sir Charles Mountford trying to excuse murder by pleading temporary insanity, saying, "Anger quite removes me from myself: / It was not I, but rage, did this vile murder" (I.iii.50-51).[17]

If the hypothetical Stoic, whom everyone condemned, was supposed to be utterly without anger, he was equally supposed to be invulnerable to pain, including such pains as pity and grief. According to the common anti-Stoic view, as stated by William Temple in "Of Health and Long Life," "To be a Stoic, and grow insensible of pain, as well as poverty or disgrace, one must be perhaps something more or less than a man." The acceptable ideal, once again, was the perfect balance. As Burton said, "There's an art of not being too unhappy, a medium to be kept" (p. 535). "I am of Seneca's mind, he that is wise is temperate, and he that is temperate is constant, free from passion, and he that is such a one is without sorrow: as all wise men should be" (p. 539). The evil consequences of emotional intemperance provided a favorite theme for playwrights and story tellers. Seneca's plays were frequently about people who had ruined their lives by giving way to passion. Spenser's Red Cross Knight almost succumbed to despair. Shakespeare's passionate Romeo continually dismayed the reasonable friar by his emotional intemperance--perpetually up too high or down too low.[18] Of Timon of Athens, another victim of emotional excess, Apemantus said, "The middle of humanity thou never knewest, but the extremity of both ends" (IV.300).

The problem, as usual, was how to achieve the desired balance. One suggestion for mitigating pity and grief was to avoid false sentimentality and, instead, take action. As Seneca said, "The wise man, therefore, will not pity, but will succour."[19] Other advice, often drawn from Plutarch or Seneca, was to try to reason oneself, or others, into a sense of proportion. Sometimes there is the irritating sort of consolation Hamlet's mother offered him when she reminded him that it is necessary to accept the laws of nature: "Thou know'st 'tis common. All that lives must die" (I.ii.72). Sometimes we are told to cheer ourselves by remembering that the wheel of fortune goes up as well as down. Robert Southwell (1561-95) in his lyric "Times goe by turnes" tells us that "the lopped tree in time may grow againe. . . . The soriest wight may find release of paine. . . . Times goe by turnes . . . From fowle to faire: from better happe, to worse."[20] Burton offers the distant comfort that although "thou art a poor servile drudge, the dregs of the people, a very slave, thy son may come to be a Prince" (p. 516). Another grim sort of cheer was to remind oneself that however bad one's luck might have been, it could, statistically, have been even worse. Therefore, as Burton says, "Comfort thyself with other men's misfortunes. . . . Consider the like calamities of other men; thou wilt then bear thine own the better. . . . Be thankful for that thou hast" (pp. 495-96). Joseph Hall suggests that we "compare the good things we have with the evils which we have not, and others groan under" (VII, 506, 519-20, 564, 627). Gonzalo in The Tempest comforts his shipwrecked friends by remarking that they are lucky they were only shipwrecked and not drowned (II.i.1-9). Duke Senior, on learning the story of Orlando and Adam, points out to his friends, "Thou seest we are not all alone unhappy. / This wide and universal theatre / Presents more woful pageants than the scene / Wherein we play in" (AYLI, II.vii.136). Finally, when all other consolation failed, it was as necessary for the Christian as for the Stoic to learn to accept the will of God with patience. As Burton said, "If it may not be helped, it must be endured" (p. 855).

Trying to avoid losing one's temper over trifles and endeavoring not to be shattered by calamity, though aspects of temperance, can also be listed under the heading of patience or fortitude. A more commonly recognized kind of temperance is the moderation of greed or desire, learning to stop wanting what we do not have. According to the Epicureans, a tranquil life came from learning to vanquish not only fear but also hope, not to wish for future benefits but to make the most of things as they are. (Seneca, Ep. CXV.18, describes the ideal life as being free from desire and free from fear.) Fulke Greville (1554-1628), who showed the usual Christian dislike of Epicurean naturalism or Epicurean praise of pleasure and who doubted the possibility of earthly tranquillity, referred over and over again to the twin Stoic-Epicurean evils of hope and fear. In this life it is impossible ever to "liue free from clouds of humane hope and feare" (An Inquisition upon Fame and Honour, st. 66). Because we do not accept our lot with patience, "the reines of humane hope and feare" are "laid on our neckes" as punishment (A Treatie of Warres, st. 9). Tyrants are able to rule because the wronged people, who would be invincible if they could all be of the same mind, are instead continually distracted by hope and fear (Alaham, Chorus of People). In sum, the "leaking ship of humane power and affections" is governed "by the two false rudders of hope and feare" (A Letter to an Honourable Lady, Grosart, III, 264).[21]

It is obvious, therefore, that romantic love, which consists to a large extent of wishing, is regarded by both Stoics and Epicureans as a great enemy to equanimity. However, on this subject English literature adheres to the classical view only now and then. As examples of the unreconciled conflict between the classical dream of tranquillity and the medieval idealization of romantic love, we have only to recall the way Chaucer painted Troilus's unhappy infatuation against a Boethian-Stoic backdrop and the way Shakespeare showed the headstrong Romeo ignoring the moral friar who trotted behind

him with sensible advice to "love moderately" (II.iii.93; vi.
9). We hear Philo at the beginning of Antony and Cleopatra
echoing Plutarch as he complains that "this dotage of our general's o'erflows the measure." Yet Shakespeare, who could well
see that lack of moderation would cause lovers like Romeo and
Antony much agony, did not pretend that it would have been easy
for them to be reasonable. He did not say of Antony and Cleopatra, as Dryden did in his Preface to All for Love, that "the
crimes of love which they both committed, were not occasion'd
by any necessity, or fatal ignorance, but were wholly voluntary; since our passions are, or ought to be, within our
power."[22] Nor did Burton, who found love one of the worst
causers of melancholy, pretend that reason could prevent it.
He said, "Your most grim Stoicks and severe Philosophers will
melt away with this passion" (p. 761). "There will not be
found, I hope, no, not in that severe family of Stoicks, who
shall refuse to submit his grave beard, and supercilious locks
to the clippings of a wife, or disagree from his fellows in
this point" (p. 819). Burton's axiom that even grim Stoics
would melt away with this passion was a favorite comic moral
with story tellers, a variation on the theme of Stoic pride.
For instance the pompous Angelo of Measure for Measure puts
on a facade of superiority to human passion only to demonstrate
soon after that he only belongs to the old family of Stoic
hypocrites. The ideal but unexciting middle way, expressed in
the popular Elizabethan ballad, "Love me little, love me long"
is probably exemplified by the legendary happy family life of
Thomas More, who--like a good Stoic or Epicurean--made the
best of what he had instead of hankering after the ideal.[23]
    Romantic love, however troublesome in youth, was neither
so reprehensible nor so long lasting as greed for wealth or
power. The problem of deciding how much is enough was one
that occupied all seekers after earthly tranquillity. When
the wheel of fortune became less a symbol of inevitable mutability than of lady luck or earthly desire, it was possible
to decide to stay off. However, before we start pursuing that
popular--though minor--literary theme, we need to pause to
remember that most people did not want to get off. Whereas
the Stoic-Epicurean definition of success means being content
with what we have, the usual definition of success means climbing to the top of fortune's wheel and staying there. A dominant theme of The Mirror for Magistrates, as of much Elizabethan drama, was that rich men want to stay rich, and powerful men want to stay powerful. By studying the mistakes of
those who lost their footing on the wheel, we can perhaps
learn to stay on ourselves. For most tranquillity is only a
kind of consolation prize. Young lovers like Romeo and Troilus
have no interest in peace of mind. A few ambitious climbers
may briefly pause to sigh for a quiet life while a few others
may take to praising tranquillity when they no longer have
anything else to praise. However, the fact that the dream of
Epicurean happiness is incompatible with the dream of getting

to the top of the heap, was not always apparent to story tellers
and playwrights, who freely mixed both ideals to suit their own
purposes, though generally equating a happy ending with the
satisfaction of desire.

Returning now to the problem of how to achieve a contented heart, we find greed as a malady exemplified by Joseph
Hall's Character of a malcontent who "is neither well full nor
fasting. . . . What he hath, he sees not, his eyes are so taken
up with that he wants." The malcontent's opposite is the happy
man who "can so frame his thoughts to his estate, that when he
hath least, he cannot want, because he is as free from desire,
as superfluity."[24] Burton calls the immoderate desire of gain
"the pattern, image, epitome of all Melancholy, the fountain
of many miseries" (p. 245). Thomas More in A Dialogue of
Comfort against Tribulation, reminds us, in the manner of
Boethius, that economic good fortune may only cause us anxiety
about thieves.[25] Thomas Elyot in The Book of the Governor says,
"The Philosophers called Stoici used this sentence. Great
indigence or lacke cometh nat of pouertie, but of great plentie,
for he that hathe moche shal nede moche."[26] In other words,
the more we have, the more we want.

Happiness means learning to stop wishing, avoiding the
glamorous but dangerous mountain top and instead living safely
and tranquilly in the humble valley. By reducing our desires,
staying outside the battle, being content with what we have,
we can come as close as is decently possible to heaven on earth.
"Art thou poore, yet hast thou golden Slumbers: Oh sweet content!" sang Thomas Dekker, who might have been describing Chaucer's povre widwe.[27] The old Cynic-Stoic-Epicurean-Christian
dream of the happy simple life, which had among its many early
praisers Virgil, Horace, Seneca, and Boethius, keeps turning
up. Sometimes the dream is classified by casual commentators
as Epicurean, sometimes as Stoic, the dividing line being a
fine one, especially when one considers that sixteenth- and
seventeenth-century users of the theme were not much interested
in being either Stoics or Epicureans. Although Epicureans had
less difficulty than Stoics or Christians in justifying a
retired life, because they had less tendency to identify virtue
with a social conscience, those Stoics or Christians who had
become disillusioned with society or with their chances of
doing any good in it, might feel justified in moving to the
country. Life far from the court was praised, sometimes as
being more virtuous, sometimes as being more pleasant than life
on the wheel of desire. When the simple life is thought to be
more conducive to virtue, the tendency is to call it Stoic; but
when it is regarded as the pleasant life, it is called Epicurean. Let us not, however, forget William Temple's remark that
"the most reasonable of the Stoics made the pleasure of virtue
to be the greatest happiness, and the best of the Epicureans
made the greatest pleasure to consist in virtue."

William Temple, who--at the end of the seventeenth
century--praised the retired life so well, nevertheless spent

the earlier part of his career in public service, thus illustrating the never-solved conflict between duty to society and
desire for personal tranquillity.  Thomas More, at the beginning of the sixteenth century, depicted an imaginary world
where unchanging tranquillity was the social ideal--an ideal
that has not appealed to many a critic.  In his Utopia he
described a whole society organized to promote peace of mind
rather than greed or ambition or power.  The Utopians, who
had discovered the way to have the good life on earth, lived
with a Cynic or early Christian simplicity that included not
bothering with private property.  Like good Horatians they
knew how much wealth was enough and how to enjoy what they had.
In their world, aggressive individualism had no place, since
they were not interested in accumulating the superfluities that
serve only to bolster self esteem.  Although pleasure was what
they wanted, for them the highest pleasure came "of the exercise of virtue and the conscience of good life" (p. 92).  Since
all cooperating members of society were Stoic-Epicurean happy
men, only one step removed from Christian humanism, there was
no need for the virtuous sage to withdraw from the world in
search of tranquillity.  The Epicureanism of Utopia was, of
course, purged of ideas that were repugnant to Christians.  In
contrast with this peaceful world, described in Book II of the
Utopia, there is the aggressive everyday world we see in Book
I, the world we all know, with everyone climbing on the wheel,
social injustice everywhere, peace of mind nowhere.[28]  Among
objections to the Utopian solution, two major ones have been
that such a life would be boring and that it would be lacking
in freedom.  The Utopians, who were forced to live the tranquil
Horatian life whether they liked it or not, generally approved
of the system, while most non-Utopians have preferred to continue climbing on the wheel of desire.[29]

In Thomas More's planned society it was possible for
everyone to bask in Horatian content because the question of
how much is enough had been settled by the authorities.  In
actual life the praiser of the Horatian simple life often turns
out to be a gentleman poet with a safe economic niche and a
classical education.  However, even a gentleman, and especially
a Tudor gentleman, might know from personal experience that
high places were not necessarily pleasant.  Though the poets
of the first half of the sixteenth century often sound as
though they were merely repeating platitudes from Chaucer or
Lydgate, they nevertheless found those themes especially
appropriate to themselves.  With feeling they could echo the
Senecan teaching that mountain tops are more vulnerable to
fortune than the lowly valley or the Lucretian thesis that it
is pleasanter to watch a storm from a safe place on shore than
from a ship at sea.  Thomas Wyatt (1503-1542), who spent much
of his life as a public servant and who knew from personal
experience about the dangers of high place, wrote poems not
only about courtly love but also about peace of mind and how
to achieve it.  One poem, "If thou wilt mighty be" is a trans-

lation of lines from Boethius advising us to conquer our desires
if we do not want to be slaves to passion. At other times
Wyatt took the same ideas from Seneca.[30] H. A. Mason, who particularly admires Wyatt's "moral-reflective" verse, thinks
highly of his ten-line translation of lines from Seneca's Thyestes (Cor. 2, "Stet quicunque volet potens . . . ").[31] These
popular lines, which compare the stresses of life at court
with the peaceful retired life that gives a man leisure to
learn to know himself, were often translated by poets of the
sixteenth and seventeenth centuries, two of the more famous
later translators being Cowley and Marvell.[32]

Wyatt's well-known "My mothers maydes when they did sowe
and spynne," which tells once again the story of the town
mouse and the country mouse, contains essentially the same
lesson as the above-mentioned passage from Seneca. In addition,
this poem has at the end a Christian moral similar to the moral
at the end of Chaucer's "Truth." Wyatt advises the friend to
whom he is writing to "Let present passe and gape on tyme to
come."[33] Like Chaucer's poem, Wyatt's combines an other-
worldly Christian moral with an old classical recipe for the
good life that might have come from Horace or Plutarch or
Boethius: Avoid greed; be content with your assigned lot;
look for happiness within yourself. The emphasis on virtue,
what some might call the Stoic note, is more marked in Wyatt's
poem than in Horace's because Horace was not gaping on the
time to come. Instead he was weighing the potentialities for
a pleasant life in the exciting town as compared with the
dull country and opting for the country. In Wyatt, as often in
writers of his time who did not set out to be scholars or original thinkers, the Stoic-Epicurean ideas that appealed were
very much the same ones that had been popular in the fifteenth
century. The new combinations to be found in More's Utopia
made no appearance.

In similar fashion, several other semi-Stoic-Epicurean
poems of the earlier sixteenth century, many included in
Tottel's Miscellany (1557) go on repeating lessons taught long
ago by Chaucer and Lydgate.[34] Although Henry Parker, Lord Morley
(1476-1556), starts a poem with a line from Cicero's Of
Duties, ("Never was I less alone than being alone,") a line
that Erasmus had quoted in The Education of a Christian Prince
(p. 244) and that Abraham Cowley's essay "Of Solitude," was
also to borrow more than a century later, and although Parker
also mentions "sage Senec" approvingly, the theme that he
develops is a familiar one often taken from Boethius, namely,
that fortune has no power over one who has a quiet mind and
accepts all fortune as good fortune.[35] A poem ("Experience
now doth shew"), by or about Edward Seymour, Duke of Somerset
(1506?-1552), one of the unlucky ones who rose to the top of
the wheel of fortune only to be flung suddenly to the bottom,
tells us, as might be expected, that high places are dangerous, that those who live on oaten cakes in poor estate are the
happy ones (Tottel, I, No. 200). A poem by Thomas, Lord Vaux

(1510-1556) called "Of a contented mynde" argues that happiness
comes from keeping our mouths shut and having a contented
mind.[36]  Henry Howard, Earl of Surrey (1517-1547), is one of
the many who translated the popular epigram from Martial (X.
47), "Marshall; the thinges for to attayne / The happy life be
thes, I finde," that sets forth the standard Epicurean recipe
for peace of mind--a simple, retired country life, with friends
to enjoy and no concern for the outside world.[37]  Tottel's
Miscellany also contains a translation of the popular passage
from the opening of Book II of Lucretius on watching a storm
from a safe place on shore (no. 196).  On the other hand, Surrey's translation of Horace's lines on "The Golden Mean" (Odes,
II.10), offers slightly more Stoic advice on choosing the
middle way and being ever prepared for the ups and downs of
fortune (Tottel, I, No's. 27, 28).  Philip Sidney was among
the other translators of the same lines.[38]  The Mirror for Magistrates has many a story illustrating the moral that "highest
hilles with tempestes bene most touched."  One example is the
tale of Humphrey, Duke of Gloucester, which teaches us "that
such as clyme the top of high degree / From Perrill of falling
nauer can be free" (p. 445, 1-7).  The final advice to other
relatives of kings is "To beare low sayle, and not to much
embrace, / The peoples loue:  for as Senec sayeth trulye: /
O quam funestus est fauor populi" (p. 459, 449-455).

When we come to the Elizabethans our first impression may
be that the praise of rural bliss is everywhere. We think of
typical songs like the anonymous lyric of 1588 that asks, "What
pleasure have great princes / More dainty to their choice /
Than herdmen wild, who careless / In quiet life rejoice, / And
fortune's fate not fearing / Sing sweet in summer morning?"[39]
We remember Robert Greene's song, "Sweet are the thoughts that
sauour of content," with its list of the usual Stoic-Epicurean
requirements for the retired happy life.  We think of the third
shepherd's song from Nicholas Breton's "Passionate Shepherd":
"Who can live in heart so glad,/ As the merrie countrie lad?"[40]
We call to mind Lodge's Rosalynde and Shakespeare's As You
Like It and Sidney's Arcadia and Book VI of Spenser's Faerie
Queene.  Then we take a second look and find that the message
is confused.  The praise of content is more likely to occur in
a short lyric or a brief episode that expresses a passing mood
than to be the major theme of an extended work.  A brief dramatic example occurs in Lyly's play Campaspe (1584) where
Diogenes--the traditional abstemious self-sufficient philoso-
pher--tells Alexander--who commonly represents greed--that
content comes from unlearning to covet[41]--appropriate advice in
this instance because Alexander fails to win the girl he is
coveting.  However, even though on this occasion Alexander con-
quers his will, we do not forget that his idea of success is to
conquer the world.  Though Lodge, the translator of Seneca, was,
in his Rosalynde (1590), possibly more serious about his Stoic-

Epicurean moralizing than most story tellers, he nevertheless
patched his morals into what was otherwise a routine success
story. The consequence is that his frequent warnings against
trusting fortune and his constant praise of retired content
are belied by the "happy" ending. At the beginning of the tale
Lodge has John of Bordeaux in his legacy warn his sons against
the dangers of climbing and has Rosalynde at court soliloquize
on the cares that wait upon a crown, telling herself that "the
greatest seas have the sorest storms, the highest birth subject to the most bale, and of all trees the cedars soonest shake
with the wind: small currents are ever calm, low valleys not
scorched in any lightnings, nor base men tied to any baleful
prejudice. Fortune flies, and if she touch poverty, it is
with her heal."[42] Later the young people have ideal happiness
in their country retreat: "They had such cates as country
state did allow them, sauced with such content, and such sweet
prattle, as it seemed far more sweet than all their courtly
junkets" (p. 85). But all this talk is only talk since as soon
as they have a chance to return to court they forget about the
country. In Chapter X of Thomas Deloney's Thomas of Reading
(c. 1599) Margaret gives her lover the bookish advice that "they
that clime vnaduisedly, catch a fall suddenly"; that "there is
none in the world poore, but they that think themselues poore:
for such as are indued with content, are rich, hauing nothing
els: but he that is possessed with riches, without content, is
most wretched and miserable" (p. 316, lines 2-3, 10-14); but
the only connection between this advice and the plot is that
the lovers forget it. Possibly we are supposed to reflect that
if they had remembered it they might have avoided disaster.

Sidney, Spenser, and Shakespeare seem to have given serious
thought to the dream of personal content and to have rejected
retirement as a proper moral choice for heroes. The Stoic side
of Sidney was more Ciceronian than Horatian or Senecan in the
sense that he considered social responsibility more important
than private peace of mind. In the Arcadia, therefore,
although the dream of a life of virtuous ease close to nature
glimmers here and there, it glimmers more faintly in the
revised portions of the story than in the earlier version. For
instance, the Old Arcadia begins with a description of Arcadia,
famous in Greece "for the moderate & well tempered myndes of
the people, who, (fynding howe true a Contentation ys gotten
by following the Course of Nature, And howe the shyning Title
of glory so much affected by other Nacions, dothe in deede help
litle to the happines of lyfe) were the onely people, w^ch as
by their Justice and providence, gave neyther Cause nor hope to
theyre Neighboures to annoy them" (IV, 1).[44] In the revised
version, this somewhat Utopian picture of a contented land has
shrunk to a description of the Arcadian shepherds as "a happie
people, wanting litle, because they desire not much" (I, 14).
Although for shepherds, already in their proper social niche,
the contented simple life is permissible, other characters have
other duties.[45] (For more on this subject see Chapter V.)

Spenser's pastoral episode in Book VI.ix of the <u>Faerie Queene</u> gives retirement the same subsidiary relationship to social responsibility to be found in Sidney's <u>Arcadia</u>. For the good old shepherd Meliboe, the retired life is the virtuous life, since that is the station into which he was born. However, the hero Calidore, who has been assigned other duties, is not permitted to escape to retirement. Nor is retirement approved even for the heroine Pastorella, once it is discovered that she is not actually a shepherdess by birth. By focusing for a time on Meliboe, Spenser is able to develop an interlude of Virgilian or Horatian content: Meliboe, somewhat like Horace's country mouse, had been led by youthful ambition to leave the country and go to the court, where he had observed the sort of courtly corruption described in "Colin Clouts Come Home Again." Having learned in time his lesson about high places, he returned to the country to live henceforth in retired content. When explaining his philosophy of life to Calidore, he moralized in the familiar Cynic-Stoic-Epicurean way on the theme that very little is required to satisfy the needs of nature, that the one who is content has enough, that those who have much are always worried about losing what they have, that ambition only undermines one's peace of mind (stanzas 17 ff). As might be expected after such an argument, Calidore wants to be allowed to stay and become a shepherd too, but Meliboe surprisingly says no. Happiness for Calidore can come only through playing well the role assigned him by heaven. Only if he accepts all fortune as good fortune can he achieve happiness. "Each hath his fortune in his brest" (29). "It is the mynd, that maketh good or ill, / That maketh wretch or happie, rich or poore. . . . wisedome is most riches. . . . each vnto himself his life may fortunize" (30). For Calidore the paradise within can come only as a reward for doing his knightly duty, part of which duty is to protect helpless peasants like Meliboe.[46] It is perhaps significant that one day, while Calidore has been neglecting duty to watch the graces dance, the good Meliboe is murdered by bandits, which suggests that in the end the Christian message prevails over the classical one, that the only place for true content is in the grave.

With Shakespeare as with Sidney and Spenser the dream of retired content is only a pleasant interlude, not a recipe for living. In <u>As You Like It</u> Duke Senior in exile meditates on the superiority of life in the forest over life at court (e.g., II.i.2-17), but when the wheel of fortune turns, he goes back to his duty at court.[47] Though old Belarius in <u>Cymbeline</u> contrasts the stresses of life at the corrupt court with his present happy retired life (III.iii), he gladly returns to court when his fortune changes. Virtuous old Gonzalo in <u>The Tempest</u> thinks how nice it would be to turn Prospero's island into a primitive paradise (II.i.143-164), but when the others go home, he goes too. Kings in the history plays sometimes pause to reflect, like a Senecan chorus, on the miseries of greatness. Henry VI in the midst of a battle sits on a mole-

hill considering how much pleasanter it would be to be a shepherd instead of a king (III H. VI, II.v). Henry IV, unable to
sleep, complains, "Uneasy lies the head that wears a crown" (II
H. IV, III.i.30-31). Henry V, before the battle (H. V, IV.i.
255-301), thinks how much happier the peasant's life is than
his, since the only thing he has that the peasant lacks is
ceremony (empty social status). In no case, however, does
Shakespeare suggest that a king would be justified in running
away from the agonies of his job. Since duty to society always
comes before selfish peace of mind, Henry VI is blamed by the
dying Clifford for having brought chaos to the country (III H.
VI, II.vi); for if he had ruled as kings should do, this disaster would not have occurred. Henry IV's complaint was part
hypocrisy, partly the just punishment of an uneasy conscience,
since he was one who had usurped the throne instead of merely
carrying out his assigned role. Henry V was only reflecting
sadly about the nature of things--while at the same time giving
us a little propaganda for the status quo. For the peasant's
happy life (unappreciated by the peasant) was made possible by
the king's devotion to duty.[48] For those whose duty required
other things of them, contented retirement was not an acceptable way of life. Even Prospero, who might well have contributed to his own overthrow by preferring to read books instead
of attending to his duty, was anxious to leave his pleasant
island and go back to being a duke.

In the seventeenth century as in the sixteenth, contented
retirement continues to be a minor theme, even though it grows
in strength. Most of the intenser religious poets pass it by.
George Herbert (1593-1633), for instance, in the traditional
Christian way relegated perfect peace of mind to the next world.
As Joseph Summers says, "His deepest and most consistent desire"
was "to live a life at one with the will of God. But he was
equally ready to recognize the reality of his momentary experience. He believed that the true state of man was 'Giddinesse.'"
Though it would be the Christian equivalent of tranquillity to
succeed in feeling confident of living at one with the will of
God, Herbert points out in "The Pulley," that the one gift that
God did not give man was rest. On earth we can expect only
"repining restlessnesse."[49] A similarly qualified attitude
toward peace of mind can be found in the writings of Sidney's
friend Fulke Greville (1554-1628), who did much of his writing
during the seventeenth century and who in some ways combines
the idealism of Sidney with the pragmatism of Bacon. In the
final stanza of his poem "Of Religion," he says: "Finde peace
in endlesse, boundlesse, heavenly things; / Place it else
where, it desolation bringes." Elsewhere he pointed out that
although once upon a time, in the virtuous golden age, earthly
tranquillity might have been a possibility, ever since the
arrival of sin, we may "as well seeke fish vpon the mountaines,
trees in the sea, as peace in flesh."[50] However, for those at
the bottom of the power structure, helpless in a world where

might makes right, Stoic remedies for fortune, which emphasize accepting what cannot be changed instead of kicking
against the pricks, may alleviate emotional distress.  His
unfinished _A Letter to an Honourable Lady_, which may or may
not have been intended for an actual unfortunate lady, explores
the problem of any powerless person forced to submit to the
rule of a tyrant.  Although the setting here is domestic, the
problem is similar to one that occurs in Greville's plays,
where the setting is political.  The helpless lady is advised
to moderate her desires, to beware of "the two false rudders
of hope and feare" (p. 264) and to look not "outwardly but
inwardly for the fruit of true peace" (p. 260).  Unjust though
it may seem, she must not rebel against her husband's treatment and must look for her reward in "the secret peace of well-
doing" (p. 270); if her husband restricts her in her estate she
can still consider "that there is none so poore, but hee may
haue liberall thoughts" (p. 274).

John Milton, like Sidney, Spenser, and Shakespeare, subordinates earthly peace of mind to social responsibility.  The
theme of retirement occurs most frequently in writers generally
classified as second string, like Burton and Hall, Herrick and
Walton, Cowley and Temple.  In the drama it often appears in
the contrast between dangerous high places and safe low places,
of which contrast Una Ellis-Fermor remarks that "the true stoic
repudiation of wealth, power and high place. . . . occupies
with the Jacobean dramatists approximately the same position
as in Seneca's drama:  it is freely professed in the form of
wistful comments, but only very rarely practised by the characters as portrayed dramatically."[51]  Examples of wistful comments are Marston's Sophonisba's "O happiness, / Of those that
know not pride or lust of citty, / Ther's no man bless'd but
those that most men pitty" (IV.i); or Webster's Vittoria's
"Oh, happy they that never saw the Court, / Nor ever knew great
Man but by report";[52] or the Duchess of Malfi's, "When Fortunes
wheele is over-charg'd with Princes, / The weight makes it move
swift. . . . There's no deepe Valley, but neere some great Hill"
(III.v.112-113, 169).  These women, who knew only too well the
miseries of high place, were also slaves to passion.  Tranquil
peace of mind had never really been important to them.

There are, however, a few dramatic characters who exemplify quiet content.  Marston's Feliche of _Antonio and Mellida_
claims to be happy because he is content with his lot, "Nor
faire, nor rich, nor wittie, great, nor fear'd: / Yet amply
suted, with all full content."  Because he is not involved in
the antics of the fools and knaves climbing on the ladder of
ambition, he is able to satirize the social scene.  In the plot
he serves a function similar to that of the chorus in Seneca's
_Thyestes_.  Having looked at other men and seen that great gifts
seem to be accompanied with great vices or other disadvantages,
he thanks heaven for his smooth brow and quiet bosom (III.i).
Like Joseph Hall's happy man, he says he has learned the vanity
of wishing, has learned to will what God wills; but his earthly

happiness does not last, for like Spenser's Meliboe, he is helpless against evil men and like Meliboe is murdered.  Once again,
the only place for true content is in the grave.[53]

Thomas Heywood (c. 1570-1641), however, does seem to toy
with the idea that a certain amount of peace on earth can be
enjoyed by the patient man.  In A Woman Killed with Kindness
we may at first consider it tragic irony when we hear Frankford platitudinizing, "How happy am I amongst other men, /
That in my mean estate embrace content" (Sc. iv. 1-14), since
Frankford does not know that he is speaking too soon, that his
best friend is about to seduce his wife.[54]  When this treach-
ery is discovered, we expect that Frankford's boasted content
will now prove fraudulent; but for once we are wrong.  Frankford turns out to be an unexciting dramatization of the patient
man who can accept what comes without losing all control.
Instead of murdering his wife and her lover in the usual stage
way, he shows clemency.  As a result, he is rewarded at the end
of the play with a quiet mind.

Thomas Dekker (c. 1572-1632), who gives us a similar picture of a patient man in The Honest Whore (discussed in Chapter
VI), has a play about Patient Grissel that contains the well-
known lyric, "Art thou poore, yet hast thou golden Slumbers: /
Oh sweet content!" (I.ii.93 ff) which develops the classic
contrast between happy poverty and the miseries of greed.  A
prose hymn on the same subject appears in "The Bel-Man of London":  "How happy, (how thrice happy) is hee that not playing
with his winges in the golden flames of the Court, nor setting
his foote into the busie throngs of the Cittie, nor running,
vp & downe, in the intricate mazes of the law, can bee content
in the winter to sit by a country fire, and in the summer to
lay his heade on the greene pillowes of the earth. . . ."[55]
Although the contrast Dekker makes between the miseries of
those eaten up with greed and the humble joys of content is
only the one we have seen often before, the difference between
his approach and that of someone like Webster is that instead
of showing the woes of a great woman like Vittoria, Dekker
focuses on the joys of patient Grissel.

It is not to be expected that contented peace of mind
should appear frequently on the stage, patience on a monument
being rather a dull subject.  Even such classicists as George
Chapman and Ben Jonson use it more frequently in short poems
than in plays, though Chapman does include in his plays some
self-sufficient men of integrity (see Chapter VI), who are
near kin, on the Stoic side, to the contented man.  Among his
shorter poems are some that teach the Stoic lesson that we are
only poor if we think we are, that even if we seem to be poor
we are actually rich, "If thou hast that, that makes thee need
no riches," or, again, "Not to haue want, what riches doth
exceed?"[56]

Lessons similar to those that Chapman could find in
Epictetus, Ben Jonson could find in Horace and other poets.
Lurking behind comedies like Volpone, or The Alchemist, or

Bartholomew Fair is Horace's favorite subject for satire, the idiotic way people destroy their peace of mind by chasing after false values. The satisfaction of greed is no recipe for happiness, whether Christian or Stoic or Epicurean. True classical happiness (sweet content) is described in Jonson's familiar Epigramme "Inviting a Friend to Supper," which promises the combined joys of a modest meal and conversation with a friend. This Epicurean recipe for heaven on earth, which appeared earlier in More's Utopia, we will meet often again. Jonson, too, was among the many translators of Martial's Epigramme XLVIII, "The Things that make the happier life, are these" and of Horace's Epode 2, "Happie is he, that from all Businesse cleere." Jonson, being himself a somewhat contentious person, was no doubt one of those who appreciated the virtues of the quiet life more in theory than in practice. His poignant elegy "On My first Son" shows him trying to console himself with Stoic-Epicurean recipes. Recollecting that the boy is lucky to have escaped the miseries of living, he thinks of how best to protect himself from ever suffering so much again. Had he remembered earlier his Stoic-Epicurean lessons, he would have known how unwise it was to hope anything for tomorrow or to give hostages to fortune by loving anything too much. He laments, "My sinne was too much hope of thee, lou'd boy," and prays for himself, "hence-forth, all his vowes be such, / As what he loues may neuer like too much." The trouble with this Epicurean lesson is that probably not even Horace or Seneca could really learn it, and certainly not Ben Jonson.[57]

Joseph Hall, sometimes called "our English Seneca," who was fond of preaching Christian-Stoic-Epicurean peace of mind as a recipe for heaven on earth, was only one more who taught the same lessons we have heard often before--even though he was a prolific writer who repeated the same thing a great many times. Like many another praiser of content, he was an upholder of the status quo who pointed out again and again the great psychological advantage of a contented heart over a discontented one. The man at the bottom of fortune's wheel is less vulnerable because he has less to lose: "While a man walks on plain ground he falls not; or if he fall, he doth but measure his length on the ground and rise again without harm" (Works, VI, 30). "The tall tree is cut down for timber; the broad tree is lopped for firewood; besides, that the tempest hath power on them both; whereas the low shrub is neither envied by the wind nor threatened by the axe" (X, 182). "A poor man, that hath little, and desires no more, is in truth richer than the greatest monarch, that thinks he hath not what he should or what he might, or that grieves there is no more to have" (VII, 481). "He is wealthy that is contented; he is poor that wanteth more" (II, 71). On this subject he even quoted Epicurus, after carefully styling him "the father of loosenes," as saying, "If a man would be rich, honourable, aged, he should not strive so much to add to his wealth, reputation, years, as to detract from his desires" (VII, 480). Once again we hear that poverty

and good health go together: "Thou couldest be content to have
the rich man's purse, but his gout thou wouldest not have" (VI,
41). Poverty has "quiet security, sound sleeps, sharp appetite,
free merriment; no fears, no cares, no suspicion, no distempers
of excess, no discontentment" (VI, 183-4). The poor man can
sleep with his doors open, is troubled neither by ambition nor
by the disappointment of false hopes, neither by the plots of
the emulous nor the traps of false friends, "but lives securely
in his homely cottage, quietly enjoying such provision as
nature and honest industry furnish him withal" (VI, 568).
"Contentment doth not lie in the coffer, but in the breast . . .
all treasures are dross to a good conscience." "He is more
happy that hath nothing to lose; then he that loseth that which
he hath" (VII, 474).[58]

Like other writers of his time, however, Hall did not offer
his praise of the simple life as a justification for running
away from it all. Believing as he did in the hierarchical system with its diversification of assigned duties, he praised
poverty partly as a way of telling the poor man to be content
with his lot. At the same time he taught that virtue included
a sense of social responsibility, that the good Christian
should have at heart not only his own welfare but also the welfare of his fellow men (VII, 486): "Solitary deserts are the
delights of Satan" (II, 393); "To sequester ourselves from the
company of the world, that we may depart from their vices, proceeds from a base and distrusting mind" (VII, 516).

Robert Burton was a different type of clergyman from Hall,
less the successful public figure, more the introspective
retired scholar, less conservative, more willing to examine
unconventional ideas. In his voluminous reading, his sense
of humor, and his thoughtful approach, he belongs in the company of men like Horace and Erasmus and Montaigne who have no
easy answers in their pockets. His aim is to find remedies that
may mitigate the agony of living, which agony is exacerbated by
the almost universal disease called melancholy, under which
heading Burton includes a broad range of disturbances from anything that momentarily troubles our peace of mind to serious
mental and emotional disorders.

In order to carry on his analysis of melancholy--its symp-
toms, its causes, its possible cures--Burton describes himself
as having adopted a mode of life that is often called Stoic or
Epicurean retirement. In his introduction he says he lives like
"Democritus in his garden . . . sequestered from those tumults
& troubles of the world . . . and in some high place above you
all, like the wise Stoick, seeing all ages, past and present, as
at one glance: I hear & see what is done abroad, how others run,
ride, turmoil, & macerate themselves in court and country; far
from those wrangling lawsuits, courts of vanity, marts of ambition, I am wont to laugh with myself: I laugh at all" (p. 14).
In some moods, when he toys with the idea that greed and ambition cause so much emotional perturbation because they are
"unnatural," there lurks in the back of his thought the old

belief that if we could only get back to a simpler form of life, we would be happier. Though he accepts, of course, the standard notion that men are, or should be, superior to beasts because men have reason, he sometimes, like Lucretius, points out that beasts may have a clearer insight than men into the things that really matter. "Beasts are better than [men] as being contented with nature. When shall you see a Lion hide gold in the ground, or a Bull contend for a better pasture?" (p. 41). Both Stoics and Epicureans had pointed out the foolishness of eating our hearts out about what other people think of us. Similarly, Burton says, "It is not another man's opinion can make me happy; but, as Seneca well hath it, <u>he is a miserable wretch, that doth not account himself happy</u>. . . . A common humour it is of all men to think well of other men's fortunes, and dislike their own" (p. 238). "No man can have what he will, he may choose whether he will desire that which he hath not: Thy lot is fallen, make the best of it" (p. 495). Quoting Epictetus as saying, "The poorer thou art, the happier thou art," he develops at length the contrast between the happy life of the countryman and the cares of the prince. "A poor man drinks in a wooden dish . . . the other in gold, silver, and precious stones; but with what success? Fear of poison in the one, security in the other" (pp. 511-14). "How happy art thou if thou couldst be content! . . . He that lives according to nature cannot be poor, and he that exceeds can never have enough: the whole world cannot give him content. . . . Thou hast enough; he that is wet in a bath can be no more wet if he be flung into Tiber . . . I say then, ('tis Epicurus advice), add no more wealth, but diminish thy desires. . . . that's true plenty, not to have, but not to want riches" (pp. 518-21).[59] However, like Horace and Montaigne, Burton is also able to turn aside from his books to look at some of the facts. He admits that poverty is not so pleasant if one is really poor, that the golden mean is one thing, grinding poverty something else. He says, "Seneca pleaded hard for poverty, and so did those lazy Philosophers: but in the mean time he was rich, they had wherewithal to maintain themselves; but doth any poor man extol it? There are those (saith Bernard) that approve of a mean estate, but on that condition they never want themselves. . . . I would to God (as he said) no man should commend poverty, but he that is poor; or he that so much admires it, would relieve, help, or ease other" (p. 523).

Burton never pretended to move in a straight line. The complexity of things kept throwing him off the track. Having admitted that it is hypocritical for a rich man to commend poverty to a poor man, he nevertheless returns to considering what a melancholy individual like himself can do to be happy; and he keeps giving himself Stoic-Epicurean answers:

All things then being rightly examined, and duly considered as they ought, there is no such cause of so general discontent, 'tis not in the matter itself, but in our mind, as we moderate our passions, and

esteem of things. . . . Saith divine Seneca, I have seen men mis-
erably dejected in a pleasant village, and some again well occupied
and at good ease in a solitary desert; 'tis the mind, not the place,
causeth tranquillity, and that gives true content. . . . No one is
hurt except by himself; and, which Seneca confirms out of his judgment and experience, every man's mind is stronger than fortune, and
leads him to what side he will; a cause to himself each one is of
his good or bad life" (p. 528).

These Stoic-Epicurean morals are by no means all that Burton
has to say on the subject of melancholy. They come mainly from
a fat section in the middle of his book with a Senecan-sounding
title: "A Consolatory Digression containing the Remedies of
all manner of Discontents." His next section is entitled "Of
Physick which cureth with Medicines." Burton was looking for
answers wherever he might find them, not preaching a fixed
doctrine.

Both Burton and Hall were careful to point out that all
the remedies for discontent that they took from the virtuous
heathen were as nothing when compared with the joys that Christianity had to offer. Even writers who failed to spell out
this qualification, no doubt assumed that it went without saying. When we notice something that we call Epicurean in the
writings of Robert Herrick (1591-1674) and Izaak Walton (1593-
1683), we do not mean that they ever went near any of the
dangerous Epicurean ideas. Herrick was an establishment clergyman, and Walton was a friend and biographer of establishment
clergymen.[60] Nevertheless, they seemed to feel no need to
involve themselves in the turmoil of their times. As private
men they settled down in retired places to enjoy what could be
enjoyed during the civil war. The picture of himself Herrick
gives in his poems makes us think he was endowed by nature
with the rare gift of equanimity, whether Christian or Stoic or
Epicurean. Instead of complaining that "here is no home," he
gladly accepted the universe, compromising with mutability by
telling us not only to hope for heaven but also to make much of
time. When he sang about "His content in the Country," he said,
"What ever comes, content makes sweet."[61] Ben Jonson, with
whose name Herrick's is often linked, was never so able as Herrick to forget the corrupt human world. Even Herrick's bishop,
Joseph Hall, could not often divorce man from his social context.

Izaak Walton, like Herrick, lived a long life and sounds
from his writings like a contented man. His withdrawal from
the business world of London was apparently voluntary. During
his last forty years he enjoyed the legendary retired life
often described in insurance company brochures, seldom met in
actual life. As a placid conventional Anglican, he saw nothing wrong with having heaven here as well as hereafter. It
does not really matter whether we call him a Christian humanist or a Stoic-Epicurean Christian; the fact is that he lived
a gentlemanly sort of virtuous simple life close to nature and
was rewarded on earth with tranquillity. Praising the golden

mean rather than poverty, he had learned the Horatian lesson that enough is enough. Piscator in Chapter I of The Compleat Angler gives us the moral:

> Sir, there be many men that are by others taken to be serious grave men, which we contemn and pity. Men that are taken to be grave, because Nature hath made them of a sowre complexion, money-getting-men, men that spend all their time first in getting, and next in anxious care to keep it: men that are condemned to be rich, and then always busie or discontented: for these poor-rich-men, we Anglers pity them perfectly, and stand in no need to borrow their thoughts to think ourselves happy. No, no, Sir, we enjoy a contentedness above the reach of such dispositions.[62]

Although we have heard this lesson often before, we are now beginning to meet writers who are taking their own advice.

As a contrast to the literary tranquillity of Walton and Herrick, we can look briefly at their untranquil contemporary John Milton, who had a notoriously difficult time trying to reconcile himself to the evil in the world and who was also encumbered with a well-developed social conscience. For him pleasure came under the heading of recreation. It had, of course, its place in the scheme of things. He said, "God himself conceals us not his own recreations before the world was built,"[63] and he tempted his friend Cyriack Skinner to take a rest from his books by arguing that heaven disapproves "that care . . . That with superfluous burden loads the day, / And when God sends a cheerful hour, refrains" (Sonnet, XXI). Like the Epicureans, and like Horace and Seneca, he placed friendship high on his list of good things and agreed with the standard doctrine that the golden mean leads to content: "Moderation in the enjoyment of temporal possessions manifests itself in the virtues of contentment, frugality, industry, and a liberal spirit." "Contentment is that virtue whereby a man is inwardly satisfied with the lot assigned him by divine providence."[64] Heaven on earth, however, the tranquil pleasure enjoyed by Adam and Eve before the Fall (see, e.g., PL, V.331-6, 450-1), was not to be expected. In this world the good life is possible only to a limited extent. In Book XI Michael gives Adam the classical recipe for making the best of things, "If thou well observe / The rule of not too much, by temperance taught" (lines 526 ff), it will be possible to mitigate somewhat the horrors of disease and death. But Adam cannot expect much. If he lives long enough, he will only be rewarded with old age, which Michael describes in terms gloomy enough for Yeats. His final advice, which might have come from Epictetus, or Lucretius, or Montaigne, is to learn to accept life or death as alike indifferent. "Nor love thy Life, nor hate; but what thou livst / Live well, how long or short permit to Heav'n."[65]

The quiet content of Herrick and Walton was also far removed from the heady bliss of Henry Vaughan (1621/2-1695),

whose "white, Celestiall thought" belonged to another world.
When Vaughan writes a poem entitled "Peace," he writes of a
"Countrie / Far beyond the stars." Even Vaughan, however--
at least in youth--had spent time mulling over Stoic recipes.
Among his translations the basic doctrine that climbing on the
wheel of desire will only result in perturbation occurs frequently, though some of his choices of subject seem a trifle
old fashioned for the seventeenth-century--more what one might
have expected from someone living in the sixteenth century or
earlier. His fondness for Juvenal and Boethius is reminiscent
of Chaucer. Among his early translations (1646) was Juvenal's
ever-popular tenth satire, which contains morals like the following: "O foolish mad ambition! these are still / The famous
dangers that attend thy will" (320-21). . . . "Vertue alone can
make a happy life. / To a wise man nought comes amisse: but we
/ Fortune adore, and make our Deity" (549-51). A number of
translations from the metres of Boethius appear in <u>Olar Iscanus</u>
(1651) and in <u>Thalia Rediviva</u> (1678). They teach us, among
other things, that all fortune must be accepted as good fortune. In I, Metrum 4 we are given the picture of the ideal
wise man: "Whose calme soule in a settled state / Kicks under
foot the frowns of Fate, / And in his fortunes bad or good /
Keeps the same temper in his bloud, / Not him the flaming Clouds
above, / Nor AEtna's fierie tempests . . . No fretting seas . . .
Nor burning thunderbolt . . . can stirre." In works of some
continental writers nearer his own time Vaughan likewise found
Stoic lessons. From the poetry of the Pole, Mathias Casimire
Sarbiewski (d. 1640),[66] he translated passages on the vicissitudes of fortune (Lib. 2, Ode 8), on the triumph of patience
over fortune (Lib. 4, Ode 13), and on the happiness that comes
from the contented simple life (Lib. 4, Ode 15). His prose
translation of "The Praise and Happinesse of the Countrie-Life"
by Don Antonio de Guevara (1490-1544) tells us that, "Whoever
Loves the <u>Country</u>, and Lives in it upon his owne. . . . he
fears no <u>discontents</u> to disturbe his <u>Peace</u>, but lives well
pleased with what <u>providence</u> gives him though never so little.
He is free from all fretting <u>cares</u>, and is fed with no mans
<u>provision</u> but his <u>own</u>. . . . But he that seeks after places of
<u>Eminency</u> will be sure to find Envy and Competitors. . . ."[67]
His translation of the "Discourse of Temperance and Patience,"
by Juan Eusebio Nieremberg, another Spaniard, contains the following excellent Stoic sentiments: "In prosperity use the first
[temperance], that is, restraine, or keepe in thy self. In
Adversity the last [patience], that is Incite, and use thy selfe
to a gallant <u>Apathie</u>, and contempt of misfortunes. . . . beleeve
with <u>Epictetus</u>, that the Quintessence of all Philosophie is
squeezed into these two. . . . beare and forbeare. . . . Why
should we Covet extraneous Goods? It is better to serve the
necessity of the time, then to be a slave to Fortune" (I, 220
ff). Presumably Vaughan translated these thoughts because he
liked them. However, the kind of lines for which he is famous
give the impression that he was greedy for more joy than a gallant

apathy could offer. For example, "The World" (1) starts with its famous image of eternity as "a great _Ring_ of pure and end-less light, / All calm, as it was bright," then drops from the sublime to describe a series of typical earthly climbers on the wheel of unsatisfied desire--the lover, the politician, the miser, the pleasure seeker. For these there is none of that bright calm. The implied lesson is that happiness means rejec-tion of the world. In this poem Vaughan gives no humanistic advice to love moderately, serve duty rather than ambition, cultivate the simple life, and make the most of harmless pleas-ures. We are back to the absolute doctrine that peace on earth is not for human beings.[68]

Andrew Marvell (1621-78), who dipped into a number of traditions, both religious and secular, made one of the best-known translations of Seneca's popular lines from the end of Act II of _Thyestes_ (_Stet, quicunque volet potens_), a trans-lation that includes the following sentiment: "All I seek is to lye still. / Settled in some secret Nest / in calm Leisure let me rest; and far of the publick stage/ Pass away my silent Age." The mood that Marvell here expresses may remind us of the opening stanza of "The Garden," with that stanza's medita-tion on the emptiness of fame and its praise of repose. But the tone of "The Garden" does not remain continuously Senecan. It passes from quiet repose to sensuous delight; earthly joy brings a foretaste of heavenly bliss; present pleasure arouses memories of the earthly paradise that might have been-- had man been wise enough to live in solitude. In the poem's laughing conclusion, "Two Paradises 'twere in one / To live in Paradise alone," we are reminded of one of the persistent obstacles to settled peace of mind--other people. The moments of delight that Marvell enjoys in a garden are only moments, not recipes for living. Similarly, in the shifting scenes of "Upon Appleton House" Marvell praises the virtuous retirement of Fairfax (st. 44 and 45), without needing to mention that most of Fairfax's life had been active. In an earlier episode of the poem (describing an earlier Fairfax) Marvell had implied that withdrawal to a nunnery was both contrary to the law of Right (st. 29) and an attempt to go against Fate (st. 31), while in a later one he disagreed with the Stoic-Epicurean cliché that high places are more dangerous than low places. For the unlucky birds, who had nested in the grass, had learned that "Lowness is unsafe as Hight" (st. 52). Even the woodland scene (st. 61-81), which recalls the solitary bliss of "The Garden," is only an episode and gives way in its turn to the final stanzas praising Maria. Marvell's delight in gardens is only one aspect of his poetry. Other aspects include "A Dia-logue Between the Resolved Soul, and Created Pleasure," in which the soul refuses Pleasure's offer of "Nature's banquet" of fruits and flowers, replying that "I sup above, and cannot stay," while in another sphere, there are poems like "An Hora-tian Ode upon Cromwel's Return from Ireland" (discussed in Chapter V) in which Marvell is more concerned with social responsibility than with personal tranquillity and praises

Cromwell for leaving "his private Gardens, where / He liv'd
reserved and austere."[69]
     Earthly content, however, was very much the theme of Mar-
vell's contemporaries Abraham Cowley (1618-67) and William
Temple (1628-99). These two writers, raised on the classics,
settled down at the end of their lives to write essays about
the small enjoyments possible in this imperfect world. Both
could point to the fact that in youth they had expressed a wistful preference for the tranquil Epicurean retired life. Both
had spent the best part of their lives in public service. Both
had retired in the end, more or less in disgust, to cultivate
their gardens. Whether their celebration of Horatian content
is sour grapes or lifelong conviction does not really matter.
Some are born contented; some achieve content. Whatever their
private religious feelings, both Cowley and Temple wrote voluminous essays unashamedly concentrating on how to have the pleasant life here and now.
     Cowley in an early poem, "The Vote," which he says he
wrote at the age of thirteen, set down his Horatian dream of
the good life. During his last years he reprinted the verses
in his essay "Of Myself," saying he still agreed with the sentiments there expressed.[70] Stanzas 9, 10, and 11 list the
things that for him make the happier life. Some items lean in
the Stoic direction, some in the Epicurean, since it is not
Cynic frugality that he admires but the pleasant golden mean.
Some honor he hopes for, based on virtue, and, in addition,
friends, books, a small house, a garden. Then he will remember that it is not how long we live that matters but how well
and will be able to accept what comes. He ends by translating
the Horatian lines, "To-morrow let my Sun his beams display, /
Or in clouds hide them; I have liv'd to Day" (p. 457). And like
many a poet before him he also translated Martial's similar
definition of the happy life (Epigram X, 47, p. 460). Among the
odes that he wrote or translated there are such remedies for
fortune as that if fortune is bad today it may be better tomorrow, that a pleasant poverty is to be preferred before discontented riches, that a well-spent life is the important thing
(II, IV, VI, p. 60 ff).
     Since his interest was in the happy life, he freely mixed
Stoic and Epicurean precepts without running into any particular conflict.[71] In his essay "Of Liberty" he defended Epicurus,
maintaining that the latter's message was that the only path to
liberty and happiness was through moderation of the appetites
(Waller, p. 385). "Of Solitude" (p. 392) begins by quoting
Cicero's lines, "never less alone than when alone" and goes
on to praise Scipio, the alleged speaker of the lines, as "the
most Wise, most Worthy, most happy, and the greatest of all Mankind" (p. 508). Scipio was all these things because "after he
had made Rome mistress of almost the whole world, he retired
himself from it by a voluntary exile" and lived a simple life as
a private man. "Of Obscurity" (p. 397) once again praises the
retired life, this time with no concern for fame, that last

infirmity of noble mind.

> I account a person who has a moderate Minde and Fortune, and lives
> in the conversation of two or three agreeable friends, with little
> commerce in the world besides, who is esteemed well enough by his
> few neighbors that know him, and is truly irreproachable by anybody,
> and so after a healthful, quiet life, before the great inconven-
> iences of old age, goes more silently out of it than he came in, (for
> I would not have him so much as cry in the exit); this innocent
> deceiver of the world, as Horace calls him, this muta persona, I take
> to have been more happy in his part, than the greatest Actors that
> fill the stage with show and noise" (p. 397).[72]

"Of Agriculture" (p. 400) again describes the idyllic
retired life, far from the temptations and vices of the court.
A little is enough to give him a life of quiet pleasure.  He
praises Virgil and Horace for their pictures of country bliss
and translates from both on the theme of contentment, including
a translation of the tale of the town mouse and the country
mouse.[73]  His essay "The Garden" is addressed to his friend John
Evelyn, who had translated the first book of Lucretius, and
appropriately contains another kind reference to Epicurus.  It
opens with the well-known statement, "I never had any other
desire so strong and so like to covetousness as that one which
I have had always, that I might be master at last of a small
house and large garden" (p. 424).  "Of Greatness" is reminiscent
of Herrick's description of content in the country.  Cowley
wants, "a little convenient estate, a little cheerful House, a
little Company, and a very little Feast" (p. 429).  In "Of
Myself" Cowley remarks, after the manner of Lucretius or Horace
[Odes III.29, end] that, "I met with several great Persons,
whom I liked very well, but could not perceive that any part of
their Greatness was to be liked or desired, no more than I
would be glad or content to be in a Storm" (p. 458).[74]

It has been pointed out that both Herrick and Cowley looked
back to pre-revolution days as the golden age.[75]  But something
had gone wrong with the comfortable assumption, which may have
flourished for a while after 1588, that the destiny of England
and the will of God were one and the same.  Now for a disillusioned Royalist who wanted to keep his faith in an ordered
universe there was nothing to choose but Job's comfort--which
is also standard Stoic comfort--to go on believing in the existence of a benevolent long-term plan while admitting that at
the present time the details of the plan were obscure.  Those
who could afford the luxury, could leave the system to take care
of itself while they retired to the country, telling themselves
that all fortune must be accepted as good fortune and that they
must concentrate on making the most of each day.

William Temple, even though he was not a Royalist, also
believed in cultivating his garden and may conceivably have been
slightly more skeptical than Cowley about a well-ordered moral
universe.[76]  Like a well-bred nineteenth-century agnostic he made
the proper conventional genuflexions toward the established reli-

gion and kept his private thoughts to himself. Probably, however, he was no more consistent in his beliefs than the rest of
us. If he defended the Epicureans and in his later essays put
a heavy emphasis on Epicurean tranquillity, we should not forget
that his years as a diplomat gained him a reputation for unusual
moral integrity. His Epicureanism was more Horatian than Machiavellian. Though he may not have been able to identify narrow
English custom with the laws of nature, he had not abandoned the
search for underlying moral principles. (See Chapter V.)

As an example of the fact that an interest in Epicureanism
may have different effects on different people, we can notice
that Cowley followed those modern Epicureans who were interested
in the new science,[77] while Temple, who was not impressed by
these new-fangled ideas, still clung to the Stoic belief that
the proper study of mankind is man, a conviction that led him
to defend the losing side in the battle of the Ancients and
Moderns. In the sense that his writing concentrates on how to
have the good life on earth, and does not talk about heaven,
he seems far away from the otherworldliness of Sidney and Spenser. But in the sense that his ideals of happiness and his
standards of right conduct can almost be explained in terms of
Virgil and Horace or Cicero and Seneca, he still has much in
common with these high-minded Elizabethan poets. His political career, which seems to have been motivated more by duty
than by ambition, was quite in line with the ideals of Roman
and medieval political theorists--however much it may have differed from the practice of actual politicians, ancient or modern.
He wrote works on political subjects as well as on gardens; and
if he retired to the country, he did so, like Horace and Seneca,
after serving his time in the political world. If his Epicurean skepticism about the point of it all seems at times
stronger than his Stoic optimism, he has Horace and Seneca as
precedents.[78] Just as his attitude toward contemporary science
was outmoded, so his attitude toward politics was outmoded,
Machiavelli having long since displaced Cicero. Temple's popularity in the eighteenth century[79] is less an indication that he
spoke for the future than of the fact that a surviving remnant
of backward-looking humanists continued to hope that one of
these days there would be a return to normalcy.[80]

Though Temple's classical mix may have included a larger
number of frankly Epicurean ideas than Philip Sidney's classical mix, it was still a mix. What Horace once said of himself,
Temple might well have echoed: "At times, I'm the Practical
Man, / The heroic, Stoical Man, who takes Part in Life, / And
Care of Truth, and Charge of inflexible Virtue. / At times, I
slip off unseen to the opposite side, / To fit the world to
myself, not me to it."[81]

As with Cowley there are hints from Temple's early life
that Stoic-Epicurean ideas of content appealed to him when he
was young. The letters Dorothy Osborne wrote to him during
their courtship contain suggestions that the contented retired
life sometimes came up for discussion. The "Character" of him

written by his sister Lady Giffard makes such remarks as that he
"said he was made for a farmer & not a courtier, & understood
being a shepheard & a gardener better then an Ambassador" or
that "those who knew him little thought him rich, to wch he used
to answer pleasantly that he wanted nothing towards it but an
estate, & was realy soe in haveing all he car'd for."[82]  A moralizing passage in one of his early romances makes him sound
like a good Elizabethan Senecan.  His hero, described as one
"whose pastime was his businesse and content his ambition,"
reflected while watching his hawks "that fly wee high or low
wee must all at length come alike to the ground; if there bee
any difference that the loftyer flight has the deadlyer fall."[83]
A passage in an early essay shows that after pondering on the
things that make a happy life he had already settled on the
golden mean.

> To bee all passion is to bee a beast, but to have none is to bee a
> block.  Theese are all the notions I have of contentment, wch I
> beleeve cannot bee enjoyed in excesse without being more or lesse  ·
> then a man, and in degree is competent with all stages of mind or
> fortune; in the meane time wee fancying some strange Chimaera of
> pleasure to bee signifyed by this word, no marvell if wee never find
> it, because tis nothing but fancy, never meeting it in thinges wee
> have, makes us allwayes imagine tis in thinges wee want, and this
> spurrs us on to weary our selves in the pursuite of (what) we might
> as well or better obtain by standing still . . . tis a just punish-
> ment that whilst wee seeke after a good which is impossible, wee are
> hinder'd from enjoying that wch is possible.  Methinks a man search-
> ing for happinesse through the glass of fancy upon the table of for-
> tune is like one looking for a peice of gold through a multiply-
> ing glass. . . . Honor and content consist both in meere opinion
> onely the difference is, the first consists wholly in others opinion,
> the last wholly in ones owne (pp. 160-61).

These are the same ideas to be found in Hall or Burton.
    One cannot help suspecting that Temple like Burton put a
high price on content because he knew what it was to be
afflicted with melancholy.  His sister reports that he was pain-
fully addicted to sudden fits of low spirits, to be accounted
for, if at all, only by the influence of the weather.  If reason were needed, watching the politicians destroy his best
efforts and losing all seven of his children would have been
enough to depress anyone.[84]  And so he said, at the end of his
essay "Upon Poetry," "When all is done, human life is at the
greatest and the best, but like a froward child, that must be
played with and humoured a little to keep it quiet till it falls
asleep, and then the care is over" (Monk, p. 203).  The melancholy sentiment, which might have come from Lucretius or from
Seneca or from many a Christian Stoic, becomes faintly Epicurean when the emphasis is shifted from patient acceptance of
unpleasantness, or hope for sleep as an escape, to concentra-
tion on what can be done to humor the child and keep it quiet
while it is awake.

In his essay "Of Health and Long Life" Temple says,

When I was young and in some idle company, it was proposed that every
one should tell what their three wishes should be, if they were sure
to be granted: some were very pleasant, and some very extravagant;
mine were health, and peace, and fair weather; which, though out of
the way among young men, yet perhaps might pass well enough among
old: . . . Let the philosophers reason and differ about the chief
good or happiness of man; let them find it where they can, and place
it where they please; but there is no mistake so gross, or opinion
so impertinent (how common soever), as to think pleasures arise from
what is without us, rather than from what is within (pp. 275, 277).[85]

The best recipe Temple knows for health and long life is the
Epicurean one: "great temperance, open air, easy labour,
little care, simplicity of diet" (p. 280).

His essay "Upon the Gardens of Epicurus, or of Gardening"
illustrates how far a prudent gentleman might go at the end of
the seventeenth century in openly defending the ideas of Epicurus and Lucretius, along with those of the less controversial
Virgil and Horace. Leaving aside the cosmic sort of questions
that interested Thomas Hardy or A. E. Housman--questions of
pointless accident and indifferent gods--it merely sets forth,
copiously and pleasantly, the time-honored prescription for
heaven on earth. If specifically Christian remarks are not much
in evidence, there is nothing to prevent Temple's good sister
Lady Giffard from insisting that they are really implied. The
analysis of the causes of melancholy and the suggested cures
are the long accepted ones. Like others in the Stoic-Epicurean
tradition, Temple usually does not concern himself with woes
that have an outside cause, whether physical or social. His
essays are addressed to gentlemen like himself who have everything but happiness because they are forever driven by their
restless passions, particularly by greed and ambition. They do
not know how much is enough. Temple, a great phrase maker,
observed that among all creatures man alone "is born crying.
. . . lives complaining and dies disappointed." After shopping
around among the Stoics and Epicureans he came up with the following conclusions:

All agreed the greatest temper if not the total subduing of passion,
and exercise of reason, to be the state of the greatest felicity; to
live without desires or fears, or those perturbations of mind and
thought which passions raise; to place true riches in wanting little,
rather than in possessing much, and true pleasure in temperance,
rather than in satisfying the senses; to live with indifference to
the common enjoyments and accidents of life, and with constancy upon
the greatest blows of fate or of chance; not to disturb our minds with
sad reflections upon what is past, nor with anxious cares or raving
hopes about what is to come; neither to disquiet life with the fears of
death, nor death with the desires of life; but in both, and in all
things else, to follow nature, seem to be the precepts most agreed
among them (Monk, pp. 1, 6).

Like practically everyone else, he rejected the early Stoic
insistence that the mind could completely control the body and
openly defended the Epicureans for recognizing that the body is
there and not to be ignored. He went on to say, "All the different sects of philosophers seem to have agreed in the opinion
of a wise man's abstaining from public affairs . . . above all,
they esteemed public business the most contrary of all others to
that tranquillity of mind which they esteemed and taught to be
the only true felicity of man. . . . For this reason Epicurus
passed his life wholly in his gardens" (Monk, p. 10). As if he
had a foreknowledge that the nineteenth-century historian Thomas Macaulay would attack him as a defector from duty, he
defended his choice of life.

> As the country life, and this part of it more particularly, were the
> inclination of my youth itself, so they are the pleasure of my age;
> and I can truly say that, among many great employments that have fallen
> to my share, I have never asked or sought for any one of them, but
> often endeavored to escape from them into the ease and freedom of a
> private scene, where a man may go his own way and his own pace, in
> the common paths or circles of life (Monk, p. 34).

His last quotation in this essay is from Horace's contented
man's prayer (here given in Bovie's translation): "What my
friend, do I pray for? For what I now have, / Or even less;
that I live out the rest of my days / In my own sweet way, if
the gods mean me to survive / A while longer" (Epistle I.18,
104). It is easy to imagine that the aging William Temple,
whose lifelong tendency to skepticism had been hardened by experience, should have had difficulty entering into the ambitious
political hopes of the young Jonathan Swift. Why should anyone
deeply convinced of the vanity of human wishes want to encourage
anyone else to waste his energies climbing on the wheel of
desire? The accident of birth had given Temple more political
power and influence than Swift could ever have hoped for. Yet
he had given it up to stay at home and tie up his apricots.
Perhaps by the time Swift came to write about the Houyhnhnms he
too might have settled for health and peace and fair weather,
but that was too much to expect when he was still under thirty.

Sir George Savile, Marquis of Halifax (1633-95), belongs
in this chapter only in that he recommended content to his
daughter as an answer to the problem of being a woman. He himself had a certain resemblance to Temple in that he was another
uneasy adjustor to changing times. In politics he was even more
important than Temple and like Temple tried to apply high-minded
ancient ideals to a world that did not want them. Though he was
a pragmatist and a skeptic, he nevertheless refused to stop
believing in principles and could not be made into a well-
behaved party man. His retirement from politics came about not
because he had rejected the world but because he had refused to
play the game according to the new rules. Like many a skeptic,
however, he did not believe in flouting custom. Though he could
well see that few marriages were made in heaven, he did not

shock his times by writing idealistic divorce tracts in the Miltonic mode. Rather, he advised his daughter to adjust herself to the system. Since statistically he could see that her chances for a happy marriage were no better than average, he loaded her down with Stoic advice on expecting the worst-- though he did not bother to give similar advice to his son, who was equally likely to make an unhappy marriage and had equally little chance of making a legal escape. Though the son, it is assumed, might comfort himself elsewhere, Halifax did not choose to encourage his daughter to do likewise. So he told her to consider the probabilities and not be surprised if her husband turned out to be a libertine or a drunk or a niggard or a man of uncertain temper. Equanimity was the goal. She should remember that what can't be cured must be endured. "You are therefore to make your best of what is <u>settled</u> by <u>Law</u> and <u>Custom</u>, and not vainly imagine, that it will be <u>changed</u> for your sake."[86] Having faced the worst, she should also learn to moderate her desires, since nature can be satisfied with very little. "Remember that <u>Children</u> and <u>Fools</u> want every thing because they want Wit to distinguish: and therefore there is no stronger Evidence of a <u>Crazy</u> <u>Understanding</u>, than the making too large a Catalogue of things necessary, when in truth there are so very few things that have a right to be placed in it. Try everything first in your <u>Judgment</u>, before you allow it a place in your <u>Desire</u>; else your <u>Husband</u> may think it as necessary for him to deny, as it is for you to <u>have</u> whatever is unreasonable" (Raleigh, p. 26). Giving Stoic advice to other people has always been one way of bolstering the <u>status</u> <u>quo</u> and preserving our own peace of mind.

Though John Dryden (1631-1700) made a few bows to humble content, it was not one of his favorite themes. His contribution came mainly as a translator. There he did his work so effectively that some of his versions of Horace are the scraps that everyone knows. Especially there is his "Horace. The Twenty-ninth Ode of the Third Book. Paraphras'd in Pindaric Verse."

> Happy the man, and happy he alone,
>  He, who can call to-day his own;
>  He who secure within, can say:
>  "To-morrow do thy worst, for I have liv'd to-day.
>  Be fair, or foul, or rain, or shine,
> The joys I have possess'd in spite of fate are mine. . . .
>  Content with poverty, my soul I arm;
>  And virtue, tho' in rags, will keep me warm. . . . (st. viii, ix).[87]

To avoid ending the chapter and the century with an over emphasis on sweet content, I shall mention that there were the usual number of people who were interested in other things. We do not find hymns to Stoic-Epicurean content in John Bunyan (1628-1688) or Samuel Pepys (1633-1703). Bunyan was too poor to be interested in philosophizing about poverty. Stoic moderation had no place in his passionate desire to win his way to

heaven. Pepys was busy enjoying the material things of life.
Using his wits to acquire his money and care for his property,
he seemed to enjoy climbing on the wheel of desire.

Not even country mice want to be country mice all the time.
Even Horace had a habit of making short jaunts to Rome, and the
placid Herrick sometimes complained about dull Devonshire.
Thomas Shadwell (1642-92) in his play <u>Bury</u> <u>Fair</u> (1689) had his
two clever young men, Bellamy and Wildish, debate the relative
pleasures of country <u>vs</u>. town, ending the argument mainly in a
draw (III.iii). If we leap ahead to the twentieth century we
notice Lytton Strachey still posing the same problem in a letter
to Lady Ottoline Morrell (24 February 1916). "The country is
certainly the place for peaceful happiness--if that's what one
wants! I think one wants it about half the time; and the other
half <u>unpeaceful</u> happiness. But happiness <u>all</u> the time."[88]

If we look at the people who wrote so well about tranquillity we observe that none of them were actually sitting around
twiddling their thumbs. They were all--among other things--
hard-working writers engaged in trying to say what they had to
say. Thus they fill rather well a prescription for happiness
set down by one twentieth-century psychologist, who says, "The
process of solving problems or reducing errors in the cyber-
netic sense is the essence of pleasure. But while the object
of problem-solving is to achieve stability, a stable state is
not itself the source of pleasure. Rather, the joy of living
is to be found in confronting a problem and doing something
about it."[89] Bishop Thomas Sprat (1635-1713) in his <u>The</u> <u>History</u>
<u>of</u> <u>the</u> <u>Royal</u> <u>Society</u> revealed himself as a seventeenth-century
praiser of the joys of problem solving.[90] For the achievement
of true equanimity, he said, there was nothing like a labora-
tory. Those who engaged in scientific experiments, so he
dreamed, would benefit society on the one hand and bring happiness to themselves on the other. In "the management of the
privat <u>motions</u>, and <u>passions</u> of our <u>minds</u>:" we will receive
far more help from "a constant cours of <u>innocent</u> <u>Works</u>" than
from "all the rigid praecepts of the Stoical, or the empty
distinctions of the <u>Peripatetic</u> <u>Moralists</u>."

> The <u>Art</u> of <u>Experiments</u>. . . . has power enough to free the <u>minds</u>
> of men from their vanities, and intemperance, by that very way which
> the greatest Epicure has no reason to reject, by opposing pleasure
> against pleasure. . . . What room can there be for low, and little
> <u>things</u> in a <u>mind</u> so usefully and successfully employd? What <u>ambitious</u>
> <u>disquiets</u> can torment that man, who has so much glory before him, for
> which there are only requir'd the delightful <u>Works</u> of his <u>hands</u>? What
> dark, or melancholy passions can overshadow his <u>heart</u>, whose <u>senses</u>
> are always full of so many various <u>productions</u>, of which the least
> progress, and success, will affect him with an <u>innocent</u> <u>joy</u>?

Turning a blind eye to the vanity of human wishes, Sprat seemed
to hope that the experimental scientist could also succeed in
being a Stoic-Epicurean happy man, a new Adam. He should have
remembered that the wheel of fortune goes round and round and

140

that Adam's sojourn in Paradise was only for a season.

Chapter IV. Notes

[1]"Though Ye Suppose all Jeopardies are Passed," Complete Poems, ed. Henderson. See also "The Bouge of Court," and the final stanzas of "Magnificence." Stephen Hawes (d. 1523) in his long "Pastime of Pleasure" treats fortune in much the same mixed way as Lydgate and Chaucer, with fortune sometimes a Christian reminder of mutability, sometimes an instrument of moral correction, sometimes another name for destiny.

[2]Ed. Campbell, p. 132, line 107 ff; see also pp. 143, 1-7; 153, 274-80; 154.

[3]Works, ed. Boas. See also the choral song on the revolutions of time at the end of Act II. For discussion of various sixteenth-century plays on the theme of fickle fortune, see Farnham, Medieval Heritage. Farnham says of Thomas Lodge's The Wounds of Ciuill Warr, Liuely set forth in the true Tragedies of Marius and Scilla (c. 1588), "very little happens that is not referable merely to the perilous chances of high place" (p. 377).

[4]Essayes, I.19, trans. Florio (quoted from Everyman, 440, p. 80). See Spencer, Death and Elizabethan Tragedy, p. 61.

[5]Anatomy of Melancholy, ed. Dell and Jordan-Smith, pp. 126, 239, 241, 493, 494, 541. See Colie's discussion of the Anatomy as a consolatio philosophiae (Paradoxia Epidemica, pp. 437-38).

[6]Works, ed. Wynter, I, 97, 207; VI, 18, 207, 313; VII, 56, 460, 464, 466, 472-73, 508, 563. Quotations, unless otherwise cited, are from this edition.

[7]Ode II.3, Works, ed. Herford and Simpson, VIII.

[8]Poems, ed. Howard, p. 58, st. 5. In another poem Davies likens contentment in this life to virgins whom "all the world have sought, but none enjoy'd" ("A Contention betwixt a Wife, a Widow, and a Maid" (Silver Poets, ed. Bullett, Everyman, 985, st. 27).

[9]For a good explanation of historical Stoic philosophical attitudes toward the passions, see Edelstain, Meaning of Stoicism. See also Haydn, p. 474. On Elizabethan theories of passion see Campbell, Shakespeare's Tragic Heroes. On the inconsistencies of various moralists in their treatment of the passions, see Ornstein, Moral Vision, p. 41 ff. And for a careful distinction among various sixteenth-century meanings of such words as "reason," "passion," "will," "apathy," see Levi, French Moralists, pp. 7-39.

[10]Some commentators try to draw a neat dividing line between the Aristotelian golden mean on the one hand and the Stoic condemnation of all passion on the other. For example, Campbell says, "The fundamental difference in the treatment of the passions in the Renaissance was a difference inherited from the conflicting attitudes of Stoics and Peripatetics in regard to

the passions. The Stoics considered all passions as evil in themselves. The Peripatetics taught that passions were evil if they were not governed by reason" (Shakespeare's Tragic Heroes, p. 70). Battenhouse says, "Literary opinion was on the side of Aristotle and the Platonists, as opposed to the Stoics. That is to say, it was held by most authors that man's passions are beneficial, provided they are kept temperate" (Marlowe's Tamburlaine, p. 227). See Zanta, pp. 214-23, for a discussion of the way in which Lipsius in the Manuductio (1604) explains the calm of the Stoic sage so as to accommodate it with Christian teaching. English writers do not seem to have adopted this complex line of reasoning. For Cicero's exposition of the golden mean, see De Officiis, I.xxix.102.

11Tr. Hudson, p. 39.

12Ep. I.i.105-108, Satires and Epistles, trans. Bovie.

13Columbia Milton (CM), XVII, 209.

14Resolves, Temple Classics, First Century, No. 39; see also No. 62, "Of the Temper of Affections."

15Le Bourgeois Gentilhomme, II.iv.

16The moral is stated in II.iv.34 and v.16.

17Quotations are from A Woman Killed with Kindness, ed. Van Fossen.

18See III.iii.109 ff for some of the friar's Stoic platitudes against despair.

19"De Clementia," ii.6.3 (Moral Essays, Vol. I). Cf. Cicero, "Why pity rather than give assistance if one can?" (Tusculan Disputations, IV.xxvi.56). See Arnold's discussion of Stoic views on grief, p. 336 ff. Zanta explains the distinction Lipsius makes in La Constance (1583) between pity and mercy (compassion and misericorde) and contrasts, on the subject of passion, as on other topics, the subtleties of Lipsius with the practical approach of Du Vair (see, e.g., p. 291 ff).

20Quotations are from Poems, ed. McDonald and Brown, p. 57.

21Quotations are from Poems and Dramas, ed. Bullough, except for A Letter to an Honourable Lady, which is from Works, ed. Grosart, Vol. III.

22Quoted from Four Tragedies, ed. Beaurline and Bowers, p. 196.

23For Stoic views on love and marriage, see Arnold, pp. 317-18.

24Heaven upon Earth and Characters of Vertues and Vices, ed. Kirk, pp. 178, 165. Cf. Felltham's "Content makes Rich," Resolves, Second Century, No. 86.

25Utopia, ed. Warrington, Everyman, 461, pp. 328-29.

26Ed. Watson, Everyman, 227, p. 245. Shakespeare has Portia in The Merchant of Venice exhibit a slightly skeptical attitude toward this moral. When she makes her first appearance on stage, complaining of being in an irritable mood, she does not care for Nerissa's pedantic lecture on being contented. (Nerissa's word for the balance between too little and too much, incidentally, is "competency," which appears everywhere in eighteenth-century writing.) Portia, as skeptical as Horace, points out that there is a big difference between knowing what reasonable action is and being able to behave reasonably (I.ii).

27(Patient Grissel, I.ii.93 ff), quoted from Dramatic Works, ed. Bowers, Vol. I.

28That there is a considerable strain of Stoic and Epicurean thinking in the Utopia has frequently been noticed. See, e.g., Adams, Better Part of Valor, p. 133 ff, and "Philosophic Unity"; Surtz, "Defence of Pleasure," "Epicurus in Utopia," and Praise of Pleasure.

29Samuel Chew describes an early poem of More's on the subject of fortune. Here fortune throws from her wheel such former favorites as Alexander, Darius, and Julius Caesar but has no power over the poverty of Socrates, Pythagoras, and other philosophers (pp. 47-48). Similarly Erasmus in The Praise of Folly ironically describes Folly as ridiculing wise men because they refuse to worship fortune and never grow rich (p. 103).

30And possibly even from Epictetus. Mason says, "If none of his poems had survived, we should still have the letter in which he recommended to his son, 'the good opinion of moral philosophers, among whom I wold Senek were your studye and Epictetus, bicaus it is litel to be euir in your bosome,'" Humanism and Poetry, p. 138. Wyatt also translated Plutarch's "On Tranquillity of Mind," (1528); for comment see Thomson, Sir Thomas Wyatt and "Sir Thomas Wyatt: Classical Philosophy and English Humanism."

31Quoted above p. 92, n. 36.

32See Mason, pp. 181-86, 234-35.

33No.197, line 101. Quotations are from Collected Poems, ed. Muir.

34Ed. Rollins.

35Quoted from Ashmole Ms. 48 in Hebel and Hudson, eds., Poetry of the English Renaissance.

36From The Paradise of Dainty Devices (1576-1606), ed. Rollins, No. 89.

37For a full discussion of this theme see Rostvig, Happy Man, I, 81-83. See also Mason, pp. 62-63, 252, 254.

38Poems, ed. Drinkwater, p. 226. For Surrey's translation, see Poems, ed. Jones, p. 34.

[39] Ault, _Elizabethan Lyrics_, pp. 122-23.

[40] _Works in Verse and Prose_, ed. Grosart, I, 6, and _Plays and Poems of Robert Greene_, ed. Collins, II, 308.

[41] _Complete Works_, ed. Bond, Vol. II.

[42] Ed. Greg, p. 25. Quotations are from this edition.

[43] _Novels of Thomas Deloney_, ed. Lawlis, p. 316, lines 2-3, 10-14. Quotations are from this edition.

[44] Quotations are from _Works_, ed. Feuillerat.

[45] The well-known song, "O sweete woodes, the Delighte of Solitarynes" comes from the _Old Arcadia_ (IV, 157-58). In stanza two the song compares worldly corruption with solitary bliss in the same passing mood that occurs in the "Blow, blow, thou winter wind" of _As You Like It_.

[46] West comments on this passage in "Spenser and the Renaissance Ideal of Christian Heroism," p. 1027.

[47] Although _As You Like It_ contains many laments over fickle fortune of the kind that appear in Lodge's _Rosalynde_ (see, e.g., I.ii.34-50), Shakespeare used the idea of ever-changing fortune as a convenient plot device. In this play, those who start at the bottom, end at the top. (In _The Malcontent_, IV.v.155-65, Marston jests with the same idea.) For a list of Shakespearean references to fortune see Samuel Chew, _Pilgrimage of Life_, p. 53 ff.

[48] Erasmus in _The Christian Prince_ describes the good prince as mulling over public problems while others sleep (pp. 182, 244, 246). Spenser has an old knight moralizing over his wounded son in such a way as to combine classical reflections on the vanity of wishing (since we can never see the consequences of getting our wish) with advice to those of low degree to be content with their stations. The stanza concludes, "Let none therefore, that is in meaner place, / Too greatly grieue at any his vnlucky case" (FQ, VI.iii.5). Quoted from _Poetical Works_, ed. Smith and De Selincourt.

[49] _George Herbert_, p. 187. Quotations are from _Works_, ed. Hutchinson.

[50] _A Letter to an Honourable Lady_, Grosart, III, 256. For discussions of this work and of Greville's carefully limited Christian Stoicism and his skeptical attitude toward earthly peace, see Rebholz, _Fulke Greville_, pp. 26, 33-35, 85, and Joan Rees, _Fulke Greville_, pp. 195-213. Greville will be discussed further in Chapters V and VI.

[51] _Jacobean Drama_, p. 24.

[52] _White Devil_, V.vi.262-63. Quotations are from _Plays of John Marston_, ed. Wood, and _Complete Works of John Webster_, ed. Lucas.

53Caputi, John Marston, Satirist, p. 136, describes Feliche as "unmistakably . . . Neo-Stoic of Marstonian stripe." Finkel-pearl, John Marston of the Middle Temple, says that Feliche "clearly lacks the quality on which he most prides himself, contentment" and that "withdrawal and inner contentment are impossible in a world where evil and folly reign" (p. 142).

54There is a similar ironic episode in the subplot. Sir Charles Mountford, in a happy mood a moment before he is arrested, says, "All things on earth thus change, some up, some down; / Content's a kingdom, and I wear that crown" (Sc. vii.7-8, ed. Van Fossen).

55Quotations are from Dramatic Works, ed. Bowers, and Non-Dramatic Works, ed. Grosart, III, 71.

56"To liue with little," lines 1-8; "Of plentie and freedome in goodness," lines 1-4, Poems, ed. Bartlett. The source of many of these lines has been traced to Epictetus; see Bartlett, pp. 243-44, 450.

57Quotations are from Works, ed. Herford and Simpson. Rostvig's Happy Man studies in detail the various ramifications in seventeenth- and eighteenth-century English poetry of ideas growing out of Horace's Epode 2. See also Mason, p. 267 ff, and McEuen, Classical Influences, especially the chapter on Horace, for examples of other seventeenth-century poets who wrote on such themes as being content with little, maintaining tranquillity by freeing oneself from desire and fear, preparing oneself ahead of time for fortune's inevitable shifts. For emphasis on the Christian aspect of "On My First Sonne," see Kay, "Christian Wisdom."

58On all this, Haller comments, "Steeped in Seneca's smooth and engaging moralizings, he shows how easily a prosperous man could compound Calvinism and stoicism into the theory that all was for the best in the best of all possible worlds" (Rise of Puritanism, p. 327).

59It should be noted that this popular bit of advice from Epicurus, transmitted by Seneca, is usually called Stoic. One familiar expression of it is Thomas Carlyle's sentence: "The Fraction of Life can be increased in value not so much by increasing your Numerator as by lessening your Denominator" (Sartor Resartus, Ch. IX).

60Musgrove, Universe of Robert Herrick, emphasizes the standard Elizabethan world picture lying behind Herrick's poems. Quotations are from Poetical Works, ed. Moorman.

61Rostvig puts his use of content in the Stoic tradition, with some Epicurean slips. See pp. 140-41.

62Ed. Keynes, Modern Library, p. 36.

63 Tetrachordon, CM, IV, 85.

[64]See "Prolusion VII," CM, XII, 263-4; Christian Doctrine, CM, XVII, 223, 275-81.

[65]See Knott, "Milton's Heaven," for a discussion of heaven as "the theological if not the dramatic center of the poem."

[66]See Rostvig, I, 91 ff, 270 ff.

[67]Works, ed. Martin, I, 124 ff. Quotations are from this edition. For the poetry, see also Complete Poetry, ed. Fogle.

[68]For a discussion of Vaughan as a traditional thinker, see Simmonds, Masques of God.

[69]Quotations are from Poems and Letters, ed. Margoliouth, Vol. I. For some of the recent complex discussions of Marvell's garden poems see D. C. Allen, Image and Meaning, pp. 93-153; Wallace, Destiny His Choice; Colie, 'My Ecchoing Song'; and Friedman, Marvell's Pastoral Art.

[70]Essays, Plays and Sundry Verses, ed. Waller, p. 547.

[71]See Hinman, Abraham Cowley, pp. 167-75; Rostvig, I, 298-306; Mayo, Epicurus, p. 166 ff.

[72]Mason points out (p. 185) that much of this last quotation is Cowley's version of the popular lines from Seneca (stet quicunque volet potens) that also attracted Wyatt and Marvell.

[73]See Rostvig, I, p. 101.

[74]Among the minor poets who wrote on the theme of retired content, Rostvig discusses Katherine Philips (1631-64), the Earl of Roscommon (1633?-85), Charles Cotton (1630-1687), John Norris (1657-1711), John Rawlet (1642-1686), Thomas Flatman (1637-1688), and William Wycherley (1640-1716) (I, 346-82). See also her discussion of John Denham (1615-1669) (I, 237-239) and John Pomfret (1667-1702) (I, 299).

[75]Musgrove, p. 27; Hinman, p. 75.

[76]See Marburg, Sir William Temple and Monk, ed., Five Miscellaneous Essays by Sir William Temple.

[77]Hinman, pp. 166-67.

[78]For an attempt to define the hairline that separates Stoic from Epicurean thoughts on retirement, see Rostvig, I, 53 ff. These philosophical distinctions seldom troubled men of letters.

[79]See Monk, pp. viii, xxiv.

[80]The following evaluation of Temple is by a nineteenth-century historian, George William Prothero: "He was debarred both by his virtues and his defects--by his impartiality, his honesty, and his want of ambition--from taking an active part in the disgraceful politics of his time. But in the foreign relations of his country he was intimately concerned for a period of fourteen years, and in all that is praiseworthy in

them he had a principal hand.  He cannot be called great, but
he will be remembered as one of the ablest negotiators that
England has produced, and as a public servant who, in an unprin-
cipled age and in circumstances peculiarly open to corruption,
preserved a blameless record" (Ency. Brit., 11th ed.).  His
"want of ambition" and his preference for being good rather
than great place him in the Stoic tradition.

[81]Epist. I.i.13 ff, Satires and Epistles, trans. Bovie.
See Fraenkel, Horace, p. 254 ff, for a discussion of Horace's
Epicureanism.  See Mayo, pp. 90-95, for a discussion of Temple's
"neo-Epicureanism."

[82]Early Essays and Romances, ed. Moore Smith, pp. 29-30.

[83]"The Constant Desperado," Early Essays, p. 42.

[84]See Early Essays, p. 594; Monk, p. xvi.

[85]Works of Sir William Temple, II, 274-312.

[86]"The Lady's New-Year's Gift; or Advice to a Daughter,"
Complete Works, ed. Raleigh, pp. 9-10, 26.

[87]Quoted from The Best of Dryden, ed. Bredvold, pp. 212-
16.

[88]Holroyd, Lytton Strachey, II, 150.

[89]Mark, "The Good Life and the Aging Brain."

[90]Third Part, Section XIII (History of the Royal Society,
ed. Cope and Jones, pp. 342-45).

## Chapter V.  The Law of Nature

If Christians considered Stoicism slightly less reprehensible than Epicureanism, it was partly because the Stoics
believed in a planned universe, ruled by fate--whatever that
might mean.  Stoic peace of mind came as a reward for good conduct, which meant cooperating with the eternal plan, willing
what God willed.  Cooperating with nature's law, even though it
included paying due heed to the physical facts of life, meant,
above all, obeying the unwritten moral laws, which were presumed
to be both universal and obvious--to all right-thinking persons,
that is.  The stumbling block comes, of course, in the definition of a right-thinking person; for when right-thinking people
are the ones who identify ideal moral law (the way things ought
to be) with custom (the way things are), Stoic morality supports
the status quo; but when right thinking persons are rebels who
decide that custom has deviated from the true moral law, Stoic
morality may be used to oppose the system.  The sad fact is that
even if the moral law is by definition supposed to be fixed and
unchanging, the only thing about it that actually remains fixed
is the belief that the law is there.  Over the centuries those
who cling to their unswerving faith in the existence of absolute
moral law find themselves in continual friction not only with
other definitions of the law but also with skeptics who doubt
the existence of absolutes of any kind.  And over the centuries,
for one reason or another, the definition of what the moral law
decrees is continually being refurbished.

At one end of this chapter John Skelton (born around 1460)
gives gratuitous moral advice in the medieval Stoic mode to
Henry VIII, while at the other end George Savile, Marquis of
Halifax (1633-95), mixes Stoicism with skepticism, pragmatism,
and Epicureanism in a way that sometimes looks ahead in the
direction of the Utilitarians, sometimes back toward Skelton.
Yet, with all their differences, both writers insisted there
was an unwritten moral standard by which kings should rule themselves.  Implicit in the work of both is some version of the
following doctrine that Fritz Caspari sets down in connection
with his discussion of Thomas Starkey (1499?-1538).  "The law
in the state corresponds to divine reason in the soul of man;
it is based on universal natural law and is implemented in each
state by a special body of law which corresponds to its particular needs and conditions.  The rulers of the state are not
above but under the law, and it is their duty to administer
it."[1]  In spite of general agreement on the existence of basic
principles, however, Skelton and Halifax were separated by
nearly two centuries during which the moral law had undergone
violent strain.  Where Skelton could base his ideas of the law
on tradition and custom, identifying Christendom with the world,
and never doubting that private morality and political morality
live under the same roof, Halifax's law was becoming amorphous--
even though Halifax insisted it ought to be as obvious to everyone else as it was to him.  Though he gave it such new names as

"reason of state" and "the true interest of the commonwealth,"
frankly putting the good of England rather than the good of
Christendom at the top of his system of priorities and making
religion, in the Machiavellian way, serve the needs of politics,
yet he had not abandoned the belief that his judgments were
based on some absolute standard.

To notice some of the ramifications of ideas about the
law of nature between Skelton and Halifax is not, of course,
to move in a straight line, partly since there is no requirement that the basic assumptions of popular writers be logically
consistent, partly because there were a number of basic assumptions available. Depending on the bias of the individual
writer, the scholastic tradition is sometimes dominant, sometimes the humanistic, sometimes custom, sometimes reason, with
the water occasionally muddied still more by admixtures of fate
and the stars. In some literary works nature, mindful of poetic
justice, rewards the good and punishes the evil, while in other
works the ways of nature (or providence) are inscrutable.
Although the good man always remembers that it is his overriding
duty to find out what the law is and obey it, he also finds that
a law of nature has a certain resemblance to a soap bubble.
Just as a really good one seems to be afloat, it runs into some
obstacle and bursts. When that happens Donne is heard complaining that all coherence is gone or Yeats mourning that things
fall apart.[2]

John Skelton's morality play "Magnificence" (ca. 1515) is
about a king who, having allowed himself to be deluded by false
notions that he can be a law unto himself, is speedily punished by being flung to the bottom of fortune's wheel. Luckily
for him, he reforms soon enough to live the rest of his days in
wealthful felicity. This is a play that teaches the apocryphal,
but nevertheless highly popular, moral that good and bad deeds
will be rewarded with earthly good or bad fortune, a teaching
which has already turned up here and there in Chaucer's "Monk's
Tale" and Lydgate's "Fall of Princes" and which will reappear in
Elizabethan and Jacobean drama, where it is sometimes called
poetic justice. Poets who stop to think twice will occasionally
recall another law, taught by Boethius among others, that
reminds us there is no necessary connection between good fortune and good deeds. Skelton, at one point in his play, takes
note of this Christian-Stoic teaching, making the abstraction
Adversity remark, "Yet sometimes I strike where is none offence,
/ Because I would prove men of their patience." Occasionally,
too, Skelton reminds us in the Boethian way that all fortune
must be accepted as good fortune. For example, Lady Poverty,
when she comes to chasten the king, Magnificence, after his fall
from fortune's wheel, thus advises him: "All that God sendeth,
take it in gre; / For, though you were sometimes of noble
estate, / Now must you learn to beg at every man's gate," advice
which, on the one hand, with its "All that God sendeth, take it
in gre," brings echoes from Hoccleve and from Chaucer's "Clerk's
Tale," and which, on the other, with its, "Now must you learn to

beg at every man's gate," looks ahead to the woes of King Lear.[3]

Success in life when defined Stoically as learning to accept what comes is, however, only a minor theme of the poem, easily drowned out by worldly advice on how to stay on fortune's wheel by learning to play the game correctly. The king, who starts out with the false idea that since he is a king he can forget the rules, has to be taught his proper place in the scheme of things and has to learn which rules apply to him. The framework is the familiar medieval hierarchical universe where everyone has his assigned place and his assigned duties.

An important theme of the play, likewise medieval, is the conflict between reason and fancy, which, in earlier works, was typified by the debates between Alexander and Diogenes, with Alexander, the king, always wanting to follow his unbridled will or fancy while Diogenes, the philosopher, continually tells him that he can be free only if he follows reason. (See p. 53.) In Skelton's play the philosopher, Wealthful Felicity, counsels the king to follow the golden mean, to temper freedom and liberty with reason or measure, to obey the classical rules for the proper use of riches.[4] Magnificence, however, prefers to go with Fancy, who soon delivers him into the hands of Poverty and Adversity. These teach him that since he has broken the rules, he must accept the consequences. This play, however, has a happy ending on earth; for Lady Poverty, with an eye on both worlds, counsels Christian-Stoic patience: "Put your will in his will, for surely it is he / That may restore you again to felicity" (p. 227), by which she means neither Christian felicity in heaven nor Stoic peace of mind but wealthful felicity on earth. Her advice is so successful that at the end of the play Magnificence is once more at the top of fortune's wheel and able to moralize sanctimoniously about mutability.

If Skelton's rules for kings who want to be both happy and wealthy have some classical roots, they nevertheless have a strong medieval flavor. But in the work of Erasmus (1469?-1536) and Thomas More (1478-1535) the classical flavor is becoming more assertive. Both men belong to the long family of Christian humanists whose faith includes an implicit belief in the existence of unwritten moral laws, a dislike for the contemporary habit of equating natural law with what is familiar, and a conviction that the laws of nature can best be discovered by studying the works of selected ancients. As Alexander Pope phrased it, "To copy nature is to copy them." Like such a later humanist as Jonathan Swift, they attacked the perennial worship of pride and greed and tried to persuade the world to follow reason, as they defined it.[5] Since Plato, Cicero, and Seneca were among their favorite mentors, many of their teachings are allied to the Stoic tradition. As satirists Erasmus and More, like Swift, made it plain that they were familiar with the ways of the world and were quite aware that there was little hope of any large improvement, but as idealists they obviously also clung to the ancient belief that through reasonable arguments erring mortals may be persuaded to choose the path that

points toward wisdom and virtue.  As Seneca said, "It is enough
for me if every day I reduce the number of my vices, and blame
my mistakes.  I have not attained to perfect health, nor indeed
shall I attain it" (De Vita Beata, XVII.3-4).  None of the
three was likely to forget that he was a Christian and that
perfect virtue, whether personal or social, is not to be
expected on this earth.  But the impossibility of achieving the
ultimate goal does not mean that all effort is pointless.  In
varying ways they were all involved in the active life of social
duty.  If Erasmus managed to maintain the larger independence of
a citizen of the world, he still thought it worth his while to
write The Education of a Christian Prince.  Fritz Caspari, on
one occasion, goes to far as to say that Erasmus "believed in
the perfectibility of man by his own effort" and "exclaimed that
in our efforts to reach the limits of humanity and approximate
God we should imitate Prometheus."[6]  As Christian humanists,
Erasmus, More, and Swift shared somewhat similar definitions
of reason.  They all believed that essential truths (the moral
laws) are relatively few and relatively easy to comprehend, and
they all disapproved of abstract or theoretical prying into
God's secrets,  Where Erasmus and More ridiculed the complex
speculations of the Scholastic thinkers, Swift made fun of the
mathematicians and theoreticians of his day.  Swift and More,
however, both approved of what they considered useful or practical applications of knowledge--making two blades of grass grow
where one grew before.  Like the Stoics, all three associated
health and happiness with the simple life.  All hated war.  And
all subscribed to the humanistic belief that virtue needs to be
taught.  Their methods of teaching were sometimes direct, sometimes oblique.
     If in the Christian fools at the end of Erasmus's The
Praise of Folly, in the happy citizens of More's Utopia, and
in Swift's Houyhnhnms we are shown some facets of the ideal,
these paragons--whether of faith or of reason--are held up to
us less with the expectation that we will be able to approach
perfection than for the purpose of reminding us what possible
goals there are, of showing us how far we have deviated, and of
pointing us in the right direction.
     A few words about Erasmus are included here mainly as
preamble to a discussion of his friend Thomas More.  The three
works to be mentioned, his Adages, his The Praise of Folly, and
his The Education of a Christian Prince, contain variations on
a number of the same basic ideas, even though in the Adages and
The Christian Prince the teaching is straightforward whlle in
The Praise of Folly we have to adjust to shifting angles of
vision.  His Adages, which was one of his most popular works,
was full of quotations from the classics, including long-
accepted Stoic lessons in fortitude and self-control (see Chapter VI).  But it included as well the standard contemporary
identification of the law of nature with the hierarchical system,
since Erasmus, like many another humanist, was radical only in
certain areas.  The Adages warn us, for instance, against dis-

turbing the fitness of things: "For example, if a wife would rule her husband, if the scholar would teach his master, if the commons would tell their prince, what he had to do, finally if the affection or sensuality would guide reason" (sig. 58[5]).[7]

In The Praise of Folly we are sometimes made to look at ourselves and our distorted system of values from the lofty viewpoint of the Epicurean gods, a rational perspective from which almost all human activity appears laughable. At other times Folly takes the attitude of the experimental scientist, shrewdly describing the way things look to the worldly observer intent on exposing the difference between what men actually do and what they profess to do. She laughs at the folly of war, at the pride of the legendary Stoic wise man, at the vain studies of the scholastic theologians, at the greed of the merchants, at the self-love and worldly pride of kings and courtiers, to mention only a few of her targets. But at the same time, here and there, she gives us oblique glimpses of the ideal. And in spite of her ridicule of Stoic pride, she sometimes assumes the attitude of the Stoic in Horace's Satire III.iii for the purpose of reminding us of the gap between our ideal and our practice.[8] Echoing the popular confrontation between Diogenes and Alexander, she points out to us that we would only revile any wise man who might drop from the sky to tell us "that the person whom the world has accepted as a god and a master is not even a man, because he is driven sheeplike by his passions; that he is the lowest slave, because he willingly serves so many and such base masters" (pp. 37-38).[9] She contrasts the way things are now with the way they were in the golden age when there was no need for such experts in complexity as grammarians, dialecticians, rhetoricians, or lawyers. Then "they had too much piety to search out, with a profane curiosity, the secrets of nature . . . deeming it a sacrilege for mortal man to try to know more than is proper to his station" (p. 44). And at a later point she describes for us the heavy burdens that would rest on the shoulders of a true prince--one reason why there are so few of them. For the true prince, unlike the aforementioned person whom the world accepts as a god and a master, would have to "further the public, not his private, interest and give his mind to nothing except as it concerns the general good" (pp. 93-94). Elsewhere she pretends to argue that we should accept the fact that Jupiter kindly put into our makeup more passion than reason to the end "that the life of mankind should not be sad and harsh," pointing out that in the unequal struggle between reason, imprisoned "in a cramped corner of the head" and the passions which govern all the rest of the body, reason "shouts out her prohibitions" and "dictates formulas of virtue. But the passions simply bid their so-called king go hang himself" (pp. 22-23). All the while, however, we are quite aware that we should reject the easy choice, heeding instead the classical teaching she has just ridiculed, namely that "wisdom is no other than to be governed by reason." Convincing though Folly's

worldly arguments may sound from the experimental point of view
of later times, we are supposed to see through her advice for
getting along in the world as it is and, ideally, to emulate
the Christian fools. But if we are not among the few who are
able to aim at perfection, we can at least try to rule ourselves by reason and concentrate on furthering the public, not
our private, interest.[10]

The Education of a Christian Prince, which emphasizes
social virtue, belongs to the long tradition of books describing the ideal ruler--the political version of the Stoic wise
man--who, because he rules himself by reason and is above selfish personal desires, cannot fail to rule others justly.[11] This
work, like the others mentioned, illustrates that in his social
thinking Erasmus was influenced not only by such Christian
teachers as Aquinas and by such Greeks as Plato, Aristotle, and
Plutarch, but also by such Romans as Cicero and Seneca, Cicero's
De Officiis being one of the many books he edited. Born says
that Erasmus leaned heavily on the philosophy of the later
Stoics because of "the high degree of morality inherent in the
doctrines" and "the universality of its thought" (p. 98). Zanta
emphasizes that Erasmus, like other humanists, was interested in
Stoic morality, not in Stoic metaphysics (pp. 75-94). Some of
his Stoic leanings are suggested by such opinions as that all
men are united by their human nature and that war is contrary
to man's true nature as a reasoning creature.[12]

Erasmus, whose good advice for Christian princes was
echoed hopefully by many another literary man, though largely
ignored by actual princes, was himself something of a Stoic
sage--even if he made no pretence to Stoic equanimity. As an
international scholar and citizen of the world he resembled the
wise man whose home is everywhere. Although he lived in a
Europe that was growing increasingly nationalistic, he continued
to dream the old dream of one world, which for him meant one
Christendom. As often happens to wise men, his allegiance to
the laws of nature (as he defined them) brought him into conflict with those engaged in factional disputes; for, as might
be expected, he communicated best with those who could appreciate his complex mode of thinking. His mixture of Christian
and classical idealism was no more tuned to the actualities of
power politics and ambitious climbing on the wheel of fortune
than such idealism ever is.

Thomas More, who, at the time of writing the Utopia was
thinking along some of the same lines as Erasmus in The Praise
of Folly, gives us ironical pictures of the disparity between
rational, but Utopian, ideals and the foolish ways of the actual
world. Book I, which concentrates on the unpleasant social and
economic condition of contemporary Europe, has this in common
with the final section of Swift's "Modest Proposal" that it
offers some serious half-way reforms that imperfect human beings
might conceivably adopt. Book II describes for us a hypothetical never-never land where reason and common sense dominate as
they never do in the world we know. Although the peaceful,

prosperous, highly regimented, uneventful life of the Utopians, with its quiet pleasures and its avoidance of luxury, presents an old classical and Christian ideal, it is an ideal that has had as little popular appeal as Swift's land of the Houyhn-hnms.[13]

One thing we notice is that the highly disciplined Uto-pians do not feel regimented, since they solve the eternal con-flict between individualism and cooperation in the ideal Christian-Stoic way. The truly reasonable or virtuous person does not desire anything that conflicts with the law of nature (or the will of God). Since the Utopian social system is a better reflection of a rational ideal (of a Christian-humanistic type) than we are ever likely to see on earth, and since most Utopian citizens are truly reasonable, there is no conflict here between social conformity and individual desire. Such a perfect world and such perfect people, as More well knew, are to be found only in Utopia. In the world as we know it, the per-fectly rational wise man is as rare as the Christian saint; and imperfect mortals can hardly expect to build the City of God on earth. The middle position of the Roman Stoics, how-ever, in which we aim as best we can toward the impossible ideal is not excluded.

In the purer air of Utopia where wise men abound it is not necessary to regard life on earth merely as a period of penal servitude. Living according to nature here means living as pleasantly as possible, since Utopian pleasures are harmless ones that do not jeopardize life in the next world. If the Utopians are Epicureans, their Epicureanism is of the long-accepted mixed variety that excludes such notions as a universe ruled by accident or a life that ends with death. As we saw in the last chapter, they had worked out a system whereby every-body--not just the lucky few--could enjoy a semi-Christian, Horatian good life. And since it is Utopia, where all people agree on what they mean by the truth, all agree that the aim of life is the pursuit of happiness and that happiness comes from virtue. "They define virtue to be life ordered according to nature, and that we be hereunto ordained of God. And that he doth follow the course of nature, which in desiring and refus-ing things is ruled by reason."[14] Fortunately, as befits those who live in what may approximate the uncorrupted state of nature that existed in the Golden Age, they are of one mind too on what they mean by virtue and reason, their insights not having dete-riorated as a result of corrupt living.

Although they all agree without difficulty on their defi-nition of reasonable conduct, they do not rely entirely on their own common sense to keep them on the path of virtue. They also rely on tradition and authority.[15] In the beginning King Utopus, the ideal combination of king and wise man, established the commonwealth. Since then the aim of government has been to preserve things exactly as he left them. The Utopians, who do not have the idea that things can be improved by being changed, realize that they have the good life and are content as they are. Since they are not climbing on the wheel of fortune, individuals do not desire greater wealth or power and neither does the country. Since wars are contrary to reason and the laws of nature, they are avoided or quickly terminated.[16] Any device that will end a war quickly is considered reasonable. Prattle about honor is unreasonable.

One problem, that of an expanding population, they solve in a manner that seems reasonable to them--given the Utopian premise that there is only one truth and that the Utopians are always operating in accordance with virtue and reason. Like the conquering Romans, who had argued that the destiny of Rome was the will of God, or the Christians, who believed that the destiny of Christendom was the will of God, or the nineteenth-century imperialists, who talked about the white man's burden, the Utopians, as colonizers, are only doing what seems reasonable to them. Since they do not want anything to change in their own country and therefore have to keep the population stable, they require excess members of the commonwealth to emigrate to neighboring uncultivated areas. When they move into a country that has "much waste and unoccupied ground," they consider that by improving the productivity of the land they are implementing the law of nature; but if the unenlightened inhabitants refuse to accept them peacefully, they then feel justified in using force, no doubt on the theory that those who refuse to cooperate willingly with virtue and reason simply have to be dragged along kicking (p. 70). If that line of reasoning now seems unreasonable, it only means that definitions of reason and virtue change.

Thomas More, who did not, of course, believe that definitions of virtue change, thought that the closer we adhere to first principles, the better. Since he, like other humanists, thought that over the years both church and state had deviated greatly from common sense, he refused to identify certain aspects of the current system with the law of nature, thus putting himself on the same side of the fence as that later humanistic radical, John Milton, when the latter inveighed against the league between error and custom.[18] It was not that More and Milton had the same ideas but that both wanted to get back to reason and the law of nature. Less daring thinkers did as Thomas Elyot did and identified an idealized version of the current system with the way things ought to be.

Since to the Utopians--even if not to Europeans--it was obvious that pride and greed and complexity are contrary to nature, they were happy with their own simple, highly regimented lives. Although all right-thinking members of the commonwealth willingly obeyed the rules, those few who refused to cooperate were speedily punished by the state.[19]

Just as Utopians reduced the commodities of everyday living to the minimum, so they organized their society along far less complicated lines than Europeans did. Their social system, though hierarchical, was hierarchical after the manner of the family and was thus closer to the systems described by

Aristotle or Augustine or Erasmus than to the elaborate system of convoluted interrelationships and hereditary duties that characterized contemporary European society.  Utopian social distinctions, less rigid than those insisted on by many six-teenth-century writers, did not try to maintain that the occu-pation into which one was born should be one's only choice.  In Utopia, for those who could demonstrate ability, there was at least a small opportunity to change one's trade.  Nor did the level-headed Utopians, who had not wandered far from first prin-ciples, require learned legal and religious intermediaries to explicate for them the complexities of truth.  Incidentally, it is worth mentioning that astrology was something they had never heard of.

The unconventional back-to-reason approach of More's Utopia is not the attitude apparent in most sixteenth-century popular writing, since it takes time for unaccustomed ideas to begin fermenting.  The typical sixteenth-century definition of the law of nature is the conservative one given us by Thomas Elyot (c. 1490-1546) in The Book of the Governor (1531), which generally identifies nature with the familiar medieval hierarch-ical system that is often associated with Aquinas.[20]  The elab-orate hierarchical organization was a medieval superstructure, added to a Roman Stoic groundplan that in turn incorporated many ideas from Aristotle.  This Roman or Panaetian-Stoic groundplan is the common variety of Stoicism, propagated by Cicero in his ever-popular Of Duties, a Stoicism that is often nowadays simply called humanism.  To forget that humanism is largely Stoic is to put too heavy an emphasis on Stoicism as individualism and to overlook the fact that the Stoic tradition includes not only the idea of personal allegiance to the higher moral law (variously defined) but also, on occasion, something very like the idea of "my country right or wrong."  It all depends on one's point of view.  Panaetian and Posidonian Stoi-cism, which have tended to promote patriotism (variously defined) as the highest duty, include such ideas as that man is by nature a social animal, that duty to society comes before self interest, that at birth we are assigned a certain social part to play, and that virtue means playing that part to the best of our ability.  The Roman conception of an organic uni-verse--with everything related to everything else--developed in time into the full-fledged medieval conception of a hierarchi-cal universe--with various categories subordinated to one another.[21]  A favorite figure of speech from the organic con-ception compares nature or the state to an animal, a familiar example being the fable of the belly and the members that Shakespeare used in Coriolanus.[22]  This animal comparison con-tinues to occur in sixteenth- and seventeenth-century writing side by side with figures of speech that put heavier emphasis on the hierarchical idea.
Another ancient metaphor, again expressing the idea that

158

universal cooperation (or harmony) is the law of nature, is the one used by Dryden in the first and last stanzas of "A Song for St. Cecilia's Day, 1687." A variation of this metaphor appears in John Davies's Orchestra (1596). Here virtuous action means participating in the harmonious dance of the universe. In Davies's poem, Antinous attempts to persuade the chaste Penelope that joining in a dance would be an act of virtue, an obedience to universal law, since dancing, "a moving all in measure" (st. 23), began with the birth of time and will last as long as time. Generated by love, it keeps all parts of the physical world moving in concord--the wheeling stars, the jarring elements. And when the dancing stars return at last to "the points whence first their movings were, . . . The axletree of heaven shall break in twain" (st. 36), or, as Dryden phrases it, the trumpet of doom "shall untune the Sky."[24] The Christian implication that the end of the cycle (sometimes called the Platonic year) will coincide with the end of the world is a modification of the older idea of repeating cycles of time, which will be revived by such later poets as Shelley and Yeats. Davies, like most Christians and like Cicero, makes disparaging allusions to the Epicurean teaching that everything is compacted of "undivided motes" that "concur by chance" (st. 20), and follows Cicero in employing a Stoic argument from design of the kind usually associated with the eighteenth century. He compares the universe to a clock, as well as to a dance, as he sets forth the accepted doctrine that reason, not chance, "the first impulsive cause and mover was" (st. 115; see also 116). Whether the universe is seen as a great dance, however, or as a great animal or a great chain, the moral is always the same: cooperation is the law of nature.

Cooperation, or duty, was the lesson Thomas Elyot taught. Since he was not one who believed in fighting windmills, he accommodated himself to the fact that most people identified the way things ought to be with custom. Instead of trying to convert the aristocracy to a life of plain living and high thinking, he concentrated on reminding the men at the top that their birth had assigned them duties of civic responsibility that required an appropriate education. It had always been a Stoic doctrine that virtue needs to be taught. Though men born at the top were presumably endowed at birth with more potential virtue and better insight into truth than those lower on the scale, still their natural gifts might be corrupted by a poor education. When Elyot said, "God gyueth nat to euery man like gyftes of grace, or of nature, but to some more, some lesse, as it liketh his diuine maiestie" (p. 4), he was not preaching egalitarianism. He was merely saying that it was natural for those at the top to be better endowed than those at the bottom.[26]

Since virtue means living in accordance with the laws of nature (pp. 62, 209), the gentleman must be instructed in what these laws are.[27] Because Elyot blandly assumed there was no conflict between the laws of nature, the wisdom of the ancients,

and the contemporary system, he recommended that a modern
gentleman be educated through the study of such writers as
Plato, Aristotle, Cicero, Seneca, and Erasmus.[28] Like Erasmus's
Education of a Christian Prince, which was one of his source
books, Elyot's The Book of the Governor was another in the long
line of descendants of Cicero's Of Duties, updating Cicero and
Aquinas by giving us the recipe for the ideal gentleman--
sixteenth-century version.[29] Like other moralists of his time,
Elyot, who identified the good Christian with the good citizen,
hoped to persuade the men in power to put duty to the state
above personal ambition. Though it is obvious that what moralists preached and what courtiers practised were not necessarily
the same, nevertheless, when we consider the popularity of
Elyot's work, we can assume that what he was saying was what
people liked to hear.

Under a moral system that assumes the heavenly computers
have already assigned every person to an appropriate place and
that defines virtue as doing the job nearest us, there is no
need to worry about developing our hidden potentialities. Such
qualities as ambition, covetousness, desire to build up our own
self-importance are contrary to reason and nature, not to mention being likely to upset the applecart. The same lessons that
are taught learnedly by Elyot are illustrated through specific
examples in the Mirror for Magistrates. From stories about the
lives of famous Englishmen who came to grief, magistrates could
learn the danger of following their own inclinations instead of
the moral law.[30] Although a number of stories in the Mirror
still attribute catastrophe to the blind workings of fortune,
the authors emphasize poetic justice whenever they can find
any.[31] Even if it is a general rule that anyone at the top of
the wheel is likely to find himself suddenly at the bottom,
simply because it is axiomatic that high places are the most
vulnerable (p. 87, lines 93-97; p. 445, lines 1-7), the Mirror
also preaches that those who reach the top by "high clymyng,
brybyng, murdring, lust and pryde" (p. 84, line 49) are especially likely to be thrown down.[32] It is no accident that first
among the sins listed is high climbing, since nothing is so
likely to unbalance the hierarchical system as everyone's wanting to play first fiddle. The rebellious blacksmith, one high
climber who fell from the ladder, dutifully recited the lesson
his fall had taught him, "Was never rebell before the world, nor
since, / That could or shall preuayle agaynst his prynce" (p.
409, lines 190-96). A little earlier he had also moralized that
no one can rule in a commonwealth who has not first learned to
rule himself (p. 407, lines 134-40). A prose section addressed
to the reader emphasizes that the way things are is the way God
wants them to be, "In my iudgement there is no mean so good
either for the common quyet of the people, or for gods free
choyse, as the naturall ordre of enheritauns by lineal dyscent:
for so it is left in gods handes, to creat in the wombe what
prince he thinketh metest for his purposes" (p. 419, lines 9-
18).

When kings are brought low, it requires only a little inge-
uity to discover that somewhere along the line they have sinned
against nature.  James IV of Scotland, killed at the battle of
Flodden, is made to confess that "Both law, and nature doth me
accuse / Of great vnkindnes: that I should take part / Against
my brother, and his liege refuse" (p. 484, lines 26-28).  Richard III, now living in hell "whereas is no order" is characterized as having been in life "disorderly and vnnatural" (p. 371,
lines 8-11, 22-24).[33]

Although in the Mirror as in Chaucer's "Wife of Bath's
Tale" and Elyot's Book of the Governor one finds an occasional
expression of the apparently egalitarian idea that a virtuous
man is a natural gentleman, "All be he poore as Iob" (p. 123,
lines 50-56), it is not safe to assume that superior moral
virtue justifies anyone in moving out of line.  It merely means
that the true gentleman is the one who knows his place and who
is sufficiently rewarded by the consciousness that he is carrying
out the will of God.  Again we are encountering the old Boethian moral that success in life means a contented heart, not
necessarily a full coffer.  The ideas in the Mirror do not
startle in the way those in the Utopia do.  If there is, as
Farnham suggests, less emphasis than in medieval works on the
seemingly arbitrary wheel of fortune and more on the idea that
worldly misfortune comes as a punishment for misdeeds, the
change indicates that the authors of the Mirror were less sophisticated as thinkers than Boethius.  Sophisticated or not,
their stories were popular.  Theodore Spencer says at least
thirty Elizabethan plays took their plots from the Mirror (pp.
62-63).  These plays demonstrate again and again the havoc
caused by those who try to defy current interpretations of the
laws of nature.

Seneca's plays, likewise contain expressions of the oft-
repeated moral that to be a good governor one must first have
learned to rule oneself.  Agamemnon in Trojan Women states the
theme that echoes through many an Elizabethan work:

> Never has for long
> Unbridled power been able to endure,
> But lasting sway the self-controlled enjoy.
> The higher fortune raises human hopes,
> The more should fortune's favourite control
> His vaulting pride, and tremble as he views
> The changing fates of life, and fear the gods
> Who have uplifted him above his mates.
> By my own course of conquest have I learned
> That mighty kings can straightway come to naught.[34]

Gorboduc (1561-2) shows us the tragedy that results when
kings forget the laws of nature, letting will have control
instead of reason.  The old king in this play goes against
nature by abdicating power to his sons before the proper time,
i.e., his death.  The sons, in the first place, are too young
to rule.  (The recent reign of Edward VI had proved no excep-

tion to the medieval adage: Unhappy the kingdom ruled by a
child.)  Secondly, the king upsets the fitness of things by
giving the younger child a share of what the older considers
his by right.  The total result is chaos: resentment by the
older, ambition on the part of the younger, civil war, brother
murdering brother, a mother murdering her son, the people murdering the king and queen.  Throughout the play wise coun-
selors underscore the moral: In Act I the king is reminded
"That Nature hath her ordre and her course, / Which being broken doth corrupt the state" (I.ii.218-222; see also 156-60,
330-332; and V.i.1-7).  At the end of Act III the chorus
laments the consequences of uncontrolled passion, "No rule of
reason, no regarde of right. / No kindely loue, no feare of
heauens wrath" (Chorus, 2-3).[35]

This play, like many another, exhibits various old but
interesting confusions.[36]  It suggests that a moral law of
nature, less firm than a physical law, can temporarily be broken.  Although no one so far has broken the physical law that
all men are mortal, unnatural people often tamper successfully
with the ideal moral system--which in Elizabethan times was
usually the hierarchical system.  In Elizabethan plays nature or
providence usually restores the proper balance in due time, but
sometimes not before there have been violent upheavals.  Once
due order has been disarranged, anyone is likely to be injured--
the innocent as well as the guilty, since the total plan is more
important than any person.  Although it sometimes happens in
popular works that nature or providence is made to operate as an
obvious instrument of moral correction--punishing the bad and
rewarding the good--it sometimes also happens that nature operates in the Boethian way, according to inscrutable laws of her
own that seem to disregard the individual.[37]

The doctrine that the way things are is the way God wants
them to be and that any disarrangement of the established system constitutes a violation of the law of nature is obviously
a way of defending the status quo and is not a doctrine that a
reformer like Milton will be willing to accept.  Nor is the
uncritical doctrine of a popular playwright to be confused with
the thoughtful treatment found in Richard Hooker's Of the Laws
of Ecclesiastical Polity (1593).  Hooker's concern as a theologian was to justify the Church of England not only as an established fact of life but also as a manifestation of reason and
the law of nature.  C. S. Lewis calls the work "the fullest and
most beautiful expression" of the medieval conception of natural
law.[38]  In addition to carrying on the system of Aquinas,
Hooker's work helped provide a bridge between the natural law
of the Middle Ages and the natural law of the eighteenth century.  By modifying or simplifying the system so as to distinguish, in the old Stoic way, between things essential and things
indifferent, Hooker not only made it possible to justify a
national church but also provided a means whereby the church and
the state after the civil war could adjust themselves to changed
conditions without having to cut all ties with the past.[39]  Just

as the Romans had transformed universal natural law into the
destiny of Rome and the Christians had changed the destiny of
Rome into the destiny of Christendom, so, with the breakup of
Christendom into national states and national churches, each
nation was seeking to prove it was still conforming to cosmic
reason.  Richard Hooker provided the necessary blueprint for
the English church.

This preamble does not mean to imply that Hooker was any
more hypocritical than the rest of us.  It merely illustrates
the powerful desire we have to justify what we do in terms of
a universal moral law.  Though ingenuity can always find a way
of interpreting the law to fit the facts, the belief that it is
necessary to do so at least slows down the eternal rush toward
chaos--just as faith in a grammar book slows the rate of language change.

Hooker, like others who belonged to the Thomistic-
Ciceronian tradition, saw the universe, as C. S. Lewis has
remarked, as a constitutional monarchy.  Neither an arbitrary
God nor an arbitrary king belonged to the proper nature of
things.  Consequently, the first book of Ecclesiastical Polity
develops the argument that everywhere in the universe there is
law: God has set laws for himself, which he obeys.  Angels have
laws.  Nature has laws.  The laws of nature, under whose juris-
diction man comes, are discoverable through the light of reason,
and ought to be obeyed--if one is wise.  "Obedience of creatures
unto the law of nature is the stay of the whole world" (I.iii.
2).[40]

In answer to the usual question about how we can be sure
what the law decrees, Hooker follows the tradition of Aquinas
which says only God and the angels have an infallible insight
into what the law really says.  Men always have to operate in
something of a fog.  To help them they have, on the one hand,
divine law, known through revelation, which they must accept
on faith, and, on the other hand, they have laws concocted by
human beings (positive law).  Although these human laws ought,
ideally, to be based on the law of nature, there is always the
possibility that somewhere along the line a slip occurred.
Hooker describes human law as "that which out of the law either
of reason or of God, men probably gathering to be expedient,
they make it a law" (I.iii.1).[41]  Men, not being infallible,
did the best they could, used what helps they could, "probably gathered."  Hooker, like the Roman Stoics, thought of the
wise man in actual life as someone only travelling toward the
distant goal of mathematical perfection.  Though all men needed
education and instruction in order to develop their "natural
faculty of reason" (I.vi.5), wise men were raised above other
men "by proceeding in the knowledge of truth, and by growing
in the exercise of virtue" so that they aspired "to the greatest conformity with God" (I.v.3).  Hooker leaves open the question of how virtuous a person has to be before he can safely
consider himself self directed, saying, "At what time a man may
be said to have attained so far forth the use of reason as

sufficeth to make him capable of those Laws whereby he is then
bound to guide his actions; this is a great deal more easy for
common sense to discern, than for any man by skill and learning
to determine" (I.vi.5).

In this reliance on common sense, Hooker adopts the usual
Stoic maneuver, giving us a classic restatement of Cicero's
recipe for recognizing universal truth.  If one happens to be
one of those rare beings--like Adam before the Fall or an inhabitant of More's Utopia--with an uncorrupted mind and mature
judgment, one need only be exposed to truth to detect it.  The
laws of reason, Hooker says,

> are investigable by Reason, without the help of Revelation super-
> natural and divine. . . . The knowledge of them is general, the
> world hath always been acquainted with them; according to that which
> one in Sophocles observeth concerning a branch of this Law, 'It is no
> child of to-day's or yesterday's birth, but hath been no man knoweth
> how long sithence.'  It is not agreed upon by one, or two, or few, but
> by all.  Which we may not so understand, as if every particular man in
> the whole world did know and confess whatsoever the Law of Reason doth
> contain; but this Law is such that, being proposed, no man can reject
> it as unreasonable and unjust.  Again, there is nothing in it but any
> man (having natural perfection of wit and ripeness of judgment) may by
> labour and travail find out" (I.viii.9).

In other words, if a wise man, someone "having natural perfection of wit and ripeness of judgment," discovers a law of nature
and proposes it for general acceptance, the law--if it is a true
one--will immediately appear reasonable and just to other people.  Unfortunately, as Milton found when he tried to argue that
divorce for incompatibility was only reasonable and just, familiar ideas are more likely to sound reasonable and just than
unfamiliar ones.  In Hooker's time, the law of nature was generally identified with the hierarchical system, which system
Hooker probably had in mind when he stressed the need for a
sense of proportion and "the knowledge of that which man is in
reference unto himself, and other things in relation unto man"
(I.viii.6).  Hooker did not, however, find it necessary to
spell out the system in all the minute detail employed by other
writers of the period.  Though he assumed such general proposi-
tions as that the spirit was superior to the body and man superior to woman, he avoided becoming excessively specific.  Like
Thomas More he used the old ideas with something approaching
eighteenth-century freedom, emphasizing the importance of being
able to distinguish between things essential and things indifferent, a qualification that left plenty of leeway for new
interpretations.

Richard Hooker's scholarly thinking was, of course, for
other scholars.[42]  It is unlikely that writers of imaginative
works sat mulling over his judicious explanations with the
intention of putting them into their plays and stories.  In
fact, there were only a few popular writers who indicated an
awareness that the law of nature is a ticklish concept.  It is

interesting, for example, to contrast the conventional political attitudes that Philip Sidney (1554-86) revealed in the
Arcadia with the more skeptical and pragmatic ones of his
friend Fulke Greville, Lord Brooke (1554-1628).  Although they
both agreed that an ideal system would follow the patterns laid
down by Cicero, Erasmus, and Elyot, Sidney was much more optimistic than Greville about the possibility that such ideals might
be approached on earth.  The Arcadia illustrates his humanistic
faith that virtue can be taught and repeats some of the same
lessons that appeared in Gorboduc.  There is the same emphasis
on social responsibility and on playing our assigned roles,
the same exemplification of the chaos that results when a king
puts private peace of mind ahead of duty to society.  One major
cause of the trouble in the Arcadia is that the elderly King
Basilius has been unwilling to accept his fate, which is another
way of saying that he does not want to submit his will to the
will of God.  In an effort to avoid a prophecy, he leaves his
throne and goes off to live the simple pastoral life.  Such a
choice, as Aquinas had pointed out and as Elizabethan literature reminds us over and over again, is not permissible for
kings.  He soon becomes an example of the adage that a king who
fails to rule himself in accordance with the laws of nature
cannot rule others.  For not only does he neglect his kingdom,
he puts his personal desires ahead of the good of his family
and lets his passions win such ascendency over his reason that
he develops an insane and ridiculous infatuation for the young
Prince Pyrocles disguised in woman's dress.  Meanwhile, his
middle-aged wife, whose ingrained female tendency toward wil-
fulness had been kept in check as long as her husband was exercising proper authority, has so far lost her sense of the fitness of things that she too has become enamored of Pyrocles,
whom she recognizes to be a man.  Though she cannot govern herself, she can still lecture her husband:  "Remember the wrong
you have done is not onely to me, but to your children, whom
you had of mee: to your countrey, when they shall finde thei
are commanded by him, that can not commaund his owne undecent
appetites: lastly to your selfe, since with these paynes you do
but build up a house of shame to dwell in."[43] Parents led
astray by their own passions cannot be expected to set a fit
example for their children.  Paragons of virtue though Pamela
and Philoclea are, even they toy briefly with the idea of
marrying without parental consent.  The disorder, in addition
to infecting the royal family, has spread throughout the commonwealth, with ambitious nobles causing peasant uprisings and
civil wars.  Chaos everywhere.

In contrast to Basilius, who let personal desire interfere
with duty, Sidney introduces King Euarchus, an ideal ruler of
the sort that Aquinas or Erasmus could have approved.  In addition to being the father and uncle of the two cousins, Pyrocles
and Musidorus, Euarchus is a literary descendant of the good
king Theseus in Chaucer's "Knight's Tale," somewhat as Pyrocles
and Musidorus, like Chaucer's Palamon and Arcite, are ideal

young courtly heroes. One consequence of the general moral confusion is that the young heroes find themselves, toward the end
of the story, in trouble with the law, while King Euarchus,
thought to be an impartial outsider, is appointed their judge.
When he discovers their identity, instead of disqualifying himself, he subordinates his private feelings to selfless abstract
justice: "Euarchus that felt his owne miserie more then they,
and yet loved goodnesse more then himselfe withall, when he had
heard the uttermost of that their speach tended unto: he com-
maunded againe they should be carried away" (II, 204). Although
he finds them guilty because he judges as well as a good man
can--using the light of reason alone--he is only human, with
the usual imperfect human insight into truth. He is not in command of all the facts. Fortunately for him, providence inter-
feres before harm is done, arousing the supposedly dead Basilius from his drugged sleep and opening his eyes not only to
the light of day but also to a proper sense of proportion.
Quickly straightening out the tangled plot, Basilius returns to
his throne to carry out his assigned duty.

Sidney's conception of a well-run commonwealth is closer
to the ideals of Thomas Elyot than to the Utopia of Thomas More.
Here, as in Chaucer's "Knight's Tale," war is a noble exercise,
with no hint of the Utopian suggestion that war is contrary to
nature. Nor is there any of the Utopian dislike of magnificent display, since Sidney obviously accepts it as axiomatic
that we can tell who the important people are by looking at
their fine clothes.[44] Similarly, there is no social mobility;
shepherds who know their places are noble shepherds, while
clowns with unsuitable notions of self importance are automatically ridiculous.

Though we do not know whether Fulke Greville in youth
shared Sidney's faith that virtue can be taught, we do know that
his many years of practical experience in the conduct of government eroded whatever illusions he might once have had about
man's ability to construct and maintain a just society on earth.
His plays, which reflect his political thinking, give us no
glimpse either of a Utopia where reason actually rules or of an
Arcadia where it may conceivably be reinstated. We are shown
only disintegrating societies where a temporary equilibrium,
achieved by compromising with principle, is the most that can
be expected. Although Greville is sometimes described as a
Machiavellian, because of his practical approach to politics,
sometimes as a Calvinist, because of his doubts about man's
ability to help himself, sometimes as an Augustinian, because
of his awareness that life on earth is intended as a period of
penal servitude, we may also notice that he has affinities with
the tradition of Boethius.[45] Unlike many of the popular writers of his time, he does not illustrate poetic justice in oper-
ation and does not believe that the ways of providence are easy
for man to comprehend. As he says, in A Treatie of Warres,
"In this spheare, this wildernesse of euils, / None prosper
highly, but the perfect diuels" (st. 63).[46] Like Augustine and

like Erasmus's Folly, he puts the golden age firmly in the past, before the fall; "for surely, if it had beene Gods intent / To giue Man here eternally possession, / Earth had beene free from all misgouernment. / Man (as at first) had bin mans nursing brother, / And not, as since, One Wolfe unto another" (st. 45).[47]

Like Boethius, and like Seneca, he continually reminds us that the wheel of mutability is part of the total inscrutable plan.[48] He says, in A Treatie of Warres, that all states "haue their growing, and declining states, / Which with time, place, occasion bounded are" (st. 39). Men go round and round on the wheel of fortune--beggars growing rich, rich men poor, kings becoming school masters, a potter a king (st. 40); and God "sends War, commotion, tumult, strife, / Like windes and stormes, to purge the ayre and earth; / Disperse corruption, giue the World new life" (st. 43). For "euen in Warre, the perfect type of hell; / See we not much more politicke celerity, / Diligence, courage, constancy excell, / Than in good Arts of peace or piety?" (st. 29). Moreover, if one kingdom should flourish forever and one family reign forever, and one people have peace, and nobility, if authority, prosperity, and gain should remain fixed "and not endure vicissitudes of Fate" (st. 35), "God would in time seeme partiall vnto some" (st. 36) and the weeds of peace "would ruine Nature, and Men monsters make" (st. 37). In other words, like Boethius he believes that the workings of evil serve an ultimate purpose and that in the end they "proue to the good but like those showres of raine, / Which, while they wet the husbandman, yet multiply his gaine."[49]

His explanation of Sidney's purpose in the Arcadia, whether or not it actually was Sidney's intent, gives us a clue to what he himself was trying to do, in a more limited way, in his own plays. He says Sidney was trying "to represent the growth, state, and declination of Princes, change of Government, and lawes: vicissitudes of sedition, faction, succession, confederacies, plantations, with all other errors, or alterations in publique affaires."[50] In Greville's plays the emphasis is on showing political conditions that have led to chaos. There are no representations of ideal rulers, no suggestions that providence will provide solutions. The plays end with the survivors stumbling along, in the human way, as best they can. In Mustapha the country is ruled by a tyrant, in Alaham by a weak king; in both the failures of the rulers have caused the mob to rise in revolt. Both plays end with a wise counselor deciding, for the good of the country, to oppose the mob and try to shore up the regal power, not because the monarchical form of government necessarily conforms best to the law of nature but because in the present situation it is most likely to promote the greatest good of the greatest number. As Achmat says in Mustapha, "Whether our choyce, or Nature gaue vs Kings, / The end of either was the good of all" (V.iii.84-88). Achmat makes his decision on utilitarian grounds. And in Alaham the

Chorus of People at the end of Act IV defends adherence to the moral law as the best policy, for when the leaders disregard virtue--e.g., when a son revolts against his father--the people are taught to do likewise and to rebel. Similarly, Greville, in his comments on Sidney's Arcadia, considers Basilius' retirement to be ill advised from the practical point of view; for the king, by removing himself from his kingly "pomp and apparatus," is likely to become a creature of scorn, vulnerable both to domestic discontent and to the ambition of foreign powers (Smith, pp. 13-14). Nor, from the standpoint of what might be expected, does Greville think it likely that such a wise and disinterested prince as Euarchus would arrive in the country. The more probable outcome would be the arrival of some prince willing to take personal advantage of the internal confusion. In other words, if the Arcadia had ended the way Greville's plays end, there would have been no providential happy ending.

Turning from politics to private virtue, Greville says that in the Arcadia Sidney would also represent "in the subjects case; the state of favor, disfavor, prosperitie, adversity, emulation, quarrell, undertaking, retiring, hospitality, travail, and all other moodes of private fortunes, or misfortunes" (Smith, pp. 15-16). It is these "moodes of private fortunes, or misfortunes," especially misfortunes, that concern Greville in his unfinished A Letter to an Honourable Lady. The problem of the relation between justice and power is universal, the same one that troubled Boethius. As Greville says, in this world, where written (or positive) law is generally preferred to unwritten equity, where custom takes precedence over the law of nature, where strength is more important than right (Grosart, III, 269), the chief remedy for the weak who are unjustly treated by the strong is the consolation of philosophy. In the case under discussion, the tyrannical husband who is mistreating his wife is condoned by society because he has strength on his side. The powerless wife is advised by Greville, on the one hand, not to try to imitate her husband or to usurp his authority because "it is most true that ages and sexes haue their distinct lawes" (p. 247), and, on the other hand, to remember that the time when "the vnwritten lawes blot out the written" will not come in this life (p. 267). Having pointed out to her that since she is weak she will be wise not to tamper with decorum, he then devotes most of the letter to the kind of lessons in Christian-Stoic patience that are frequently given to those who have no other choice.

Greville's tough practical insistence on trying to make the best of a bad situation that will never become permanently better sets him apart from the idealism of most writers in the humanistic tradition. When we turn to his contemporary, Edmund Spenser (1552-1599) we are back again in the fictional world where those who have been properly educated in virtue are likely to triumph over the vicious. Although the heroes of The Faerie Queene are only now and then concerned with social problems, the social world when it does appear is, of course, the familiar

hierarchical world where virtue means doing our duty as members
of the established order. A well-known identification of nature
with the customary system occurs in Book V where the just hero
Artegall maintains the status quo against a rabble-rousing giant
who is trying heretically to argue that justice means dividing
all things equally.[51] Artegall, like Thomas Elyot, et al,
explains that the existing system is a manifestation of the
will of God and should be left alone. In line with Hooker and
Aquinas, Artegall points out that since the giant, unlike God,
cannot pretend to have unclouded insight into all the minute
workings of the universe, he should leave alone things that he
cannot hope to understand (V.ii.32 ff).

If virtue means supporting things as they are, it is
obvious that we should all study to be content with our assigned
lots. Cooperation is a virtue; self-aggrandizement a vice.
The chain of ambition in Book II (vii.46) reaches from heaven to
hell. Those who think they can reach an earthly heaven by
climbing the golden chain are much more likely to find they have
slipped down to eternal hell. An unnatural woman is, by definition, one who does not know her place; such a one for instance,
is Radegund, in Book V, who should have realized that it is
improper for women to wage aggressive war. Anyone who neglects
due order as flagrantly as she does can be expected to be
untrustworthy in all areas. She defeats Artegall only by fighting unfairly; then, while she is holding him prisoner, she
defies the unwritten law (the gentleman's code) by making her
knightly captive do woman's work. In the just universe of The
Faerie Queene, it is not to be anticipated that providence will
allow such an imbalance to continue long, and shortly thereafter
justice is restored. Meanwhile Artegall, like Sidney's heroes
and heroines in prison, has an opportunity to strengthen his
fortitude with Stoic maxims of the Senecan type (V.v.38). (See
Chapter VI.)

Shakespeare was another for whom morality customarily
meant playing one's assigned role. The familiar discussions of
Shakespeare and the Stoicism of Seneca that focus on Stoicism
as self-sufficiency should not make us forget that the common
form of Stoicism in Shakespeare's time was that of Cicero's Of
Duties--with its sundry accretions.[52] Before concentrating on
that topic, however, it is necessary to look at some of the
related issues that cloud the picture. First among these is the
problem of fate--its significance and its relation to the law of
nature. As noted in earlier chapters, popular usage gave the
term an imprecise meaning, often interchanging it with the word
"fortune." Although like fortune it was presumed to be an
instrument of providence and to act only in accordance with the
overall plan, nevertheless from the point of view of the individual it often seemed to act as a mischievous or malignant
free agent. In Romeo and Juliet fate behaves as arbitrarily as
chance in a Hardy novel, despite the pious attempts of the
friar to prove that everything is for the best. In this play
we faintly suspect Shakespeare of using the irony of fate

as one means of justifying all the plot's improbable tragic
coincidences, much as Molière in L'Avare gaily caps the absurd
series of coincidences that conclude his comedy by having someone marvel over the power of heaven to work miracles.  Although
the tension is hieghtened if we think of Romeo and Juliet as
star-crossed lovers, the rest of the plot makes it clear that the
lovers are not entirely fate driven and that Shakespeare does
not blame every gory detail in the play on benevolent providence.  If everyone were fate driven, the warring factions would
be as helpless as Romeo and Juliet, which means that the sacri-
ficial victims could have no influence on the future course of
events.  Instead of assuming that Shakespeare is attributing
everything to the stars, we must conclude that he is merely
introducing a little popular astrology as seasoning.

The following quotation from Walter Ralegh's History of
the World (1614) shows how a thoughtful Christian might try to
reconcile some of the logical conflicts caused by faith in the
stars:

> But in this question of fate, the middle course is to be followed:
> that as with the heathen we do not bind God to his creatures, in this
> supposed necessity of destiny; so on the contrary, we do not rob
> these beautiful creatures [the stars] of their powers and uses.  For
> had any of those second causes despoiled God of his prerogative, or
> had God himself constrained the mind and will of man to impious acts
> by any celestial enforcement, then sure the impious execution [i.e.,
> wicked inclinations] of some were justifiable.  But that the stars
> and other celestial bodies incline the will by mediation of the sensi-
> tive appetite, which is also stirred by the complexion, it cannot be
> doubted. . . . The heavenly bodies . . . make in us habits, complex-
> ions, and dispositions. . . . But that either the stars or the sun
> have any power over the minds of men immediately it is absurd to
> think, other than as aforesaid, as the same by the body's temper may
> be affected.[53]

As Ralegh's remarks indicate, the matter of starry influence leads to the question of the relation between fate and free
will, on which subject Shakespeare's stand, though conventional,
is not necessarily clear.[54]  Since complex theological explanations were no doubt as confusing to theatre goers of Shakespeare's time as they were to Chaucer's Troilus, Shakespeare
leaves them alone.  It was enough that the experts had proved
that although a good providence has everything carefully planned,
nevertheless we are still responsible for our own behavior.
Though villains like Edmund in Lear or Cassius in Julius Caesar,
who insist they are not ruled by the stars, are obviously mistaken and turn out to be more star-driven than they had
thought, yet they are also made to answer for their misdeeds and
not allowed to blame their wrongdoing on the eternal plan.[55]

With Shakespeare as with others, "fate" is an ambiguous
word with many meanings, some Stoic, some not.  When fate is
identified with mischievous fortune or with the avenging furies
or with some vague malignant power with a petty interest in

detail, it is not necessarily Stoic. However, when fate is
another name for the orderly process of nature, "unalterable
law," the agent of a benevolent master plan from which there
is no escape, it has some Stoic antecedents.[56] This plan,
which governs the course of history as well as the lives of
individuals, can be temporarily disrupted, even though it cannot be permanently altered. The individual who is pulverized
in the machinery may take Boethian comfort from the thought
that his misfortunes are a necessary part of the total incom-
prehensible picture. However, this sort of Job's comfort is
a last resort that Shakespeare generally avoids, preferring
where possible to identify the law of nature with the current
system and to show some connection, however tenuous, between
violation of the law and misfortune. Even at his most pessimistic, as in _Lear_ or _Troilus_ _and_ _Cressida_ or _Timon_ _of_ _Athens_
he does not completely abandon the idea that the law is clear,
even though harsh. At times the punishment for violation seems
excessive to those of us who are tender hearted and who think
fate should have taken extenuating circumstances into account.
We dislike seeing innocent people caught in the catastrophe
and sympathize more with the sufferers than with the system.
But the law seems to be that the system must go on. Meanwhile,
the individual, whether Christian or Stoic, can theoretically
find ultimate reward in his own virtue.

And so we return to the idea that virtue means playing our
assigned role, which is another way of saying that all the
world's a stage. Somewhat illogically, however, the assignment
of roles usually applies to a social niche rather than to a
moral niche--even if some people, especially bastards, seem to
have been assigned the moral role of villains. Since villains
are generally punished for persisting in their seemingly
ingrained villainy, the presumption is that they were originally free to be virtuous if they had made the necessary extra
effort. To want to change one's social role, however, is reprehensible. A king, who has been assigned at birth to the role
of active leader, may not choose for himself the vocation of
scholar. A good general may not aspire to become a king. A
servant must never put his own interests ahead of his master's.
A wife must remember that her husband's will is the law.[57]

Over and over again we watch the tragic consequences of
violating the social order. _Richard_ _II_ and the _Henry_ _VI_ plays
show us what happens when a king fails to behave like a king,
thus tempting ambitious subjects to move out of place. Though
Henry VI might have preferred to be a saint instead of a ruler,
he was not free to change his role. He was free only to will
what God willed. Richard II, in a different way, also lost his
sense of proportion. Like Skelton's Magnificence, he forgot
that though a king he was only a part of the social organism,
with the result that when he failed to rule himself, attempting
instead to make his own will into the law, he came tumbling
down. It was after he had neglected his duty that he tried to
console himself with what are often called Senecan platitudes,

telling himself that having lost his kingdom he would now have
less care, that he could still be as great as Bolingbroke by
serving God (or virtue), that his rebellious subjects had
revolted against God in revolting against their king, that there
is no evil to him who has learned that death is no evil (III.
ii.92-103).[58] Had Richard been someone lower on the social
scale, one whose main function was to learn to be content, these
sentiments would have been praiseworthy. Though Richard
deserved to be punished, yet Bolingbroke, the instrument, was
not excused for his part in unsettling due order. In addition
to causing him personal loss of peace of mind, his ambition
ultimately brought calamity to the whole country; and even
though it took nearly a century of civil war for nature or the
master plan to regain control, nature had the last word. If
innocent people were crushed in the process, that was only to
be expected.

Over and over the pattern is repeated. Order is violated;
chaos results; nature (or providence) restores order. Sometimes, as in Richard III or Macbeth, the focus is on the dis-
rupter, sometimes, as in Romeo and Juliet, on the innocent
victims. In Romeo and Juliet the political chaos in Verona is
the major cause of the tragedy; for here as in Gorboduc and in
Sidney's Arcadia, disorder in the state has the side effect of
contributing to disorder in the individual. Romeo and Juliet,
far more than the young lovers in the Arcadia, forget that reason should guide the passions and that children should obey
their parents. By giving way to passion and by marrying without parental consent, they neglect due order and thus make themselves especially vulnerable to fate or fortune.

As we watch inexperienced youth defying the system, we
always hope that they may for once succeed, though we know in
our bones that they will fail. Shakespeare, like Chaucer,
teaches us the received doctrine while at the same time making
us sympathize with some of those who take chances with the law.
His Brutus in Julius Caesar is another example. From the highest motives, Brutus makes the wrong choice. As the play unfolds
we realize that he is making the mistake of trying to divert the
destiny of Rome; for in this case, as it turns out, Antony and
Octavius are on the side of history. Idealistic though Brutus
is, his insight into the designs of destiny is imperfect.
Guided too much by reason alone, he manifests Stoic pride and
deludes himself with the belief that he understands truth.

This play illustrates the way different aspects of Stoicism
can conflict with one another. The acceptable Elizabethan kind,
which emphasizes conformity to the status quo and selfless performance of duty, is found side by side with the unacceptable
brand, labeled Stoic pride. Brutus is something of a stage
Stoic, with too much faith in individual self-sufficiency.
Though high minded, he is as great a menace to the system as
Cassius, the skeptical, less altruistic, Epicurean. Brutus,
the noblest Roman of them all, is not necessarily good for
Rome. The play likewise illustrates once more the ambiguous

role of fate--controlling and not controlling at the same time. Cassius, who represents the Elizabethan idea of an Epicurean, at first insists that we are free, that the stars have no influence over our actions. ("The fault, dear Brutus, is not in our stars . . ." [I.ii.139-41]). Yet later he comes to realize he was mistaken, saying, "You know that I held Epicurus strong / And his opinion. Now I change my mind / And partly credit things that do presage" (V.ii.76-78).[59] To us it is plain that throughout the play fate is working the strings while we also see plainly that Brutus and Cassius are morally responsible for what they do. When they die, though they die after the high Roman manner, yet they die as failures, as monuments to the folly of trying to go against nature's plan.

Hamlet, on the other hand, is a success. Though he too loses his life, he loses it in the process of restoring order and is thus on the side of the angels, as the Stoic Horatio strongly implies when he prays that "flights of angels sing thee to thy rest" (V.ii.371). The fact that Hamlet is also instrumental in causing the deaths of several relatively innocent bystanders does not seem to be held against him. When the system is out of joint, it is inevitable that innocent people will be hurt. Though Hamlet does not enjoy the role to which he has been assigned and complains bitterly, he does not seriously try to escape. Shortly before the end, in a mood of what is usually called Stoic resignation, he signifies that he has achieved the ability to accept all fortune (or fate or providence) as good fortune, to face death or life with equal calm, as he says, "If it / be now, 'tis not to come; if it be not to come, it / will be now; if it be not now, yet it will come: / the readiness is all. Since no man knows aught / of what he leaves, what is't to leave betimes?" (V.ii.230-35). "The readiness is all." The important thing is not whether we win but how we play the game.[60]

_Troilus and Cressida_ is another play that illustrates the confusion that results when people try to ignore the rules of the game. Ulysses' famous degree speech (I.iii.74 ff) expounds in detail the standard doctrine that virtue means everyone in his proper place; and the action demonstrates that when democracy and selfish individualism take over, as they have in the Greek camp, the effect is chaos. Had there been cooperation among the Greeks instead of a philosophy of every man for himself, the Trojan War would have been over long ago.[61]

_Lear_, too, among all its complexities, gives us variations on the theme that virtue means conformity to the laws of nature. Once again the laws are perverted, only in due time to reestablish themselves without concern for individuals. Edmund's Epicurean or Machiavellian attempt to defy the conventional laws in favor of his own interpretation, plausible though it may sound to him, proves, as is usual with such heresies, to be a mistake. A misbegotten son, trapped through the accident of birth, Edmund, like Malory's Modred, destroys his own father.[62] Though seemingly cursed at birth with an abnormally large evil streak, he is nevertheless punished for his villainy, The implacable system, which fails to excuse his inability to distinguish between right and wrong, at the same time punishes his father for having followed will instead of reason in begetting him--clearly the implication of Edgar's comment that "the gods are just, and of our pleasant vices / make instruments to scourge us" (V.iii.170).

In contrast to the moral Edgar, whose unclouded insight allows him to function as a chorus character, some of the others see incorrectly because their moral sense, for one reason or another, has been corrupted. In addition to the skeptical Edmund, who feels himself an outcast and refuses to subscribe to conventional values, there is Gloucester, whose pleasant vices have slightly fogged his moral spectacles, and Lear, whose judgment has been perverted by flatterers. None of these, to use Hooker's words, has the necessary "natural perfection of wit and ripeness of judgment" needed for apprehending the laws of nature. Gloucester, who is unable to distinguish his good son from his bad, complains, when disaster falls, that human beings are no more to the gods than flies are to wanton boys, seeming, under stress, to be adopting the Epicurean doctrine of cosmic pointlessness. As he sees it, if the gods are good, they should reward good people with good fortune and bad people with bad fortune. Leaving aside the question of whether or not he and Lear are without sin, there is still the question that troubled Seneca and Boethius, the question of why evil befalls good people. The standard answer, of course, is that "good men are shaken in order that they may grow strong."[63] Success is measured not by good fortune but by the quality of one's performance. Fortunately for Gloucester's soul, he is at least saved from despair and suicide by Edgar who, like Boethius's Lady Philosophy, persuades him that he must patiently accept the will of the gods without presuming to understand nature's plan. In words reminiscent of Hamlet's "the readiness is all," Edgar warns his father that it is not for him to decide when the time is ripe for him to die. "Ripeness is all" (V.ii.8).[64] Lady Philosophy had argued that the good man's reward is peace of mind while the bad man loses not only his peace but also his humanity, becomes an animal. The comparison of Lear's daughters to animals has often been remarked.[65] And Hardin Craig has argued that the "aged Lear . . . ultimately . . . achieves a calm."[66]

If we shift from Seneca and Boethius to Cicero and Aquinas, we will remember that because Lear is a king, and therefore supposedly endowed at birth with superior potential insight into truth, his deviations from the laws of nature are especially heinous. Like Gorboduc or like King Basilius in Sidney's Arcadia, he leaves his appointed place with the consequence that there is disorder in the commonwealth--children forgetting their duty to their parents, servants forgetting their duty to their masters, war in the state. Like Skelton's Magnificence, Lear has to be reeducated into a proper sense of the fitness of

things.[67] At the beginning of the play he has a disproportion-
ate sense of his own self importance, forgetting that he like
everyone else is only one part of the great design. When
Goneril and Regan flatter him ridiculously, he sees nothing
comic. When Cordelia refuses to give him more than his due he
is furious. Like Richard II he considers himself above the
law, forgetting that when he ceases to have the power of a king,
he will no longer be treated like a king and that when he
upsets due order by retiring from his duty and setting the
child above the father, he must be prepared to accept the consequences. He forgets that even a king is only a human being
and subject to the physical facts of life. Because of his
unbalanced judgment, he, like Timon, is unable to make a correct assessment of people, and like Timon and Romeo he responds
to any situation with passion rather than reason. Lear, who
has somehow acquired the notion that kings are intrinsically
different from other human beings, has to learn what Richard
II also found out, that kings are only mortal (cf. R.II III.
ii.160 ff). It is a lesson that he learns only gradually.
When the wise fool tries to teach him good sense, he cannot
listen: "The tempest in my mind / Doth from my senses take all
feeling else / Save what beats there. Filial ingratitude!"
(III.iv.12). Though he has disregarded the rules in giving up
his kingdom, he expects his daughters to obey them and is
shocked when he finds that his children can be ungrateful. Next
he learns that though a king he will get wet if he stays out in
the rain. It is only gradually that he learns such old
Christian-Stoic lessons as that all men are brothers, that very
little is needed to satisfy the needs of nature, and that no
man is immune to the vicissitudes of fortune.[68] Out in the
storm, where he learns what it is like to be a poor naked wretch
(III.iv.28), he gradually admits that under his fine clothes he
is no more than such another "poor, bare, forked animal" as
Edgar (III.iv.105). Summing up the lesson he has learned from
nature, so different from the earlier false education he had
received from flatterers, he says that now he has learned from
experience what it was like "when the rain came to wet me once,
and the wind to make me chatter; when the thunder would not
peace at my bidding," that it has occurred to him that he is
"not ague-proof" (IV.vi.98-107). The final lesson about the
nature of earthly things comes with the pointless death of Cordelia. Seneca could have told him not to be surprised. Apparent accidents are a normal part of the order of nature, kings
being no more immune than other men.

Lear's folly in giving up his throne brings chaos to the
state, while Macbeth's villainy has the same effect; and both
plays end with providence restoring the balance, busily filling
vacant positions with colorless organization men.[69] Just as
Gloucester in Lear loses his sense of a meaningful universe and
says that men to the gods are no more than flies to wanton boys,
so Macbeth loses peace of mind and comes to think life no more
than a tale told by an idiot, signifying nothing. A punishment

for those who subvert order is to believe that there is no such
thing.

Even magnificent individuals like Antony and Cleopatra
have to be sacrificed to the system. Although in <u>Julius Caesar</u>
Antony was on the side of history, in <u>Antony and Cleopatra</u> he
demonstrates the tragic effect of following personal desire
instead of selfless virtue, having forgotten not only that
reason should govern passion but also that men should rule
women. Although at any particular moment in the play the
poetry may make us forget these tiresome old platitudes, a nag-
ging voice in the pit of our stomachs keeps saying that we cannot for long continue to break the rules. Perhaps because of
the influence of the courtly love tradition, Shakespeare shows
much sympathy for those who err through an excess of romantic
love, seeming almost to say that the exciting people are the
ones who break the rules and accept the consequences; nevertheless, it is the unexciting obedient ones who survive in a system that does not care for rampant individualism.

Similarly the system has no room for unenlightened self
interest. Although Enobarbus seems throughout to represent the
voice of reason in contrast to Antony's passion, nevertheless
he too deviates from true reason; for he deserts his duty. For
him, as for Chaucer's Griselda or Shakespeare's Kate in <u>The
Taming of the Shrew</u>, virtue is tied to his relation to his
master. Just as Griselda and Kate can only be virtuous by willing what their husbands will, so Enobarbus can only be virtuous
by being loyal to Antony. It is his duty to go down with the
sinking ship. When he tries to substitute for his duty what
Bacon calls "wisdom for a man's self," he loses his peace of
mind, falls into despair, commits suicide.

Though old ideas about the laws of nature were fading in
the actual seventeenth-century political arena, they still
lingered on the popular stage in the works of such writers as
Chapman, Heywood, Marston, Webster, and Ford.[70] In the theatre
it was still taken for granted that the hierarchical system was
the natural one; that virtue meant willingly playing one's
assigned part; that superior moral insight was the birthright
of those at the top, who therefore had to meet higher standards than those at the bottom; that nature, if sometimes slow
to act, would not for long permit tampering with the system.
Although lip service was given to the idea that there is an
unwritten moral law lying behind all valid human law, individuals were seldom encouraged to set themselves up as authorities on this law. If a king, whose insight was supposed to be
the best, should corrupt his insight by living viciously and
hence proceed to act against the moral law, subjects were
never--before the fact--justified in rebelling. After the fact,
of course, a successful rebellion might be explained as having
been part of nature's plan.

George Chapman (c. 1559-1634) was an intellectual who
liked to dabble in the fashionable learning of his time--notably

Platonism and Stoicism--but who generally used his learning to support the familiar system, a possible exception being his attitude toward moral self-sufficiency. In Chapman's Stoicism, which has been studied at length,[71] the usual distinction between good Stoics, who subordinate personal self interest to social duty, and bad Stoics, who insist on their moral and emotional self-sufficiency, sometimes appears blurred, possibly because some of Chapman's heroes also seem to be related to Marlowe's hero villains, who make no pretence of subordinating individualism to social conformity.[72] As a result, we are left in some doubt whether we are supposed to admire Chapman's best-known hero, Bussy d'Ambois, or to regard him as a bad example.[73] It is possible to argue for either side. In his later plays Chapman was usually less ambiguous, making it clear that he adhered to the conventional interpretation of virtue as doing one's duty in the pattern.

A difference in attitude between Chapman and Marlowe is suggested by Chapman's continuation (1598) of "Hero and Leander"; for in Chapman there is less passion than in Marlowe, more law and order. The Goddess Ceremony, otherwise known as the traditional system, descends to chastise Leander for his irregular behavior with Hero, decreeing that since the lovers have violated propriety by trying to be a law unto themselves, they must pay the penalty (lines 112-54). Among Chapman's other non-dramatic poems there are a number of free translations of Stoic passages from Virgil and Epictetus.[74] In the lines "Pleasd with thy place" (Bartlett, p. 449), which also appear in The Revenge of Bussy d'Ambois (III.iv.58-75), there is an elaboration on a passage from Epictetus (Discourses IV.vii.6-11), in which Chapman sets forth in complex language the familiar doctrine that virtue means playing one's assigned part, that those who refuse to play their parts will only be crushed, that freedom means willing what God wills, and that selfish individualism is a bad thing. Here the intellectual Chapman expands lines from Epictetus into a convoluted argument that turns out to be a lesson he might have learned from Thomas Elyot or any number of other people.

Where Chapman differed from conservative thinkers like Elyot, however, was that he sometimes implied that his heroes were justified in relying entirely on their own interpretations of the law of nature. Idealistically Chapman here failed to consider the ambiguous nature of "reason." If in the Byron plays the traditional Ciceronian or Erasmian point of view seems to be dominant, in the other plays something more cosmic is implied. In the Byron plays the exciting but selfish individualism of the hero-villain Byron is less admirable than the dull social responsibility of the virtuous king, Henry IV, who belongs to the same family as all the other good kings in the literature of the time.[75] But the well-known Epictetan passages in The Revenge of Bussy (III.iv.58 ff, IV.i.131 ff) in which the virtuous hero Clermont expounds the doctrine that it is man's duty to submit his private will to "great Necessity,"

refer to a law of nature that is larger and more vague than
patriotic duty. In this play, where the corrupt world of
Henry III bears no resemblance to an ideal state, Clermont
guides himself by his inner light. Another example is Chabot
in Chabot who has such confidence in his personal interpretation of a problem in foreign relations that he mistakenly stakes
his whole career on the theory that the king will obviously
agree with him. Cato in Caesar and Pompey shows a similar self-
confidence when he asks, "But is not every just man to himself
/ The perfect'st law?"(IV.v.71-2). But in this latter play, at
the same time, Chapman puts a long speech in the mouth of the
Stoic philosopher Athenoderus (V.ii.70-85) which is reminiscent
of other traditions in which the truth is less plain, traditions
such as those of Augustine or Boethius that warn us that the
laws of nature are not easy for man to comprehend. Athenoderus
says, "The gods' wills secret are, nor must we measure / their
chaste-reserved deeps by our dry shallows. . . . For this giant
world, / Let's not contend with it, when heaven itself / Fails
to reform it." The implication is that it is a tragic mistake
to hope for justice in this world.

Although Cato, Chabot, and Clermont are all obviously
intended as virtuous characters whose Stoic self-sufficiency
Chapman presents sympathetically, even if tragically, he does
condemn the egoism of Byron; and with Bussy D'Ambois it is possible to argue either that Bussy like Chabot expected too much
of this world or that like Byron he had too much pride. Part of
his fascination comes from the fact that he is a puzzle. Is he
a Hamlet, or is he a Macbeth, a servant of destiny or an ambitious climber? Though he makes fine Stoic speeches, he sometimes appears to be a sham Stoic--a slave to passion. Whether
Chapman made him a sham Stoic on purpose, as a bad example, or
whether he was only in this early play following the contemporary fad for Senecanism and had not yet gone deeply into Stoic
thinking, the fact remains that the message is not clear.[76]

For example, there is the hocus-pocus treatment of fate
that assigns fate the malignant and ambiguous qualities of fortune or Old English wyrd. If fate is meant to be an instrument
of providence, then providence seems to behave in a disreputable
way. However, fate is actually only serving as a plot device,
since something that is fated needs no further motivation.
Bussy asks why Monsieur should suddenly now, after all these
years, take an interest in him: It must be fate. If fate has
now decreed that he should suddenly be raised from obscurity
and placed in a high place, well, so be it (I.i.128-43). In
fact, fate singles out a hitherto virtuous man, arbitrarily puts
him at the top of fortune's wheel, and lets us watch him destroy
himself. If we like, we can read the play as a moral lesson on
the old Senecan or Boethian theme that high places are more vulnerable to fortune than low ones.[77] Or we can read it as a sermon against Stoic pride: Bussy's false pretence to being self-
sufficient is exposed and his cloistered virtue shown to be per-
ishable in the dust and heat, even though Bussy is allowed to

die like a hero.

Fate here is so powerful that it gobbles up morality, leaving few traces of the Stoic doctrine that a man is always free not to sin. No Goddess Ceremony descends to lecture the lovers on their irregular behavior. Instead, as with Chaucer's Troilus and Shakespeare's Romeo, the courtly love code twines itself into the pattern, with Bussy and the friar sometimes appearing as virtuous servants of true love (i.e., passion), sometimes as the helpless victims of fate. When the Guise and Monsieur appear as fate's ministers (V.iii.62), we suspect fate of being deliberately mischievous. The whole purpose of having Bussy come to his end through a series of deliberately fated accidents is to give him a chance to make his final exit on a high Stoic note.

It may be that Bussy thinks of himself as a self-sufficient Stoic while Chapman all along intends us to see through him. In the hodge-podge of pseudo-Stoic arguments that Bussy uses when defending himself to the king for having engaged in a duel, there is a possibility that Chapman intends irony throughout. It is also possible that he is merely delighting in his own versatility. Bussy's argument is that by breaking the king's law and righting his honor in a duel, he is obeying a higher law. "When I am wrong'd, and that law fails to right me, / Let me be king myself (as man was made), / And do a justice that exceeds the law." Then, says he, if I can't right the wrong myself, the king should step in and if necessary set aside the written law, "and do a right, exceeding law and nature. / Who to himself is law, no law doth need, / Offends no law, and is a king indeed" (II.i.194-204). This is the sort of argument Chapman's colleague John Marston liked to put in the mouth of sham Stoics.[78] If Chapman is seriously arguing that a king is a law unto himself, above both "law and nature," then he is siding with the skeptical Machiavellians rather than with the Stoics. Easier explanations are either that he was demonstrating the fallacies of Stoic pride or that he was concentrating on writing a successful stage piece.[79] In The Revenge of Bussy, Bussy's ghost uses this same argument as he incites Clermont to hasten his revenge: "What corrupted law / Leaves unperform'd in kings, do thou supply, / And be above them all in dignity" (V.i.97-99). Yet again we cannot be sure that Chapman is more sympathetic with Bussy's impatience than with Clermont's reasons for delay, even though Bussy's speech seems superficially to be similar to Cato's insistence that the just man is "to himself the perfect'st law," for Bussy is not necessarily a just man.

Unlike Hamlet, who approaches his last scene talking about a divinity that shapes our ends, Bussy fails to link fate with anything that sounds like a benevolent providence--whatever Chapman may have done. Bussy says, "Fate is more strong than arms, and sly than treason, / And I at all parts buckled in my fate" (V.iv.39-40). Although he, like Hamlet, is prepared to accept what cannot be avoided, he is one who defies fate instead of patiently accepting it as the will of God.

Again in the Byron plays (<u>The</u> <u>Conspiracy</u> <u>of</u> <u>Charles,</u> <u>Duke</u>
<u>of</u> <u>Byron</u> and <u>The</u> <u>Tragedy</u> <u>of</u> <u>Charles,</u> <u>Duke</u> <u>of</u> <u>Byron</u>), though
less than in <u>Bussy</u>, inexorable fate is treated as something
quirkish to be distinguished from the orderly progress of
nature.   Fate, here as in many another play, concerns itself
with petty details that can in no way be altered.   La Brosse
(a good character, even though a magician) heightens tension
by lamenting that he can foresee his fate but not change it
(<u>Conspiracy</u>, III.iii.1-19).   On the other hand, it appears once
again that the order of nature can be temporarily, though only
temporarily, diverted from its course.   Before nature finally
rights things, Byron is allowed to cause a great deal of political trouble.[80]

Chapman was not, of course, the only playwright who
used fate for dramatic rather than philosophical purposes.
Star-crossed lovers and star-crossed villains were common prop-
erty.   Thomas Heywood (c. 1570-1641) in <u>A</u> <u>Woman</u> <u>Killed</u> <u>with</u>
<u>Kindness</u> has the villain Wendoll blame fate for his own lack of
self control.   "What sad destiny / Hath such command upon my
yielding thoughts? / I will not.   Ha!   Some Fury pricks me on;
/ The swift Fates drag me at their chariot wheel, / And hurry
me to mischief" (Sc.vi.100-104).   This implication that the
fates deliberately cause mischief, like Bussy's remark that fate
is more sly than treason, is neither Christian nor Stoic.   It is
something out of folk mythology, an excuse used by people who do
not wish to accept responsibility for their own acts.[81]   Neither
Wendoll nor Bussy is, after all, a person with unobstructed
moral vision.

Characters whose virtue safely follows the Ciceronian-
Stoic mode--such as Shakespeare's Henry V or Chapman's Henry IV
or Marston's Scipio (in <u>Sophonisba</u>)--have no quarrel with fate.
Though John Marston (1576-1634) larded his plays with miscellaneous Stoic bits and pieces, some sympathetic, some unsympathetic, he consistently pictured the good ruler as one who
could rule others because he had submitted his own will to the
will of God (the law of nature).   In spite of his many Senecan
quotations, sometimes supporting, sometimes ridiculing individual self-sufficiency, Marston's basic groundplan was the conventional Ciceronian one that emphasized selfless social duty.
To support the ideal that seemed to him only common sense,
namely, that everyone should concentrate on performing his
assigned task instead of climbing on the ladder of personal
ambition, he frequently used satire, partly because as a nostal-
gic backward looker, he found it difficult to adjust to changing
times, otherwise known as the way of the world.

As a gentleman's son himself, he scorned those trying to
move up the ladder, got into trouble for making fun of James I's
carpet knights, and once described his fellow satirist Joseph
Hall (the future bishop) as a swineherd's brat.   Though after
leaving Oxford he spent a number of years at the Middle Temple
(where his father was a member) presumably studying law and
preparing to follow in his father's footsteps, he for some

180

reason abandoned the law and took instead to writing plays.  One can surmise that among other reasons his moralistic preference for the law-of-nature ideal brought him into conflict with the complexities of actual legal practice.[82]  His time as a playwright was likewise short; for after a brief brilliant career as a poet and dramatist, he left London in his early thirties to enter the church, having had, like Molière's Misanthrope, enough of the ways of the contemporary world.  Possibly as a churchman he was able to carry out his own ideals, concentrating on selfless duty rather than on personal ambition, for unlike John Donne he never became Dean of St. Paul's and unlike Joseph Hall, he never became a bishop.

This biographical detail is included because of its tie-up with the theme of natural law in Marston's plays, where Machiavellian opportunists are continually juxtaposed against Ciceronian idealists.  While virtuous characters insist on obedience to the unwritten moral law, villains, who maintain that kings are above the law, defend their own activities on the grounds of expediency.  For Marston's relativistic villains, whatever succeeds is good.  From the plays we can gather that Marston would scarcely have agreed with Francis Bacon that "we are much beholden to Machiavel and others, that write what men do and not what they ought to do," for he was always satirizing people for not conforming to nature as he defined it.  His low opinion of lawyers is briefly suggested in the last act of The Dutch Courtesan, a play, incidentally, which also contains one or two casual mentions of Tully's Offices, the bible of Ciceronian Stoicism.  Elsewhere, though Marston customarily preaches Ciceronian doctrine without bothering to mention Cicero, he frequently mentions Seneca, whom he accepts less implicitly.

A brief glance at four of Marston's plays will show a combined Ciceronian-Senecan (or Erasmian) ideal underscored again and again.  In the early pair of Plays, Antonio and Mellida and Antonio's Revenge (occasionally described as Senecan because of their form) Ciceronian doctrine is sometimes preached directly, sometimes implied by means of social satire, even though the total effect is ambiguous because Marston seems to be going in too many directions at once--satirizing the corrupt court, idealizing social responsibility, laughing at pretensions to Stoic imperturbability, capping a comedy with a revenge play--to name only some.  In Antonio and Mellida, the comedy, we meet Antonio's father, Andrugio, a just ruler who is destroyed by the machinations of his devious enemies and who describes a true king as one "that dares doe aught, save wrong, / Feares nothing mortall, but to be unjust."  As a good Christian this king does not pretend to be morally self-sufficient, he "sits upon Joves footestoole, as I doe, / Adoring, not affecting majestie."  His reward is the just man's reward, "the silver crowne / Of cleare content" (V.iv).  Unfortunately for Andrugio's equanimity, it is not quite so stable as he pretends.  Not only does he easily lose his temper when alive, but after he has been murdered, at the beginning of Antonio's Revenge, he

entirely forgets his Stoicism and becomes simply a Senecan
revenge-minded ghost who recites at the end of the play a law
of nature that is neither Christian nor Stoic: "Sons that
revenge their fathers blood, are blest" (V.vi).

In _Antonio's Revenge_, with Andrugio dead, the mouthpiece
for Stoic doctrine becomes Pandulpho Feliche, a virtuous private man who tells the villainous ruler Pietro that a subject
must obey a king as long as the king commands "just and honorable things,"[83] that a king becomes a tyrant when he considers
himself free to do other than noble deeds, that a king should
be praised not for doing what he can do but for doing what he
should (II.ii). In addition to preaching Ciceronian doctrine
to the king, Pandulpho tries himself to live up to the Boethian or Senecan ideal of accepting all fortune as good fortune, insisting that he is a free man because he carries his
freedom within (I.v; II.ii). However, the corrupt world is too
much for his professed Stoicism. When his son, Feliche, is
murdered, he joins Antonio's revenge plot.[84]

Marston' satirical picture of the corrupt world in which
the good men are either destroyed by the evil ones or else must
themselves forget morality to fight fire with fire, left him in
something of a dilemma as a Christian. Although Pandulpho was
able to say of his murdered son, "Thrice blessed man that dyeth
just" (IV.v), he knew that he himself, once he had become a
murderous revenger, could no longer be considered virtuous. It
is notable that Marston, unlike some other writers of revenge
plays, was troubled by the dilemma. Instead of killing off
Antonio and Pandulpho and leaving the audience to surmise that
heavenly justice would treat them leniently, he sent them,
rather lamely from the dramatic point of view, to repent their
sins in religious retirement. Although their crimes had benefited society, they as individuals were tarnished. Marston,
the moralist, was evidently not happy with the Machiavellian
doctrine that political morality and personal morality are two
different things. In _The Malcontent_ and _Sophonisba_ he tangled
again with the problem.[85]

In these plays, however, he avoided having his good characters commit murders. In _The Malcontent_, where the good Duke
Altofront, disguised as Malevole, the Malcontent, has some
resemblance to Feliche of _Antonio and Mellida_ (see Chapter IV)
in that both rail at social evils, their names indicate a basic
difference. Feliche claims to be the contented Horatian happy
man who stays aloof from the evil court, while the Malcontent,
on the other hand, is by definition discontented; and Malevole,
under his disguise, has more than selfish personal happiness on
his mind. As a good governor in the Ciceronian tradition, he
must regain his throne in order to carry out the social duty
assigned him at birth. Though his methods of easing out the
usurping duke and outwitting the Machiavellian villain Mendoza
are devious, he commits no crimes and acts in the best interests
of the foolish multitude. In the end he even treats Mendoza
with clemency. As contrasted with Mendoza, an ambitious climber

who is motivated only by personal ambition, Malevole, like
Andrugio, is only doing his duty; for he was appointed a ruler
by God and remembers that his own will is subsidiary to the will
of God, that his whim is not the law. At the end of the play he
says that when great men "observe not Heavens imposd conditions,
/ They are no men, but forfeit their commissions."[86]

Sophonisba, Marston's Roman tragedy, brings us more variations on the same theme. This play, about the war between
Rome and Carthage, gives us Marston's Jacobean interpretation
of Stoic virtue. Although the story is told from the Carthaginian point of view, we soon realize that providence is on the
Roman side. The play exemplifies, with a Christian twist or
two, the Roman Stoic doctrine that the destiny of Rome is the
will of God. The Carthaginians, although fated to lose, are
shown, nevertheless, also as sinners who bring merited destruction on themselves by deviating from the moral law. In the play,
the elder Scipio, the Roman general and one of Cicero's favorite symbols of patriotic virtue, exemplifies the ideal good
governor, although as a character he, like Chaucer's Theseus,
is only slightly involved in the action. The hero is the Carthaginian Massinissa, Sophonisba's first husband, who has his
system of moral priorities well in order.[87] In spite of his
love for Sophonisba, he puts his duty to Carthage first, leaving his bride on his wedding night at the call of his country.
However, when the Carthaginian politicians betray him and try
to poison him, and when even Sophonisba seems to have deserted
him in favor of Syphax, Massinissa goes over to the Roman side,
arguing Stoically that "a just mans contry Jove makes everywhere" (III.ii). Once having sworn allegiance to Scipio, he
keeps his word, even though Sophonisba has to be sacrificed as
a consequence.[88]

Syphax, in contrast to Massinissa, is a pure opportunist.
In the beginning, out of anger at being rejected by Sophonisba,
he deserts Carthage to join Scipio. Later, when the devious
Carthaginians hold out Sophonisba as lure, he returns to Carthage. Unlike Massinissa, who always puts virtue first, Syphax
is depicted throughout as a slave to passion. Perverting the
Stoic doctrine that only the good man is free, Syphax says "Hee
that may onely do just act's a slave." Massinissa, whose virtue makes him almost a Christian, never boasts that he is self-
sufficient. Rather, he hopes that because he is a just man
"angels" will fight on his side; and Marston, the dispenser of
poetic justice, sees to it that they do (V.ii).

To exemplify the acceptable Stoic doctrine that only the
good man is free, that death is no evil if one dies with integrity, Marston inserts the story of Gelosso, a Carthaginian who
sets his conscience above politics. Having failed to persuade
the Carthaginian politicians not to forsake the moral law, not
to break their faith with Massinissa, Gelosso refuses to give
up his own moral freedom. Obeying his conscience, he warns
Massinissa of the plan to poison him and as a consequence is
himself executed as a traitor. Before he dies he clearly states

the anti-Machiavellian moral: "I am bound to loose / My life but not my honour for my country. . . . The Gods assist just hearts, & states that trust / Plots before <u>Providence</u> are tost like dust" (II.i).[89]

Contrasted with Gelosso are the immoral Carthaginians like Carthalon; like Sophonisba's father, Asdruball; and like the villain Syphax. All these argue for expediency rather than integrity. Carthalon, saying that governmental decisions must be based on policy rather than on abstract principles, disclaims--at the same time--all free will, blaming God for the existence of evil. Unlike Gelosso, who sees no conflict between accepting his fate and following virtue, Carthalon blames fate for his own lack of integrity and argues that "he that gives way to <u>Fate</u> is wise" (II.i). Asdruball, defending the plan to betray Massinissa, says, "Thou know'st, a statist must not be a man" (II.ii). In other words, a politician is not expected to obey the same moral system as a virtuous man in private life. A moment later Asdruball becomes what may be meant by a "Stoic-Machiavel." Having defended political expediency, like a Machiavel, he then claims to possess godlike self-sufficiency, like a Stoic. Perverting Stoic doctrine, he claims immunity to fortune because he knows how to manipulate his chances, and immunity to passion because he is not troubled by such benevolent emotions as pity (II.iii). He is not, of course, immune to such selfish passions as ambition. Marston points the contrast between the real Stoic, Gelosso, and the Stoic frauds, Carthalon and Asdruball, by showing us the way all three accept defeat. Gelosso exits saying, "Thou canst but kill a weake old honest man." Carthalon and Asdruball, having lost all dignity, leave the stage loudly blaming each other for their misfortunes (II. iii).

Sophonisba, the title character, though she dies nobly in Stoic fashion, is not depicted throughout as an uncomplicated Stoic like Gelosso. Had she been, there would have been no story. Since she is a vacillating woman, guided more by passion than by reason, concentrating at first more on getting what she wants than on subordinating her personal desires to the public welfare, she contributes to the catastrophe. Later, when she is persuaded to sacrifice her own desires in favor of political expediency, she again makes a wrong choice since by neglecting the moral law she only succeeds in hastening the defeat of Carthage. Only when she drinks poison at the end does she finally achieve integrity. At the beginning of the play there is a hint that she has too much pride, and she herself frankly admits that she knew when she followed her own desires in choosing Massinissa as a husband rather than Syphax that she was bringing discord to Carthage (I.ii). In Act II, when the Carthaginian politicians are debating about strategy, she vacillates between keeping faith with Massinissa and allowing herself to be used as a political pawn. Although she at first goes along with the good Gelosso, arguing eloquently that there should be no discrepancy between public poiicy and private

morality, she immediately afterwards allows herself to be persuaded that for reasons of the alleged public good she must
subordinate her own integrity to practical politics. Not wishing to admit that she has now lost her moral freedom, she
goes on talking like a Stoic, insisting that she will accept
all fortune as good fortune, that misfortunes are sent as a
test of virtue. All this comes under the heading of what T. S.
Eliot in "Shakespeare and the Stoicism of Seneca" calls "cheer-
ing oneself up." Significantly, Gelosso is disgusted by her
hypocrisy.[90] Next, although she has agreed to accept Carthaginian policy, she tries to avoid keeping her word to Syphax.
Much of the rest of the play is devoted to her Clarissa-like
attempts to stay out of his bed. In the end, though Massinissa rescues her from Syphax, Scipio considers her a threat to
Rome and orders that she be turned over to him. Now, at last,
she chooses integrity over vacillation. To preserve Massinissa's honor and her own freedom, she drinks poison, leaving
Massinissa, at the end of the play, singing her praises as one
whose virtue was able to triumph over the blows of chance or
fate.[91]

The two famous plays of John Webster (born c. 1570-80)
again show the tragic consequences of breaking the moral law.
Even though various innocent minor characters are sacrificed
as helpless victims, it is plain that the major characters have
all in some way brought catastrophe on themselves. By giving
way to passion, or by deviating in some other way from reason
and virtue, they have lost their sense of the fitness of things.
To be sure, some seem to us more guilty than others. Just as
Macbeth seems to deserve punishment far more than Lear, so
Vittoria seems far more guilty than the Duchess of Malfi. The
rule seems to be, however, that any deviation from nature is
risky and that there will be no clear relation between the
gravity of the crime and the severity of the punishment.

Although Webster focuses attention on corruption in high
places, he does not suggest that since this is the way of the
world we had better accommodate ourselves to the facts. Rather
he seems to be saying that although this is the way it is, this
is not the way it ought to be, the ideal being still the conventional one described by Thomas Elyot. Had Webster been completely skeptical about a just universe, he need have made no
attempt to show evil doers receiving punishment and could have
ended his plays with the villains carolling happily as they rode
off into the sunset. Moreover, although he may not have dealt
out perfect poetic justice, he did not, on the other hand, go
all the way with Boethius in asserting that the ways of providence are inscrutable and that there is no necessary relation
between good deeds and good fortune. If Webster's world is for
most of the action the same old world that Horace or Juvenal or
Boethius knew, with the evil ones flourishing, the good ones
suffering, yet at the end there is the customary Elizabethan
suggestion that nature is beginning to restore the balance.

With Webster, as with these other playwrights, the medieval

code of courtly love, which operates on completely different
principles from the unromantic law of nature, confuses the
message. Courtly love, with its emphasis on individualism and
passion, does not mesh well with the Ciceronian emphasis on
cooperation and moderation. Thomas More, it may be remembered,
had no courtly love in the Utopia. If playwrights had been
scholars instead of playwrights they might have confined themselves in a single play either to love or to law; but as it was,
they seldom tried seriously to reconcile the conflict. Instead,
they wrote one scene at a time, concentrating on whatever point
was appropriate at the moment, with the consequence that our
attitude toward Webster's lovers wavers between sympathy and
condemnation. If at one moment we are inclined to agree that
love should conquer all, at the next we are wondering whether
selfish passion should take precedence over social responsibility. The White Devil shows clearly that giving way to passion
leads to crime and brings about chaos. Though Flamineo acts
the devil's part in engineering the evil, the others are plainly
responsible for their own actions and have to accept the consequences.

Several times in the play we are reminded of the familiar
doctrine that great men are especially required to steer themselves according to the moral law and to set examples for those
below. In Act I Cornelia--one of the few good characters--says,
"The lives of Princes should like dyals move, / Whose regular
example is so strong, / They make the times by them go right or
wrong" (I.ii.279-81).[92] A little later Francesco hints to
Brachiano that he is not following nature, not remembering that
he is supposed to play the role of eagle and keep his eye on
the sun, or virtue. Unfortunately, says Francesco, "Some Eagles
that should gaze upon the Sunne / Seldom soare high, but take
their lustfull ease, / Since they from dunghill birds their prey
can ceaze" (II.i.50-52). Next it is the conjuror who fails in
his attempt to remind the over-excited Brachiano of his social
role. "Both flowers and weedes, spring when the Sunne is warme,
/ And great men do great good, or else great harme" (II.ii.55-
56). Brachiano, however, puts selfish desire above social duty,
thereby causing great harm. At the beginning of the play we
may be inclined to believe a depraved character like Lodovico
when he complains that justice in the world applies only to
underlings like himself, not to great evil doers like Brachiano,
an idea with which Boethius might have agreed; but Webster ends
the play by showing us Brachiano, Duke of Milan, tumbling off
the wheel of fortune.

While the selfish passion of Brachiano and Vittoria is so
harmful to others that we consider their downfall only just,
the lovers in The Duchess of Malfi get far harsher treatment
than they seem to deserve in a just universe. They too, however, have made themselves vulnerable by taking chances with the
system. We cannot listen to their specious arguments for putting desire above reason without suffering from the same anxiety
we feel when listening to Romeo or Antony. Though we long to be

told that the system will make allowances for special circumstances, we fear we shall get no such comfort. The Duchess,
overlooking the fact that she has been assigned the role of
prince and that as a public person she is not free to marry
where she likes, has to conceal her marriage from general
opinion as much as from her brothers.[93] Antonio too, for all
his virtue and his genuine love for the Duchess, falls slightly
from perfect wisdom when he allows himself to be tempted by
ambition. The punishment, admittedly, seems to us excessive,
just as the punishments of Juliet and Desdemona seem excessive.
It is the system that goes on.

The play begins and ends with its focus on the corrupt
great men, the villainous Cardinal and Ferdinand, whose evil
influence has long been infecting everything around. When they
are finally brought low, at the end of the play, order in the
state begins to reassert itself. Meanwhile, however, they have
caused great harm, two of their victims being Antonio and the
Duchess. Just as Romeo and Juliet are partly sacrificed to the
general chaos, partly the causers of their own woe, so the
Duchess and Antonio are mainly destroyed by the Cardinal and
Ferdinand but partly contribute to their own misfortunes. By
introducing even an insufficient connection between misdeed and
misfortune, Webster is lining himself up with Elizabethan tradition. The tradition of Boethius made no such requirement.
Antonio's feeling that he should have stayed away from high
places and avoided ambition is suggested by his dying advice
that his son should "flie the Courts of Princes" (V.iv.84).
Moralizing in the medieval way on the folly of high climbing,
he says,"In all our Quest of Greatnes. . . / (Like wanton Boyes,
whose pastime is their care) / We follow after bubbles" (V.iv.
75-77). At the very end of the play, as Antonio's friend Delio
stands surveying the array of corpses, he suggests in Stoic
terms that the one thing that really matters is "integrity of
life." Though it is clear that he is talking primarily about
the fallen great men, Ferdinand and the Cardinal, who forgot to
keep their gaze on the sun, failed to be "lords of truth," he
may also refer to Bosola; and possibly too he is implying sadly
that his friend Antonio made a serious mistake when he slipped
from perfect wisdom and let himself be tempted with the thought
of rising out of his assigned place in the social scheme.

Bosola is the character who sometimes finds the universe
meaningless. When his attempt to save Antonio fails, he seems
to see everything that happens as pointless accident, complaining that "we are merely the Starres tennys-balls" (V.iv.63).
Though he may be talking here like Shakespeare's Gloucester or
Sidney's Cecropia, he is not necessarily speaking for Webster.
Earlier in the play he is obviously one of those whose ability
to perceive truth has been corrupted by vicious living. Combining characteristics of the stage Machiavel with those of the
stage Epicurean and always making a faulty assessment of the
nature of things, he looks cynically at society, where it seems
to him--as it did to Lodovico in The White Devil--that great

men are above the law and that conventional morality is only
nonsense.  Having no sense of social responsibility, he thinks
only of self interest, which tells him to cling to the coattails
of Ferdinand and the Cardinal and to commit whatever crimes the
brothers demand.  While under their orders, he seems to feel no
personal guilt for what he does, laying, instead, all the blame
on them.  The death of the Duchess, however, brings about at
least a partial change of heart, making him switch his allegiance to Antonio, though he continues to act like a stage
Machiavel, still doing evil, even if now with the hope of bringing about good.  When he tries to turn aside the course of fate
and has his plans go wrong, he blames the stars.  There is a
possibility, however, that at the same time he learns humility;
for while blaming the stars for their failure to aid his plans,
it may occur to him in the Boethian way that their plans are not
necessarily the same as his.  At any rate, from the point of
view of the plot, Bosola is the chosen instrument for finally
bringing down the wicked brothers and starting the return of
order to the state; and his death speech implies that he has by
now revised his earlier ideas about the nature of things, since
he advises others not to be afraid "to suffer death, or shame,
for what is just."  Instead of his earlier skeptical relativism,
he now seems to believe in an absolute value called justice and
to see the emptiness of the worldly values he had earlier
thought all important, thus implying with Delio that integrity
of life is what matters.

     John Ford (1586-?1639) in The Broken Heart likewise writes
about kings and courts and the dangers of breaking the moral
law.  If his focus is less on the social scene at large than on
the morality of personal relations, yet at the end of the play
fate once again makes a clean sweep and turns the country over
to new rulers.  Once more there is an imperfect fusion of popular literary ideas about the laws of nature, courtly love, and
the power of fate.  A law of nature is broken; catastrophe
results; innocent people as well as guilty are harmed, but in
the end order marches on.  Side by side with such traditional
Stoic precepts as that breaking promises is contrary to natural
law and that anger is inimical to peace of mind is the conflicting law of courtly love that decrees no one should recover from a
broken heart.  Meanwhile, inexorable but quirkish fate goes on
its own way, working out a plan that may have been responsible
for the entire action.

     One cause of the misery in the play comes from a broken
promise--Ithocles's failure to let his sister marry the man to
whom her father had betrothed her.  Ithocles, who is not a bad
man, is merely one more example of a character made to pay
severely for having made a wrong decision.  Except for this
grievous mistake, which was made some time before the play
begins and which he sincerely repents, he is presented as a
good man.  The villain--if there is one--is Orgilus, the man
he has wronged.  Orgilus, like one of Seneca's passion-driven
characters, is the angry man bent on revenge whose uncontrolled

188

anger is treated as a reprehensible passion. His inability to recover from a broken heart, however, is considered admirable.

Side by side with the broken law, which presumably need not have been broken, goes the theme of inexorable fate, interpreted for us by the philosopher Tecnicus, who takes the place of a Senecan chorus. As a result of his communication with the Delphic oracle, Tecnicus at various times utters prophesies or makes wise comments, for here, as in <u>Romeo</u> <u>and</u> <u>Juliet</u>, there is a suggestion that the stars are interested in politics and are going to elaborate lengths to bring a new blood line to the throne of Sparta (IV.iii.11 ff).[94] From this point of view, all the individual tragedies are only parts of fate's plan, which means that Ithocles's broken promise and Orgilus's anger are part of the plan and not their fault--an idea, however, which is not suggested. What we actually have is fate used as a theatrical device for heightening suspense. Though Orgilus, like Bosola, proudly thinks he can bend fate to his own uses, it turns out, as is usual in such cases, that he is wrong. In spite of Tecnicus's warning, "Tempt not the stars, young man; thou canst not play / With the severity of Fate" (I.iii.1), Orgilus proudly boasts, "Ingenious Fate has leap'd into mine arms, / Beyond the compass of my brain. Mortality / Creeps on the dung of earth, and cannot reach / The riddles which are purpos'd by the gods" (I.iii.178 ff). Here he speaks more truly than he realizes, as Tecnicus points out later in the play, saying, "Much mystery of fate / Lies hid in that man's fortunes; curiosity / May lead his actions into rare attempts. / But let the gods be moderators still; / No human power can prevent their will" (III.i.54-58).

And so fate brings about the inevitable catastrophe that allows Ford to show us one noble character after another accepting death as no evil, dying with proper stage fortitude. The murdered Ithocles accepts death as "a long-look'd for peace" (IV.iv.69); Orgilus, slowly bleeding, says, "Welcome, thou ice, that sitt'st about my heart" (V.ii.154); Calantha, dying of a broken heart, smiles (V.iii.98). Now that the stage has been swept clear, the country can be turned over to the good prince Nearchus. Order marches on. The modern reader of the play, however, feels vaguely dissatisfied, possibly because the relation between political morality and private morality is never made entirely logical. The careless way in which the old conventions are now being used suggests that they are rapidly becoming dead clichés.

If we want to know what a popular Jacobean-Caroline preacher was saying during the years that these playwrights were writing, we can listen to Joseph Hall (1574-1656), whose purpose as a moralist was to tell us how we ought to behave without the dramatist's need to show the tragic consequence of failing to follow his advice. Though he has been called "Our English Seneca," he was not necessarily an aggressive defender of Stoic self-sufficiency, even though he had moments when he set

up conscience as the highest guide for right conduct. "What
doest thou hear from the bird in thy bosom?" he would ask.
"If thy conscience acquit thee, and pronounce thee guiltless,
abdure thy forehead against all the spite of malice. What is
ill fame but a little corrupted unsavoury breath?"[95] Since he
was a bishop as well as a scholar, however, he knew very well
that men have to live in society as well as with their own consciences. Using an analogy from Ptolemaic astronomy, he tried
to suggest that a good man might exercise a certain amount of
integrity even when caught by fate in a corrupt society.
"Happy are they who (like unto the celestial bodies, which
being carried about with the sway of the highest sphere, yet
creep in their own ways) keep on the courses of their own holi-
ness against the swinge of common corruptions" (II, 406-7).[96]
When he descended from these lofty spheres to contemporary
England, however, Hall lined up with the Aristotelian-Panaetian-
Ciceronian tradition that identified nature and virtue with
patriotic responsibility. For him the will of God, the law of
nature, and the English system were all the same. "Whatever
politic philosophers have distinguished betwixt bonus vir and
civis, I say, that as a good man cannot be an ill subject, so a
lewd man can no more be a good subject, than evil can be good"
(V, 114-15). In other words, he was digging in his heels
against those who were arguing that private morality and political morality were not necessarily the same.[97] He was also
opposing those who argued that the contemporary hierarchical
system was not necessarily the law of nature. "Nothing, say we,
can be more disorderly than the confusion of your democracy; or
popular state if not anarchy" (IX, 19). Once again we hear the
arguments proving that subordination is the order of nature.
In the supernatural world "there is a subordination of spirits,
some higher in degree, some inferior to others. . . . If we
look up into heaven, there is the King of Gods, the Lord of
Lords; higher than the highest; if to the earth, there are monarchs, kings, princes, peers, people. If we look down to hell,
there is the prince of devils. They labour for confusion that
call for parity" (II, 382). Once again we are told that virtue
means playing the part assigned us by providence. "The world is
a large chessboard: every man hath his place assigned him: one
is a king; another a knight; another a pawn; and each hath his
several motion: without this variety, there could be no game
played. . . . There is no estate in this world which can be universally good for all. . . . The great Housekeeper of the world
knows how to fit every palate with that which either is or
should be agreeable to it. . . . We are ill carvers for ourselves: he that made us knows what is fit for us" (VI, 362-3).
Hall frankly states that, "One man's virtue is another's vice;
so, boldness in a woman, bashfulness in an old man, bounty in
a poor man, parsimony in the great, are as foully unbeseeming,
as boldness in a soldier, bashfulness in a child, bounty in the
rich, parsimony in the poor, are justly commendable" (VII, 592).
"Perhaps there may be a better head for policy upon plebeian

shoulders than the governor's: shall that man leave his rank,
and thrust into the chair of government?" (VII, 596). Elsewhere he says, "It will be meet for us to consider, that as we
are made to serve all, so only in our own station: there can be
no order without a due subordination of degrees and diversity
of vocations" (VIII, 152). "If mean men should bear the minds
of great lords, no servile works would be done. . . . If, contrarily, great persons had the low spirits of drudges, there
could be no order, no obedience, because there should be none
to command" (X, 171-72). "There cannot be a greater shame than
to see servants ride on horseback, and princes walking as
servants on the ground" (V, 99).

Again and again he argues that to put country above self
is only to do the natural thing, that "natural bodies forsake
their own place and condition for the preservation of the
whole" (VII, 463), that self-sacrifice is a virtue practised
even by the heathen, that "we shall as soon extinguish both
grace and nature as quit this compassionate sense of the common calamities" (VII, 50). "Patriots of all times have
respected" country "above their parents, their children, their
lives" (VI, 71). "Even civilly the king is our common father;
our country our common mother: nature hath no private relations
which should not gladly give place to these" (I, 490). It is
the duty of every citizen to yield "personal inconveniences. . .
to public mischiefs" (II, 239). "Faithful statesmen, overlooking private respects, must bend their eyes upon public dangers, labouring to prevent a common mischief, though with the
adventure of their own" (II, 258). "The ready way for private
persons to procure peace, is, that every one should be willing
to let fall his own interest for the advancement of the public"
(VI, 636-37). Given Hall's identification of the law of nature
with patriotic responsibility, it is not likely that he would be
sympathetic with private individuals who thought the present
system had deviated from the truth and needed to be put back on
the right track. At first glance it might be tempting to say
that he represented the old way of thinking while Milton represented the new. At second glance one realizes that Hall's way
of thinking is a constantly recurring one, just as Milton's is.
To look no farther ahead than the eighteenth century is to see
similarities between Hall's frame of mind and Edmund Burke's.
At any rate, Hall had no sympathy with those who having "sucked
the breasts of our common mother, upon a little dislike . . .
have spit in her face" (VII, 69). He still held to the belief,
sometimes called medieval, that if everyone would only obey the
laws of nature--as he defined them--we would have the city of
God on earth or the perfect commonwealth. "O let prince and
people meet in the ambition to be . . . a righteous nation. . .
. First, let God have his own. . . . Then for men: Let us give
Caesar his own: tribute, fear, subjection, loyalty; and, if he
need, our lives. Let the nobility have honour, obeisance,
observation. Let the clergy have their dues and our reverence.
Let the commons have truth, love, fidelity in all their trans-

actions. Let there be . . . just balances, just weights. . . .
Let there be no grinding of faces, no trampling on the poor . .
. no swallowing of widows' houses, no force, no fraud, no per-
jury, no perfidiousness" (V, 230-1). Any tampering with "dis-
tances and proportions of respects" meant danger. "Popular
states may ring the changes with safety, but the monarchical
government requires a constant and regular course of the set
degrees of rule and inferiority" (X, 159).

The monarchical government was for him the most natural
government, the surest protection against anarchy (I, 341; V,
147, 329, 341). To support his arguments he drew examples from
the Bible, of which he said, "certainly there can be none such
mirror of princes under heaven as this." In his <u>Contemplations</u>
of "that which God hath thought good to say of kings; what they
have done, what they should have done; how they sped in good, in
evil" (II, 141) he argued in the traditional way that a king,
though above human law, could expect direct punishment from
God for any transgression (I, 350). Even on the touchy question of what a subject should do if the king commanded something that the subject considered immoral, Hall stuck to the
old view that obedience to one's superior in the hierarchy was
the main thing. He even said, "that which authority may sin
in commanding is done of the inferior, not with safety only,
but with praise" (I, 504, 523; II, 70, 112). Perhaps that was
the line of reasoning Bosola followed when he was carrying out
the commands of the Cardinal and Ferdinand.

Hall, like others, used the analogy of the belly and the
members in support of "legal and universal justice," which he
called

> the apparent mother and nurse of public peace: when governors and
> subjects are careful to give each other their own; when both con-
> spire to command and obey for the common good; when men frame their
> lives to the wholesome laws of their sovereigns, not more out of fear
> than conscience; when respect to the community carries men from par-
> tial reflection upon themselves; as, contrarily, distractions and
> private ends are the bane of any state. When the head and members
> unite their thoughts and endeavours in the centre of the common good:
> the head to devise and command, the eyes to see, the ear to hear, the
> palate to taste, the heart to move, the bellows of the lungs to blow,
> the liver to sanguify, the stomach to digest, the guts to export,
> the hands to execute, the tongue to talk for the good of this natural
> commonwealth of the body; all goes well and happily: but if any of
> these parts will be gathering to themselves, and obstructions grow
> within, and mutinous distempers arise in the humours, ruin is threat-
> ened to the whole. If either the superior miscommand, or the infe-
> riors disobey, it is an affront to peace. I need not tell you, that
> good laws are the walls of the city, the sinews of the politic body,
> the rule of our life, the life of our state; without which men would
> turn brute, yea, monstrous; the world were a chaos, yea an hell. It
> is wisdom that makes laws; it is justice that keeps them. (V, 222-23)

"It is not for subjects to poise the prince's charge in the

scales of their weak constructions, but they must suppose it
ever to be of such importance as is pretended by the commander"
(I, 523).  If that is Stoic self-sufficiency, it is morality of
the type followed by Chaucer's Griselda when she let her husband do as he liked with her children.  Hall's definition of
freedom, therefore, must be seen as freedom to play our assigned
role.  "See how free the good man is; he doth what he will; for
he wills what God wills, and what God would have him will" (V,
397).  Since God has willed the present system, the good man
should not rock the boat with intemperate criticism or demands
for change (V, 393-406).

Like many of his conservative contemporaries, Hall was a
middle-of-the-road man.  For instance, he distinguished in the
customary Christian way between just and unjust wars, maintaining that the only just grounds of war were religion and the
commonwealth and believing that when the nation had righteousness on its side it could expect a victory like the one of 1588
(V, 272).  The most unjust war, on the other hand, was civil
war, an upsetting of the ordered scheme of things (VII, 52-3;
V, 629; VI, 660; X, 149).  Similarly, he followed middle-of-the-
road thinking when he identified truth with common sense, in
opposition to those who claimed to have special insight into the
way things ought to be.  And just as the Roman Stoics had distinguished between things essential to virtue and things indifferent, so Hall, like Hooker, distinguished between things
necessary to salvation and things indifferent.  "Neutrality in
things good or evil is both odious and prejudicial; but in matters of an indifferent nature is safe and commendable" (VII,
529).  It is the essence of Stoicism to believe that we are
adhering to obvious objective truth while all the time we are
being as subjective as any skeptic.

The identification of natural law with the hierarchical
system extends, of course, to the family as well as to the
state.  A husband who does not rule his children and his wife
firmly, even though benevolently, is unnatural.  Disobedience
in a child, he said, is a "foul and unnatural" sin (I, 492).
"Ingratitude is odious in any man, but in a child monstrous"
(I, 492).  The point of this long summary of Hall's conventional
ideas about the order of nature is to emphasize that a man who
has been used as an example of the new Senecanism as opposed to
the old Ciceronianism, who has been called a Puritan bishop, who
has been hailed as a precursor of eighteenth-century latitudi-
narianism, nevertheless continues to preach the humanistic ideal
of virtue as social responsibility and the integration of the
individual into the pattern that we associate with the tradition
of Cicero's Of Duties.  As opposed to the political realists--
the Machiavellians, the skeptics, or whatever we choose to call
them--he still thinks the moral order of the universe is plain
for every man to see, that it is identical with an idealized
version of the way things are, and that there is no conflict
between political or public morality and private virtue.

Robert Burton (1577-1640), though more of a skeptic and

less of a public relations man than Hall, nevertheless shared
the same conservative social attitudes. As is to be expected
of a man with a skeptical turn of mind, he had little faith
that changing the system would bring much improvement, and on
the question of religious controversy he sided pretty much with
Hall:

> We that are University Divines especially, are prohibited all curious
> search, to print or preach, or draw the Article aside by our own sense
> and comments, upon pain of Ecclesiastical censure, I will surcease
> and conclude with Erasmus of such controversies: Let who will dis-
> pute, I think that the laws of our ancestors should be received
> with reverence, and religiously observ'd, as coming from God; nor
> is it safe or pious to invent or spread evil suspicion as to the
> public authority. And should any Tyranny exist, if unlikely to
> drive men into wickedness, 'tis better to endure it than resist it
> by sedition.[98]

In the early part of his book he satirized topsy-turvy contemporary morality from much the same point of view that Hall used
in his <u>Virgidemiarum</u> and <u>Mundus Alter et Idem</u>. Burton said
that if Democritus were to look at the modern world he would
laugh to see how the fitness of things had been forgotten,
would laugh "To see wise men degraded, fools preferred; one
govern towns and cities, and yet a silly woman over-rules him
at home; command a Province, and yet his own servants or children prescribe laws to him, as Themistocles' son did in Greece;
<u>What I will (said he) my mother wills, and what my mother wills,
my father doth</u>. To see horses ride in a coach, men draw it;
dogs devour their masters; towers build masons" (p. 55). Like
Hall he emphasized a place for everyone and everyone in his
place.

> But because mortal men want many things, therefore, saith Theodoret,
> hath God diversely distributed his gifts, wealth to one, skill to
> another, that rich men might encourage and set poor men a-work, poor
> men might learn several trades to the common good. As a piece of
> arras is composed of several parcels, some wrought of silk, some of
> gold, silver, crewel of divers colours, all to serve for the exorna-
> tion [or embellishment] of the whole; [as] Music, is made of divers
> discords and keys, a total sum of many small numbers: so is a Com-
> monwealth of several inequal trades and callings. (p. 527)

A little earlier on the same page he referred to Epictetus's
advice to play the game as well as we can. "If thou canst not
fling what thou wouldest, play thy cast as well as thou canst.
. . . Conform thyself then to thy present fortune, and cut thy
coat according to thy cloth: be contented with thy lot, state,
and calling, whatsoever it is, and rest as well satisfied with
thy present condition in this life. . . . And as he that is
invited to a feast eats what is set before him and looks for no
other, enjoy that thou hast, and ask no more of God than what he
thinks fit to bestow upon thee" (p. 527).
        By playing our part in the pattern we resolve the apparent

conflict between fortune, fate, and free will. Unlike the playwrights, who liked to show fate as all powerful, Burton, like
Aquinas, drew a dividing line between God's plan and man's freedom. "Although the Stoicks absolutely deny it, and will have
all things inevitably done by destiny, imposing a fatal necessity upon us, which we may not resist; yet we say that our will
is free in respect of us, and things contingent, howsoever (in
respect of God's determinate counsel) they are inevitable and
necessary" (p. 147). Though he blamed Seneca and other Stoics
for believing in "Stoick Fate . . . inevitable necessity" (pp.
930-31), he also praised Seneca for pointing out that nature is
another name for God. When defining his own position he
referred to Scaliger, Calvin, Minucius, and Seneca. "As Scaliger defines, Nature signifies God's ordinary power; or as Calvin writes, Nature is God's order, and so things extraordinary
may be called unnatural: Fortune his unrevealed will; and so we
call things changeable that are beside reason and expectation.
To this purpose Minucius, and Seneca well discourseth with them
[philosophers and deists]. They do not understand what they
say; what is Nature but God? Call him what thou wilt, Nature,
Jupiter, he hath as many Names as Offices. It comes all to one
pass, God is the fountain of all, the first Giver and Preserver,
from whom all things depend. God is all in all, God is everywhere, in every place" (pp. 929-30). There is nothing extraordinary about Burton's position on the relation between God,
nature, fate, fortune, and free will, nor in his condemnation
of Stoic fate and the "Chaldaean Astrologers of old" (p. 930).
Probably his contemporaries who wrote for the theatre would
privately have agreed with him. For dramatic purposes, however,
they often found it convenient to treat fate as some sort of
evil, interfering, free agent that took a malignant pleasure in
making things go wrong.

John Milton (1608-1674) was some thirty years younger than
Hall and Burton. Though his ties to the system of Cicero and
Aquinas and Hooker were more tenuous than theirs, they were not
completely broken.[99] Even if practical men were coming to prefer Machiavellian definitions of natural law, Milton's affinities were still with the Stoic tradition. Where he differed,
however, from such a conservative as Joseph Hall was in refusing to identify truth with custom. Like Erasmus and Thomas
More, though not necessarily with the same ends in mind, he
argued that contemporary society, having deviated a long way
from the true laws of nature, needed to be put back on the
track. Consequently he battled against the identification of
custom (the way things are) with the law of nature (the way
things ought to be), and in spite of his various sneers at
Stoic pride he leaned in the direction of moral self-
sufficiency. Like the Stoics he believed that it takes a virtuous man really to arrive at truth and that virtue has to be
carefully nurtured through a proper education--one requirement
that kept him from being an egalitarian. Though he did not

think kings were necessarily better endowed with virtue than
other men, he did not consider everyone's insight as good as
everyone else's.  In fact, he did not think that many people
could interpret reason as well as he could.  When arguing a
point, he sometimes based his arguments on what seemed plainly
reasonable to him, sometimes on the authority of the Bible,
sometimes on what he regarded as the consensus gentium.  As a
master craftsman he knew how to promote an idea once he had
taken it up.  In youth he was possibly more confident of his
insight into the laws of nature than he was when old, and during his active years in politics he hoped to see the will of
God--as he interpreted it--prevail.  In later life, like many
another, he tried to resign himself to accepting the will of
God without presuming to understand it very well.

His attitude toward social organization is in some ways
reminiscent of Thomas More's in the Utopia, where a hierarchical system, loosely modeled on the family, still left room for
gifted people to change their places.  Although in Milton's
writing there is no suggestion that he planned to level all the
ranks, and although he, like other humanists, emphasized doing
one's social duty rather than climbing on the wheel of ambition,
yet he did not always equate the rank assigned by social custom
with the rank assigned by God.  If on such things as the position of women he went along with the usual thinking of his
time, he nevertheless broke with traditionalists like Hall by
insisting that people at the top had to demonstrate superior
virtue in order to justify their right to stay where they were,
even going so far as to suggest that kings and bishops might
not be a necessary part of the natural order.  His insistence on
virtue as the mark of true nobility links him once more with the
tradition of Cicero and Erasmus.[100]

Though custom equated nature with the rigid medieval hierarchical system, Milton often preferred to go back to the
looser authority of Aristotle and to use vague phrases like "the
principles of reason," "the true welfare of every Christian,"
"our own dignity rightly understood."  Since his attacks on
Stoic pride did not cure him of the humanist's tendency to
expect a great deal of the human animal, there is even an occasional suggestion that he thought society ought to be composed
only of those mythical virtuous beings whose inward self-
government was sufficient to make external compulsion unnecessary.  Like any Stoic he failed to suffer fools gladly and dis-
dained the miscellaneous rabble for its inability to distinguish
between liberty and license.

Though Milton's ideal man belongs in the next chapter, Milton's big difference from traditionalists like Hall comes from
his greater faith in the individual.  Where Hall put his heaviest emphasis on cooperation, Milton came down a little more
strongly on the side of personal integrity.  Writers in the
Aquinas tradition, like Hall, tended to believe that if a custom had endured a long time it had some hidden link with the
laws of nature and should be changed very warily.  Distrusting

arguments that a custom should be changed merely because it
seemed unreasonable, they insisted that those at the top had
been put there as part of God's plan and had generally been
endowed with superior insight.  If for some reason these leaders
turned out to be tyrants or proved otherwise unfit, it should
still be left to God to solve the problem.  For Hall, civil war
was never justified.  Milton, however, argued that a king who
did not demonstrate superior virtue was no true king.  In The
First Defence of the English People (1651) he said, "There is
no right of succession by the law of nature, no king by the
law of nature except him who excels all the rest in wisdom and
courage; and all kings else are such by force or faction, contrary to nature, being fit rather to be slaves" (CM, VII, 273).
That the king ought to be the same as the wise man was not a
new idea.  Chaucer's Theseus, More's King Utopus, Shakespeare's
Henry V were all examples of the wise man as king.  Milton's
ideal king, as described by Christ in Paradise Regained, was,
like Shakespeare's Henry V, a servant to the commonweal, the
one who stayed awake worrying while the careless peasant slept.

> a Crown,
> Golden in shew, is but a wreath of thorns,
> Brings dangers, troubles, cares, and sleepless nights
> To him who wears the Regal Diadem,
> When on his shoulders each mans burden lies;
> For therein stands the office of a King,
> His Honour, Vertue, Merit and chief Praise,
> That for the Publick all this weight he bears.  (II.458 ff)[101]

Christ continues his lecture, after the manner of Erasmus in The
Education of a Christian Prince or the medieval Diogenes when
explaining true freedom to Alexander, by arguing that in another
sense the true king is the man who knows how to rule himself,
that only the wise and virtuous man can properly rule others.

> Yet he who reigns within himself, and rules
> Passions, Desires, and Fears, is more a King;
> Which every wise and vertuous man attains:
> And who attains not, ill aspires to rule
> Cities of men, or head-strong Multitudes,
> Subject himself to Anarchy within,
> Or lawless passions in him which he serves.

In thus identifying the good king with the Stoic wise man, Milton was fighting a last humanistic battle against the ever-
growing tendency of practical politicians to forget even to
apologize for divorcing political expediency from standards of
private morality.
     In earlier days, the radical Milton had actually thought it
possible to enforce the old-fashioned doctrine that a king is
accountable to the laws of nature and is in no sense a free agent
whose own will is law or whose own whim is the will of God.
Unlike such a conservative moralist as Hall, who confined himself to reminding the people at large to accept the decrees of

authority as the will of God, Milton insisted that authority
ought to identify the will of God with the welfare of the public.  One eloquent statement of his all-for-one, one-for-all
doctrine occurs in Of Reformation (The Second Book).

> Looke what the grounds, and causes are of single happines to one
> man, the same yee shall find them to a whole state, as Aristotle both
> in his ethicks, and politiks from the principles of reason layes down:
> by consequence therefore, that which is good, and agreeable to mon-
> archy, will appeare soonest to be so, by being good, and agreeable to
> the true wel-fare of every Christian, and that which can be justly
> prov'd hurtfull, and offensive to every true Christian, wilbe evinc't
> to be alike hurtfull to monarchy: for God forbid, that we should
> separate and distinguish the end, and good of a monarch, from the
> end and good of the monarchy, or of that from Christianity.  (CM,
> III, 37-9)

The idea that everybody from the king down to the peasant
should be continually checking his actions against the guiding
moral law was not new.  The new thing was that as the hierarchical system became less rigid, inferiors became more vocal in
criticizing the morality of their superiors.  Where the earlier
rule had been that morality for servants (and wives and children) consisted in obeying their masters, now Milton was saying
that masters were no longer masters when they forgot the moral
law.  Though Milton's Eve clearly erred when she depended on her
own reasoning powers instead of listening to her husband, there
was for her no conflict between obeying her husband and obeying
the law.  Whether Milton would have condoned the obedience of
Chaucer's Griselda is another question.  Where he clearly differed from a conservative like Hall was on the question of what
a good subject should do if the king should command something
contrary to moral law.  From a practical point of view, he made
a distinction between what one subject acting alone could do
and what was possible for a number of subjects acting together.
The individual could only make a moral protest and accept his
punishment.  As long as he wished to remain a subject, he had
to accept the existing situation: "When the King shall command
things constituted in Church, or State, obedience is the true
essence of a subject, either to doe, if it be lawful, or if he
hold the thing unlawful [i.e., contrary to the law of nature],
to submit to that penaltie which the Law [i.e., positive law]
imposes, so long as he intends to remaine a subject."  A rebel
who wishes to consider himself moral must come to terms with the
doctrine that "obedience is the true essence of a subject."  One
way to do that is to argue that the subject is absolved from his
duty when the king, by failing to obey the higher law, proves
himself no true king.  A number of subjects acting together have
obviously more chance of enforcing such an argument than a single objector.

> Therefore when the people or any part of them shall rise against the
> King and his authority executing the Law in any thing establish'd
> civil or Ecclesiastical, I doe not say it is rebellion, if the thing

commanded though establish'd be unlawfull, and that they sought
first of all due means of redress (and no man is furder bound to
Law) but I say it is an absolute renouncing both of Supremacy
and Allegeance, which in one word is an actual and total depos-
ing of the King, and the setting up of another supreme authority over them. (The Tenure of Kings and Magistrates [1649], CM,
IV, 31-2)

Milton's attempt to argue that the governments of states
ought to be able to stand the test of reason--as defined by Mil-
ton--expanded easily to include a similar argument for the governments of families. His efforts to clear away some of the
unreasonable clutter that had accumulated around the institution
of marriage roused him to eloquent attacks on custom:

Error supports Custome, Custome count'nances Error. And these
two betweene them would persecute and chase away all truth and
solid wisdome out of humane life, were it not that God, rather
then man, once in many ages, cals together the prudent and Religious counsels of Men, deputed to represse the encroachments,
and to work off the inveterate blots and obscurities wrought
upon our mindes by the suttle insinuating of Error and Custom.
(The Doctrine and Discipline of Divorce [1643], CM, III, 368)

Opposed to error and custom is that confusing and useful
word "nature." Obviously Milton, unlike Shakespeare, did not
identify nature with custom--at least not when he was arguing
for change. In a later section of his defense of divorce he
cited the familiar and generally accepted doctrine that man-
made laws should not run counter to the basic laws of nature
and then went on to state it as a law that questions of like
or dislike result from "the guiltless instinct of nature" and
are "not within the Province of any Law to reach." When
"guiltless instinct" instead of "selfless duty" is taken as
the prime factor, the law of nature is bound to take on a different color. Ignoring the fact that he was changing his terms,
Milton referred to Socrates in support of his argument that it is
an error to suppose "that Law may bandy with nature, and tra-
verse her sage motions"; and thus, having made a general statement that most people would have accepted, he then went on to
give a specific interpretation that caused shock. Arguing that
to forbid the divorce of people who dislike each other is contrary to nature, he said, if "law and nature are not to goe contrary, then to forbid divorce compulsively, is not only against
nature, but against law" (III, 500-01). For those who accept
Milton's definition of what is natural, the argument is convincing. For those who have some other definition of nature,
such as that it is natural for married people to dislike each
other, or that it is natural to make the best of the cards we
have been dealt, or that it is natural for children to obey
their parents, the argument may appear to have a flaw in it.
However reasonable Milton's arguments in favor of divorce may
now seem, most people of his time preferred to go on identify-

ing nature with custom.[102]

It was axiomatic, of course, that the laws of nature ought not to conflict with the Bible. Joseph Hall had written volumes of commentary on Bible history, always finding plenty of support for his arguments in favor of the contemporary status quo. Milton, too, could find Biblical precedents for his somewhat more radical arguments. By pointing to the example of Joseph in Egypt he could defend the idea that a man of merit might move to the top of the political ladder (Christian Doctrine, CM, XVII, 243). When arguing for divorce he said he had concluded from his study of the Gospel "that the great and almost only commandment of the Gospel, is to command nothing against the good of man, and much more no civil command, against his civil good" (Tetrachordon, CM, IV, 136-7). Instead of looking for specific rules and regulations, he was looking for large general principles and was thus lining up not only with such earlier humanists as Erasmus and More but also with the coming eighteenth-century tendency to loosen the tight Elizabethan definitions of the laws of nature.

Although Milton inveighed against custom and was suspicious of authority, he continued to draw the conventional dividing line between Stoic pride and Christian humility; for human beings always needed to remember that their own efforts could never lead them to final answers. He may possibly have had more faith in the potentialities of human reason at the time of writing the Areopagitica (1644) than he had when he produced Paradise Regained (1671); but, although in the Areopagitica his frame of mind was far removed from that of the skeptic who doubts the existence of moral absolutes, although he believed that truth--even if not yet completely deciphered-- was there for the searching, although he rebelled at the notion that authority will decide for us which things it is safe for us to know, and although he was not afraid of change, he nevertheless did not--even at this time--pretend that all truth could be discovered by the light of human reason: "When every stone is laid artfully together, it cannot be united into a continuity, it can but be contiguous in this world" (IV, 342).

When he was seriously chasing truth, Milton, like the Stoics and like humanists in general, usually had in mind truth as applied to human conduct rather than abstract speculative knowledge. When he was only talking about astronomy instead of politics he was quite willing to side with the skeptics or the fideists. In Paradise Lost Raphael told Adam that all he really needed to know was that "which best may serve / To glorifie the Maker and inferr / Thee also happier" (PL, VII, 115-17). To speculate about the operations of the universe and to admire them was all right; to understand them was neither essential nor possible (PL, VIII, 166-68). When we come to Christ's attack on Stoic pride in Paradise Regained we are reminded of Folly's similar diatribe in The Praise of Folly. Once again we are given a good summary of the standard Christian objections to Stoicism, namely its belief in self-sufficiency and its definition of God

as nothing more than the implacable law of nature.  Once again
the primitive Stoic straw man is tumbled by someone who himself
embodies the ideals of later Stoicism.  In reply to Satan's
praise of what the Gentiles had learned "by Natures light" (IV,
228), Christ denied that such learning was true wisdom.  Of the
Stoics he said,

> The Stoic last in Philosophic pride,
> By him call'd vertue; and his vertuous man,
> Wise, perfect in himself, and all possessing
> Equal to God, oft shames not to prefer,
> As fearing God nor man, contemning all
> Wealth, pleasure, pain or torment, death and life,
> Which when he lists, he leaves, or boasts he can,
> For all his tedious talk is but vain boast,
> Or subtle shifts conviction to evade.
> Alas what can they teach, and not mislead;
> Ignorant of themselves, of God much more,
> And how the world began, and how man fell
> Degraded by himself, on grace depending?
> Much of the Soul they talk, but all awrie,
> And in themselves seek vertue, and to themselves
> All glory arrogate, to God give none,
> Rather accuse him under usual names,
> Fortune and Fate, as one regardless quite
> Of mortal things.  Who therefore seeks in these
> True wisdom, finds her not, or by delusion
> Far worse, her false resemblance only meets,
> An empty cloud. (IV. 297-321)

If Milton here in old age has lost some of his faith in
the human animal, his earlier preference for reason as opposed
to custom had contributed its mite toward the general shake-up
of Elizabethan verities that was characteristic of the seventeenth century.  His faith that there must be a fairly large
portion of truth in what seemed reasonable to a good man like
himself stemmed from the same tradition that later produced a
similar self-confidence in Rousseau.  If the two men arrived at
different conclusions, that is only what a skeptical observer
would expect.

Milton was not the only man of his time with his own ideas
about the laws of nature.  By his side were the Levellers,
whose insights into truth led them to argue that the laws of
nature gave everyone certain natural rights, a startling idea
that later came to be accepted as axiomatic.[103]  Meanwhile the
Diggers were interpreting "the laws of nature as a communal
right to the means of subsistence" (Sabine, p. 491).  On the
continent the Dutchman, Hugo Grotius (1583-1645), sometimes described as the father of international law, had been basing new
legal arguments on old Roman Stoic principles.  Divorcing
natural law from its medieval dependence on providence, he said,
as C. S. Lewis puts it, that the law of nature "would be equally

binding even if we supposed that no God existed."[104] Though
the world of the seventeenth century was no longer the one
world of the Roman empire or the one world of Christendom, the
old Stoic dream of one world still hovered in the background.
Just as the Romans had tried to work out a legal system based on
the general principles underlying seemingly divergent local customs, so Grotius and others hoped to find the general principles underlying the laws of various nations.  These principles,
which he called the law of nations, would not necessarily be
the same as the laws of nature, any more than Roman law was necessarily the same.  A margin for human error always had to be
left.[105]  It was hoped, however, that when a lowest common
denominator had been found, one had come close to a basic law.
In addition to the consensus gentium, there were the other traditional ways of looking for the basic unwritten laws, namely
by using reason and common sense.  The important thing was that
the old Stoic belief in the existence of absolute moral truth
was being adapted to changing times, was being freed from some
of the particular interpretations it had acquired during the
Middle Ages.  Grotius, with his belief in the existence of universal moral or legal principles, stood on the opposite side
of the fence from the skeptics who had no such faith.

A contemporary of Grotius, George Herbert's brother, Lord
Herbert of Cherbury (1583-1648), is sometimes classified as a
sort of ur-Deist who lived before his time and who carried his
confidence in human reason to the point of arguing that truth
was largely available without the need for special revelation or
expert interpretation.  His interest, however, was less in moral
or political problems than in the question of how we know that
God exists.  Just as Grotius had disentangled the law of nature
from providence and had distinguished between the law of nations
(the consensus gentium) and the law of nature (known intuitive-
ly), so Cherbury, de-emphasizing revelation, had sometimes
looked for the lowest common denominator (the consensus gentium) among the beliefs of various religions and sometimes had
set up right reason (intuition) as the key to truth.[106]

Opposed to the believers in absolute moral law, available
through reason, were the skeptics or fideists, among whom there
were conservative thinkers as well as members of the avant
garde.  Just as it was common for conservative Christian writers
to emphasize the insufficiency of human insight and to prefer
custom or authority or revelation to so-called reason,[107] so
among lawyers there were various shades of opinion about whether natural law existed and if it existed to what extent it
was related to written law.  Although there were only a few
skeptics who refused to give lip service to the standard doctrine that just human laws must not run counter to the laws of
nature, there still remained the problem of how to recognize
natural law.  Where human law was non-existent or not clear, how
was true justice to be known?  Which clue to ideal justice was
the best, authority or reason or custom?  In the hierarchical
system, which endowed God's minister, the king, with special

insight, the king's deputy, the Lord Chancellor, was supposed to be able to resolve legal disputes by direct reference to abstract justice or equity.[108]  Those who accepted this point of view believed that whatever the king's court decided was automatically right.  Skeptics, for other reasons, might also accept the king's decision as the last word, since from their point of view absolute truth was unreachable and an arbitrary decision had to be made somewhere.  Francis Bacon as a lawyer inclined to this point of view.  His often-quoted remark that "we are much beholden to Machiavel and others, that write what men do and not what they ought to do" was one way of saying that he like Hobbes preferred to define the laws of nature as the way things are rather than as the way things ought to be.  Like Hobbes, too, he was willing to give the king--or the king's court--more arbitrary authority than suited the upholders of the common law.[109]  John Selden (1584-1654), however, another lawyer who was likewise skeptical about natural law, felt safer relying on written authority and on the common law tradition than on the Lord Chancellor.  Denying that he was born with innate ideas about right and wrong, he said in his Table Talk, "I cannot fancy to myself what the law of nature means but the law of God.  How should I know I ought not to steal, I ought not to commit adultery, unless somebody had told me so?"  And of the idea that any judge has an intuitive feeling for equity, he said, "Equity is a roguish thing.  'Tis all one as if they should make the standard for the measure we call a foot the chancellor's foot."  It is not surprising that Selden, who was wary of change and preferred to side with Coke and other upholders of the common law, should have found himself disagreeing with some of the opinions of the optimistic Grotius.[110]

Thomas Hobbes (1588-1679), that arch skeptic, gave the old Stoic term "law of nature" a somewhat Epicurean flavor.[111]  It will be remembered that the Epicureans, who did not believe in the existence of universal, unchangeable justice, tied definitions of law and justice to local and current ideas of the general welfare and said that these ideas might change with changing circumstances.  Definitions of justice depended on definitions of mutual security.[112]  For Hobbes, also, definitions of moral and political law depended on definitions of mutual security.  As he followed a line of reasoning that seemed to him more logical than the methods that such predecessors as Hooker and Aquinas had used to arrive at the commonly received definitions of the laws of nature, he concluded that the fundamental principle behind human behavior was not some altruistic ideal like Stoic or Christian brotherly love and the desire to cooperate with the total scheme but rather the egoistic need for physical self-preservation.  In the end, however, he argued for something like the golden rule as the best policy, since self-preservation, namely, living at peace, requires us to give up our right to molest other people and consequently to learn to do as we would be done by.  According to Sabine,

> The laws of nature really meant for Hobbes a set of rules according
> to which an ideally reasonable being would pursue his own advantage,
> if he were perfectly conscious of all the circumstances in which he
> was acting and was unswayed by momentary impulse and prejudice. . . .
> The power of the state and the authority of the law are justified
> only because they contribute to the security of individual human
> beings. . . . This clear-cut individualism . . . makes Hobbes's
> philosophy the most revolutionary theory of the age.  (pp. 461, 467)

Though the individualism of people like Milton was probably not
so "clear-cut" as that of Hobbes, it is well to remember that
the Stoic tradition as well as the Epicurean stressed individualism, that individualism, in fact, was the coming thing and
was spreading everywhere like strains of influenza.

Aside from his skepticism about conventional definitions
of the laws of nature, Hobbes differed from the Stoics and Epicureans in that he was no primitivist.  In sharp contrast to
the idealized classical picture of the golden age stands his
famous unpleasant description of the original state of nature.
Where the early or primitive Stoics thought that if every man
would live in accordance with the laws of nature there would be
no need for other laws, Hobbes said that men in a state of
nature would be ruled by such natural passions as partiality,
pride, and revenge, which passions would not be sins because
there was yet no law forbidding them.  Life in accordance with
nature would be so nasty that men would have to give it up and
set some artificial law-making authority over themselves.  In
order to survive, they would have to give up their right to be
"natural."  As a political writer Hobbes got somewhat the same
treatment as Machiavelli.  Though he was publicly castigated,
his ideas in time became commonplaces; and, ironically, his
theories were often made palatable by being given a sugar coating of conventional-sounding Stoicism.[113]

Hobbes's successor, John Locke (1632-1704)--who was actually born nearly fifty years later--is generally credited with
enormous influence on succeeding generations and was possibly
better able to get a hearing because by the time he came the
climate had changed and because he was one of those apostles of
good sense who do not express their ideas in an irritating way.
In putting across his political message he was sufficiently
ambiguous to keep commentators differing even up to the present
time about what he was actually saying.  On the one hand he is
credited with carrying on the long tradition of political
thought that is associated with Aquinas and Hooker.  As Sabine
says,

> Through Hooker Locke was joined with the long tradition of medieval
> political thought, back to St. Thomas, in which the reality of moral
> restraints on power, the responsibility of rulers to the communities
> which they ruled, and the subordination of government to law was axio-
> matic. . . . The chief mark of his genius was neither learning nor
> logic but an incomparable common sense by which he gathered together
> the chief convictions, in philosophy, politics, morals, and education,

that the experience of the past had generated in the more enlightened minds of his generation.  (p. 523)[114]

Although the natural law tradition of Aquinas and Hooker was based
on the Stoic idea that there is such a thing as innate moral law,
Locke, as a writer on psychology, is famous for his attack on
the notion of innate ideas.[115]  Part of the inconsistency
results from his use of the old familiar words with new meanings attached, for he was often propagating ideas similar to
those of Hobbes by wrapping them in the language of Hooker.[116]
Instead of identifying the rules of politics with ideals handed
down by authority or tradition, he, like the Machiavellians,
sometimes believed in deriving political theory from an empiri-
cal study of what men actually do, while, like Milton, he at
other times identified what seemed logical to him with the laws
of nature.  Like Hobbes he argued "that the natural condition of
man is the pre-political state of nature, which is the state of
war; that man's first care and most natural desire is to be safe;
and that the end of government, since it is established by con-
tract, is essentially to secure the members in their lives, liberties, and possessions."[117]

Although history shows us that succeeding generations are
continually throwing away the absolute verities of their ancestors in order to substitute new ones of their own, yet at any
particular time there are only a few naughty children who
boldly compare the laws of nature to the emperor's new clothes.
It is more common to insist that the laws are there, even if
not yet perfectly discovered.  Like Descartes's wax or Shelley's
cloud, they change but they cannot die.  The new law that was
struggling to replace the old law was that everything should
revolve around the individual.[118]  Increasingly natural law was
coming to mean natural rights.  The old order, which had decreed
that there is a place for everyone and that everyone should stay
in his or her place, that identified freedom with the freedom to
cooperate willingly with the established order, and that considered it contrary to nature to follow personal desire instead of
selfless social responsibility, had lingered longer among literary men (whether playwrights or preachers) than among the practical men of the world; and as time passed these old ideas continued to linger in the minds of bookish people.  Throughout the
eighteenth century the attempt to reconcile the old with the new
found writers trying to prove that self love and social were the
same, that unbridled laissez-faire would in the end contribute to
the greatest good of the greatest number, that from the long-
range point of view everything was for the best.

During the closing decades of the seventeenth century William Temple and George Savile, Marquis of Halifax, give us examples of thoughtful bookish statesmen who tried to adapt their
humanistic early training to a changing world.  Though both have
been accused of varying degrees of religious skepticism, there
is no necessary connection between religious skepticism and political opportunism.  Both men persisted in believing that England

should guide itself by some higher standard than immediate expediency.  Though they were willing to re-examine old assumptions and to re-define the laws of nature, they were not willing to substitute narrow self interest or blind party loyalty for what they defined as principle.  Though they may not have seen eye to eye with Aquinas or Hooker, they were still devoted to the Ciceronian ideal of patriotic responsibility.  It is not surprising, then, that they ran into conflict with the practical politicians.

Although the years that William Temple (1628-1699) spent as a diplomat gave him plenty of opportunity to ruminate on the disparity between the way things are in government and the way things ought to be, he was no more ready than that other skeptic, his admired Montaigne, to abandon the search for moral standards.  In much the same way that Montaigne in "Of Cannibals" had looked for the laws of nature underlying the customs of Brazil and had found, or thought he found, the same basic principles that had been set down by the ancient Romans, so Temple when reading about such far-off places as China and Peru kept looking for the basic moral principles underlying divergent customs.  Wherever he looked he found evidence to support his theory that reason and the law of nature are everywhere the same--by which he meant that wherever he looked he could find something resembling the good old Ciceronian principles on which he had been raised.  A remark like the following, from his essay "Of Heroic Virtue," indicates that he was thinking along the same lines as Grotius.

> From the orders and institutions, the laws and customs of these empires and states, the sages of law and justice in all countries endeavour to deduce the very common laws of nature and of nations, as well as the particular civil or municipal of kingdoms and provinces.[119]

When Temple described China and the teachings of Confucius, he might just as well have been expounding the old Roman ideal of selfless cooperation; and Thomas Elyot would certainly have approved of the following sentiments:

> The bent of his [Confucius'] thoughts and reasonings running up and down this scale that no people can be happy but under good governments, and no governments happy but under good men; and that for the felicity of mankind, all men in a nation from the prince to the meanest peasant, should endeavour to be good and wise, and virtuous, as far as his own thoughts, the precepts of others, or the laws of his country can instruct him.  (p. 114)[120]

Continuing to use Stoic terminology to describe Confucius, Temple went on,

> The chief principle he seems to lay down for a foundation and builds upon, is that every man ought to study and endeavour the improving and perfecting of his own natural reason to the greatest height he is capable, so as he may never (or as seldom as can be) err and swerve

from the law of nature in the course and conduct of his life.  (p. 115)

When Temple turned from his study of China to look at Peru, he might almost have wandered into Thomas More's Utopia, except that the emphasis on the simple life was missing.  The Peruvians, like More's Utopians, had arrived at the laws of nature through the use of reason.  Here the rule was "that every man should live according to reason, and consequently neither say nor do any thing to others that they were not willing others should say or do to them; because it was against all common reason to make one law for ourselves, and another for other people: and this was the great principle of all their morality" (p. 126). Reason, in other words, had taught men the golden rule but had not taught them all the class privileges that Europeans assumed were part of the nature of things.  Temple, like other humanists, was hoping to find the large simple principles underlying local customs.  From his study of Peru he concluded "that human nature is the same in these remote, as well as the other more known and celebrated parts of the world . . .that the same causes produce everywhere the same effects" (pp. 133-34).

The golden rule and the golden mean were two of Temple's guiding principles.  As a mild Stoic, mild Epicurean, mild skeptic he belonged in the company of such men as Montaigne and Horace.  Though he may have made little use of the word "providence," he followed the common middle-of-the-road practice of rejecting both blind chance and absolute fate.  Of fortune he said in an early essay,

> Wee say shee is blind when the truth on't is tis wee that are soe, our ignorance gives her a name; when wee cannot discover the cause of any effect, either because the way is darke or wee are purblind, tis but beeleeving there is none, and then comes fortune in, like a cypher that signifies nothing and yet you may make it stand for whatere you please.[121]

Of fate he said in "Of Heroic Virtue," that the Stoic belief in predestination was something that appealed to men as a "refuge in the uncertain conditions or events of life under tyrannical and cruel governments.  So as some Roman authors observe, that the reigns of Tiberius, Caligula, and Nero made more Stoics in Rome, than the precepts of Zeno, Chrysippus, and Cleanthes" (Monk, p. 155).  It would seem, then, that he took the moderate view that although cooperation with the laws of nature will both promote the general welfare and conduce to individual peace of mind, belief in inexorable fate will only be an excuse for making no effort.

As a practical statesman Temple tangled with the politicians because of his habit of trying to act like a Stoic man of integrity.  As John Marston had shown in his plays, those who try to live according to the Stoic doctrine that reason and virtue are everywhere the same and refuse to admit any conflict between political duty and personal virtue have difficulty adjusting to the practical world where political virtue tends to be identified with uncritical obedience. Though Temple's insistence on having a conscience of his own made him something of a nuisance to the practical men, his reputation for integrity could serve their purpose on occasion. When the king, for instance, wished to impress a foreign power with the rectitude of his intentions, he could send Temple to negotiate a treaty. But when the king had other plans in mind, he could move Temple aside. In the end, Temple retired to the country to work on his garden.[122]

George Savile, Marquis of Halifax (1633-95) was another who tried to combine some of the old with some of the new, who tried, in other words, to reconcile Cicero with Machiavelli and Hobbes. Even more than Temple he moved in the top political circles. Like Temple he was a moderate religious skeptic without being a complete moral relativist; and like Temple too he accepted as a matter of course his hereditary role as public servant, only to find that in the end he was eased off the political stage for refusing to accommodate himself to the new game of party politics. Though he has a reputation as a pragmatist who based his political theories on a hard knowledge of the facts, he nevertheless clung at the same time to the old law-of-nature ideal. The new wrinkle was that instead of identifying the law of nature, as many Elizabethans did, with a specific social or political system, he left the ideal sufficiently ambiguous to be adaptable to change. An example of the way he managed to sound more cynical than he was is shown by his use of the word "interest." When he insisted that the proper foundation of politics is interest, he sounded on the surface like the very opposite of a Stoic idealist. Soon we learn, however, that "interest" means public interest--not self interest or selfish individualism. By the "true interest" of the commonwealth Halifax had in mind some sort of amorphous, ever-changing, yet ever-objective standard rising above the exigencies of party politics.[123] If the government would only base its policies on the "true interest" of England instead of allowing itself to be swayed by special-interest groups, it would avoid some of the muddles it had stumbled into. Following his own teaching, Halifax had the habit of voting according to principle instead of according to party--a failing that did not endear him to the party politicians. For all his sophisticated worldly skepticism, he had not broken his ties with the old-fashioned humanistic tradition.

A few illustrations from his well-known "The Character of a Trimmer' will illustrate some of the ramifications of his thinking about the law of nature.[124] The section headed "The Trimmer's Opinion of the Laws and Government" starts out sounding like Hobbes, saying laws are "the Chains that tye up our unruly passions, which else, like wild Beasts let loose, would reduce the world into its first State of Barbarism and Hostility" (p. 50). Soon, however, he shifts from talking about the laws as something dictated by expediency to saying, in the idealistic way, that they are dictated from above. "All Laws

flow from that of Nature, and where that is not the Foundation,
they may be legally impos'd, but they will be lamely obeyed:
By this Nature is not meant that which Fools and Madmen misquote
to justify their Excesses; it is innocent and uncorrupted
Nature, that which disposeth Men to chuse Vertue, without its
being prescribed" (p. 50). He goes on to remind us that Roman
law was based on "Patterns of good laws" taken by the Romans
"even from those they had subdued" and that through their admirable laws the Romans still reign. Then, becoming a practical
man again, he says that "no Prince is so Great, as not to think
fit, for his own Credit at least, to give an outward, when he
refuseth a real worship to the Laws" (p. 51). From the practical point of view, likewise, Halifax recognized that good laws
are only good if well administered, that putting them into
practice requires a recognition of the difference between "Men's
Nature as it is" and men's nature "as it should be" (p. 54).
Unlike Hobbes, he was against trusting a king with absolute
power, preferring the old argument that a king is free if he
wills what the law wills. To a good king the laws are not
really fetters. Indeed, "to such as would make them their
choice as well as their practice they are Chains of Gold." "A
good and wise Governour, tho' all laws were abolish'd, would, by
the voluntary direction of his own Reason, do without restraint
the very same things they would have enjoined" (p. 56). Once
again the good governor is identified with the wise man. Once
again we are presented with the ideal of the commonwealth as a
great animal in which "the King and Kingdom ought to be one
Creature" (p. 56). Again we hear that the prince should look on
himself as "God Almighty's Deputy upon Earth" (p. 57) and are
told that "a Prince who doth not allow his thoughts to stray
beyond the Rules of Justice hath always the blessing of an
inward quiet" (p. 58).

Sometimes instead of "interest" or "nature" he talks about
"reasons of state." These too are vaguely indefinable, yet
supposed to be self evident. "When all is said, there is a
Natural Reason of State, an undefinable thing, grounded upon
the Common Good of Mankind, which is immortal, and in all
Changes and Revolutions still preserveth its Original Right of
saving a Nation, when the Letter of the Law perhaps would
destroy it; and by whatsoever means it moveth, carrieth a Power
with it, that admitteth of no opposition, being supported by
Nature, which inspireth an immediate consent" (p. 60). Skeptics
like Hobbes and Selden might have raised their eyebrows at such
sentiments, though they might have nodded approval at the way
Halifax combined idealistic generalizations with practical
advice of the kind often called Machiavellian. Though as an
idealist he kept reiterating that the aim of government should
be to promote the "true interest" of England, as an experienced
statesman he knew the ideal could only be approached by taking
account of the way men actually behave.

If the efforts of sensible men managed to keep England on
the right track, there would be no need for nature to interfere

from outside.  If men became careless, however, destiny would
find it necessary to take a hand; and the ways of destiny are
not necessarily pleasant.  Who would expect to hear this skeptical worldly statesman once again setting forth the doctrine, so
popular with Elizabethan dramatists, that although wicked or
foolish men may temporarily divert the nation from its proper
course, nature will not for long permit the good of the commonwealth to be violated?  In the section entitled "The Trimmer's Opinion in Relation to Things Abroad," he says,

> Mistakes, as all other things, have their Periods, and many times
> the nearest way to Cure is not to oppose them, but stay till they
> are crusht with their own weight: for Nature will not allow any
> thing to continue long that is violent; violence is a wound, and as a
> wound must be curable in a little time, or else 'tis Mortal, but a
> Nation comes near to be Immortal, therefore the wound will one time
> or another be cured, tho perhaps by such rough Methods, if too long
> forborn, as may even make the best Remedies we can prepare, to be
> at the same time a Melancholy Contemplation to us.  (p. 98)

Nature here is no sentimental kind mother, any more than she
was in _King Lear_.  When nature is restoring order from chaos,
she has no respect for persons.

To stay on the good side of nature, Halifax recommends following the golden mean.  His Trimmer is a middle-of-the-road
man, one more example of a Stoic-Epicurean-skeptical compromise.  Just as writers primarily interested in peace of mind
had combined the Epicurean desire for quiet pleasure with a
Stoic faith in a planned universe, so Halifax, with his emphasis on patriotic responsibility, combines a faith in a moral
law, pointing toward the way things ought to be, with an experimental willingness to keep an eye on the way things are.  When
he ends "The Character of a Trimmer" by describing his moderate
hero as a defender of such vague abstractions as "Nature, Religion, Liberty, Prudence, Humanity, and Common Sense" (p. 103),
Halifax leans in the old-fashioned Stoic direction, just as he
does when describing a "reason of state" as something immortal
that inspires immediate consent.  But when he derives his definition of "true interest" from a continuing reassessment of the
way things are, he is looking ahead to the time when "true
interest" will frankly be given the relativistic Epicurean-
Utilitarian definition of the greatest good of the greatest
number.[125]

If conservative statesmen like Temple and Halifax were
not yet ready to preach rampant individualism, some of their
contemporaries among the comic dramatists seemed to be declar-
ing that the true law of nature is selfishness and that success
in life simply means staying on top of fortune's wheel.[126]  In
_The Man of Mode_ by George Etherege (1634-91) the law of the
jungle--aside from a faint suggestion that we should seize the
day--seems to decree that women who do not know how to look
after themselves deserve their punishment.  While we are asked
to admire the heroine, Harriet, because she knows the rules

of the game of self interest and knows how to play her cards,
we are not expected to waste sympathy on females who are foolishly soft hearted.  The title character, Sir Fopling Flutter,
is ridiculed not because his ideals are ridiculous but because
he goes to extremes in his foppishness.  A sense of decorum,
which to Hooker had meant "the knowledge of that which man is
in reference unto himself, and other things in relation unto
man" here seems to be merely a fashionable status symbol.
Although there are a few old-fashioned doctrines about order
and woman's place in Bury Fair by Thomas Shadwell (1642-92),
we are more familiar with such plays as Love for Love and The
Way of the World by William Congreve (1670-1729) where the idea
that virtue means playing well our assigned part in life has
been reduced to an artificial convention.  In these plays the
older generation, represented by Sir Sampson and by Lady Wish-
fort, is considered fair game for the younger one because the
old people are behaving in ways inappropriate or "unnatural"
for their age.  The young ones who do the successful exploiting
are admired for their superior dexterity in rising to the top
of fortune's wheel.  Any such antique notion as duty to their
assigned roles is conspicuously lacking.

Chapter V.  Notes

¹Humanism and the Social Order, p. 121.  See also C. S.
Lewis, p. 284.

²See Ornstein, "Donne, Montaigne and Natural Law."

³Complete Poems, ed. Henderson, pp. 224, 226.

⁴The Stoics of the Roman period, it will be remembered,
had modified the primitive Stoic emphasis on Cynic poverty,
stressing instead the golden mean between excessive liberality
and excessive stinginess and emphasizing that it is the duty
of a wealthy man to do good with his wealth (see p. 8).  The
medieval and Renaissance doctrine that each station in life has
its appropriate virtues had grown out of the classical idea
that a person does not live for himself alone but for society.
Because of the emphasis on the golden mean in Skelton's play,
the influence of Aristotle is sometimes emphasized.  See
Farnham, pp. 216-33; Daiches, I, 220.  Recent writers, however,
have called attention to the Roman (e.g., Cicero and Horace)
and medieval intermediaries.  See Heiserman, Skelton and
Satire, p. 77, and Harris, Skelton's Magnyfycence, pp. 139-44.

⁵See, e.g., Erasmus, Christian Prince:  "A goodly part
of crime arises from the one fact that everywhere wealth is
exalted and poverty is scorned.  The prince will therefore make
an effort to see that his subjects are rated according to their
worth and character rather than their material wealth" (p. 225).

⁶Humanism and the Social Order, p. 39.

⁷Proverbs or Adages, ed. Starnes.  On medieval elements
in Erasmus's thinking see Clarence Miller.

⁸See Praise of Folly, trans. Hudson, p. xxi.  Quotations
are from this edition.

⁹Christian Prince, p. 134.

¹⁰For a recent intensive analysis, see Rebhorn, "Metamor-
phosis of Moria."

¹¹A typical statement from this tradition emphasizes that
"a kingdom is a wonderful thing if each has his own place, if
each performs his own peculiar duties" (p. 236).  See Raab,
English Face of Machiavelli, pp. 8-29.

¹²See Christian Prince, pp. 249-57.  For bibliography and
a brief summary of Roman Stoic and Christian dreams of one
world and the brotherhood of man, see Adams, Better Part of
Valor, pp. 6-9, 166, 211.

¹³For discussion of the Utopia, see Surtz, Praise of Pleasure, and the introduction to his edition of Utopia.

¹⁴Utopia and a Dialogue of Comfort, ed. Warrington, Everyman, 461, p. 85.  Quotations are from this edition.

[15]A passage in A Dialogue of Comfort shows More tangling with the old problem of how to tell a true insight from a false one.

> God may cast into the mind of a man, I suppose, such an inward light of understanding that he cannot fail but be sure thereof. And yet he that is deluded by the devil may think himself as sure and yet be deceived indeed. And such a difference is there in a manner between them as is between the sight of a thing while we be waking and look thereon, and the sight with which we see a thing in our sleep while we dream thereof. (p. 265)

The discussion is long, for More well sees--as Spenser's Red Cross knight did not--that it is not always easy to know whether we are asleep or awake. As a middle-of-the-road man, he recommends applying a variety of tests before accepting an apparently clear and distinct idea as a true one.

[16]Pp. 107-117. See Adams, pp. 136, 149-50.

[17]Raitiere argues that this Utopian defense of war is meant to be taken ironically ("More's Utopia and The City of God").

[18]See Seebohm, Oxford Reformers, pp. 348-52; Surtz, "Logic in Utopia"; Adams, pp. 137-39; P. R. Allen, "Utopia and European Humanism."

[19]See Adams, pp. 34-35; Chambers, Thomas More, p. 131 ff. Chambers says, "From Utopia to the scaffold, More stands for the common cause, as against the private commodity of the single man, or even the single kingdom" (p. 266).

[20]For Elyot's outline of the system see Boke Named the Gouernour, ed. Watson, Everyman, 227, pp. 3-4. See also Major, Sir Thomas Elyot; Lovejoy, Great Chain; Spencer, Shakespeare and the Nature of Man; Tillyard, Elizabethan World Picture; Haydn, Counter-Renaissance, pp. 293-324.

[21]See Boas, Rationalism, pp. 311, 409-39.

[22]Some earlier users of the body analogy had been Aristotle, Livy, Plutarch, John of Salisbury, Aquinas, and Erasmus. See Keeton, Shakespeare's Legal and Political Background, pp. 234-35, 238; Erasmus, Christian Prince, pp. 114-16, 236.

[23]Quoted from Orchestra, ed. Tillyard. See also Tillyard, "The Cosmic Dance," Elizabethan World Picture; Finney, "A World of Instruments"; de Santillana, Origins of Scientific Thought, p. 84; Erasmus, Christian Prince, pp. 91-92; 115-16.

[24]Quoted from Poems and Fables of John Dryden, ed. Kinsley.

[25]On the great year, the great dance, and the argument from design, see Cicero, De Natura Deorum, II.20.51 ff, II.5.15; and "Scipio's Dream," De Re Publica, VI.21.24 ff.

[26]Cf. Erasmus, Christian Prince, pp. 154, 170, 212-13.

[27]Two examples from Elyot will indicate the difference between what the Stoic means by "nature" and the definition based on observation that the pragmatist may have in mind.  An observor, trying to arrive at laws of nature by noticing what most people do, may conclude that it is natural for the seller to try to delude the buyer or for the recipient of benefits to grow restive under the debt immense of endless gratitude. Elyot, however, like other idealists, says, "He [Tully] . . . proueth, sayenge, Nature is the fountayne whereof the lawe springeth, and it is accordinge to nature no man to do that whereby he shulde take (as it were) a praye of a nother mannes ignouraunce" (p. 209).  (See Cicero, De Officiis, III.v.21-26.) Or, he says, as Shakespeare does later in "Blow, blow thou winter wind," "The most damnable vice and moste agayne iustice, in myne oppinion, is ingratitude, commenly called unkyndnesse. All be it, it is in diuers fourmes and of sondry importaunce, as it is discribed by Seneca in this fourme.  He is unkynde which denieth to haue receyued any benefite that in dede he hath receyued.  He is unkynde that dissimuleth, he is unkynde that recompenseth nat.  But he is moste unkynde that forgeteth" (p. 186).  (See Seneca, "On Benefits," I.x.4, Moral Essays, Vol. I.  See Gouernour, p. 195, for Elyot's definition of jus- tice in terms of the four Stoic virtues.

[28]See Gouernour, pp. 47-48, 62, 145, 183-84; Buckley, Atheism in the English Renaissance, p. 13; Bush, Renaissance and English Humanism, pp. 57-63; Major, pp. 28-29, 33, 53, 141-44, 163-65.

[29]For more on Elyot's ideal man see Chapter VI.  According to Theodore Spencer, Cicero's Of Duties, which was also much read in the sixteenth century, "represents the official sixteenth-century doctrine concerning the behavior of man as a governor.  It was universally read; apart from many editions in Latin, there [were] at least eleven editions of the work in English between 1534 and 1616, and no sixteenth-century trea- tise on government was without some indebtedness to it" (Shakes- peare and the Nature of Man, p. 41).  See also Baker, Dignity of Man, p. 295.

[30]See Raab, pp. 14-22, for a summary of the traditional Tudor attitude toward kings.

[31]The amended title page of the 1571 edition reads, "A MYRROVR for Magistrates, Wherein may be seene by examples passed in this realme, with howe greueous plagues, vyces are punished in great princes and magistrates, and how frayle and vnstable worldly prosperity is found, where Fortune seemeth moste highly to fauour" (ed. Campbell, p. 15).

[32]Farnham, Medieval Heritage, pp. 281-91, emphasizes the increase (over Boccaccio and Lydgate) in the number of stories that show a cause and effect relationship between misdeeds and misfortune.

[33]See Farnham, p. 285 ff.

[34]Line 259 ff, trans. Miller, Complete Roman Drama, Vol. II.

[35]Quoted from Specimens of the Pre-Shaksperean Drama, ed. Manley, II, 211-72. For a discussion of the mixtures of influences on Gorboduc, among them Seneca and Boethius, see Bacquet, "L'Imitation de Sénèque dans 'Gorboduc.'"

[36]Cf. Cleanthes' Hymn, discussed in Chapter I.

[37]See Farnham, p. 355; Spencer, Shakespeare and the Nature of Man, p. 61; Reese, Cease of Majesty, pp. 71-74. For a discussion of the connection between Stoic law, Christian providence, and poetic justice, see Battenhouse, Marlowe's Tamburlaine, p. 124 ff. See also Herndl, The High Design.

[38]English Literature in the Sixteenth Century, p. 49; see also pp. 451-63.

[39]See Sabine, History of Political Theory, pp. 439-42, and d'Entreves, Natural Law, pp. 44-47.

[40]Quotations are from Works, ed. Keble. See Spencer, Shakespeare and the Nature of Man, pp. 6-7; Baker, Dignity of Man, p. 234; Hoopes, Right Reason, pp. 123-32.

[41]The word "expedient" frequently appears in Stoic writing and carries, as here, the older meaning of "fit" or "proper" in an absolute sense rather than the later meaning of "useful" or "politic." See OED.

[42]For other writers who set forth contemporary ideas about natural law, see Lewis, pp. 288-89; Spencer, Shakespeare and the Nature of Man, p. 3 ff; Farnham, p. 336.

[43]Works, ed. Feuillerat, II, 94.

[44]However, a song in the Roman-Stoic mode by Boulon (IV, 143) explains that the proper use of riches is "To holde these worldly thinges in such proportion, / As let them come or goe with even facility."

[45]For discussions of Greville's religious views, see Rebholz, Life of Fulke Greville, and Joan Rees, Fulke Greville.

[46]Poems and Dramas, ed. Bullough. His ideal state and his ideal ruler, neither of which he expected to see in actual fact, belonged, like Sidney's, to the Ciceronian tradition. See Maclean, "Fulke Greville: Kingship and Sovereignty," and "Fulke Greville on War"; Rebholz, p. 148.

[47]Cf. the argument of the evil spirits in Alaham, "Chorus Tertius A Dialogue of Good and Evil Spirits."

[48]See, e.g., Caelica LXIX; Mustapha, "Chorus Tertius of Time: Eternitie."

[49]Alaham, "Chorus Tertius," lines 107-8. See Joan Rees, pp. 132, 156.

[50]*Life of Sir Philip Sidney*, ed. Smith, p. 15.

[51]See Caspari, pp. 190, 199.

[52]See, e.g., Cunliffe, *Influence of Seneca*; T. S. Eliot, "Seneca in Elizabethan Translation," *Selected Essays*; Lucas, *Seneca and Elizabethan Tragedy*; but also see Spencer, *Shakespeare and the Nature of Man*.

[53]*Works*, II, 29-30. For discussions of various Renaissance attitudes toward astrology, see D. C. Allen, *Star-Crossed Renaissance* and Elton, *"King Lear" and the Gods*, p. 149 ff.

[54]For a discussion of the complex way in which an intellectual like Justus Lipsius explained the relation between fate and free will, see Zanta, pp. 182-83, 227-31; Haydn, p. 436; Hinman, *Abraham Cowley's World of Order*, pp. 75-76.

[55]Cf. the following lines, quoted by Clark in "Samuel Daniel's 'Complaint of Rosamond,'" p. 155: "But fate is not prevented though foreknowne. / For that must hap decreed by heavenly powers, / Who worke our fall, yet make the fault still ours."

[56]See Cicero, *De Divinatione*, I.iv.125-26; Seneca, *Ad Helviam*, VIII.3; Cicero has a defender of portents in *De Divinatione* state: "According to the Stoic doctrine, the gods are not directly responsible for every fissure in the liver or for every song of a bird; since, manifestly, that would not be seemly or proper in a god and furthermore is impossible" (I. lii.118). Cicero also points out that Panaetius, unlike the other Stoics, including Posidonius, doubted the efficacy of divination (I.iii.6). Zanta, pp. 46-73, discusses the way in which the Protestant reformers tried to distinguish between predestination and fate. More recently Gustave Lanson and Paul Tuffrau have distinguished between determinism and fatalism by saying that determinism leaves no place for miracles or human liberty or chance and differs from fatalism, which limits itself to asserting that a distant event is inevitable (*Manuel D'Histoire de la Littérature Française*, pp. 775-76). The OED, less dogmatic, says under fate (sense 1) that "all events, or some events in particular, are unalterably predetermined from eternity." Its listings indicate the variety of meanings the word may have in popular usage.

[57]See Spencer, *Shakespeare and the Nature of Man*, pp. 73-74, 92, 108, 154-61; Keeton, *Shakespeare's Legal and Political Background*; Reese, *Cease of Majesty*.

[58]See Farnham, p. 415; Keeton, pp. 225-47. See RII.III. iv.33-47 for a conversation between the king's gardeners underscoring once more the importance of "law and form and due proportion." The Duchess of Gloucester illustrates the popular attitude toward the relation between virtue and social position when she says to Gaunt, whom she is trying to goad into revenging her murdered husband, "That which in mean men we entitle

patience / Is pale cold cowardice in noble breasts" (I.ii.34-
35).

[59]Quotations are from Complete Works, ed. Kittredge.

[60]See Craig, "Shackling of Accidents," p. 18; E. V. Cunningham, "Ripeness is All," Woe or Wonder, pp. 7-13; Haydn, p. 635.
Even Othello, though generally more psychological and Senecan
than Ciceronian and political, includes a suggestion that by
violating social propriety Desdemona and Othello have made
themselves vulnerable.  It is obvious that Desdemona causes
shock when she marries a Moor and marries him secretly, thus
defying propriety as her father sees it and displaying a rash-
ness that fills us with the same apprehension that Juliet's
does.  The Senecan part of the lesson illustrates the dire
effects of letting passion gain control.

[61]See Spencer, Shakespeare and the Nature of Man, pp. 111-
21.

[62]See Elton, p. 131 ff, for bibliography on the attitude of
Shakespeare's age toward bastards.

[63]See Seneca, "De Providentia," I.iv.16, Moral Essays, Vol.
I; Bradley, Shakespearean Tragedy, p. 30 ff; Farnham, p. 443;
Elton, p. 165 ff; Presson, "Boethius, King Lear, and 'Maystresse
Philosophie.'"

[64]See Haydn, p. 643; Cunningham, pp. 7-13; for Elton's
different interpretation of this passage see pp. 100-104.
Edgar's advice against suicide, though more Christian than
Stoic, is classical in its emphasis on staying at one's
assigned post until released.  See Cicero's "Dream of Scipio,"
where Scipio is forbidden by his father to leave his place
before his appointed time (De Re Publica, VI.15).  See also De
Senectute, XX.73; Tusculan Disputations, I.30.74, as well as
Plato, Phaedo, 61, 62; Epictetus, who usually emphasizes that
death is always available, also says, "Men as you are, wait upon
God.  When He gives the signal and releases you from this service, then you shall depart to Him; but for the present be content to dwell in this country wherein He appointed you to
dwell" (Disc., I.ix).  On the subject of ripeness for death,
Seneca says: "Your son himself was ripe for death; for he lived
as long as he needed to live. . . . There is no uniform time
for old age" (Ad Marciam, XXI.4).

[65]See Bradley, pp. 218-19; Spencer, Shakespeare and the
Nature of Man, p. 142; Mack, King Lear in Our Time, p. 117;
Presson, "Boethius," p. 416.

[66]"Shackling of Accidents," p. 16.

[67]See Spencer, Shakespeare and the Nature of Man, pp. 145-
46, and Haydn, p. 306; Ornstein compares Lear's education to
Job's education, Moral Vision, pp. 272-73.

68For bibliography and discussion of the <u>natura</u> <u>paucis</u> <u>contenta</u> tradition, see Elton, p. 125, n. 22.

69See Bush, <u>Renaissance and English Humanism</u>, p. 98; Campbell, <u>Shakespeare's Tragic Heroes</u>, pp. 98, 104, 238; Spencer, <u>Shakespeare and the Nature of Man</u>, pp. 154-61.

70For similar ideas in Jonson and Beaumont see Evans, "Sejanus and the Ideal Prince Tradition"; Hamilton, "Irony and Fortune in <u>Sejanus</u>"; and Finkelpearl, "Beaumont, Fletcher, and 'Beaumont and Fletcher.'"

71See Schoell, <u>Etudes sur L'Humanisme</u>; Bartlett, ed., <u>Poems of George Chapman</u>; Wieler, <u>George Chapman</u>; Ennis Rees, <u>Tragedies of George Chapman</u>; Ornstein, <u>Moral Vision</u>, Presson, "Wrestling with this World."

72See Battenhouse, "Chapman and the Nature of Man."

73For differing views see Wieler and Ennis Rees. Among those who have admired Bussy's individualism are Leech, "'The Atheist's Tragedy'"; and Schwartz, "Seneca, Homer, and Chapman's <u>Bussy D'Ambois</u>." Leech says, "Bussy stands in intellectual stature above Sejanus, even above Macbeth because--along with his restlessness and fiery will--he has from the beginning a sure realization of the vanity of the prizes offered" (p. 526). Schwartz says, "Far from being a Christian tragedy, Bussy is a Senecan one. . . . Bussy goes down because the blind and random world in which he lives inevitably destroys the virtuous" (p. 164).

74On Chapman's Stoic reading, see Schoell, Bartlett, Wieler. Among his favorite books were Plutarch's <u>Morals</u> and compilations like Erasmus's <u>Adages</u>.

75See Wieler, pp. 67, 77. Quotations are from <u>Plays and Poems</u>, ed. Parrott, Vol. I.

76See Wieler, p. 36; Ennis Rees, p. 31.

77On fate and fortune in <u>Bussy D'Ambois</u> see Wieler, pp. 41-43; Ennis Rees, p. 42.

78See Ch. VI. For another interpretation of this passage, see Ornstein, <u>Moral Vision</u>, pp. 55-56; Haydn, pp. 493-95. In <u>Chabot</u> the father-in-law reminds the king that a ruler has in his own breast a chancellor above the law (IV.i.110-11), that the king, in other words, is supposed to possess an innate sense of justice. But Chabot's trial had been an obvious perversion of both written and moral law while Bussy's case is less clear.

79Perkinson, "Nature and the Tragic Hero," emphasizes that Chapman was a playwright, not a philosopher, and that "dramatic problems led him to draw upon his acquaintance with Stoicism" (p. 277).

80For further discussion of Chapman, see Chapter VI.

[81]Quotations are from the Revels Play edition by Van Fossen. For a discussion of Heywood's affirmation in his plays of the traditional Elizabethan idea of order, see Ribner, _Jacobean Tragedy_, pp. 50-70.

[82]See Wood, ed., _Plays of John Marston_, I, xv ff. (Quotations are from this edition.) Also see Finkelpearl, _John Marston_; for comment on Marston's devotion to abstract justice, see pp. 85, 123-24.

[83]On this theme in Marston see Finkelpearl, pp. 22-23, 192.

[84]See Finkelpearl's discussion, pp. 151-159, which emphasizes the influence of Calvinism on Marston's view of the world. For an interpretation of the play as a parody, see Ayres, "Marston's _Antonio's Revenge_."

[85]Caputi argues that _The Malcontent_ is an exposition of Marston's Neo-Stoic philosophy (p. 148 ff).

[86]For Caputi's discussion of Altofront as critic, protagonist, and judge, see p. 188 ff and 198. Finkelpearl emphasizes that "Despite [Malevole's] high moral standards, he has learned the black arts required to manipulate men" (pp. 185-92).

[87]For an example of Cicero's treatment of Massinissa, as well as the Scipios, as a Stoic hero, see _De Senectute_, X.34; on the Scipios see _De Officiis_, II.76; III.15 and _De Re Publica_ (only book VI of which was known in Marston's day). On the contribution of Petrarch to the high reputation of the Scipios during the Renaissance, see Cast, "Aurispa, Petrarch, and Lucian."

[88]For discussion of the Stoicism of this play, see Ure, "John Marston's _Sophonisba_."

[89]See Ornstein, _Moral Vision_, p. 159. For the Erasmian doctrine that "a mere promise" from a prince "is more sacred than an oath from anyone else," see _Christian Prince_, p. 239. Cicero says, "'When a man enters the foot-race,' says Chrysippus with his usual aptness, 'it is his duty to put forth all his strength and strive with all his might to win; but he ought never with his foot to trip, or with his hand to foul a competitor'" (_De Officiis_, III.x.42).

[90]But see Caputi, who says, "The play is designed to define and heighten progressively the impressiveness of Sophonisba's and Massinissa's Stoic virtue" (p. 241 ff).

[91]Finkelpearl, who calls Sophonisba "Marston's one authentic Stoic," points out that such perfection cannot endure on earth and that Massinissa represents the limited form of Stoic virtue appropriate for those who would cope effectively with the evil world (pp. 241-45).

[92]Erasmus says great harm is done to mankind when either

celestial bodies or great princes wander from their true courses (<u>Christian</u> <u>Prince</u>, p. 248). Quotations are from <u>Works</u>, ed. Lucas, Vols. I and II.

[93]On this point see Bradbrook, <u>Themes</u> <u>and</u> <u>Conventions</u>, pp. 198-200. For a contrary view see Ornstein, p. 141. See Bogard, <u>Tragic</u> <u>Satire</u>, p. 43, for a discussion of the pattern of Websterian tragedy as the struggle and defeat of the individual trying to escape "the laws of the norm."

[94]Cunliffe emphasizes the influence of Seneca on Ford's use of fate and the stoic submission with which his characters die (pp. 114-15). Quotations are from <u>John</u> <u>Ford's</u> <u>Dramatic</u> <u>Works</u>, ed. de Vocht.

[95]<u>Works</u>, ed. Wynter, VII. 46.

[96]Cf. Fulke Greville: "Some would haue vs imitate the spheres, who carried about with the violent course of the First Mouer, doe yet steale on in their naturall with slow and vnsensible motion" (<u>Letter</u> <u>to</u> <u>an</u> <u>Honourable</u> <u>Lady</u>, pp. 261-62).

[97]Cf. Cicero: "This, then, ought to be the chief end of all men, to make the interest of each individual and of the whole body politic identical" (<u>De</u> <u>Officiis</u>, III.v.26). See Raab, <u>English</u> <u>Face</u> <u>of</u> <u>Machiavelli</u>.

[98]<u>Anatomy</u> <u>of</u> <u>Melancholy</u>, ed. Dell and Jordan-Smith, p. 964.

[99]See Hoopes, p. 188, and Madsen, "Idea of Nature in Milton's Poetry."

[100]See Cicero, <u>De</u> <u>Officiis</u>, II.xii.42, and Erasmus, <u>Christian</u> <u>Prince</u>, pp. 170-72. For an account of changing conceptions of natural law in the seventeenth century, along with a brief summary of the natural law concept, see Sirluck's discussion in the "Introduction" to the Yale edition of Milton's <u>Prose</u> <u>Works</u>, Vol. II; on Milton and natural law and Christian liberty see Lewalski, "Milton: Political Beliefs and Polemical Methods, 1659-60." Quotations are from the <u>Columbia</u> <u>Milton</u> (CM), ed. Patterson.

[101]For references--in Aristotle, Cicero, Seneca, and Marcus Aurelius--to the idea that a prince should be preeminent in virtue, see Born's notes to Erasmus, <u>Christian</u> <u>Prince</u>, pp. 58, 67-68, 79-80, 170-72.

[102]Though in other contexts Milton defends control of the passions, here he argues that it is dangerous and harmful to compel "natures resistless sway in love or hate" (III, 501).

[103]See Sabine, pp. 484, 489; Woodhouse, <u>Puritanism</u> <u>and</u> <u>Liberty</u>.

[104]P. 49; see also Sabine, pp. 421-33; Cassirer, <u>Myth</u> <u>of</u> <u>the</u> <u>State</u>, pp. 165-68; d'Entreves, p. 52; Muller, <u>Freedom</u> <u>in</u> <u>the</u> <u>Western</u> <u>World</u>, p. 232; Keeton, pp. 67-93.

220

105See Cox, Locke on War and Peace, pp. 144-45.

106Cf. Cicero, Tusculan Disputations, I.xiii.30. Hutcheson, ed., Lord Herbert of Cherbury's "De Religione Laici," says, "Herbert, though the point has rarely been appreciated, did not claim absolute completeness for natural religion; he merely asserted the folly of attempting to enforce universal faith in possible truths which, not being 'natural' and hence discoverable by 'right reason' could not secure universal assent" (p. 79). See also Sidney Lee, ed., Edward Lord Herbert of Cherbury, Autobiography.

107On Jeremy Taylor (1613-67), for instance, see Hoopes, pp. 168-70.

108An example of sixteenth-century humanistic faith in reason, combined with a Christian reminder of the ultimate limitations of human reason, can be found by looking back at John Davies' Nosce teipsum: Of Humane Knowledge (1599). On the one hand, in the section headed "That the soule is a thing subsisting by itself without the Bodie" Davies compares the soul's method of reaching decisions to the methods of "our great wise Empresse, that now raignes" (p. 127, st. 5). Although the queen uses her subject's pains to help her gather the information on which to base a judgment, yet

> when she sits to iudge the good and Ill,
> And to discerne betwixt the false and true,
> She is not guided by the Senses skill,
> But doth each thing in her owne Mirror view.
> Then she the Senses checks, which oft do erre,
> And euer against their false reports decrees;
> And oft she doth condemne what they preferre,
> For with a powre, aboue the Sense, she sees. (p. 128, st. 6

p. 129, st. 1)

Similarly, in the section on "The intellectual powers of the soule," he argues that the soul is not "a blanck where nought is writ at all," that "nature in mans hart her lawes doth pen" (p. 163, st. 1-2). Later still, however, he inserts the orthodox qualification that the soul's desire for knowledge can never be completely satisfied on earth, that "in this life no Soule the truth can know" (p. 169, st. 1). Quotations are from Poems, ed. Howard.

109Works of Bacon, ed. Spedding, III. 430; Raab, pp. 74-76. On Bacon's anti-Stoicism, see Anderson, Francis Bacon. See also Vickers, Francis Bacon, pp. 60-95.

110See "Law of Nature," and "Equity," Table Talk, ed. Reynolds, pp. 101, 61.

111See Mayo, Epicurus in England, p. 142; Cox, pp. 20-21.

112See Zeller, Stoics, Epicureans, and Sceptics, p. 463.

113On the tendency of present-day writers on international

law to lump together the natural-law doctrines of "Grotius on the one hand, and . . . Hobbes and Locke on the other," see Cox, pp. 146-47. See Raab's chapter, "Harrington, Hobbes, God and Machiavelli," pp. 185-217, for a discussion of James Harrington's formulation of new laws of nature that combined economic determinism with the ideas of Machiavelli.  Raab says, "From: 'what sort of government does God want us to have?' the basic political question had largely changed to: 'what sort of government would be best for us, given our present circumstances?'" (pp. 214-15).

[114]See also Muller, pp. 66, 309-10.

[115]An Essay Concerning Human Understanding, ed. Yolton, I, chs. 2-3 (pp. 9-43).

[116]See Sabine, p. 529; Cox; Laslett, ed. John Locke, Two Treatises of Government; Abrams, ed., John Locke, Two Tracts on Government; Seliger, "Locke's Natural Law and the Foundation of Politics."

[117]Cox, pp. 174-75, 194-95; see also Armstrong, "Cambridge Platonists and Locke on Innate Ideas"; Greene and MacCallum, eds., Nathaniel Culverwell, An Elegant and Learned Discourse of the Light of Nature, pp. xiv-xlviii.

[118]According to Sabine, "a theory of society in terms of individual interests was in Locke's day a foregone conclusion. The whole drift of the theory of natural law was in this direction" (p. 525).  Hobbes and Locke "fastened on social theory the presumption that individual self-interest is clear and compelling, while a public or a social interest is thin and unsubstantial" (p. 529).

[119]Five Miscellaneous Essays by Sir William Temple, ed. Monk, p. 105.  See also Monk's introduction, p. xxx.

[120]Temple is not, of course, the only one to have noticed the parallels between Confucianism and Stoicism.  See, e.g., McNeill, Rise of the West, pp. 226-27, 230-31, 265.

[121]Early Essays and Romances, ed. Moore Smith, pp. 156-57.

[122]For a brief summary of Temple's life and work see James Sutherland, English Literature of the Late Seventeenth Century, pp. 223-26.

[123]Raab, pp. 242-54.

[124]Quotations are from Works, ed. Raleigh.

[125]See Sabine, p. 522.

[126]Dryden will be discussed in the next chapter.

# Chapter VI.  The Wise Man

The noble, sad, and ridiculous ideal of the Stoic wise man keeps floating ahead of us, ever out of reach, as over the centuries we continue devising new recipes for transforming ourselves into well-balanced, well-adjusted, rational animals with a well-developed sixth sense known as a sense of proportion that will show us in an instant both how to promote the good of the world and how to be ourselves wise and good and happy, and therefore successful, human beings.  At times we think that if we would only work together hard enough to maintain the established pattern, the world would operate smoothly with everyone happy in his appropriate place.  At other times we suggest the exact opposite.  If everyone were truly free to follow his inner light, all of us would be wise citizens of one world.  In the sixteenth and seventeenth centuries the accepted doctrine continued to be, more or less, the medieval one that the wise man is the man who knows his place.

Then as always the picture was complicated by such factors as that doctrines preached by moralists are seldom the same as the way of the world, that what looks ideal to one person looks silly or evil to another, and that practical people are ever quick to adapt the ideals of the moralists to their own ends.  Therefore, before going on to examine serious ideals of the wise man, we must make a feeble effort to dispose of that travesty variously known as a Stoic villain or a Stoic Machiavel.  When we find the ambitious self-seeking hero villains of Marlowe's plays described as Stoics, we must remember that from the Christian point of view a Stoic might be a villain because his claims to emotional imperturbability and to moral self-sufficiency marked him as an unfeeling atheist.[1]  On closer look a so-called Stoic villain usually turns out to be a deliberate caricature of a Stoic made up of popular misconceptions, whether the playwright himself shared the popular view or whether he was merely relying on a stock response.  One example of a villain sometimes characterized as Stoic is Marlowe's Barabas, who is so described partly because he lacks such tender feelings as pity, love, and sympathy, partly because when he realizes the game is up he accepts the consequences without whining.  To suggest that Barabas demonstrates Stoic fortitude both by accepting the unjust human condition and by shaking his fist at the stars is to forget that Stoic fortitude is based on Stoic optimism and that Stoic optimism denies the idea of cosmic injustice.  The morality of The Jew of Malta is better seen as the law of the jungle, or at least as that of a medieval beast fable.  When it is a question of such passions as greed, ambition, hate, and anger, Barabas is anything but passionless.  Until he is overthrown by seemingly capricious providence, which he probably calls bad luck, it never occurs to him to accept his fate with equanimity.  Nor does he at any time classify wealth as something indifferent--not essential to peace of mind--or think to comfort himself in the Boethian manner by reflecting that his enemy the wicked governor will be his own punishment, that everything that happens is part of nature's plan, and that his essential responsibility is to maintain his integrity.

So much for the so-called Stoic villain, who is not part of our subject.  When we turn to look at serious treatments of the wise man, we are surprised at how slowly--in this period of ferment--the ideal changes.  Even so daring an admirer of Stoicism as Chapman usually adheres to long accepted attitudes.  The change--if there is one--comes in Dryden's time as much from the fading vitality of sixteenth-century doctrines about the laws of nature as from a deliberate reassessment of the definition of a good man.  When duty dwindles into decorum, the letter is likely to be obeyed while the spirit changes.

As always, it is necessary to keep in mind that the mathematically perfect wise man is only "a dazzling abstraction."[2] With some few exceptions, therefore, the wise man to be discussed here will be the struggling good man of the Roman Stoic tradition who is doing his duty as best he can, given his human limitations.  Among legitimate exceptions are Milton's Adam before the Fall and his Christ of Paradise Regained.  Christian humanists had long recognized that the traditional Stoic virtues were appropriate both for God and for Adam in his sinless state.

If we start with Erasmus, we will meet many of the variations on the wise-man theme that will still be turning up a century or two later.  Folly in The Praise of Folly, who sometimes speaks from the point of view of the average person, at times mocks the wise-man ideal, making traditional fun of the godlike self-sufficient Stoic, who, she says, is in reality only "a senseless block, completely alien to every human feeling." Although at this point we are expected to agree, a little later when she also ridicules so-called wise men for being incompetent at such activities as war and money making, we realize that her own system of values is now askew.  At other times, in other veins, she looks ironically back at human history to remind us of the vanity of human wishes, and in this mood-- both classical and Christian--she concentrates on the disparity between what men in their pride have hoped to do and what history has actually brought about.  Her ridicule begins with Plato's ideal philosopher king and finishes with the good emperor Marcus Aurelius who "by leaving behind such a son as his, . . . certainly harmed the state more than he had benefited it by his good management."  Others whose influence she says was ultimately more harmful than helpful were the Catos, Brutus, Cassius, the Gracchi, Cicero, and Demosthenes.  But if she here sounds like a Skeptic or like a pragmatic Machiavellian, in a later passage, when she lists the qualities that a sensible prince should avoid, because they interfere with the pleasant life, she also gives us an oblique portrait of the ideal Erasmian Renaissance prince:

One who grasps the helm of great affairs must further the public, not

his private, interest and give his mind to nothing except as it concerns the general good; he must not deviate a finger's breadth from
the laws of which he is author and executor; he must himself be war-
rant for the integrity of all officials and magistrates; he is one
person who is exposed to all eyes, and like a favorable star he has
power, by the good influence of his conduct, to bring salvation in
human affairs; or like a fatal comet he may bring destruction in his
train. The vices of other men are not so deeply felt or so widely
communicated. A prince is in such a position that if he lapses ever
so slightly from honesty, straightway a dangerous and vital infec-
tion spreads to many people.[3]

This picture is similar to the one that Erasmus gives in his
_Education of a Christian Prince_, the well-accepted recipe for
the good ruler in the Ciceronian tradition of patriotic responsibility, the Christian-Stoic prince who, having received a
proper education in virtue, now rules himself and his kingdom
in accordance with the laws of nature, and who, though making no
pretence to be a god, nevertheless tries to imitate a God who
loves moral virtue and who willingly cooperates with his own
laws.[4]

Where Folly sometimes turns accepted moral values on their
heads, Erasmus's popular collection of _Adages_ gives us in
straight didactic form such commonly accepted teachings about
social duty as the following:

No man can be a good ruler, unless he hath been first ruled. Certes
nothing is truer, than this proverb, both because no prince, no
ruler, no master can well do his office, unless he first were a subject and under the correction either of his parents, tutors, gover-
nors, or teachers. And also because a man must first rule his own
lusts, and be himself obedient to right reason, ere he can well
govern other.[5]

In addition to advising rulers, the _Adages_ also contain
generalized Stoic lessons gathered from such moralists as Seneca and Epictetus:

Nothing saith Seneca is so hard but man's mind can overcome it. . . .
It is too late sparing at the bottom. This sentence of Seneca is
worthy to be written upon the doors of all those houses. . . . Seek
not soft things lest hard things happen unto thee. Sustain and
abstain. This sentence is worthy to be written upon all doors, posts,
walls, yea in every corner wheresoever a man casteth his eye. The
author of it is Epictetus. By the first we be taught, strongly to
bear adversity, and by the second to abstain from all baleful pleasures and pastimes. . . . The wise man carrieth about with him his
goods. By this is signified, that those only be indeed and truly ours,
which be within, as learning and virtue. (30 ff)

The Stoic admonition to learn both to abstain and to sustain is one that echoes through the literature of this period.[6]
Writer after writer reminds us that prosperity can be quite as
challenging to spiritual health as adversity. Spenser tells us

that "the strong through pleasure soonest falles, the weake through smart" (F.Q., II.i.57). Bacon, in his essay "Of Adversity," says, "The virtue of prosperity is temperance; the virtue of adversity is fortitude; which in morals is the more heroical virtue. . . . Certainly virtue is like precious odours, most fragrant when they are incensed or crushed: for prosperity doth best discover vice; but adversity doth best discover virtue." And Joseph Hall says, "Of the two [pleasure and sorrow], I confess it harder to manage prosperity, and to avoid hurt from good. Strong and cold winds do but make us gather up our cloak more round more close: but, to keep it about us in a hot sunshine, to run and not sweat, to sweat and not faint, how difficult it is!" (Works, VI, 216).[7]

In Book Two of Thomas More's Utopia, where the general emphasis is on prosperity, the lesson of temperance has been learned, and there is a careful avoidance of baleful pleasures and pastimes. The good rulers, who are themselves obedient to right reason, govern wise citizens who willingly play their assigned roles, avoiding the excesses of pride and greed. Content with their simple lives, they have solved the difficult problem of knowing how much is enough.[8]

A Dialogue of Comfort against Tribulation, on the other hand, shows us how the good man sustains adversity. This book, written when More was in prison at the end of his life, discusses the moral problems of persons no longer able to identify whole-hearted loyalty to the ruling powers with virtuous action. The fictional dialogue is between two Hungarians momentarily expecting their country to be invaded by the Turks. Although they assume that a Turkish victory, if it happens, will be part of God's plan and that their own so-called Christian society will only be suffering just punishment for sin, nevertheless they as individuals will still have a certain measure of freedom, in the Stoic sense that the good man is free. Loss of political or physical freedom will not mean loss of spiritual freedom, since they can still maintain their own integrity. And even if the earthly city has fallen to the enemy, the heavenly city is still an achievable goal. To prove their worth and gain their reward, however, they must continue to exercise their spiritual muscles. Although the Dialogue inevitably reminds one of Boethius' Consolation, there is the difference that More's Hungarians are comforting themselves with hopes of reward after death while Boethius was only hoping to attain present peace of mind. Boethius could be successful if he could somehow convince himself that everything was for the best in terms of the total plan and that his own performance as a good man was satisfactory. More's Hungarians, who can have this same earthly peace of mind if they will gladly bend their wills to the will of God, can, in addition, hope for eternal peace in heaven.

As aids in perfecting their wills they quote not only St. Paul but also Seneca, who teaches them that if as captives they are forced to do work they dislike they can still triumph by

doing gladly what they will have to do anyway. "The thing that
we see we shall needs do let us always to put our goodwill
thereto." Meanwhile, St. Paul teaches them that "in the patient
and glad doing of our service unto that man for God's sake . . .
we shall have our thank and our whole reward of God" (p. 367).
They remind themselves that stone walls do not a prison make,
that a prisoner "while his will is not longing to be anywhere
else, he is, I say at his free liberty to be where he will,
and so is out of prison too" (p. 373), that the real prisoner
is the man who, even though a prince, is slave to his own lusts.

     As a point of interest, before going on to Thomas Elyot,
we should notice that in this work More, following Augustine,
parted company with the Stoics on the question of suicide, even
though in the Utopia he handled it in the classical manner.
Cato Uticensis, who committed suicide rather than submit to
Caesar, and who was a favorite Stoic hero with many writers,
including Chapman and Addison, was accused by More of displaying "plain pusillanimity and impotency of stomach" (p. 259).[7]

     If More in his own life reached the point at which loyalty
to a higher principle required him to say no to the course of
contemporary history, his friend Thomas Elyot went on conscien-
tiously trying to adjust the old humanistic ideals to the contemporary facts. Since his mildly hopeful point of view was the
one that prevailed as a model for some time, it may be well to
review a few obvious points. First, for Elyot, as for More and
Erasmus and practically everyone else, the ideal man does not
exist in a vacuum but rather is part of the hierarchical system
which assigns to everyone a particular place with particular
duties. Second, the wise man is not expected to be perfect but
only to do the best he can in his allotted place. Third, the
whole Stoic tradition is an attempt to defend as "natural" a
mode of behavior which other schools of thought consider highly
"unnatural." Hence we have the Stoic fondness for paradoxical
expressions. Specifically, the Stoics try to teach that unsel-
fishness is natural, that following nature means doing our duty,
whether duty be defined as submitting our will to the will of
God, or working for the good of mankind, or thinking first of
our country, our social class, or even our family. The main
stream of Roman Stoic education in virtue has tended to mean
education in teamwork. If man is by definition a reasonable
animal, then it ought to be possible to persuade him to forget
selfishness and instead to cooperate voluntarily with the laws
of nature, which laws have often been identified with the laws
of society.

     Erasmus did what he could to persuade princes to follow
virtue. Elyot turned his attention to the nobles, whose
inclination to go their own way in pursuit of ambition and
greed was quite as pervasive as the tendency of princes to confuse their own wills with eternal law. In simple terms, Elyot
believed that through the right education it would be possible
to improve the quantity and quality of public-spirited gentlemen.[10] In an attempt to identify inherited gentility with

innate virtue, he said,

> In the begynning. . . . the persones were called gentilmen, more for
> the remembraunce of their vertue and benefite, than for discrepance
> of astates. Also it fortuned by the prouidence of god that of those
> good men were ingendred good children, who being brought up in ver-
> tue, and perceiuinge the cause of the aduancement of their progeni-
> tours, endeuoured them selves by imitation of vertue, to be equall
> to them in honour and autoritie; by good emulation they retained stille
> the fauour and reuerence of people.[11]

Since his idea of a virtuous man was someone on the model
of an idealized Cicero or Marcus Aurelius, the best education
was obviously one based on their writings or on the writings of
those who either influenced them or were influenced by them.
Hence he particularly recommended some parts of Aristotle's
Ethics, Cicero's De Officiis, Erasmus's Education of a Christian Prince, and the works of Plato.[12]  Of Elyot's definition
of wisdom, Major says, he goes back to "the famous definition
of the Stoics (which he gives in Cicero's phrasing): 'Sapience
is the science of things diuine and humaine, which considereth
the cause of euery thing, by reason whereof that which is
diuine she foloweth, that which is humane she estemith ferre
under the goodnes of vertue.'"[13]  Major also emphasizes the
influence on Elyot of Quintilian's ideal of the good orator who
should be "a kind of Roman wise man, who may prove himself a
true statesman, not by discussions in retirement, but by personal experience and exertions in public life."[14]  Elyot's
dream was that the country should be well supplied with this
kind of wise gentleman, "ayding . . . in the distribution of
iustice in sondry partes of a huge multitude. . . . as Jesus
Sirach sayeth, The multitude of wise men is the welth of the
worlde" (Governour, p. 16).  Caspari, summing up Elyot's contribution, says, "His great achievement was the adaptation of
the humanistic ideal of man and society to English needs and
conditions: he created a new social norm which the English ruling class, then in its most formative period, could and did
adopt as its own" (p. 86).
The humanistic ideal of man was also propagated by Richard
Hooker, who, like Erasmus, encouraged the good man to study
wisdom and try as far as he could to imitate God, who was, of
course, Hooker's law-abiding God.  "By proceeding in the knowledge of truth, and by growing in the exercise of virtue, man
amongst the creatures of this inferior world aspireth to the
greatest conformity with God."  By referring his doctrine back
to Plato, Hooker neatly avoids any association with Stoic pride.
"With Plato what one thing more usual than to excite men unto
the love of wisdom, by shewing how much wise men are thereby
exalted above men; how knowledge doth raise them up into heaven;
how it maketh them, though not gods, yet as gods, high, admirable, and divine?" (I.v.3).  This ideal wise man can be classed
either as a Platonic abstraction or as a Christian saint.

Among the several varieties of possible wise men--pure ones and blends--there were plenty of examples from which story tellers, poets, playwrights, and essayists might choose. Philip Sidney in his _Arcadia_ introduces the good king Euarchus to exemplify the social virtue of the responsible ruler and illustrates the personal virtue of Christian-Stoic fortitude through the behavior of the young heroes and heroines when they are in prison.[15] Euarchus also exemplifies personal integrity, for when justice requires him to set aside his personal feelings and condemn his son and his nephew to death, Sidney likens his "sad assured behaviour" to that of Cato when he "killed him- selfe withall" (_Works_, II. 204).

Pamela and Philoclea in prison, like Thomas More's Hun- garians in _A_ _Dialogue_ _of_ _Comfort_, console themselves with the idea that by accustoming themselves to suffering they may strengthen their spiritual muscles and demonstrate their mettle: "All feares & terrors were to them but summons to a battaile, whereof they knew before hand they would be victorious" (I, 474). Using familiar Stoic arguments, Pamela says, "A shippe is not counted strong for byding one storme" (I, 503); "Hope is the fawning traitour of the minde, while under colour of friendship, it robbes it of his chiefe force of resolution" (I, 508). Pyrocles and Musidorus, under arrest, give themselves similar counsels of resolution: "Let not our vertue now abandon us; let us prove our mindes are no slaves to fortune, but in adversitie can tryumph over adversitie" (II, 129). The two young heroes, therefore "(fortifying courage with the true Ram- pier of patience) did so endure, as they did rather appeare gov- ernours of necessitie, then servaunts to fortune" (II, 163). Fortitude, for Sidney as for Thomas More, excludes the right to commit suicide. When Pyrocles (less advanced on the scale of virtue than Philoclea) tries to convince her that since he has failed so badly he can only show true courage by dying, she answers him with the same argument that Shakespeare's Edgar gives Gloucester: "It is not for us to appoint that mightie Majestie, what time he will help us. . . . And therefore to prejudicate his determinacion is but a doubt of goodnes in him, who is nothing but goodnes" (II, 109-11).[16]

Sidney was only one of many who taught the Boethian lesson, sometimes refreshed with quotations from Seneca and Epictetus, that the good man accepts all fortune as good fortune. Surrey praises Wyatt for his upright life and his ability to accept his fortune ("Of the death of Sir T. W. the Elder"). Thomas Hoby's translation of Castiglione's _Book_ _of_ _the_ _Courtier_ des- cribes the Duke of Urbino as overwhelmed with every sort of calamity and yet bearing everything "with such stoutnesse of courage that vertue never yeelded to fortune. But with a bold stomacke despising her stormes, lived with great dignitie and estimation among all men: in sicknesse, as one that was sounde, and in adversitie, as one that was most fortunate" (p. 123). John Florio's translation of Montaigne's _Essayes_ helped spread the popular Senecan doctrine that "there is no evill in life,

for him that hath well conceived, how the privation of life is
no evill" (I.19). Thomas Lodge's Rosalynde describes a franklin
who, having lost both his sons at once, yet "as a man of courageous resolution took up the bodies of his sons without shew of
outward discontent," for which courage the hero Rosader commends
him, "I see thou scornest fortune with patience, and thwartest
the injury of fate with content" (p. 18). Duke Robert in Chapter XIII of Thomas Deloney's Thomas of Reading, upon learning
that he is to lose his eyes, says, "The noble mind is neuer conquered by griefe, nor ouercome by mischance" (p. 335).

Edmund Spenser, like Sidney, endowed several of his heroes
with miscellaneous Stoic virtues. The righteous Artegall, in
addition to belonging to the same family of good magistrates as
Sidney's Euarchus, is similarly given an opportunity to demonstrate how the true hero sustains adversity. When he is cap-
tured by the underhanded Radegund, he refuses sympathy on the
ground that "to a courage great / It is no lesse beseeming well,
to beare / The storme of fortunes frowne, or heauens threat, /
Then in the sunshine of her countenance cleare / Timely to ioy"
(V.v.38). Guyon, the knight of temperance, adheres to the Roman
or Christian Stoic middle way as he distinguishes expertly
between too much passion and too little. Though too wise to
rush into senseless battles, he can be roused by anger in
defense of virtue; and if he is immune to immoderate desire,
either for gold or for women, he is not lacking in benevolence.
Like such classic Stoic heroes as Hercules, Ulysses, and Aeneas,
he has an assigned goal to reach, difficulties to overcome,
temptations to withstand.[18]  That Spenser followed the tradition that endowed not only Virgil's hero but also several of
Homer's with Roman Stoic virtue is indicated by his letter to
Walter Ralegh, in which he says that in fashioning his prescription for a "gentleman or noble person" he has followed "all
the antique Poets historicall, first Homere, who in the Persons
of Agamemnon and Vlysses hath ensampled a good gouernour and a
vertuous man, the one in his Ilias, the other in his Odysseis:
then Virgil, whose like intention was to doe in the person of
Aeneas."

Spenser, like many another moral story teller, frequently
puts forward his Stoic lessons by using negative examples and
has Guyon meet various people who have destroyed their peace of
mind by giving way to passion. Early in the book he comes upon
Amavia, whose immoderate grief causes her to commit suicide
when her husband dies (II.i.36); and in Stanza 57 the moral is
underscored: Behold what happens when passion robs reason of
her sovereignty. "The strong through pleasure soonest falles,
the weake through smart." Canto IV tells the sad story of the
rash young man who is so maddened by fury that he commits murder. Long before we met these negative examples in Book II,
however, we had been introduced in Book I to the headstrong
Red Crosse Knight, whose reckless self-confidence was always
leading him astray. In the very beginning, instead of listening to Una's counsels of moderation, he rushed into the cave of

error, "full of fire and greedy hardiment." But even if he
thought he had conquered error, he was soon making the mistake
of deserting Una to follow Duessa and shortly afterwards was
overcome first by pride and then by despair. He is one more
example of someone either up too high or down too low. Fortunately, he learned in time that he needed instruction in
self-discipline.

Side by side with the humanistic idealism of Sidney and
Spenser there was, of course, the actual world as it was known
to experienced men of affairs like Bacon and Greville. Bacon
in his essay "Of Great Place" ruminates at first over the
strange desire men have for a power that will rob them of peace
of mind, referring, in this section, to the popular passage
from Seneca's Thyestes on the impossibility of learning to know
oneself while occupying a high position. But instead of condemning ambition as a sin or pretending that the only requirement is to do one's duty in one's assigned station, he accepts
the fact that "all rising to great place is by a winding stair"
and tries to emphasize that "power to do good is the true and
lawful end of aspiring." His practical advice on how to reach
the top and stay there includes advice on how to exercise power
with integrity.

Fulke Greville, like Bacon, divided the ideal from the
possible, and though he perhaps spent more time than Bacon
indulging in melancholy reflections on the disparity between
the two, he still devoted much energy, both as a public servant
and as a poet, to the problem of choosing the best apparent
solution in a wicked world whose ultimate purposes are hidden.[19]
In spite of his Christian, or Stoic, awareness of the emptiness
of wealth, place, and honor, he continued as a courtier to pursue these goals, while at the same time trying to manage the
areas of his own responsibility with rectitude. In his writings he more than once makes the distinction between perfect
virtue, available to none or few, and the practical conduct that
will result in the greatest happiness of the greatest number.[20]

In A Treatie of Humane Learning he looks at human knowledge and considers it worthless from the ultimate point of
view, only an aspect of pride or a manifestation of pedantry.
At the same time, however, he follows the humanistic tradition that divides the proud knowledge that leads us either to
pry into God's secrets or to engage in scholastic quibbling from
the practical knowledge that will help us improve our conduct
(st. 3, 4, 30-34, 82). Instead of technical information about
what is meant by a lyric mood, he says, let music "instruct me
rather, how to show / No weeping voyce for losse of Fortunes
goods." Let geometry, instead of showing me how to measure the
earth, "instruct me, how to measure / What is enough for need,
what fit for pleasure" (st. 32) Like Seneca and like Joseph
Hall he praises the plain style: "Those words in euery tongue
are best, / Which doe most properly expresse the thought" (st.
109). "The true art of Eloquence indeed / Is not this craft
of words, but formes of speech, / Such as from liuing wisdomes

doe proceed; / Whose ends are not to flatter, or beseech, / Insinuate, or perswade, but to declare / What things in Nature good, or euill are" (st. 110). Poetry and music, he says, should serve a useful purpose, such as moving the passions to goodness or bravery or teaching us "order vnder pleasures name" (st. 111-14).[21] Arithmetic, geometry, astronomy should emphasize the practical rather than the theoretical (st. 116-19); and in general he, like Milton, believes that the purpose of learning is not to "dazell the earth with visions infinite; / But nurse the World with Charitable food, / Which none can doe that are not wise and good" (st. 142). For in spite of his disdain for curious or theoretical knowledge, he has the usual humanist belief that most of us need education in virtue and dare not trust the untutored impulse. He divides "Gods Children" (st. 63) who need no tutors from the majority who will be wise to conform as well as possible to the book of God and to the established order, subordinating the individual to the general "that private hearts may vnto publike ends / Still gouern'd be, by Orders easie raines" (st. 93). Where he differs from contemporaries like Joseph Hall is in failing to pretend that the familiar social system necessarily represents the ideal state and in failing to set up as an achievable standard the Ciceronian model of the good governor--even though he does refer to Sidney as "this Britane Scipio" (Life, p. 127). He, like others who are aware that custom has a way of deviating from the original plan, suggests that from time to time the two ought to be compared. "Once in an age let Gouernment then pease [weigh] / The course of these traditions, with their birth" (st. 101).

Just as he distinguishes between a learning that cannot help us to arrive at ultimate truth and a learning that may be useful in practical conduct, so he evaluates the desire for fame and honor from a practical point of view. The desire for worldly distinction is not so reprehensible, he thinks, as the Stoic's proud boast of moral self-sufficiency and claim of immunity to the desire for fame; worldly pride is not even so bad as the pride of the humanistic wise man who strives to imitate God. The latter Greville compares to the pride of the first Adam, "Since to be like his Maker he affected, / And being lesse still thought himselfe neglected" (st. 20, 33, 34). But the ordinary worldly desire for reputation may benefit society since we may do good deeds through a desire for fame (st. 20-21). To pretend that our motives are ever pure is only a form of Stoic pride; for the Stoics are "all foule within, yet speake as God were there" (st. 22).

The distinction between private virtue and worldly pragmatism appears again in his two plays, Mustapha and Alaham. Mustapha, the title character, is one of "God's children" who like a Christian Stoic asserts his freedom not to do evil and accepts the will of God without pretending to understand fate. Specifically, he accepts assassination, asking, "Shall we, to languish in this brittle Iayle, / Seeke, by ill deeds, to shunne ill destinie? / And so for toyes, lose immortalitie?"

(IV.iv.137-38); for, as he asserts a little later, "all Fates
are from aboue / Chain'd vnto humors that must rise, or fall. /
Thinke what we will: Men doe but what they shall" (IV.iv.179-
81).  And so at the end he is praised by Achmat as one "that
neither hop'd nor fear'd, / [one who] Seeing the stormes of Rage
and Danger comming, / Yet came" (V.ii.31-33).  Mustapha's sister likewise refuses to compromise with evil and loses her life
for trying to prevent the murder of her brother.  As her first
speech in the play indicates, she is an example of constancy or
Christian fortitude.  Meditating on the difference between
those who feed at fortune's breast and those who feed at virtue's, she says of the latter, "Their minds grow strong against
the stormes of fortune, / And stand, like rockes, in Winter
gusts vnshaken; / Not with the blindnesse of desire mistaken"
(II.iii.7-11).

The self-sacrificing virtue of Mustapha is of little benefit to society, however; and in contrast to him we have the less
perfect virtue of the good councillor Achmat, whose primary
concern is the good of the state.  Although at the beginning of
the play he sometimes talks like a Stoic man of integrity, in
the end he makes the pragmatic decision to go on serving the
tyrannical monarch in the hope of restoring order and protect-
ing the country from the chaos that would result if the out-
raged mob should gain control.[22]

If Mustapha presents the difficulty of trying to balance
private virtue with social benefit, Alaham leans more heavily
in the direction of political expediency.  Where Mustapha is
admired for accepting his fate and sacrificing himself, the
weak king in Alaham who passively accepts what he calls his
fate is not presented as an admirable character.  His weakness
brings harm to the state.  In this play the good councillor
Mahomet, who, like Achmat, remains alive at the end presumably
trying to restore some order, is not given any markedly Stoic
characteristics and is obviously a pragmatist who is only trying to find the best temporary solution in an evil world.[23]

A Letter to an Honourable Lady, although it may have been
written at an earlier time when Greville was feeling more sympathetic with Stoic ideas (see Rebholz, pp. 33, 35, 85, 328),
is not really in conflict with his later thinking since it deals
exclusively with private virtue.  The mistreated wife, who is
told to remember "afflicted Iob, in whom the excellent wisedome
of constancy is figured" (Grosart, III, 270) is offered such
standard remedies for fortune as the reminder "that there is
none so poore, but hee may haue liberall thoughts" (p. 274),
that "affliction is rather a spurre than a bridle" to devotion
(p. 274), that it is still possible for the sincere conscience
to enjoy the pleasure of "peace within, and fame without," that
it is man's error not to seek "rest in that fortune vnder which
hee liues; but in change, which is euer in the power of others"
(pp. 274-75).  At the end he reminds her of the classical distinction between Caesar, the restless man of ambition, and
Scipio, the retired man of virtue (p. 293), with Scipio obvi-

ously the model to be admired.

Though Bacon and Greville, as men who knew the world and who combined skepticism with their humanism, saw clearly the wide gap between what men do and what they ought to do, many a poet, ignoring the daily obstacles in the way of moral virtue, hymned the praises of the good and happy man. Samuel Daniel (1563?-1619), who, like others, had a way of combining, in a suitable Christian framework, the Stoic emphasis on duty with the Epicurean emphasis on pleasure, has a debate between a Stoic Ulysses and a hedonistic Siren in which Daniel has Ulysses argue that "natures of the noblest frame / These toyles and dangers please, / And they take comfort in the same / As much as you in ease."[24] A poem "To the Lady Margaret, Covntesse of Cvmberland," begins with a clear echo of Lucretius (opening of Book II) that nevertheless contrives to sound Stoic:

> He that of such a height hath built his minde,
> And rear'd the dwelling of his thoughts so strong
> As neither Feare nor Hope can shake the frame
> Of his resolued powres, nor al the winde
> Of Vanitie or Malice, pierce to wrong
> His setled peace, or to disturbe the same;
> What a faire seate hath he from whence hee may
> The boundlesse wastes, and weildes of man suruay (lines 1-11).

As the poem goes on, praising the countess for her "wel-tun'd" mind (line 116), it ends, of course, on a properly Christian note. Another poem, "To the Lady Lvcie, Covntesse of Bedford," states that "all happinesse remaines confind / Within the Kingdome of this breast of ours" (lines 54-55), a sentiment that makes us think of Edward Dyer's (d. 1607) "My mind to me a kingdom is, / Such present joys therein I find. . . . I seek no more than may suffice. . . Lo! thus I triumph like a king, / Content with that my mind doth bring." But where Daniel's thought is a small part of a lengthy discourse on the nature of true glory, Dyer's much anthologized short poem calmly describes the poet himself as having already achieved that enviable state of equanimity that allows him to be pleased with his own virtue and to accept all fortune as good fortune. This poem provides a classic sixteenth-century example of what sounds very much like Stoic self-sufficiency. Henry Wotton's (1568-1639) "The character of a happy life," on the other hand, merely sets up an ideal without pretending to have attained it and keeps the man who is lord of himself within humble Christian limits. How happy, he says, the man "whose passions not his masters are; / Whose soul is still prepared for death." Thomas Campion's (1567-1620) "The man of life upright," though it also describes an ideal rather than a state achieved by the poet, yet depicts the Christian pilgrimage to heaven as a tranquil Epicurean journey, with the struggles, whatever they may have been, all in the past. This happy man, "whose silent days / In harmless joyes are spent, / Whome hopes cannot delude, / Nor sorrow discontent. . . . Hee onely can behold / With unaffrighted eyes / The horrours of the deepe / and terrours of the Skies" as he scorns "all the cares / That fate, or fortune brings." In contrast, George Herbert's "Constancie," another description of the ideal man, emphasizes the pursuit of duty more than the settled pleasure of accomplishment. It starts out by inquiring "Who is the honest man?" and goes on to list the virtues of the Christian of integrity, depicting the just man as one constantly on the path of virtue but not necessarily content with his own performance, even though he is one "Whom neither force nor fawning can / Unpinne, or wrench from giving all their due," one who can bear trials calmly, though not necessarily easily, who cannot be tempted and who obeys true virtue as his sun instead of requiring man-made laws to guide him. This honest man is always being faced with difficult practical decisions, and though he "still is right," he also "prayes to be so still."[24] Though all of these poems have behind them the same groundwork of classical aphorisms, the message nevertheless varies with the individual treatment.

Shakespeare who followed the uncontroversial practice of sneering at Stoics while at the same time endowing a number of his minor characters, as well as a few of his major ones, with acceptable Stoic qualities, gives us in the good Henry V the ideal king from the school of Cicero and Aquinas,[25] and has Antony eulogize the dead Brutus as "the noblest Roman of them all," one in whom the elements were so mixed "that Nature might stand up and say to all the world, 'This was a man.'" This description, though not always applicable to Shakespeare's Brutus when alive, nevertheless expresses the Roman ideal of the good man as one who devotes his life to the common welfare.[26] The complex Hamlet, who has some Stoic qualities among the rest, has the highest regard for the well-balanced Horatio, who frankly models himself on Stoic lines and even uses as an excuse for wanting to commit suicide that he is "more an antique Roman than a Dane" (V.ii.351). Hamlet's well-known description of his friend (III.ii.70-79) gives us the character of the ideal Stoic as private man; and though we know too little about Horatio to know the basis for this praise, we do know that Shakespeare's audience enjoyed hearing about the man of life upright who accepts all fortune as good fortune, the man "that is not passion's slave," the one "whose blood and judgment are so well commingled" that he is not perturbed by the ups and downs of chance that unsettle the rest of us.[27] Another Shakespearean version of Stoic virtue is the good servant Adam in As You Like It who does his work well for the sake of the work and not for the reward, as Orlando points out, saying, "O good old man, how well in thee appears / The constant service of the antique world, / When service sweat for duty, not for meed!" (II.iii. 56). Other examples are Kent and Edgar in King Lear.[28] Kent, like the Adam of As You Like It, is the good man in the role of faithful servant, one whose occasional bursts of temper come

under the heading of being angry in a just cause, while Edgar,
who is almost too good to be true, shows us how the good man
sustains adversity.  Holding him on the human side of perfect
virtue is only his slight tendency to slip into the smugness of
Stoic self-sufficiency, a fault, however, that he himself is
quick to recognize.  At the beginning of Act IV he is briefly
carried away with satisfaction in his own fortitude.  Thinking
he has finally hit bottom, he laughs at fortune and taunts the
air, "Welcome then, / Thou unsubstantial air that I embrace! /
The wretch that thou hast blown unto the worst / Owes nothing
to thy blasts."  Fortune, however, who has not finished her
game with Edgar, quickly responds with such a blast that he is
completely humbled and has to confess, "The worst is not / So
long as we can say 'This is the worst.'"  By continually profit-
ing in this way from the lessons of misfortune, Edgar goes on
developing his spiritual muscles, demonstrating a constancy
which is almost as rare among Shakespeare's characters as it is
in life.

Patience is a virtue we like to recommend to others, but
which we ourselves impatiently reject.  In Romeo and Juliet the
Friar only irritates Romeo when he says, "I'll give thee armour
to keep off that word [banishment]; / Adversity's sweet milk,
philosophy."  The Epicurean Cassius taunts the Stoical Brutus
with the reminder that he is momentarily forgetting his own
doctrine: "Of your philosophy you make no use / If you give
place to accidental evils" (IV.iii.145).  Coriolanus tries telling his stout Roman mother that misfortune gives her a chance
to show her mettle: "You were us'd / To say extremity was the
trier of spirits; / That common chances common men could bear; /
That when the sea was calm, all boats alike / Show'd mastership
in floating" (IV.i.3).  In Measure for Measure the Duke's
advice to Claudio to "be absolute for death" (III.i.5-41) is an
aria on Montaigne's Senecan theme that "there is no evil in
life for him that hath well conceived how the privation of life
is no evil.  To know how to die doth free us from all subjection and constraint."  However much the audience may have
enjoyed this speech, Claudio is not the man to appreciate it.
Brabantio in Othello reacts as Shakespeare's characters often
do when Stoic advice is offered to them.  When the Duke, trying
to comfort him for the loss of his daughter, suggests he try
smiling at fortune because "the robb'd that smiles steals something from the thief," Brabantio throws back the hint that the
Duke might take a little of his own advice.  "So let the Turk of
Cyprus us beguile: / We lose it not, so long as we can smile"
(I.iii.199 ff).

Shakespeare's treatment of suicide, like his treatment of
Stoic ideas in general, varies with the demands of the particular situation.  When Edgar in Lear persuades his father to go
on living until God decides the time is ripe for him to die, he
gives the same sort of Christian advice we heard in More's Dialogue of Comfort or Sidney's Arcadia.  In a Roman play like
Julius Caesar or Antony and Cleopatra, however, suicide is

treated as a dignified exit when the game is no longer worth
the candle.  Sometimes, even in a Roman play, we have it both
ways.  In a brief exchange between Brutus and Cassius just
before the last battle, Cassius asks Brutus what he will do if
their side should lose.  Surprisingly, Brutus gives the
Christian-sounding answer that he will bear with patience what
providence sends and not destroy himself as Cato did.  A
moment later, however, when Cassius asks if he is then content
to be led in triumph through the streets of Rome, he reverses
himself, swearing he never will go bound in Rome (V.iii.95-115),
which promise he makes good when he kills himself two scenes
later saying, "It is more worthy to leap in ourselves / Than
tarry till they push us" (V.v.24-25).

Ben Jonson was another, like Shakespeare and Erasmus and
Horace, to name only three, who sometimes laughed at the Stoic
wise man, sometimes admired him.  In Bartholomew Fair the laughter predominates.  Among the various forms of human idiocy presented for our delight there is the pompous fool (familiar in
academic circles) who considers that because he can quote Horace
he is a wise man.  The complacent Justice Overdo, who thinks
himself exceedingly superior, has nevertheless managed to get
himself put in the stocks.  Sitting there, he tries to comfort
himself with the act of imperturbability: "In the mid'st of this
tumult, I will yet be the Author of mine owne rest, and, not
minding their fury, sit in the stockes in that calme, as shall
be able to trouble a Triumph" (IV.i.43-45).  Several scenes
later, when asked by Wasp how he is taking his affliction, he
pontificates, "I doe not feele it, I doe not thinke of it, it
is a thing without mee.  Adam, thou art aboue these battries,
these contumelies.  In te manca ruit fortuna, as thy friend
Horace saies.  Thou art one, Quem neque pauperies, neque mors,
neque vincula terrent. . . ."  "What's heere?" says Quarlous,
"a Stoick i' the stocks?  The Foole is turn'd Philosopher" (IV.
vi.95-103).  At the end of the play the proud Justice Overdo,
required to face the fact that he is only a fool like the rest
of us, is counseled to "remember you are but Adam, Flesh, and
blood!  you haue your frailty, forget your other name of Ouer-
doo" (V.vi.96-98).

Presumably Overdo's tag from Horace was one with which
every schoolboy was sadly familiar, one which, out of context,
was doubtless memorized as schoolboys of the early twentieth
century used to memorize Kipling's "If."  A translation is worth
quoting in full because even if Horace when he wrote it had his
tongue partly in his cheek, this sort of definition of the well-
rounded wise man, complete in himself, whether taken from Horace
or Virgil or someone else, keeps being alluded to.  "Who, then,
is free? / The wise man alone, who has full command of himself, /
Whom poverty, death, or chains cannot terrify, / Who is strong
enough to defy his passions and scorn / Prestige, who is wholly
contained in himself, well rounded, / Smooth as a sphere on
which nothing external can fasten, / On which fortune can do no
harm except to herself."[29]

Though Justice Overdo, whose name clearly suggests he has forgotten the golden mean, is ridiculous, Jonson does not always make fun of the wise man. In the Apologetical Dialogue following The Poetaster, the author [Jonson?], claiming to be superior to the tongues of detractors, says, "The Fates haue not spun him the coarsest thred / That (free from knots of perturbation) / Doth yet so liue, although but to himselfe, / As he can safely scorne the tongues of slaues: / And neglect Fortune, more than she can him," and so on. The Roman tragedies have a few virtuous minor characters who stand in obvious Stoic contrast to the self-seeking major characters. Near the beginning of Sejanus a satirical description of the art of climbing at court has Sabinus telling Silius that the two of them have been left behind because they "are no guilty men, and then no great" (I.i.12). The chorus character, Arruntius, calls on the spirits of Cato and Brutus as symbols of integrity, praising Cato in typically Stoic terms: "Where is now the soul / Of god-like CATO? he, that durst be good, / When CAESAR durst be euill; and had power, / As not to liue his slaue, to dye his master?" (I.i.89-92). In Catiline the virtuous Cato argues that "to iust men, / Though heauen should speake, with all his wrath at once, . . . we should stand vpright, and vnfear'd" (IV.i.29-32). Later Cato addresses Cicero as "good MARCUS TULLIUS (which is more, than great)" (V.i.99). Similar sentiments appear in some of Jonson's non-dramatic poems. "Epistle XIII. To Katherine, Lady Aubigny" contains the line "for he, that once is good, is ever great" (52) Of this poem Maren Sofie Rostvig says, "A better example of the Stoicism which leads to a desire for the retired life could scarcely be found."[30] Lady Aubigny's love of virtue in no way fills her with Stoic pride. As a faithful and obedient wife, she understands her place in the hierarchical system; for though she is praised for choosing a life of integrity "Farre from the maze of custome, error, strife" (60), she is also praised for loving "him you should," and for "depending on his word and will" (113 ff). Like Chaucer's Griselda and Shakespeare's well-tamed Kate, her concept of virtue includes knowing her place.

Jonson has no objection to Stoic virtue, as long as it is combined with what he considers a sense of proportion, which is another way of saying that virtue means conforming to the laws of nature as Jonson, the Jacobean humanist, defines them. Many of the fools in his comedies are fools simply because they have lost sight of what is fitting. The greedy minor characters in Volpone and The Alchemist deserve the exploitation they get because their values have gone askew. Husbands like Sir Politic Would-be and Littlewit and Overdo who forget that wives need proper supervision, deserve their medicine. Extremists of any kind, from Morose to Overdo, receive no sympathy. People like Kitely (Every Man in his Humor) and the Would-bes in Volpone who overlook the obvious to search for complicated answers provoke Jonson's humanist risibilities. Like many a middle-of-the road Stoic he believes that a salient characteristic of the wise man is common sense.

John Marston's varieties of wise men cover virtually the
same spectrum as those of Shakespeare and Jonson.[31] As we have
already seen (Chapter V), he gives us examples of the Horatian
contented man (Feliche in Antonio and Mellida), of the proud
Stoic whose claim to imperturbability will prove false (Pandulpho Feliche in Antonio's Revenge), of good Ciceronian public
servants (Andrugio in Antonio and Mellida, Duke Altofront in The
Malcontent, Scipio, Geloso, and Massinissa in Sophonisba), and
of the sham Stoic who is really a self-seeking villain (Asdruball in Sophonisba). In his early plays, Antonio and Mellida
and Antonio's Revenge, Marston runs head on into the difficulty of putting Stoic characters of the self-sufficient type
at the center of the action. Andrugio in Antonio and Mellida,
who is a rather common variety of confused Stoic, was, before
his banishment, a good Ciceronian ruler; and now, in retirement,
he tries to comfort himself with Senecan boasts about the contented heart of the virtuous king. Since he has really no
heart for the retired life, however, these boasts immediately
prove false at the mention of his enemy, the Genoese. "That
very word / Unkings me quite, makes me vile passions slave" (IV.
i). When we meet him again as a bloody-minded ghost in Antonio's Revenge, he is anything but a Stoic.[32]

Though basically a good character, and one with some Stoic
characteristics, Andrugio is not consistently a Stoic paragon;
and no more is Sophonisba--until her final scene. (See discussion in Chapter V.) Though sometimes she displays Stoic fortitude, she is also sometimes a slave to passion and sometimes
merely a vacillating female. In Act II (i), before letting the
politicians talk her into a dishonorable decision, she tries to
maintain her integrity by reciting a Stoic speech that makes
her sound as steadfast as Sidney's Pamela: "What evill / Is
there in life to him, that knowes lifes losse / To be no evill.
. . . Without misfortune Vertue hath no glorie." And, like
Shakespeare's Brutus, who was not always so perfect as Antony
made him sound when he was dead, she obviously seems a paragon
to Massinissa when she has heroically given her life to save his
honor. It is not only a good ending to the play but also under-
standable that he should at that point apostrophize her as "thou
whom like sparkling steele the strokes of Chance / Made hard and
firme; and like wild fier turnd / The more cold fate, more
bright thy vertue burnd." . . . (V.iii). In actuality, however,
Massinissa himself and Scipio, both of whom illustrate selfless
patriotic duty of the Ciceronian type, are the truly admirable
characters. (See Chapter V.)

We are so used to the well-worn joke on Stoic pride which
consists of showing someone making fine speeches about how
little he or she minds the blows of fortune or how immune he or
she is to passion, all as a preamble to being flattened a
moment later by sudden misfortune or maddened by anger at some
frustration, that we are a little surprised to find Thomas

Dekker quite seriously presenting us with patient characters who
have mastered the delicate art of accepting all fortune as good
fortune. Not only did he write a play called Patient Grissil,
which ends with the smug husband advising others to test their
wives in the same way,[33] but also in his two plays about The
Honest Whore he included a patient minor character, Candido,
whose patience endures to the end. At first glance Candido
seems too good to last, just another example of a Stoic fraud.
His superhuman patience acts as a sort of attractive nuisance,
provoking other characters to see if they can shake his calm.
For instance, when he needs his gown to go to the Senate house,
his wife, for no particular reason, refuses to give up the key
to his chest. Instead of losing his temper, however, he keeps
cool and finds another solution. At the end of Act V, Part I
(ii.488 ff) we hear him, with his equanimity still intact, making a last speech full of the kind of Christian and Stoic moralizing we associate with the Boethian tradition. Patience, he
says, is a godlike virtue that the good Christian should try to
imitate, a virtue which brings content, makes one immune to
wrongs, gives freedom to the prisoner or the slave, makes beg-
gars equal with kings, and supplies the remedy for a shrewish
wife. By the end of Part II this good man has so pleased the
duke that the latter takes him back to court with him, saying,
"No Armour's like the minde, / A Patient man's a Patterne for a
King" (V.ii.493 ff). It is on this idealistic note that the
play concludes.[34]

Of all the playwrights, George Chapman is the one most
noted for his dabblings in Stoicism.[35] Though he managed to
keep his interest within safe Christian bounds, he nevertheless liked to flirt with the Stoic dream of moral self-
sufficiency and included among his non-dramatic poems a number
of translations that show his interest in what makes an upright
man. There is "Virgils Epigram of a good Man" that identifies
the rare "good and wise man" as one whose inner strength keeps
him "chearfull and secure," who goes on his way "in himself,
worldlike, full, round, and sure," immune to what great men may
do or what the mob may think (p. 227). There is "For Good
Men," a translation from Epictetus, expounding the doctrine
that since God is good, everything that happens to a good man
is good (pp. 236-7). Likewise from Epictetus come "To Yong
Imaginaries in Knowledge," which discusses the art of self
control and the need to "sustain and abstain" (p. 450), and "A
Great Man" (p. 228), which describes "A great and politicke
man (which I oppose / To good and wise)," who "is neuer as he
showes. / Never explores himselfe to find his faults." According to Ennis Rees, Chapman's most important philosophical poem
is "Euthymiae Raptus," a poem that describes the purpose of
education as learning to imitate God, which means learning to
rule ourselves before we try to rule others (p. 184 ff). The
reward of true learning is peace of mind. All these poems
show that side of Chapman that may be said to adhere to the

Boethian tradition since all of them concentrate less on the
wise man as good governor than on the wise man as moral individual. However, when Chapman started endowing the heroes of
his plays with miscellaneous Stoic qualities he ran into the
ancient problem that the man who tries to follow his conscience
alone is likely to find himself in conflict with other people
with other ideas.

Part of the puzzlement over what Chapman was trying to do
in Bussy d'Ambois comes from our inability to be sure whether
he was deliberately showing us a somewhat confused man of
integrity or whether as playwright he was himself somewhat
confused. Confused or not, this play is generally regarded as
Chapman's only successful stage piece. Its hero, Bussy, is
sometimes described as a Stoic, sometimes as a slave to passion,
since we are not quite sure whether he is intended as a good
example or as a bad example.[36] Like Marston's Sophonisba,
Bussy certainly makes his final exit in high Stoic fashion,
which does not preclude the possibility that during his journey he may have stumbled once or twice from the high moral
path. Among the many ways of interpreting him, one is to see
him as a good man destroyed by a corrupt society, a man who
nevertheless triumphs because he maintains his integrity and
refuses to compromise with evil. Another way is to see him
as a victim of Stoic pride, a man too prone to confuse the
impulses of his own heart with the laws of nature. A third way
is to see the play as showing a hero who knows how to sustain
but not how to abstain. Before he came to court, when he lived
retired in the country, he was able to maintain his virtue; and
at the end, when he is destroyed by his enemies, he demonstrates
his fortitude and dies with dignity. In between, however, he is
overcome by the temptations of a life of prosperity and becomes
a slave to passion. Although Bussy has often been compared to
Marlowe's Tamburlaine, perhaps he should also be compared to
such much-tempted and sometimes fallible heroes as Malory's
Lancelot or Spenser's Red Cross Knight. Less consistently
self-sufficient than the Stoicized Ulysses, he yet manages to
triumph in his death like the Stoicized Hercules.[37]

By choosing a story based on history, Chapman had to
accept the fact that his hero's death was brought about through
his love affair with Montsurry's wife. If Chapman attached any
blame to this episode, however, he seems to have attached it
all to Tamyra, who was made to fling herself at the gentlemanly
Bussy. She was the one who lamented that when she lost her
virtue she lost her peace of mind and then tried to put the
blame for her passionate temperament on fate and the blame for
her weakness on the nature of women (III.i.63-86). Chapman
never gave any clear indication that he thought his hero had any
faults.

At the beginning of the play, when the virtuous hero first
comes to the corrupt court, he meditates in a classical fashion
on the difference between the way things are and the way things

ought to be, complaining that "Fortune, not Reason, rules the
state of things," that reward and honor go to the wrong people,
that the only virtuous people are the poor ones, that the great
ones are merely hollow shams who have forgotten how unimportant
a thing man is. The only safe guide, says he, is virtue. But
if Bussy thinks his virtue is safe, we do not necessarily have
to accept his opinion. The answer is not clear cut. Perhaps
we must be content with taking one scene at a time, without
trying to impose an uncomfortable unity upon the whole play.
In the beginning it is obvious that Bussy's plain-talking virtue
is exactly the new sensation that a jaded court is looking for.
The king grows lyrical over the idea that back in the age of gold
all men must have been like Bussy. He even goes so far as to
say Bussy's virtue makes him the equal of a king (III.ii.90 ff).
The king's brother, Monsieur, takes Bussy into his service,
giving him a large gift of money, but soon learns he cannot
buy his integrity. And Tamyra, hitherto a faithful wife, is
so overcome by the spectacle of Bussy's virtue that she throws
away her own.

Though Bussy certainly has a passionate side, there is no
clear suggestion that Chapman condemns him as a slave to passion or even blames him either for his love for Tamyra or for
his quick temper. The Stoic emphasis on emotional calm was
never very popular. The Christian moralists had long justified a righteous anger in a good cause; and the courtly love
tradition had its own definitions of virtue, which did not
include equanimity. When Bussy loses his temper in defense of
his honor and engages in a duel that causes the deaths of five
people, he clearly feels himself justified and expects the king
to exonerate him by obeying the law above the law. All we know
is that circumstance (here called fate), using the evil Monsieur
as its instrument, brings about Bussy's murder, and that Bussy
accepts his fate standing up, asserting as he dies that to him
life or death are alike indifferent.

Among Chapman's other more or less Stoic characters the
next most controversial one is Byron, the title character of
The Conspiracy of Charles, Duke of Byron and of The Tragedy of
Charles, Duke of Byron. Obviously a victim of false Stoic
pride, Byron is better at asserting self-sufficiency when fortune is favoring him than in demonstrating fortitude when
things go wrong. As a man who claims to be a law unto himself,
he stands in contrast to his king, Henry IV of France, who
represents the ideal Christian prince in the tradition of Cicero's Of Duties. Unlike Byron, Henry can rule others because
he knows how to rule himself. His function as a king is to
cooperate with the laws of nature. Byron, although he likes
to think of himself in Stoic terms, makes the mistake of identifying freedom with lack of restraint, not with self discipline;
and when it comes time to die he demonstrates none of Bussy's
godlike courage.[38] A comment by Epernon at the end of Act IV of
the Tragedy points the moral: "Strength to aspire is still
accompanied / With weakness to endure . . . his state still is

best / That hath most inward worth" (IV.ii.305).

If Henry IV is the ideal wise man as king, Clermont D'Ambois, the hero of The Revenge of Bussy D'Ambois, is the ideal wise man as private gentleman.  Since Clermont, unlike Bussy, is a purely fictitious character, it is generally considered that he was deliberately invented as a mouthpiece for Stoic doctrine and that Chapman somehow lost sight of the fact that he was writing a revenge play.  As Una Ellis-Fermor said long ago, "Chapman has brought him into the plot to fulfill an act of vengeance which no sixteenth-century gentleman could have neglected but no stoic would have considered worth performing" (pp. 69-70).  In other words, Chapman made the dramatic mistake of putting at the center of the action a passive type of Stoic who believes that since whatever is is right there is nothing to do but accept without surprise whatever happens, remembering always that for the good man all fortune is good fortune.[39]  As a result Clermont has been classified by the critics as a lifeless Stoic stick.[40]

Clermont's virtue, though dull, is mainly of the well-accepted, uncontroversial sort.  His Stoicism comes into conflict with his Christianity only when he commits suicide upon learning that his friend the Guise has been assassinated. Though Epictetus had said that whenever we are tired of the game of life we are welcome to leave, the usual Christian attitude has been that we should wait until God decides it is time.[41]  Since suicide was a popular dramatic device, however, Chapman here may have been more interested in ending his play with a punch than in defending suicide.  The case is different in Caesar and Pompey, where Cato's high-minded suicide is the central act of the play.  Differing from those Christians like Augustine and Thomas More who condemned Cato, Chapman followed Plutarch, Seneca, and others who treated him as a Stoic hero. Chapman's Cato, like his Clermont, is generally classed by the critics as a Stoic bore.  The play, which is frankly elaborated around the text from Plutarch that "only a just man is a free man," has its characters at one point sitting around discussing "the strange opinion of the Stoic philosophers . . . that only the good man is free," with Cato, of course, defending the Stoic position.  One freedom that the good man has is the freedom not to go against his conscience; for when pushed to the wall, he can always die.  Cato, to enforce this point, quietly commits suicide rather than submit to Caesar.[42]  But Chapman, not choosing to leave Cato to the spare Stoic reward of a good conscience, departs from Plutarch to have Cato couple his defense of the just man with arguments for a belief in life after death.  The implication is that Chapman, like Addison later, sent Cato off to a Christian heaven.[43]

In Chapman's last play, The Tragedy of Chabot Admiral of France, while the title character, Chabot, is obviously a virtuous hero, there has been some argument as to whether he should be called a Stoic hero.  Wieler (pp. 130-31) classifies him as a Stoic, emphasizing such qualities as Chabot's belief

that it is more important to be good than to be great, his
sense of patriotic responsibility, his notion that both king
and subject have common obligations to the state, in other
words, his creed that selfless duty not selfish ambition should
be the motivating force. Ribner, arguing that in this play
Chapman renounced Stoicism to reassert the moral vision of
Bussy D'Ambois, says that Chabot gives us one more example of
the inability of a good man to survive in a corrupt world
(p. 19). Falsely accused of treason, falsely condemned by a
judge who is more responsive to political pressure than to
abstract justice, Chabot dies of a broken heart--even though
finally pardoned by the king. Though the play was set in the
France of Francis I, its point was equally applicable to the
England of James I. Arguing that Stoics are not crushed by
temporary reversals of fortune and do not die of broken hearts,
Ribner thinks that if Chabot had been a Stoic he would have
retired from the world like his father-in-law instead of throwing
in his lot with society. Undoubtedly Chabot's father-in-law is
in the play for the purpose of underscoring the Stoic-
Epicurean lesson that the good man who would survive must avoid
the wheel of fortune--or the world of power politics. Chabot,
an impractical idealist who thinks he can be both good and
great, is destroyed because he cannot bend.[44] He is a tragic
version of Molière's comic Misanthrope. In some ways, also, he
resembles Pompey of Caesar and Pompey, another character who
was falsely accused of being "too great to be truly good" (V.i.
136). Pompey said to his wife just before his death, "Let us
still be good, / And we shall still be great" (V.i.181-82). In
that play the point of view of Chabot's father-in-law is
expressed by Cato in his final warning to his son, "not to
touch / At any action of the public weal" (V.ii.108), in other
words, to fly the courts of princes.

What we have to remember is that there are Stoics and
Stoics, but very few pure Stoics. The main Roman tradition,
which included not only Cicero but also Epictetus and Marcus
Aurelius, emphasized social duty. Ideally the world should be
a place in which everyone accepts his assigned job; a king
should conform to the model of the Henry IV of the Byron plays.
Unfortunately the actual world has a tendency to operate on the
principles described by Machiavelli, and not all would-be Stoics
have sufficient equanimity to go on bearing the way things are.
If Marcus Aurelius tried to persuade himself that "to be vexed
at anything which happens is a separation of ourselves from
nature," Cato chose death rather than life under Caesar. Though
Chabot possessed neither perfect Christian patience nor perfect
Stoic fortitude, he did have a stiffnecked Stoic objection to
moral relativism.

Chapman's complicated experiments with self-sufficient
Stoic heroes like Clermont and Cato were not imitated by his
fellow dramatists. Usually a character in a Jacobean play who
is classified by the critics as Stoic confines his Stoicism to
such things as self-control and patience in adversity which do

not conflict with his Christianity. Such a character is Charlemont in Cyril Tourneur's The Atheist's Tragedy, or, the Honest
Man's Revenge, who has been called a "Senecal Man" because he
masters his passions and accepts misery with Christian
patience.[45] In the play he stands in contrast to his villainous atheistical uncle, D'Amville, an Epicurean Machiavel who
tries to manipulate fortune for his own ends. When D'Amville
murders Charlemont's father and marries Charlemont's betrothed
to his own son, Charlemont leaves revenge to providence; and by
thus failing to take matters into his own hands in the usual
Elizabethan-Jacobean stage fashion, he puts himself in the same
class as the patient Master Frankford in Heywood's A Woman Killed
with Kindness. The morality of the play, however, is largely
that of a bourgeois-Christian folk tale; for virtue is required
neither to be its own reward nor to wait for a heavenly reward:
the hero wins the girl and the gold here and now. After the
patient hero and heroine, Charlemont and Castabella, have successfully undergone various trials, with periodic assistance
from providence, they are allowed to live happily ever after.
As a reward for patiently refusing to defend themselves in court
and uncomplainingly submitting their heads to the axe, they are
miraculously saved when their wicked uncle accidentally brains
himself, thus leaving them in possession of all they had formerly
lost, and more: titles, wealth, each other. Charlemont is the
sort of self-satisfied prig who might have provoked the risibilities of Ben Jonson; and the Christian-Stoic speech he makes
to his cousin Sebastian when the latter visits him in prison is
remarkably similar to the speech Jonson's Justice Overdo makes
from his seat in the stocks. Sebastian asks Charlemont if he
is drooping and dejected and gets the standard reply that stone
walls do not a prison make, that his heart is impervious to
scorn, that he is a king because he knows how to rule himself.

> I have a heart above the reach
> Of thy most violent maliciousness,
> A fortitude in scorn of thy contempt--
> Since Fate is pleas'd to have me suffer it--
> That can bear more than thou hast power t'inflict.
> I was a baron; that thy father has
> Depriv'd me of. Instead of that I am
> Created king. I've lost a signory
> That was confin'd within a piece of earth,
> A wart upon the body of the world.
> But now I am an emp'ror of a world,
> This little world of man. My passions are
> My subjects, and I can command them laugh,
> Whilst thou dost tickle 'em to death with misery. (V.iii.33)

Steadfast constancy in adversity is likewise the characteristic that sometimes earns for female characters in the plays of
John Webster and John Ford the epithet "Stoic." In commenting
on Webster's The Duchess of Malfi, David Daiches says,

> Traditional satire of Court life, the theme of the Machiavellian
> man and the cruelties and luxuries of Italy, the revenge theme,
> and the notion that in moments of ultimate crisis even evil charac-
> ters can redeem themselves by a stoic dignity—all these threads
> are woven together by Webster and given color and strength by the
> morbid splendor of his verse. . . . Even the masque of madmen . . .
> stops short of the ridiculous because Webster keeps our eyes fixed
> on the stoical duchess who, made to sup her fill of horrors, retains
> the dignity to say 'I am Duchess of Malfi still.'[46]

That sums up well the situation of many a character whose life
was by no means Stoic but who was able to meet suffering and
death with fortitude. It is for that reason that even Vittoria
of The White Devil is sometimes described as Stoic.[47] Eugene
Waith in discussing Calantha of Ford's The Broken Heart speaks
of the "Stoical suppression of her personal feelings in the
interest of the popular good."[48] What we have in all these
characters is aristocratic courage and dignity. There is no
suggestion that any of them was interested in so-called Stoic
philosophy.

When we turn from the popular drama to the writings of
those two thoughtful clergymen, Joseph Hall and Robert Burton,
we again meet several varieties of Stoic wise man. Joseph Hall,
whose claim to be remembered has rested heavily on his little
book of Characters of Vertues and Vices, was not interested in
the kind of purist virtue that would only hasten the revolution.
He hoped to teach people to study to be quiet. The very fact
that he did not try to draw up one simple character who represents ideal virtue with a capital "V" indicates his allegiance
to the Thomistic thesis that different stations in life require
different duties. Some men are born to the contemplative life,
some to the active; some are rich; some poor. Although Hall
includes among his characters some Christians whose concern
seems to be wholly concentrated on the other world, he spends
most of his time describing people who have to work out a compromise between looking after their own souls and getting along
with other people. If such acceptable Stoic characteristics as
patience and fortitude make an expected appearance, none of
Hall's characters can be classed as an all-out unfeeling self-
sufficient individualist.
Elaborating on his basic thesis that virtue is another name
for wisdom and that a wise man is a happy man, Hall offers for
our edification a parade of good types who have achieved heaven
on earth, or have, at any rate, learned to make the best of a
bad world.[49] His "Character of the Wise Man," which sounds from
its title as though it might describe a good Stoic, actually is
about a prudent inhabitant of the earthly city who is expertly
combining spiritual health with worldly common sense. His
recipe is to follow his conscience in such a way as not to
attract attention, to avoid the public scene and any kind of
extremism, to keep himself busy, get along with his neighbors,

and mind his own business. A believer in common sense, who
thinks that knowledge should have a moral purpose and that
important truths should be obvious, he dislikes skeptical
shilly-shallying or Puritanical hair splitting. Giving every
man his due and keeping his own passions under control, he manages to stay out of trouble.[50]

After the wise man comes a portrait "Of an Honest Man,"
in this case an ideal businessman, who would rather be virtuous
than make a profit, who would still be virtuous even if there
were no heaven. In all his dealings with others he is so
upright that he would prefer suffering himself to doing someone else an injury. If the honest man is a worldly type who
comes perilously close to moral self-sufficiency, he is coun-
terbalanced by portraits "of the Faithfull Man" and the "Humble
Man," whose focus is so entirely on the other world that they
hardly seem to belong to this one.

And so it continues, with the "Valiant Man" and the "Patient Man" displaying two facets of the Christian-Stoic virtue
of fortitude. Here is the classic picture of the good man
dealing on the one hand with adversity and on the other with
success: smiling in the face of death, preparing himself ahead
of time to meet disaster, and mastering his passions, but willingly fighting in a just cause and, when he wins, being merci-
ful to vanquished enemies, holding "it the noblest revenge, that
he might hurt and doth not." The valiant man "is so ballaced
with wisdome, that he floats steddily in the midst of all tempests." The patient man "hath so conquered himself, that wrongs
cannot conquer him." "All things befall him alike; and he goes
with the same mind to the shambles, and to the fold." Both, in
fact, would seem to have achieved Epictetan equanimity. After
these examples of fortitude comes the "True Friend," whose
virtues belong to the tradition that includes Epicurus, Aristotle, Cicero, Horace, and Seneca and whose prime quality is
that he puts his friend's welfare before his own.

While the virtues of fortitude and friendship are not
confined to any particular social class, the recipes for "The
Truly-Noble" and "The Good Magistrate" apply only to men from
the top of the social scale. Once again we meet the good
leader from the school of Cicero, Aquinas, Erasmus, and Elyot,
"the Truly-Noble," who realizes that even though he was born
great he is not truly great unless he can demonstrate his worth
by virtuous action. He must understand the proper use of
riches, must acquire knowledge, must behave in such a way as to
set a good example, must be kind to his servants, generous to
the needy, a good servant to his country, and above all a good
Christian. "The Good Magistrate" is the ideal Ciceronian official, the faithful deputy of God with his eye ever fixed on
true justice (equity). Beside these two might be placed "A description of a Good and Faithfull Courtier," contained in one of
Hall's Epistles and included by Kirk in the appendix to his
edition of the Characters (p. 200). This description, which
might well be compared with Bacon's essay "Of Great Place,"

gives us the ideal public servant in the ideal commonwealth where there is no conflict between service to God and service to the king. This ideal public servant, who cares more for integrity than for promotion, aims ever at "a wise mediocrity" and whether in favor or out of favor maintains his equanimity and his sense of proportion. These idealized portraits of great men use the opposite technique from that employed by Webster in his plays. Where Webster emphasizes the seamy side of the way things are, Hall paints the rosy picture of the way things ought to be. Behind Webster's satire stands Hall's ideal; behind Hall's ideal stands Webster's seamy actuality.

Hall's collection of Virtues closes with descriptions "Of the Penitent" and the "Happy Man," both of whom, like the Faithful Man and the Humble Man, are potential saints. While the Penitent's concern is entirely with the next world, the Happy Man succeeds in having the best of both. Once again cutting across class lines, the Happy Man is the contented Christian Stoic. Master of himself, prepared for whatever may befall, able to live untroubled by fear or desire, virtuous whether in prosperity or in adversity, he walks cheerfully, whatever his social class, along the path God has chalked out for him. If he is rich, he understands the use of riches; if poor, he lives simply and cuts down his desires. Living quietly in Horatian retirement, he guides himself by his own conscience, remembering always that his greatest business is to die.[51]

After Hall's solemn idealism it is pleasant to inhale a little of Burton's gay skepticism and tempting to quote him at length as he, in the tone of Erasmus's Folly, summarizes the arguments pro and con the wise man:

> Aristotle in his Ethicks holds to be wise and happy are reciprocal terms. Goodness and wisdom are one to the honourable. 'Tis Tully's paradox, <u>wise men are free, but fools are slaves</u>, liberty is a power to live according to his own laws, as we will ourselves. Who hath this liberty? Who is free?

> He is wise that can command his own will,
> Valiant and constant to himself still,
> Whom poverty nor death, nor bands can fright,
> Checks his desires, scorns honours, just and right. (Horace)

> But where shall such a man be found? If no where, then on the contrary, we are all slaves, senseless or worse. No bad man is happy. But no man is happy in this life, none good, therefore no man wise. (<u>Anatomy</u>, pp. 62-63)

After this Burton lists all the reputed wise men he can think of and then names people who have called them fools. In support of his favorite thesis that we are all of us mad, he singles out for special ridicule Zeno, the all-or-nothing father of Stoicism:

> The Stoick is the wise man, and he alone is subject to no pertur-

bations, as Plutarch scoffs at him, he is not vexed with torments, or burnt with fire, foiled by his adversary, sold of his enemy. Though he be wrinkled, sand-blind, toothless, and deformed; yet he is most beautiful, and like a god, a king in conceit, though not worth a groat. He never dotes, [is] never mad, never sad, [never] drunk, because virtue cannot be taken away, as Zeno holds, by reason of strong apprehension, but he was mad to say so. (p. 99)

Among the self-styled modern wise men that Burton goes on to mock, he includes both Lipsius and the Pope (p. 100). Since in Burton's view all human beings are subject to the disease of melancholy, it follows logically that anyone claiming to be immune must be made of something other than flesh and blood. "I cannot except [from melancholy] any complexion, any condition, sex, or age, but fools and Stoicks, which, according to Synesius, are never troubled with any manner of passion, but, as Anacreon's grasshopper, free from pain and flesh and blood, almost a little god" (p. 151). A few pages later he is at it again, contradicting the opinion of the Stoics "that a wise man should be without all manner of passions and perturbations whatsoever," arguing that no matter what others may say, "no mortal man is free from these perturbations: or if he be so, sure he is either a god or a block" (p. 218).

Having made clear his belief that perfect peace of mind (on earth) is impossible, Burton does not object to remedies that may alleviate the pains that come from recurring attacks of perturbation. One such remedy is Stoic rationality. If we argue ourselves into a sense of proportion, so Burton says, we will stop fretting. Like Augustine he accepts the Stoic doctrine that freedom is a state of mind: "Servitude, loss of liberty, imprisonment, are no such miseries as they are held to be: We are slaves & servants, the best of us all: as we do reverence our masters, so do our masters their superiors" (p. 529). "What I have said of servitude, I say again of imprisonment. We are all prisoners. What's our life but a prison?" (p. 530). "Banishment is no grievance at all, every land is the brave man's land, and that's a man's country where he is well at ease" (p. 531).

Even the ultimate Stoic freedom, suicide, the right to choose to leave the game when we have had enough, receives more sympathetic treatment from Burton than we might expect from a Christian and a clergyman. Though he is careful to protect himself by saying, "But these are false and Pagan positions, profane Stoical Paradoxes, wicked examples, it boots not what Heathen Philosophers determine in this kind, they are impious, abominable, and upon a wrong ground," yet he gathers more than two pages of arguments in favor of suicide from ancient writers whom he normally quotes with approval. This willingness to give sympathetic ear to forbidden doctrine may have given rise to the legend, reported by Anthony à Wood, that Burton hastened his own death with a noose in order to make his horoscope come out as predicted.

The ancient arguments set down by Burton defended suicide as a relief from incurable disease, as an escape from prison or bondage, as a defense of one's honor.

> He is a coward who dies without due cause, & a fool who lives merely to brave out his pain. . . . Seneca . . . commends Cato, Dido, and Lucretia, for their generous courage in so doing, & others that voluntarily die, to avoid a greater mischief, to free themselves from misery, to save their honour, or vindicate their good name, as Cleopatra did, as Sophonisba, Syphax' wife did, Hannibal did, as Junius Brutus, as Vibius Varius, & those Campanian Senators in Livy that poisoned themselves to escape the Roman tyranny. (p. 371)

Among the many defenders of suicide, he includes Thomas More who

> in his Utopia commends voluntary death, if he be troublesome to himself or other, (especially if to live be a torment to him), let him free himself with his own hands from this tedious life, as from a prison, or suffer himself to be freed by others. And 'tis the same tenent which Laertius relates of Zeno of old, the wise man is right to put an end to himself, if so be he is twisted by violent pain, or is mutilated, or have incurable disease, & which Plato approves, if old age, poverty, ignominy, &c. oppress, and which Fabius expresseth in effect, no one need long be miserable except through his own fault. (p. 372)

Though Burton disclaims sympathy for these "false and Pagan positions," he does, as a specialist in melancholy, openly sympathize with those whom the agonies of extreme depression have driven to suicide. And in support of his plea that suicides be treated with charity and pity, he calls on Seneca the quasi-Christian, recalling that Seneca had advised, "Be justly offended with him as he was a murderer, but pity him now as a dead man." Of those who had committed suicide, Burton says,

> What shall become of their souls, God alone can tell; His mercy may come betwixt the bridge and the brook, the knife and the throat. What happens to one may happen to any. Who knows how he may be tempted? It is his case, it may be thine. That which is his lot this day, tomorrow may be thine. We ought not to be so rash and rigorous in our censures as some are; charity will judge & hope the best; God be merciful unto us all! (p. 374)[52]

The gloomy view of the nature of things that underlies Burton's comic manner prevents the kind of Stoic optimism that appears in Hall's Characters of the Virtues or in the following pleasant but rather simple-minded ditty addressed by Robert Herrick "To Fortune."

> Tumble me down, and I will sit
> Upon my ruines (smiling yet:)
> Teare me to tatters; yet I'le be
> Patient in my necessitie.
> Laugh at my scraps of cloaths, and shun

> Me, as a fear'd infection:
> Yet scarre-crow-like I'le walk, as one,
> Neglecting thy derision.[53]

John Milton, whose high standards of personal integrity
often manifested themselves as irritability at average fools,
occasionally paused to describe the joys that reward one who
is pleased with his own performance.  Rostvig calls attention
(I, 158) to the lines in <u>Comus</u> in which the Elder Brother sings
that

> he that has light within his own cleer brest
> May sit i'th center, and enjoy bright day,
> But he that hides a dark soul and foul thoughts
> Benighted walks under the mid-day Sun;
> Himself is his own dungeon.   (380-84)

And everyone knows the lines from the conclusion of <u>Paradise
Lost</u> in which Michael tells Adam that even if he has had to
leave his earthly paradise, he can still--if he learns true
wisdom--possess "a Paradise within thee, happier farr" (XII.
587).[54]  Contented equanimity, however, was not Milton's consistent mood.  As one who could not be happy himself while the
rest of the world was on the wrong track, he frequently considered a righteous anger in a just cause to be the only proper
way of exercising right reason.  Although he never pretended to
have achieved the imperturbability of one who has attained perfect wisdom, his works suggest that he had to do lifelong battle with a persistent tendency to overvalue his own insight.
Though he castigated Stoics, he himself had a tendency to suffer from Stoic pride.  Frequently he lectures himself, as well
as other people, on the need to learn to will what God wills.
Obvious examples are Sonnet VII in which he tries to calm his
frustrated youthful ambitions by telling himself to sit still
and accept "that same lot, however mean, or high, / Toward
which Time leads me, and the will of Heav'n"; Sonnet XIX, when
he tries to remind himself that "they also serve who only stand
and waite"; and Adam's final admonition to himself, "Henceforth
I learne, that to obey is best" (PL XII.560).
During the contentious days when he hoped to see the city
of God on earth brought a little nearer through his efforts, he
sometimes tried to argue that a great man (in terms of worldly
power and reputation) ought to be the same as a virtuous man--
a dream in conflict not only with the actualities of the way
things were but also with the conventional identification of an
idealized hierarchical system with the law of nature.  Instead
of recognizing as a great man one who had been appointed to a
high position or one who had been designated a ruler through
birth, he said,

> He alone deserves the appellation of great, who either achieves
> great things himself, or teaches how they may be achieved; or
> who describes with suitable dignity the great achievements of

> others. But those things only are great, which either make
> this life of ours happy, or at least comfortable and agree-
> able as far as is consistent with honesty, or which lead to
> another and a happier life. [55]

Whereas Bacon's essay "Of Great Place" concentrates in the conventional way on "greatness" as political power, a greatness
which is likely to be attained through a combination of birth,
ability, and appropriate politicking, Milton tries to argue
that in order to be great it is also necessary to be good. His
oft-quoted declaration from An Apology for Smectymnuus that as
a poet he considers it essential to try to make his own life a
true poem, shows, according to J. W. H. Atkins, that "he
endorses the Stoic doctrine of the poet (and orator) as vir
bonus."[56]

In his treatise on education, Milton argues that study
should be for the purpose of learning what virtue is and how
we can progress, as far as is humanly possible, along the road
to perfect wisdom. For him, as for Erasmus or Hooker, the
good man's aim is to imitate a God who, early in the Christian
tradition, had acquired, in addition to his other qualities,
many of the attributes of the Stoic wise man. The Christ of
Milton's Paradise Regained is the ideal Christian-Stoic--a king
because he knows how to rule himself, free because he wills
what God wills.

As Douglas Bush points out, whenever Milton talks about
liberty, he means the Stoic liberty to cooperate willingly with
eternal law. Conceding that those who fail to discipline themselves must expect to be subjected to external restraints, he
nevertheless believes in an aristocracy of virtue that would
give the really good man--whether a reader or a ruler--large
freedom to follow his own conscience. A few of his many
remarks on liberty illustrate clearly his adherence to the doctrine that only the good man is free. In his Character of the
Long Parliament he says,

> For Liberty hath a sharp and double edge, fit only to be handled by
> Just and Vertuous Men; to bad and dissolute, it becomes a mischief
> unweildy in their own hands: Neither is it compleatly given, but by
> them who have the happy skill to know what is grievance, and unjust
> to a People, and how to remove it wisely; what good Laws are want-
> ing, and how to frame them substantially, that good Men may enjoy
> the freedom which they merit, and the bad the Curb which they need.
> (CM.XVIII.253-54)

The Spirit in Comus says, "Mortals that would follow me, / Love
vertue, she alone is free" (line 1017). In The Doctrine and
Discipline of Divorce, Milton says, "Honest liberty is the
greatest foe to dishonest licence" (CM.III.370); in the
Christian Doctrine, "Righteousness towards ourselves consists
in a proper method of self-government" (XVII.203).

His righteous attacks on dishonest licence are well known.
There is Sonnet XII, where he compares the undisciplined mob

to hogs and says again that whoever loves liberty "must first be wise and good." In the Second Defence of the English People his attack on those with false notions of liberty is accompanied by the usual moral that genuine liberty is something "which a good man alone can properly attain. . . . that as to be free is precisely the same thing as to be pious, wise, just and temperate, careful of one's own, abstinent from what is another's, and thence, in fine, magnanimous and brave--so, to be the opposite of these, is the same thing as to be a slave" (CM.VIII. 249-51). In Paradise Lost Michael explains to Adam (who before the Fall was himself wise and free) how it was that true liberty was lost when desires and passions managed to take over the government from reason (XII.83 ff).[57] As Milton well knew, however, it is the common lot of the wise man to be vilified by the confused herd. Most people fail to understand what is meant by true liberty, are willing slaves to their own lusts, and, like the "miscellaneous rabble" castigated by Christ, lack the necessary wisdom and intelligence to appreciate the rare man "who dares be singularly good" (PR.III.49-59).

Like other followers of the Ciceronian tradition, Milton seldom thinks of his wise man as cultivating virtue or peace of mind in a safe retired place. For him even such private virtues as temperance and fortitude have social consequences. Both contribute to the self-discipline necessary for the good soldier and the good citizen. A happy nation is one composed of men of life upright who abstain, on the one hand, from the temptations of the soft life or false doctrine and sustain hardship, on the other, without deviating from the path of virtue. The Lady in Comus argues that luxurious living is contrary to nature and that nature's law decrees that "every just man that now pines with want" should have "a moderate and beseeming share / Of that which lewdly-pamper'd Luxury / Now heapes upon som few with vast excess" (line 113). In The First Defence of the English People Milton attacks the argument that England was happier in the days of its kings when it was "an island swimming in Luxury" (CM.VII. 285-87). The real story, he says, was that in those days England's "moral ruin through luxury was almost accomplished that it might the more indifferently bear with enslavement." He considers it a rule that when a nation gives in to luxury and self-indulgence it is laying down its neck "for some wily Tyrant to get up and ride" (CM.III.52-53). In his "Commonplace Book" he notes that with Albert of Brandenburg the self-indulgence of habitual drunkenness had the social effect of releasing his propensity to cruelty, even when he was not drunk.

Discipline is a virtue that Milton is always preaching. Early in life, in The Reason of Church-Government, after enthusiastically praising the fine discipline of "those perfect armies of Cyrus in Xenophon, and Scipio in the Roman Stories,"[58] he goes on, quite after the manner of such an old-fashioned Christian humanist as Joseph Hall, to argue that the "discipline of a good soldier" is, "if any visible shape can be given to divine things, the very visible shape and image of

vertue, whereby she is not only seene in the regular gestures
and motions of her heavenly paces as she walkes, but also makes
the harmony of her voice audible to mortall eares" (CM.III.
184-85). In the Areopagitica he enthusiastically defends the
idea that through exposure to evil the good man can strengthen
his spiritual muscles and show that he can "see and know, and
yet abstain." In Paradise Lost he illustrates perfect self-
discipline in the Seraph Abdiel, the only one of Satan's followers able to see through his master's false, though persua-
sive, arguments, the only one able to see and know and yet
abstain (V.803; VI.171). Against Satan's confused notions of
liberty, Abdiel gives the classic rebuttal. To serve God or
nature is to be free; to serve Satan, the slave of his own passions, is to be a slave indeed.[59] And in Paradise Regained
Christ, the perfect hero, repeats the lesson once more, "Who
best / Can suffer, best can do; best reign, who first / Well
hath obey'd" (III.194). Obedience, for Christ as for Abdiel,
obviously means obedience to the higher truth, not obedience
to the might of Satan.

Milton's troublesome identification of virtue with an
unconventional social conscience was not to everyone's taste.
Among his Royalist contemporaries wisdom is frequently a quiet
private virtue, well nourished on the perennial Boethian-Senecan
remedies for fortune. Jeremy Taylor (1613-67), though somewhat
skeptical about the ability of reason alone to arrive at the
higher truth, nevertheless finds Senecan advice helpful in promoting the moral life and the maximum possible peace of mind.[60]
His phrase for a mature human being or a wise man is a "living
man." As described in Holy Dying this "living man" is one more
embodiment of the middle-of-the-road wise man who is calm, contented, free from slavery to his passions, accepts good or bad
fortune with equanimity, looks on death as a release from the
miseries of life, is not concerned about wealth (though he exercises the proper golden mean in the use of riches), lives simply, loves his friends, forgives his enemies, and obeys his
prince (I.iii.6). Though he guides himself by his own conscience, he is not one who is likely to disturb the commonwealth.

The echoes of Boethius are heard again in Richard Lovelace's well-known "To Althea, from prison" ("Stone walls do not
a prison make, / Nor iron bars a cage"). Actually this pleasant
ditty contains a classic boast of superhuman self-sufficiency.
"If I have freedom in my love,/ And in my soul am free, /
Angels alone that soar above / Enjoy such liberty." No one,
of course, ever takes Lovelace seriously enough to accuse him
of Stoic pride. Nor do they bother to make such accusations
against Roger L'Estrange (1616-1704), another Royalist who
spent time in prison and cheered himself by remembering similar
unfortunates who had fronted adversity with equanimity, among
them, "Stoicks severe we see / Make torments easie by their
apathy" (st. 4).[61] Other familiar examples are Henry Vaughan's

translations of works teaching how to be master of oneself and
so remain immune to fortune and Abraham Cowley's essay and poem
on the subject "Of Liberty."  As a disciple of Horace, Cowley
sings that only the temperate man is free, the man "Who governs
his own course with steddy hand, / . . . Whom neither Death,
nor Poverty does fright. . . ."  A little farther on he sings
that "Freedome with Virtue takes her scat, / Her proper place,
her onely Scene, / Is in the Golden Mean" (Waller, II, 385, 388).

Though Cowley and other wise men of his persuasion tried
to find peace of mind by retiring from the public scene, and
though it would hardly surprise us if the old-fashioned recipe
for a good governor were completely forgotten after the Civil
War, faint traces of it are still evident in various of the
works of Marvell, Temple, Dryden, and Otway.  Andrew Marvell,
who was himself a member of Parliament in his later years, had,
like Fulke Greville, a close acquaintance both with actual
great men and with the public scene.  Like Greville, too, he
had the complex sort of vision that allowed him to see more than
one side of a question.  Greville, who had worshipped Sidney and
looked back nostalgically to the age of Elizabeth, nevertheless
worked diligently under James.  Marvell wrote poems praising
both Fairfax and Cromwell.  Fairfax, who had withdrawn from the
public scene for reasons of conscience, becomes in Marvell's
poems something of a Senecan wise man.  The concluding lines of
"Upon the Hill and Grove at Bill-borow" praise him for retreat-
ing from high public office to his own hill and grove in words
that seem to echo the opening lines of Marvell's translation of
the popular passage from Chorus 2 of Seneca's _Thyestes_:  "Climb
at _Court_ for me that will / Tottering favors Pinacle; / All I
seek is to lye still."  Again, in "Upon Appleton House," Fairfax is praised as one who "did, with his utmost Skill, / _Ambi-
tion_ weed, but _Conscience_ till" (st. 45).  Perhaps, however,
Marvell wished that Fairfax's conscience had dictated otherwise;
for he also praised Cromwell, whose conscience permitted him to
do what Fairfax refused to do.  Again we may be reminded of
Greville who in _Mustapha_ presented sympathetically both the
virtuous prince whose strict conscience prevented him from
defending himself against his unjust father, even though the
country suffered as a result, and the practical statesman who
identified his private duty with what seemed to be the best
interests of the country.  The somewhat puzzling "Horatian Ode
upon Cromwel's Return from Ireland" may indicate an attempt on
Marvell's part to adjust notions of goodness to hard facts.
Like Horace himself, who had followed Brutus in his student
days but who in later life came to admire Augustus, and like
Virgil, whose Augustan-Stoic hero Aeneas sometimes carried out
the will of God in unappealing ways, Marvell praises Cromwell
as the chosen instrument of fate who, though he has manifested
his right to rule primarily through his superior might, nevertheless rules for the good of the commonwealth and lays his
trophies at the Commons' feet.[62]

William Temple in his essay "Of Heroic Virtue" ruminates
not only over the universal principles underlying human law but
also over the basic qualities necessary for a true hero. He
calls to mind specific examples of famous heroes, trying to
decide what it is that makes them great and where they ought
to be ranked on his scale of virtue. Though his humanistic
education inclines him to prefer heroes in the Roman Stoic mode
such as Scipio and Marcus Aurelius, he is also occasionally
interested in heroes from other cultures--just as he is interested in discovering the universal laws of nature underlying the
diverse customs of China and Peru. He says, "I do not remember
ever to have read a greater and a nobler character of any
prince than of this great Almanzor in some Spanish authors or
translators of his story out of the Arabian tongue."[63] When
he is considering the standard heroes of Western tradition, he,
like Milton, praises "the picture of Cyrus drawn by Xenophon"
calling it "the truest character that can be given of heroic
virtue" (Monk, p. 103). Alexander and Caesar are ranked lower
in the scale, both suffering from too much personal ambition.
Alexander was flawed by "his intemperance in wine, in anger, and
in lust, and more yet by his cruelties and his pride: for true
honour has something in it so humorous, as to follow commonly
those who avoid and neglect it, rather than those who seek and
pursue it" (p. 104).[64] "Caesar . . . seems to have possessed
very eminently all the qualities, both native and acquired,
that enter into the composition of an hero, but failed of the
attribute of honour, because he overthrew the laws of his own
country and orders of his state, and raised his greatness by the
conquest of his fellow-citizens, more than of their enemies"
(p. 104).

Temple here seems to be using the phrase "true honour" as
a synonym for heroic virtue, which virtue, in turn, continues to
follow the familiar pattern laid down in Cicero's Of Duties.
True honor obviously means ruling oneself in accordance with
the laws of nature. When we turn, however, from these somewhat
old-fashioned ideas about honor to honor as it appears in one
of the milder examples of the Restoration heroic play, Dryden's
Aureng-Zebe (1675), we discover that here, even for such public
men as princes, honor is seen as something narrower, less
socially conscious, more private, than what Temple had in mind.
As a virtuous prince, Dryden's Aureng-Zebe belongs only dis-
tantly to the family of Shakespeare's Henry V.[65] Although
Aureng-Zebe is not to be taken as a serious ideal in anything
like the same sense as Henry V, he does show us what kind of
stage concoction Dryden's audience was willing to accept as a
hero. That Dryden chose to make him into a hero instead of a
villain is itself noteworthy, for he might very well have produced a Marlovian hero-villain on the model of Aureng-Zebe's
historical ancestor Tamburlaine. Like Shakespeare's Henry V
and like Chapman's Bussy d'Ambois, Aureng-Zebe was a historical personage reworked to fit the contemporary fashion in heroes.
As Samuel Johnson pointed out in his Life of Dryden, it was just

as well that communication in Dryden's day was such that the
actual Aureng-Zebe, the then reigning Great Mogul of India, did
not know what was happening to him on the English stage. The
actual Aureng-Zebe was, like Dryden's hero, the third son of
the former monarch. By overcoming and destroying his three
brothers and imprisoning his father, he established himself on
the throne.[66] Unlike Dryden's hero, he was around forty when
he became emperor and was the father of grown sons. Somewhat
as Corneille had softened the Cid in order to make him into an
acceptable seventeenth-century French hero, so Dryden softened
the actual Aureng-Zebe's aggressive individualism, endowing
him--in the process--with a few Stoic characteristics, as well
as making him the romantic lover of Indamora, in accordance
with contemporary French fashions in literary love.[67]

Although Dryden did not pretend to take the ideas in his
plays as seriously as he took the ideas in his non-dramatic
works, and though in Aureng-Zebe he obviously put more emphasis
on plot and spectacle than on doctrine, he yet retained a sufficient number of the popular clichés about duty and passion to
keep the atmosphere comfortably familiar. Even if Aureng-
Zebe's definition of duty seems to be confined to the idea that
he must at all costs obey his father, yet we are given no clear
evidence that he is going to develop into an oriental despot.[68]
Dryden leaves that point conveniently vague. Although the people of India exist only as background noise, with the plot centered around a power struggle among the rulers, still it is
Morat, the villain, who boasts that his will is law.

In remodeling the actual Aureng-Zebe into a stage hero,
Dryden may have found it convenient to remember the Erasmian or
Miltonic sort of argument that the most virtuous man is the one
most fit to rule and Marvell's sort of argument that the victor
is obviously the chosen instrument of fate. Although Dryden
himself might have preferred to justify Aureng-Zebe as the eldest son and the obvious heir, the fact was that he was only the
third son and that on his way to the throne he overthrew his
older brothers as well as the younger Morat. Although Dryden
mentions the elder brothers briefly in the opening exposition,
we quickly forget them as we concentrate on watching the obstrep-
erous Morat receive the punishment suitable for one who tried to
move out of place in the hierarchy. We are told, in addition,
that Aureng-Zebe, because of his superior virtue, is his
father's favorite and that he is only making war on his brothers
in support of his father. Another spurious justification
devised by Dryden is that India has the unnatural custom of
killing the younger sons when the eldest succeeds to the throne.
Thus in fighting against his brothers Aureng-Zebe is only being
"natural" in the Hobbesian sense and fighting for his life.

In order to build up Aureng-Zebe, Dryden uses the device
of tearing down not only Morat but also the Emperor. At this
point we may think we are back in the world of Gorboduc or King
Lear or Sidney's Arcadia. The Emperor is another one of those
rulers who upset nature and bring on chaos by putting their

personal desires ahead of their social duty.  In addition to
going against fate by not wanting to serve out his appointed
time, he also demonstrates by his unnatural behavior that he is
now unfit to rule others since he can no longer rule himself.
Not only does he neglect decorum through his ridiculous pursuit
of his son's betrothed, he also shows that he has become a
slave to passion.

Aureng-Zebe, though a faithful lover of Indamora, is not
a slave to passion, even though he suffers from occasional fits
of jealousy.  Neither are the virtuous female characters, Melesinda and Indamora.  These three are contrasted with the
Emperor, with his wife, Nourmahal, and with his youngest son,
Morat, all of whom have lost peace of mind through giving way
to desire.  This psychological moral, the message of many a
Senecan tragedy, was also, in Dryden's time, a popular theme
with Racine.

None of the good characters is an emotionless Stoic stick.
To have deprived them of emotion would have deprived them of
sympathy.  Though Aureng-Zebe's jealousy is obviously a fault,
it is also obviously more a plot device for adding suspense
than a serious element of characterization.  Possibly, too, it is
a polite bow to the female members of Dryden's audience; for it
is common in literary works for female characters to triumph in
the field of virtue, as here Indamora and Melesinda do.  Melesinda, who belongs to the honorable tradition of patient Gri-
seldas, patiently sustains adversity to the very end and calmly
immolates herself on her husband's funeral pyre as if she were
a Hindu widow instead of a Muslim.  Indamora, who triumphs in
the end, has to demonstrate her mettle not only by sustaining
adversity but also by withstanding the temptations of prosperity.  First the old Emperor and then the young Morat offer her
the kingdom in return for her love, but she remains faithful to
Aureng-Zebe, in spite of his downfallen fortunes.

Aureng-Zebe's passions, except for his jealousy, are all
of the acceptable sort, such as anger in a good cause.  His
desire for honor is always subordinated to his duty to his
father.  In fact, his self-righteousness often makes him sound
irritatingly smug.  He tells Morat that he is "Fearless without,
because secure within" (III.203),[69] says to his father, "All my
designs and acts to duty lead" (III.218). . . . "So to your welfare I of use may be,/ My life or death are equal both to me"
(III.276).  For his father's sake, he says, he would even be
willing to resign everything to Morat, lead a private life, and
"leave the rest to Fate" (III.231).  At one point, when it looks
as though he may be about to die, he makes the proper Stoic or
Epicurean claim to be immune not only to fear but also beyond
the delusions of hope (IV.33).  However, when his fortune suddenly changes, giving him an opportunity for action, he quickly
substitutes courageous fortitude for quiet patience.

If Aureng-Zebe illustrates the way a good potential ruler
subordinates to the decrees of fate his private desires for
honor and power, Morat and the old Emperor show what a good

ruler should not be. At one point Aureng-Zebe has to tell his
brother he is acting more like a wild beast than a rational
creature (III.304 ff). A few moments later we hear Morat talking to his wife, Melesinda, in the language of a stage Machiavel. He says that private men may be swayed by honor or love,
"But Monarchs onely by their int'rest move" (III.422-4). He
means, obviously, not the national interest but his own private
interest. Melesinda counters with a long speech arguing that
his true interest as God's deputy requires him to gain public
love through acts of pity.[70] Naturally, as his wife, she has
no influence. Neither, at a later point, has his mother, Nourmahal, even though she happens to be advising the kind of selfish action Morat would normally take. Because he is swayed by
will alone, he boasts, "I'll do't, to show my Arbitrary pow'r"
(IV.175). He blames his father for setting him a bad example,
"If your own Actions on your Will you ground, / Mine shall hereafter know no other bound" (IV.322-23).

Although Morat has demonstrated his unfitness as a ruler,
he is allowed to reform and make a pathetic last exit. When
Indamora, who has more influence on him than Melesinda, points
out to him that "all Greatness is in Virtue understood: / 'Tis
only necessary to be good," that he should dare to be great by
prescribing laws to his wild will, he immediately sees the
light (V.83-84). However, just as he is on the point of
renouncing his desire for renown and power, though not yet his
desire for Indamora, he is drawn again into battle. His death,
soon after, is properly edifying in the Christian-Stoic mode.

The Emperor shows his lack of present fitness not only by
pursuing Indamora but also by wanting to shirk his duty. He
tells Morat he turns over to him the "drudgery of Pow'r" and
wishes for himself the careless ease of an Epicurean god--a sure
sign, even in Dryden's time, that his moral sense is askew (III.
172). "Were I a God, the drunken Globe should roul: / The little Emmets with the humane Soul / Care for themselves, while at
my ease I sat, / and second Causes did the work of Fate" (184).
Like Sidney's Basilius, however, he finds that he cannot
neglect his duty and follow his will without bringing the house
down on himself. Morat, once he has the power, insists also on
having the girl. In case we miss the point, the Emperor complains didactically, "Why was my Reason made my passion's slave?
/ I see Heav'n's Justice; thus the Pow'rs Divine / Pay Crimes
with Crimes, and punish mine by thine!" (IV.372).

As compared with a complex dramatic examination of ideas
and characters of the sort to be found in Shakespeare's Lear,
Dryden's Aureng-Zebe might well be classed as an opera. A few
well-tried ideas are tossed in to arouse the desired con-
ditioned response. When we hear that a character is a slave to
will, we know he is going to be a villain, just as in an opera
we suspect that a man is a villain as soon as we hear that he is
a baritone. Although it is obvious that the virtuous Aureng-
Zebe, the chosen instrument of fate, will be a benevolent despot
who rules as he sees fit, it is not easy to say whether Dryden

in depicting such a hero was being modern and Hobbesian or
merely following a long literary tradition.

It is not to be denied that Dryden had given thought to
Stoic ideas, just as he had studied Lucretius with interest.
The definition of Stoicism that he gives in his "Discourse Concerning the Original and Progress of Satire" (1693), in connection with his remarks on Persius, suggests that he himself
had been reading Epictetus, even if Persius had not (since
Persius died when Epictetus was only seven). Dryden says,

> The philosophy in which Persius was educated, and which he pro-
> fesses through his whole book, is the Stoic; the most noble,
> most generous, most beneficial to human kind, amongst all the
> sects, who have given us the rules of ethics, thereby to form
> a severe virtue in the soul; to raise in us an undaunted courage
> against the assaults of fortune; to esteem as nothing the things
> that are without us, because they are not in our power; not to
> value riches, beauty, honours, fame, or health, any farther than
> as conveniencies, and so many helps to living as we ought, and
> doing good in our generation: in short, to be always happy, while
> we possess our minds with a good conscience, are free from the
> slavery of vices, and conform our actions and conversations to the
> rules of right reason. See here, my lord, an epitome of Epictetus;
> the doctrine of Zeno, and the education of our Persius. (pp. 75-
> 76)[71]

Dryden was careful to point out that Persius fell into none of
the impieties and absurdities for which Christians had criticized Stoic doctrine. In other words, in Dryden's translation,
at least, controversial ideas are rare. There is no boast of
self-sufficiency, no pretense of being completely free from
passion, no discussion of immortality. Except for one couplet
in the all-or-nothing vein of the early Stoics, "Vertue and
Vice are never in one Soule: / A Man is wholly Wise, or wholly
is a Fool" (V.175),[72] we find only those ideas on which Christians and Stoics had long agreed. Persius, an idealistic, well-
to-do young man, who died young, attacked contemporary society
for its greed and materialism. He put forth such unexception-
able arguments as that the best gift one can offer the gods is
a virtuous soul, that the purpose of study is to learn what virtue is and how to practise it in the station to which one has
been assigned, that we must learn to temper our desires, that
only the good man is free, that the proper way to use riches is
to help our needy friends and observe the golden mean. In
praise of Persius, Dryden says, "He shifts not sides, like Horace, who is sometimes an Epicurean, sometimes a Stoic, sometimes an Eclectic, as his present humour leads him" (Ker, p.
77).

Even though Dryden praises the high seriousness of Persius
and somewhat blames Horace the satirist for being "commonly in
jest," his own attitude toward the old philosophies is generally closer to Horace's eclecticism than to the Stoicism of
Persius. Though he takes good things wherever he finds them,

he combines them to suit himself. He has, after all, the usual
Christian attitude that pagan visions of truth are never complete. The rest of the essay ought to convince us that Dryden
was more a judicious weigher of pros and cons than a propagandist for any ancient philosophy. His ruminations over the various merits and demerits of Horace, Persius, and Juvenal as
satirists make it quite plain that he is more interested in the
art of poetry than in any philosophy and that he still believes
that the purpose of poetry is to give pleasure. As he puts it,
near the end of the essay,

> They who will not grant me, that pleasure is one of the ends of
> poetry, but that it is only a means of compassing the only end,
> which is instruction, must yet allow, that without the means of
> pleasure, the instruction is but a bare and dry philosophy: a
> crude preparation of morals, which we may have from Aristotle
> and Epictetus, with more profit than from any poet. (p. 112)

Like Dryden's Aureng-Zebe, Otway's Venice Preserved (1682)
has a plot, faintly based on historical fact, that stresses a
conflict between a man of passion and a man of reason. In both
plays we can discern some favorite Elizabethan clichés with
their meanings almost lost. Though Aureng-Zebe as a hero has
ties with the tradition of the good governor, he has a narrow
definition of duty; and the play as a whole lacks a meaningful moral frame. The same may be said of Venice Preserved.
Since Otway's echoes of Shakespeare are obvious, it is difficult not to compare Pierre with Brutus, or Jaffeir with Romeo
or Othello. No matter how often we are cautioned to look on
the play as a domestic tragedy rather than as a political play,
we cannot help noticing the political plot and therefore cannot help feeling vaguely dissatisfied with the pathetic ending.
There is no suggestion, here, as at the end of Romeo and Juliet,
that the tragedy of the young lovers may cause the state to mend
its ways. In fact, we are given neither the optimistic feeling
that after chaos the law of nature will now be back in control
nor a clear pessimistic conclusion that the same old corruption
in Venice will merely go on and on. We forget all about the
larger scene to concentrate on Belvidera's broken heart.

Since Venice Preserved is not a heroic play, we should not
complain that it is a play without a hero. Both the main characters, Jaffeir and Pierre, are flawed; Jaffeir is a slave to
passion, Pierre, a self-sufficient Stoic. Although the ideal is
presumably somewhere between, there is no one in the play to
underscore the point.[73] It may even be that no such point is
intended and that the political corruption is less bad than
Pierre says it is. Perhaps Otway is merely using some old ster-
eotypes as a starting point from which to concentrate on confused human beings who mix their private emotions with politics.
Jaffeir feels mistreated by his father-in-law, a senator, while
Pierre is furious because another senator is using money to
entice away his mistress. Both are drawn into a conspiracy to
blow up the senate. Although we believe Pierre when he

inveighs against the corrupt Venetian senate and condemn its
double-dealing at the end, we also see the venality of the
leader of the conspirators and approve the failure of the sub-
versives.[74]

Like Shakespeare's Brutus and Romeo, Pierre and Jaffeir
are sympathetic characters, even though extremists. Like Romeo
and Othello and Antony, Jaffeir is one who loves not wisely
but too well; for though Belvidera is a paragon of wifely virtue, Jaffeir's excessive love for her makes him lose his moral
balance. Caught between love and honor, his method of solving the dilemma is to commit suicide along with the friend he
has betrayed. This unchristian behavior, which drives Belvidera mad, is not criticized by Otway any more than Shakespeare
criticized Romeo or Othello or Antony.

Pierre, obviously a stage Stoic who belongs part of the
time to the family of Shakespeare's Brutus,[75] part of the time
to the family of self-sufficient Stoic atheists, does not
include equanimity among his Stoic qualities and is continually
angry in what he considera a good cause. He is a high-minded,
morally self-sufficient, but impractical, idealist who trusts
too much to his own judgment and has too much faith in the
integrity of his fellow conspirators. Early in the play he
cites "the great Call of Nature" as justification for entering into the plot to destroy the senate and later scoffs at
Jaffeir when the latter says he is on his way to pray (I.i.162,
II.i.85).[76] When he is about to be executed he refuses to
talk to the priest, saying that his own conscience acquits him,
and, finally, since death to him is no evil, he dies laughing
(V.i.382). All this, in earlier days, would have marked him as
a villain. And perhaps he is supposed to be a villain. As the
misguided friend who leads Jaffeir astray, he obviously
receives a smaller share of sympathy than the emotional
Jaffeir.

The fact is, however, that we admire the noble deaths of
Pierre and Jaffeir and weep over the pathetic death of Belvidera without quite knowing what the play is saying, unless it
is that we should sympathize with confused human beings. The
play's popularity throughout the eighteenth century must mean
that it was finding an echo somewhere. Perhaps Pierre was seen
as a doomed freedom fighter and Jaffeir as an admirable man of
feeling. Perhaps it was the nightmare of it all that struck a
responsive chord.

Chapter VI. Notes

[1]Buckley, _Atheism in the English Renaissance_, pp. 16-18, argues that Stoicism contributes to a secularization of morals and therefore to the growth of atheism. On Marlowe's Stoic villains, see Baker, _Dignity of Man_, pp. 310-11; on the Stoic-Machiavel in Marston, see Bogard, _Tragic Satire_, pp. 89-90; Bogard also refers to the earlier blending, without philosophical basis, of stoicism and Machiavellism in _The Spanish Tragedy_ and _The Jew of Malta_ (p. 96).

[2]Herschel Baker's phrase; see _Dignity of Man_, p. 74. C. S. Lewis, in listing a dazzling series of sixteenth- and seventeenth-century literary examples, notes that "if modified in one direction" the wise man is "Milton's Christ: if in another, his Satan" (_English Literature in the Sixteenth Century_, p. 54).

[3]Tr. Hudson, p. 39.

[4]See Bush, _Renaissance and English Humanism_, p. 46 ff; Caspari, _Humanism and the Social Order_, p. 35 ff; Raab, _English Face of Machiavelli_, p. 8 ff; Erasmus, _Christian Prince_, pp. 157-201.

[5]_Proverbs or Adages_, ed. Starnes, sig. 3$^r$. See also _Christian Prince_, pp. 148-56, 160, 236.

[6]This lesson is taught by Cicero as well as by Epictetus. See, e.g., _De Officiis_, I.xxvi.90-93.

[7]Cf. Owen Felltham, "Of Sudden Prosperity," _Resolves_ I, p. 1.

[8]See Caspari, pp. 55-75. For a description of Rabelais' Pantagruel as a wise man see Nash, "Rabelais and Stoic Portrayal." Quotations are from _Utopia and A Dialogue of Comfort_, ed. Warrington, Everyman, 461.

[9]P. 259. Thomas Elyot is one who admires Cato. Major says Elyot "ventures the opinion . . . that Cato Uticensis, the Stoic hero, would have been far worthier than Achilles to have been the hero of Homer's epic" (_Sir Thomas Elyot_, p. 165).

[10]Although Elyot's reputation rests on his Ciceronian recipe for the good governor, he, like More and Erasmus, also touched on the Senecan subject of how the wise man deals with adversity. See Major, pp. 163-66; _The Boke Named the Gouernour_, ed. Watson, Everyman, 227, pp. 229, 233, 235.

[11]_Gouernour_, p. 127; see Major, pp. 23, 196-99, 201, 242, 251; Caspari, pp. 95-98. Cf. Aristotle, _Politics_ III.17; Cicero, _De Officiis_, II.12.42; Erasmus, _Christian Prince_, pp. 170-72.

[12]_Gouernour_, pp. 47-48. For a discussion of Cicero's _De Officiis_ as "the official sixteenth-century doctrine concerning

the behavior of man as a governor," see Spencer, Shakespeare and the Nature of Man, p. 41.

[13]P. 228 (Elyot's passage is from Tusculan Disputations, IV.26.57). Bush, to illustrate Cicero's humanistic outlook and ethical doctrine, calls attention to "that utterance in the De Republica which Lactantius thought well-nigh inspired, that morality is founded on the eternal law of right reason written in every human heart," and to Cicero's definition of sapientia in the De Officiis, as "the knowledge of things human and divine, which is concerned also with the bonds of union between gods and men and relations of man to man" (Renaissance and English Humanism, p. 57 ff).

[14]P. 163. For discussion of Elyot's indebtedness to "Plato, Cicero, Aristotle, Plutarch, Quintilian, Seneca, and Isocrates," see Major, pp. 28-29, 140-45. Of Quintilian, Bush says, he "said that the good orator--for posterity that meant the poet as well--must first of all be a good man" (p. 46). See also Caspari, Humanism and the Social Order, p. 6; Grant, ed. Roman Readings, p. 333.

[15]See Caspari, p. 165, for a discussion of Sidney's attempt, both through his life and through his work, to promote humanistic ideals of virtue. He calls Euarchus "Sidney's poetic image of the ideal ruler in action."

[16]In a song to the tune that all fortune must be accepted as good fortune (II, 166) Musidorus gives a familiar Stoic-Epicurean argument against the fear of death: Fear--in the particular situation in which the heroes now find themselves--serves only to destroy peace of mind. There is no reason to fear death since it is inevitable, since it is a work of nature, and since nature's works are good.

[17]Quotations are from The Book of the Courtier, trans. Hoby, ed. Henderson, Everyman, 807, p. 19; The Essayes of Michael Lord of Montaigne, trans. Florio, Everyman, 440; Rosalynde, ed. Greg; The Novels of Thomas Deloney, ed. Lawlis.

[18]On the development of Hercules into a Stoic hero see Waith, Herculean Hero, pp. 31-38. On Spenser's treatment of Agamemnon, Ulysses, and Aeneas in the Stoic tradition, see Lemmi, "Symbolism of the Classical Episodes in The Faerie Queene"; Hughes, "Virgilian Allegory and The Faerie Queene"; and Bush, Mythology and the Renaissance Tradition, p. 123.

[19]On the distinction Greville made between loving God and doing the best one could with the world, see Joan Rees, pp. 108, 110, 113; Bullough, I, 10-12.

[20]See Bullough, I, 57, 61.

[21]See Maclean, "Greville's Poetic."

[22]See Joan Rees, p. 166; Ure, "Fulke Greville's Dramatic Characters"; and Jacquot, "Religion et raison d'état dans

l'oeuvre de Fulke Greville."

[23]Ure, who analyzes the way in which Greville dramatizes the inner conflict in the souls of his characters, emphasizes that Greville's Calvinistic stress on the basic evil of man makes a strong statement of Stoic self-sufficiency impossible ("Fulke Greville's Dramatic Characters").

[24]Quotations from Daniel are from Poems and a Defense of Ryme, ed. Sprague. Quotations from Dyer and Wotton are from Elizabethan Lyrics, ed. Ault. Quotations from Campion are from Works, ed. Davis. Quotations from Herbert are from Works, ed. Hutchinson.

[25]See Spencer, Shakespeare and the Nature of Man, p. 81; Reese, Cease of Majesty, pp. 135-58.

[26]See Schoell, Etudes sur L'Humanisme, p. 99; Vernon Hall, "Julius Caesar," pp. 111-12, 124; Levitsky, "The Elements Were So Mix'd."

[27]On the various ideals of noble action reflected in Hamlet, see Levitsky, "Rightly to be Great."

[28]For a discussion of Kent, see Elton, pp. 284-92. Haydn calls Lear "a Stoic play through and through" (pp. 107-108).

[29]Satires, II.7.82 ff, trans. Bovie. Chapman's translation of "Virgil's Epigram of a Good Man" has the line, "He, in himself, worldlike, full, round and sure." The self-serving Asdruball in Marston's Sophonisba claims to be "Round in's own globe, not to bee clasp's, but holds / Within him all" (II.iii). Jonson quotations are from Works, ed. Herford and Simpson.

[30]Happy Man, I, 109-10. For recent comment on Sejanus see Evans, "Sejanus and the Ideal Prince Tradition," and Hamilton, "Irony and Fortune in Sejanus."

[31]See the discussion of The Dutch Curtezan by Finkelpearl, in John Marston of the Middle Temple, pp. 199-216. Finkelpearl shows how Malheureux, a would-be "wise man," learns a lesson about "the defects of moral absolutism in any of its forms" (p. 216).

[32]Bradbrook explains the quick shift from self-sufficiency to passion's slave as the contrast between an out-of-character chorus speech and a part of the action (Themes and Conventions, pp. 131-32). Ellis-Fermor sees Marston in these two plays as carrying on "an endless three-sided discussion of Stoicism," with Andrugio representing extreme Stoicism, Antonio representing extreme emotionalism, and Pandulpho, who rejects his earlier Stoic position to admit his grief and participate in revenge, standing for the Jacobean ideal of a mean between "continence and over-expression" (Jacobean Drama, p. 88). Caputi, John Marston, Satirist, p. 135 ff, says Andrugio struggles for "the palm of Neo-Stoic content" without attaining it. Finkelpearl, pp. 146-47, says, "The implication of Andrugio's

266

and Feliche's fluctuations is clear. Stoicism may be satisfactory as a philosophy, but it does not take into account the whole of man's nature." In addition, I suggest that Marston, who wholeheartedly praised only the Ciceronian type of Stoicism, enjoyed rousing the customary laugh by exposing the hollowness of Senecan-sounding boasts of self-sufficiency. For another of Marston's attacks on Seneca and Stoic self-sufficiency see "Satyre IIII," Scourge of Villanie (1599), ed. Harrison, line 45 ff.

33Quotations are from Dramatic Works, ed. Bowers, Vols. I and II.

34Cf. Marcus Aurelius, Meditations, XI.28, "Consider what a man Socrates was when he dressed himself in a skin, after Xanthippe had taken his cloak and gone out" (trans. H. A. J. Munro, ed. Oates, Stoic and Epicurean Philosophers).

35For some of the many discussions of Chapman's Stoicism, see Parrott, ed., Plays and Poems; Schoell; Bartlett, ed., Poems; Bradbrook; Ellis-Fermor; Spencer, Death and Elizabethan Tragedy; Battenhouse, "Chapman and the Nature of Man"; Baker, Dignity of Man and Wars of Truth; Wieler, George Chapman; Ennis Rees, Tragedies of George Chapman; Bogard; Ornstein, Moral Vision; Ribner, Jacobean Tragedy.

36See, e.g., Ellis-Fermor, p. 65; Spencer, Death and Elizabethan Tragedy, pp. 243-44; Baker, Dignity of Man, p. 304; Battenhouse, "Chapman," p. 95; Wieler, p. 36.

37The ghost of the Friar points up the resemblance to Hercules as he apostrophizes the dead Bussy: "Farewell, brave relics of a complete man! / Look up and see thy spirit made a star." See Battenhouse, "Chapman," p. 97.

38See Ellis-Fermor, pp. 65-68; Ennis Rees, pp. 7, 68, 72.

39Described at one point in the play as a "Senecal man," Clermont frequently likes to quote Epictetus--though he could have got his sentiments from any number of sources including, besides Seneca and Epictetus, Horace, Virgil, Boethius, Erasmus, and Montaigne. He demonstrates self-sufficiency by accepting all fortune as good fortune (IV.iv.42), by claiming to be rich because he desires nothing, by proving his freedom by ruling himself (IV.v.22), and by accepting his assigned place in God's plan, realizing that the universe cannot be subjugated to "such a rag of it as he" (III.i; IV.i). See Ennis Rees, pp. 115-16.

40See, e.g., Spencer, Death and Elizabethan Tragedy, pp. 251-52; Ribner, Jacobean Tragedy, p. 22. Wieler says, "Though The Revenge reveals on practically every page Chapman's complete familiarity with the Stoicism of both Epictetus and the neo-Stoics at both levels, it demonstrates at the same time that Stoicism must mean the negation of the tragic concept" (pp. 109-10). See also Bement, "The Stoicism of Chapman's

Clermont D'Ambois."

[41]For a discussion of contemporary attitudes toward suicide see Keeton, Shakespeare's Legal and Political Background,
and Spencer, Death and Elizabethan Tragedy, pp. 158-77, 242.
Spencer states that in France suicide "was excused when it was
committed in a moment of mental alienation or as a result of
intense sorrow" (p. 160), an excuse that would cover Clermont,
in case Chapman had it in mind.

[42]For discussion, see Bradbrook, p. 76; Spencer, Death
and Elizabethan Tragedy, p. 175 ff; Wieler, p. 154 ff; Ennis
Rees,p. 145 ff.

[43]He could also, of course, have found support for the
immortality of the wise man, though not for suicide, in such
a work as Cicero's "Dream of Scipio," De Re Publica, VI. Among
Chapman's Stoic characters Wieler includes Pompey as part Stoic,
part non Stoic, and Pompey's wife, Cornelia, as the only fem-
inine Stoic in all Chapman's tragedies (p. 140 ff).

[44]Chapman alludes in Bussy, V.iii.41-44, to the fable of
the proud oak tree that broke because it could not bend before
the wind.

[45]Ribner, Jacobean Tragedy, p. 91. For an extended dis-
cussion of Tourneur as a conventional Christian moralist see
Ribner's introduction to his edition of The Atheist's Tragedy.
Quotations are from this edition.

[46]Critical History, I, 331.

[47]See, e.g., Cunliffe, Influence of Seneca, pp. 111-12;
Bogard, pp. 36-37.

[48]Herculean Hero, p. 148.

[49]An idea to be found in Cicero as well as Seneca; see,
e.g., Tusculan Disputations, V.vi.16; vii.19, xiv.43, xxiii.
67, xxv.72, xxviii.82. For some examples in Seneca see De
Constantia and De Tranquillitate.

[50]References here are to Heaven upon Earth and Characters
of Vertues and Vices, ed. Kirk.

[51]Owen Felltham's poem "True Happinesse" contains a similar recipe. See Poems, ed. Pebworth and Summers, pp. 1-2. See
also Felltham's "Of Resolution," Resolves, I.2 (pp. 3-6).

[52]Cf. Colie's discussion of Donne's treatment of suicide
in Biathanatos (Paradoxia Epidemica, p. 500).

[53]Quoted from Poetical Works, ed. Moorman.

[54]See Ulreich, "A Paradise Within."

[55]Second Defence of the English People, CM, VIII, 95-7.

[56]English Literary Criticism: The Renaissance, pp. 338-
39. Grant explains this doctrine as follows: "The philosophers

held that 'the good poet must first be a good man'; so good
poetry was what made men good--and thus philosophy added its
great influence to an already existing tendency to regard
edification as the aim of poetry.  This was particularly the
view of the Stoics, the school which emphasized ethics most
strongly.  But it was also true of the rival Epicurean school"
(<u>Roman</u> <u>Literature</u>, pp. 126-27).  Bush says of Milton, "No other
English poet has so earnestly and so repeatedly dedicated himself to the classical office of poet-priest, and most of his
important poems may be regarded directly or indirectly, as
successive spiritual stock-takings" (<u>Renaissance</u> <u>and</u> <u>English</u>
<u>Humanism</u>, pp. 105-106).

57See also IX.1127; Bowra, <u>From</u> <u>Virgil</u> <u>to</u> <u>Milton</u>, p. 216
ff; Hoopes, <u>Right</u> <u>Reason</u>, p. 188 ff; Stollman, "Milton's Samson
and the Jewish Tradition."

58Both Cyrus and Scipio, it may be remembered, were familiar symbols of Stoic patriotic virtue.

59See Bowra, p. 231; Bush, p. 116; Hoopes, p. 196.

60See Baker, <u>Wars</u> <u>of</u> <u>Truth</u>, pp. 115, 241; Hoopes, pp. 168-
72; D. C. Allen, <u>Doubt's</u> <u>Boundless</u> <u>Sea</u>, pp. 121-22.  References
are to <u>Works</u>, ed. Heber, rev. Eden, Vol. III.

61Lovelace is quoted from <u>Minor</u> <u>Poets</u> <u>of</u> <u>the</u> <u>Seventeenth</u>
<u>Century</u>, ed. Howarth, Everyman, 173; L'Estrange is from "The
Liberty and Requiem of an Imprisoned Royalist," <u>Parnassus</u>
<u>Biceps</u> (1656), ed. Thorne-Drury, pp. 107-110.  An anonymous
drinking song entitled "The contented Prisoner his praise of
Sack," <u>Choyce</u> <u>Drollery</u> (1656), ed. Ebsworth, p. 93, parodies
the theme of content by praising the happy prisoner who con-
quers his fates not only with silence but also with sack and
sets himself free with drink.

62For some discussions see Margoliouth, ed., <u>Poems</u> <u>and</u>
<u>Letters</u> <u>of</u> <u>Andrew</u> <u>Marvell</u>; Daiches, I, 388; Mazzeo, "Cromwell
as Machiavellian Prince in Marvell's <u>An</u> <u>Horatian</u> <u>Ode</u>"; Baron,
"Marvell's 'An Horatian Ode and Machiavelli'"; Raab, p. 145;
and for a full discussion of Marvell's ideas on the relation
between providence and politics see Wallace, <u>Destiny</u> <u>his</u> <u>Choice</u>;
Friedman, <u>Marvell's</u> <u>Pastoral</u> <u>Art</u>, pp. 253-74; and Hayes, "The
Dialectic of History in Marvell's <u>Horatian</u> <u>Ode</u>."

63<u>Five</u> <u>Miscellaneous</u> <u>Essays</u> <u>by</u> <u>Sir</u> <u>William</u> <u>Temple</u>, ed.
Monk, p. 156.

64Cf. Seneca, "On Benefits," I.xiii.2; VII.ii.5; "On
Anger," III.xvii.1, <u>Moral</u> <u>Essays</u>, Vols. I and III.

65With primary emphasis on Stoicism as self-sufficiency,
Winterbottom argues that Dryden's tragedies show an increasing
use of Stoic ideas as time goes on ("Stoicism in Dryden's
Tragedies").  Other commentators have singled out Almanzor of
the <u>Conquest</u> <u>of</u> <u>Granada</u> for special notice as an inflated Stoic

of the "chest-thumping" type (C. S. Lewis, p. 54; Baker, <u>Dignity of Man</u>, p. 302). Waith calls him a "hard" Primitivist (p. 157).

[66]His father was Shah Jahan, best known as the builder of the Taj Mahal as a mausoleum for his favorite wife, Mumtaz Mahal (d. 1631), who was the mother of all four of his sons, including Aureng-Zebe. Her aunt, Nur Mahal or Nur Jahan, the consort of Shah Jahan's father, Jahangir, is presumably the shadow behind Dryden's Nourmahal. For historical background see Sachchidananda Bhattacharya, <u>Dictionary of Indian History</u>. For Johnson's comment see <u>Works</u>, ed. Hill, VII, 268.

[67]Although what was happening in France was not necessarily the same as what was happening in England, it is interesting to notice that in France Stoic ideas about glory and passion were undergoing changes. Anthony Levi's chapter "The Cult of Glory" (<u>French Moralists</u>, pp. 177-201) shows how personal glory changed during the sixteenth and seventeenth centuries from something a conventional Stoic would despise to something a latter-day Stoic would covet, and that passion came more and more to be classed as a virtue. In the plays of Corneille, though virtue, glory, and reason are still on one side of the fence, with passion on the other, yet some passions are considered more noble than others. Corneille's "Stoic" hero rises to heights of noble passion in defense of his honor (his external reputation), something we might expect a Stoic to class as "indifferent." Before long Corneille's contemporaries were making honor and passion "compatible with virtue" (p. 191). For a description of the patriotic hero as mechanical monster, see Nitze, "Vertu as Patriotism in Corneille's <u>Horace</u>."

[68]According to Levi, in France the law of nature was gradually developing into a "raison d'état," and the will of the king into the will of God (pp. 197-98). Where Chapman in his Byron plays idealized Henry IV of France as a good ruler in the Ciceronian tradition, Dryden may well have admired Louis XIV.

[69]Quotations are from <u>Four Tragedies</u>, ed. Beaurline and Bowers.

[70]Cf. Seneca, "De Clementia."

[71]Quotations are from <u>Essays</u>, ed. Ker, Vol. I.

[72]Quoted from <u>Works: Poems 1685-1692</u>, ed. Miner, Vol. III.

[73]In discussing Restoration comedy, James Sutherland says, "The one fixed point in Restoration comedy is the man of sense, the <u>honnête homme</u>, who has attained to his position of assured stability by a nice sense of self-control and an intelligent balancing of opposites" (<u>English Literature of the Late Seventeenth Century</u>, p. 118). In Thomas Shadwell's <u>Bury Fair</u> (1689) a good-humored exchange between the two dashing young men, both presented as men of sense, suggests a certain sympathy for romantic excess. Wildish, the hero, actually more wildish than

wild, defends lack of self-control: "I'd not give a farthing
for an appetite that can be curbed. My Stoic, I'd have my appetites high mettled, and run away with me." His staid friend
Bellamy, however, makes the old-fashioned reply. "And I must
always think a man a slave till he has conquered himself; for
my part, I had almost as lief be in subjection to another's
appetites as to my own" (I.ii.149).

[74]For a discussion of the false definition of nature
employed by the conspirators, see Berman, "Nature in Venice
Preserv'd."

[75]Algernon Sidney, as described by James Sutherland, was a
real-life example of the committed Stoic who put his conscience
first (p. 358 ff). Condemned to death in 1683 for complicity
in the Rye House plot, he was described by Burnet as "a man of
most extraordinary courage, a steady man, even to obstinacy,"
and one "who had set up Marcus Brutus for his pattern."

[76]References are to Works, ed. Ghosh, Vol. II.

# Chapter VII.  Conclusion

This is one of those conclusions in which nothing is concluded, the end of the seventeenth century being merely an
arbitrary stopping point in a continuing story.  Although the
eighteenth century will begin refurbishing some facets of
Stoicism that had been out of favor in the centuries immediately
preceding, it will also go on expressing and modifying many
long popular ideas.  There will still be writers cogitating
over the themes that had interested their ancestors, voicing
their divergent attitudes toward the possibility of peace of
mind, redefining the laws of nature, characterizing various
sorts of wise men, and ridiculing Stoic pride.  The following
scattered examples, mainly from Swift and Fielding, will suggest some of the ways these old patterns of thought continued
to adapt themselves to changing times.

If we begin with peace of mind, we can notice in passing
the youthful Alexander Pope's "Ode on Solitude" (1726), which
is one more poem that belongs, as Maynard Mack has reminded us,
to the long line of Roman and English works extolling the joys
of rural content.[1]  The "health of body, peace of mind" that
Pope here envisions as the lot of the quiet countryman, Jonathan Swift's Gulliver (1726) claims to have enjoyed briefly
during his sojourn among the Houyhnhnms (Ch. X).  Pope and
Swift, of course, also have anti-Stoic moods.  Swift elsewhere
implies, like Robert Burton (see above, p. 127) that literary
advice to reduce one's desires, especially when it comes from
those with comfortable incomes, only smacks of hypocrisy.  Monk
quotes his remark from Thoughts on Various Subjects that "the
Stoical Scheme of supplying our Wants by Lopping off our
Desires, is like cutting off our Feet when we want Shoes."[2]
And where the young Pope concludes "On Solitude" with an echo
of the popular lines from Seneca's Thyestes (Stet quicunque
volet potens), asking to be allowed to live and die "unseen,
unknown," the older and more skeptical Matthew Prior sets these
same lines at the head of his poem "An Epitaph" (1718) in which
he makes fun of the lives of a tranquil couple, now dead, whose
lack of involvement had resulted in a quietly sterile existence
that had contained, from Prior's point of view, neither much
pleasure nor much point.  On the other hand, Richard Steele
continues teaching such optimistic Boethian lessons as that
happiness comes from reducing one's desires, controlling one's
passions, and accepting all fortune as good fortune.  When he
meditates in the Classical manner on the shipwrecked Alexander
Selkirk (The Englishman, No. 26, Dec. 3, 1713) he concludes
that the happy man is the one who confines his wants to natural
necessities and that to go beyond these is only to discover
that the more we have the more we want.  Unlike such skeptical
humanists as Swift and Fielding, who go on manifesting pessimistic Christian doubts about the possibility of continuous
earthly happiness, Steele is among those sanguine Christians

who assert that a life of virtue will bring the earthly reward
of emotional tranquillity.[3]  In Spectator No. 143, Aug. 14,
1711, Steele, like earlier praisers of the man of life upright
(see above p. 234), describes a man of perfect faith who is so
thoroughly persuaded of his own worth and of another life that
he is able not only to ignore the pains of this world and to
accept calmly the ups and downs of fortune but even to live
"without fear or hope of futurity."  In contrast, Henry Fielding points out in Tom Jones (XV.i) that although quiet private
virtue may be rewarded with Epicurean tranquillity, the active
kind of social conscience that he himself values will probably
be rewarded only with contempt and may very well bring one to
poverty or even to jail.  In general, Fielding holds out little
hope of peace of mind for those forced to live in the world of
affairs but does manage to reward his heroes and heroines at the
end of Joseph Andrews (1742), Tom Jones (1749), and Amelia
(1752) by allowing them to retire to an ideal Horatian world.
Unlike most of us, these characters are able to make this choice
because they have the good fortune suddenly to acquire sufficient wealth to live as they like and have learned by experience
where to find a certain measure of earthly peace.  For example,
Parson Adams in Joseph Andrews describes the mode of life of
Mr. Wilson--to which Joseph and Fanny eventually retire--as "the
manner in which the people had lived in the golden age" (III.
iv, end),[4] while a few pages earlier Mr. Wilson himself had
expressed the conviction that the "calm serene happiness, which
is seated in content, is inconsistent with the hurry and bustle
of the world."  Since the average person would find Fielding's
solution as out of reach as the solution offered at the end of
Voltaire's Candide, the indictment of the greedy world and the
ridicule of optimistic boasts that virtue will be rewarded with
happiness both stand uncontested.  For although Voltaire leaned
somewhat to the skeptical Epicurean side and Fielding shared
Swift's Christian doubts about the probability of continued happiness in this life, their analyses of the nature of earthly
things, otherwise known as the way of the world, were similar.

     In like manner, definitions of the law of nature contin-
ued to be various, while at the same time the different interpretations had some influence on one another.  To think of the
eighteenth century is to think at once of the deists and of the
line of thought leading from such seventeenth-century writers
as Nathaniel Culverwell and Henry More to the Third Earl of
Shaftesbury, a fashion of thinking with which we associate the
resurgence of the old Stoic teaching that moral ideas are innate
and immediately available to those in whom the clear light of
reason has not been corrupted.  The eighteenth-century deist
version of this idea insists that one's sensibilities need to
be carefully nurtured; and the substitution of the word "sensi-
bility" for reason or intuition makes, of course, for a change
in flavor.  With writers in the Shaftesbury school we particu-

larly connect the idea that God is benevolent and that benevolence is a primary law of nature.  But benevolence was also
prized by writers who rejected the doctrines of the deists,
while the familiar medieval teaching that natural law assigns
to each of us a particular social niche with specific duties,
even though it was being threatened, was by no means gone.

Opposed to the deists were writers like Swift and Fielding.  Swift's admiration for certain of the ancients and his
insistence that man is capable of reason did not lead him to
accept either the notion that man's reason is sufficient to
explain to him the nature of God or the faith that the average
person will behave morally if not assured of a system of
divine rewards and punishments.  At one point in _Gulliver's
Travels_ he makes fun of the rational scholars of Brobdingnag
who refuse to believe in occult causes and who are thus totally
unable to explain the existence of such a creature as Gulliver,
whom they are forced to classify as a sport of nature (II.iii).
However, at the same time that Swift doubted the ability of
human reason to arrive at ultimate answers, he argued that an
ordinary human being who has received an adequate education
has been endowed with sufficient common sense to learn to live
in accordance with the laws of reason and nature and to recognize ordinary truth instinctively as soon as it is presented to
him.  As Gulliver remarked of one good man, "as Truth always
forceth its Way into rational Minds; so this honest worthy Gentleman, who had some Tincture of Learning, and very good Sense,
was immediately convinced of my Candor and Veracity" (II.viii).[5]
Swift, who shared with Milton the Stoic habit of dividing mankind into virtuous or wise men and knaves or fools, classified
as fools all those who did not see things in the same light
that he and his friends saw them.  As a relatively old-fashioned
moralist he continued to preach that a happy society is one in
which everyone does his duty in his appointed place, though at
the same time he defined the appointed place less rigidly than
the Elizabethans had done.  According to Arthur Case he emphasized, for instance, the necessity of a proper balance of the
three estates--king, nobles, and commons--with the king responsible for keeping the balance but possessed of less independence than kings had had in Shakespeare's time.[6]  When the
emphasis shifts from maintaining due degree to maintaining a
proper balance, the relationships have become slightly more
fluid.

In the two rational societies that Swift depicts in _Gulli-
ver's Travels_, the lands of the Houyhnhnms and of the Brobdingnagians, he has the Houyhnhnms existing somewhat as the
ancient Cynic philosophers had recommended.  These had taught
that the good life comes from living in accordance with reason
and nature and that nature is to be identified with a life that
eliminates as far as possible the superfluities of civilization.
In other ways the Houyhnhnms follow the recommendations of such
writers as Seneca, Epictetus, and Marcus Aurelius, paring down
their physical wants, avoiding ambition, greed, and other vio-

lent passions but practising friendship and benevolence and
quietly accepting life or death as part of the order of nature.
The world of Brobdingnag, on the other hand, is farther removed
from the golden age than the land of the Houyhnhnms; here the
principles so often laid down by writers in the Ciceronian tradition prevail, the general outline being that of the benevolent monarchy guided by an ideal Erasmian king endowed with a
combination of superior virtue and Swiftian common sense who
is motivated by duty to his people rather than by self-interest
and who can rule others wisely because he knows how to rule himself.

From the descriptions of both Brobdingnag and the land of
the Houyhnhnms--not to mention Laputa--it is plain that Swift
drew the usual Christian-humanist line between the kind of
intellectual prying that he, like Pope, regarded as something
on the order of "Stoic pride" and the kind of knowledge that is
based on tradition and common sense. The wise men of Brobdingnag, who, in trying to explain the existence of Gulliver, failed
to consider that there were more things in heaven and earth than
were dreamt of in their philosophy, had too much confidence in
their own self-sufficiency. And so did the mathematicians of
Laputa who tried to substitute their own logic for well-tested
tradition. But at the same time that Swift, in the usual way,
rejected some aspects of intellectual pride, he accepted some
aspects of Stoic tradition, such as the belief that the proper
study of mankind is man, the implication that there are such
things as universal moral values with simple meanings, and the
belief that rational (i.e., virtuous) people can trust their
consciences to guide them much of the way. He has Gulliver suggest that the Europeans, instead of making greedy plans to conquer the Houyhnhnms, should go to them for lessons in "the first
Principles of Honour, Justice, Truth, Temperance, publick Spirit,
Fortitude, Chastity, Friendship, Benevolence, and Fidelity" (IV.
xii). Among the Houyhnhnms there is no such thing as irony or
ambiguity. Truth is simple; lying is unknown; disputes never
arise over mere matters of opinion; and the kind of poetry in
which the Houyhnhnms excel is the didactic kind that Fulke Greville had praised, poetry that teaches ideals of friendship and
benevolence or praises "those who were Victors in Races, and
other bodily Exercises" (IV.ix). The uneventful history of the
Houyhnhnms is contrasted with that of Europe where no wars are
"so furious and bloody, or of so long Continuance, as those
occasioned by Difference in Opinion, especially if it be in
things indifferent" (IV.v). This use of the phrase "things
indifferent" takes us back to the seventeenth century and to
such earlier humanistic clergymen as Richard Hooker and Joseph
Hall, even though Swift's definition of "things indifferent"
was not necessarily the same as theirs.

Since basic truth is unambiguous, neither the Houyhnhnms
nor the Brobdingnagians have much use for lawyers; and because
the decrees of the general assembly of the Houyhnhnms are firmly
grounded on the laws of nature, the Houyhnhnms obey the laws

without coercion, for they are all rational creatures and "no Person can disobey Reason, without giving up his Claim to be a rational Creature" (IV.x). According to the Houyhnhnms, "Nature and Reason were sufficient Guides for a reasonable Animal, . . . in shewing us what we ought to do, and what to avoid" (IV. v). In other words, these creatures exemplified the Socratic ideals of Primitive Stoicism, which had asserted that for virtuous men the compulsion of man-made laws is unnecessary. By contrast, European lawyers are accused by Gulliver of subverting the "common Justice and General Reason of Mankind" under the name of precedent (IV.v). (Here, Gulliver, like the Stoics, seems to believe in such universal values as "common justice" and the "general reason of mankind.") In Brobdingnag, similarly, the king confines "the knowledge of governing . . . to common Sense and Reason, to Justice and Lenity, to the Speedy Determination of Civil and Criminal Causes" (II.vii). Since each law in this country has only one meaning, there is no need for legal experts; and all laws are expressed briefly, clearly, and simply. The prose style of the Brobdingnagians, too, emphasizes simplicity, being "clear, masculine, and smooth, but not Florid; for they avoid nothing more than multiplying unnecessary Words, or using various Expressions" (II.vii).

Fielding, who in some areas agreed with Swift, had, at the same time, professional experience in the law which made him somewhat more suspicious of abstract generalizations; and he more than once ridiculed Stoics and/or deists for their tendency to make broad statements and to disregard concrete instances. As a practical man, as well as a Christian moralist, Fielding continually warned that benevolence--much though he approved of it--had nevertheless to be tempered with prudence and, like Swift, he emphasized that morality needs the support of divine rewards and punishments. One example of the latter occurs in Joseph Andrews when Mr. Wilson recounts his adventures with a group of gentlemen who "were engaged in a search after truth, in the pursuit of which they threw aside all the prejudices of education, and governed themselves only by the infallible guide of human reason. This great guide, after having shown them the falsehood of that very ancient but simple tenet, that there is such a being as a Deity in the universe, helped them to establish in his stead a certain rule of right, by adhering to which they all arrived at the utmost purity of morals" (III.iii). In the classic manner, these fine theorists soon begin behaving in immoral ways that quickly disillusion Mr. Wilson with their abstract talk. He at once realizes, as Fielding's enlightened characters always do, that philosophy alone does not have enough teeth to enforce morality. Another of Fielding's Stoic frauds is the philosopher Square in Tom Jones who similarly talks in large terms about the laws of nature and the fitness of things and justifies Bliful's spiteful freeing of Sophia's bird to let it be devoured by a hawk on the abstract ground that "to confine anything, seems to me against the law of nature, by which everything hath

a right to liberty. . . . Can any man have a higher notion of
the rule of right, and the eternal fitness of things?" (IV.iv).
Like the abstract moralists in Joseph Andrews. Square's behavior is no better than that of other men. When he is discovered in Molly's bedroom he justifies himself by playing on the
meanings of the word "natural," saying, "I have done nothing
for which that part of the world which judges of matters by the
rule of right will condemn me. Fitness is governed by the
nature of things, and not by customs, forms, or municipal laws.
Nothing is indeed unfit which is not unnatural" (V.v). Fielding is obviously skeptical of the notion that a wise man needs
only the law of nature to guide him.

If Fielding rescues his guileless heroes from the snares
of the world and settles them in the country, he does not necessarily preach that the retired life is the more virtuous, only
that it is the one most conducive to Horatian content. Actually, the higher moral choice is the Ciceronian one which puts
social duty above personal happiness. And high among social
virtues is benevolence, tempered by prudence. Although Fielding ridicules the Philosopher Square's use of the word "reason,"
he himself uses words like "benevolence" in a relatively broad
way that shows us how earlier notions of social duty were being
reinterpreted. For instance, when Francis Bacon, in his essay
"Of Wisdom for a Man's Self" describes wisdom as a proper balance between "self-love and society," saying "be so true to
thyself, as thou be not false to others," he goes on to define
the notions of duty to oneself and to others in terms of hierarchical relationships, such as those between a master and a
servant. With writers like Fielding the relationships are
becoming slightly less definite, and we can watch the old Stoic
and Christian ideal of brotherly love beginning gradually to
loosen itself from its medieval emphasis on paying every man his
due in accordance with his degree.

Several illustrations of Fielding's willingness to relax
some notions of degree but not others can be found in Amelia,
where we are shown Sergeant Atkinson, an ideal character whom
Fielding rewards by allowing him to move up several steps on
the social ladder. Unlike the protagonist, Booth, Atkinson, who
combines prudence with virtue, is able to cope with the world
and is seldom deceived by knaves. At the same time he himself
is very conscious of his assigned place in the social scheme
and never of his own accord presumes to take liberties with his
social betters. Booth and his wife, Amelia, are congratulated
by the wise Dr. Harrison for their Christian behavior in accepting Atkinson not merely as a servant but also as a friend (see
IX.vi, end). In Atkinson's case we have an isolated instance
in which a man of merit is rewarded--although it must be admitted that part of his advancement results from the machinations
of his wife, of whom Dr. Harrison is not nearly so fond. Mrs.
Atkinson is one of Fielding's comic learned ladies whose pride
of intellect violates the laws of nature. She is also one of
the many imperfect wives who presume to set their own opinions

above those of their husbands.  And she stands in contrast to
the unlearned but wise Amelia who knows her place and continually demonstrates how the ideal wife should behave.  Although
Amelia has every reason to dominate over her  husband,  since she
is generally his superior, not only in virtue and judgment but
also in fortune, yet she submits not only to his legal authority but also to what she sincerely regards as his superior
knowledge and wisdom.  Fielding's attitude toward the hierarchical system seems to be that it ought to be flexible enough to
allow men of merit to advance in rank, but at the same time he
adheres to the traditional doctrine that an important characteristic of virtue is the acceptance of one's assigned place.
He wishes to restore the system to what he regards as the true
laws of nature, not to abolish it.

As we have just seen, there are in the eighteenth century
various examples of wise men and women.  In Gulliver's Travels
Swift presents a few people he seems to approve, among the many
he ridicules.  Extreme examples are his Houyhnhnms who resemble
absolutist primitive Stoics.  Like Thomas More's Utopians they
are all of them so wise that there is little need for government.  Like More's Utopians, too, they know how much is enough,
have learned to maintain good health by living simply, are able
to regulate the size of their population, have no desire for
change or excitement, avoid violent passions while cultivating
benevolence, and regard all members of their society equally as
their friends.  In the less perfect world of the Brobdingnagians, an ideal wise man of the Erasmian type is exemplified by
the king, who is described by Gulliver as "a Prince possessed
of every Quality which procures Veneration, Love, and Esteem;
of strong Parts, great Wisdom and profound Learning; endued
with admirable Talents for Government, and almost adored by his
subjects" (II.vii).  Another praiseworthy man, of a practical,
middle-of-the-road type, is Lord Munodi who appears in Book III.
In a land to which the modern theoreticians with their new-
fangled ideas have brought chaos, Lord Munodi alone adheres to
the basic rules discovered long ago, and, consequently, he
alone has a flourishing estate and a handsome house.
In Glubdubdrib Gulliver meets a number of ghostly heroes
from the past who help him satisfy some of his curiosity about
history.  Alexander the Great, for instance, is described in
the way Seneca, Epictetus, and William Temple had described him,
as a symbol of lack of self-control; and Caesar confesses "that
the greatest Actions of his own Life were not equal . . . to the
Glory of taking it away."  Outstanding among the real heroes is
Brutus, of whom Gulliver says he "could easily discover the most
consummate Virtue, the greatest Intrepidity and Firmness of
Mind, the truest Love of his Country, and general Benevolence
for Mankind in every Lineament of his Countenance" (III.vii,
end).  Brutus spends his time in the company of five other
heroes, all of whom can be classified as men with legendary

reputations for personal integrity. This group, which includes Brutus's ancestor, Junius Brutus, consists also of Socrates, Epaminondas, and Cato the younger. It has only one modern member--Thomas More. Later when Gulliver summons some ghosts of ideal English yeomen from the imaginary past they too turn out to possess the characteristics of the ideal patriotic Roman Stoic and are described as "famous for the Simplicity of their Manners, Dyet and Dress; for Justice in their Dealings; for their true Spirit of Liberty; for their Valour and Love of their Country" (III.viii, end).

Swift, as we have just seen, included Cato in the tiny group of heroes Gulliver met in Glubbdubdrib. And Joseph Addison's popular play, Cato, again lauds Cato in the Senecan manner, depicting him above all as a patriotic Roman for whom the victory of Caesar means the end of the Rome in which he had believed. Where Chapman's Caesar and Pompey had emphasized the psychological freedom of the good man, Addison's play has been interpreted as a contribution to the fight for constitutional liberty.[7] Where Chapman had set at the head of his play the lines from Plutarch asserting that only the just man is free, Addison chose lines from Seneca, which Pope, who in other contexts could condemn Stoic pride, paraphrased in the prologue, describing the hero as godlike Cato, virtue in human shape, "a brave man struggling in the storms of fate, / And greatly falling with a falling state," Rome's "last good man."

A female example of eighteenth-century fortitude is Samuel Richardson's Clarissa Harlowe, who, like Chapman's Cato, is free because she is good. Although the villainous Lovelace can injure her body, he cannot harm her mind, and she dies a symbol of Christian and Stoic patience whose sufferings and example will lead others in the right path. Clarissa, in addition, is one female character for whom duty means more than simple obedience to her superiors. Where her conscience requires it, she not only suffers patiently but also acts. At one point she writes boldly about the "principles that are in my mind; that I found there; implanted, no doubt, by the first gracious Planter" (Let. LXXXVI).[8] When the commands of her parents conflict with these basic principles, she places her conscience first. Since her conflict is not between her wishes and her duty but between two notions of duty, she is not in the same class with young ladies like the bride who eloped with Walter Scott's Lochinvar. But at the same time she is a step removed from a simply obedient child like Penthea in Ford's The Broken Heart, for she asserts her freedom not to go against her principles, which in this case means she must not marry someone she finds repugnant. She is caught somewhere in the middle between the loosening hierarchical system and the growing emphasis on individualism, for she does not easily disobey her family. In fact, where her conscience is not involved, she thinks she ought to obey not only her parents but also her uncles, her aunt, her brother, and her elder sister. As David Daiches has remarked, the world of Richardson's novels "is a world in which relationships are of the first importance" (II, 711).

Henry Fielding, whose attitude toward Stoicism was always ambivalent, sometimes endows his characters with admirable Stoic traits and sometimes laughs at their confused pretences to Stoic virtue or at their hypocritical Stoic facades. In general, one might say that Fielding, more often than Richardson or Swift, voices distrust of the self-sufficient kind of Stoicism that we associate with Seneca or Epictetus or even Boethius but indicates approval of the ideal of social duty that we associate with Cicero. At the same time, he shows sympathy for characters who admit their inability to cope with the world and wisely retreat, after the manner of Horace's country mouse, to some quiet rural spot. When he is making fun of boasts of self-sufficiency or emotional imperturbability, he does not exempt anyone. The benevolent but impractical Parson Adams unwittingly teaches us that bookish philosophy is not an easy guide for irrational human beings. In one episode he and a disguised Romish priest enjoy an agreeable conversation about the uselessness of riches, only to be equally annoyed when each discovers the other has not a penny to lend him (III.viii). (Similarly in *Tom Jones*, as there had been in Congreve's *Love for Love* [see above p. 88], there are smiles at "the ancient opinion, that men might live very comfortably on virtue only" [XIII. vi]). Like many another moralist, Parson Adams is adept at giving consolation to other people. When he and Joseph are tied to the bed posts while Fanny is being abducted, he advises Joseph to accept the will of God with resignation and proceeds "to enlarge on the folly of grief, telling him all the wise men and philosophers, even among the heathens, had written against it, quoting several passages from Seneca, and the consolation, which, though it was not Cicero's was, he said, as good almost as any of his works" (III.xi). His argument fails to have the desired effect. On a later occasion when he is again in the process of lecturing Joseph on the need to control his passions and submit to the will of God, he is told that one of his children has just been drowned. As is uaual in such cases, the Stoic philosopher immediately begins to cry out against fortune (IV.viii). Another ineffective preacher of Stoic platitudes is Parson Supple, the well-intentioned familiar of Squire Western in *Tom Jones*. Fielding observes that Supple's lecture on anger was "enriched with many valuable quotations from the ancients, particularly from Seneca; who hath indeed so well handled this passion, that none but a very angry man can read him without great pleasure and profit" (VI.ix).

Where Parson Adams is amiably muddle-headed, the philosopher Square of *Tom Jones* is a deliberate hypocrite who preaches Stoic doctrine for selfish ends. Like several of Fielding's other characters, he uses the mask of Stoic imperturbability as an excuse for failing to show such benevolent emotions as pity or sympathy while all the time he is actually motivated by such selfish passions as greed. He can regard Tom's broken arm with equanimity but when he bites his own tongue he loses his temper

(V.ii). When other people were quarreling, "he very calmly smoked his pipe, as was his custom in all broils, unless when he apprehended some danger of having it broke in his mouth" (V.ix). As Fielding remarks in connection with Square's adventures in Molly's bedroom, though philosophers "think much better and more wisely, they always act exactly like other men" (V.v). Two similar caricatures are of the somewhat Epicurean Colonel James in _Amelia_, who combines an admiration for Mandeville with a "mind . . . formed of those firm materials of which nature formerly hammered out the Stoic, and upon which the sorrows of no man living could make an impression" (VIII.v, end), and of the overly self-sufficient philosopher (also in _Amelia_) whom Booth meets in the bailiff's house. The philosopher reasons learnedly about the temporary nature of earthly things and about his emotional superiority to the blows of fortune but is overwhelmed when he learns that he is to be carried off to Newgate without seeing his family first (VIII.x). As Booth had just remarked to him, "we reason from our heads, but act from our hearts," for we are always at the mercy of our ruling passion.

But with all his ridicule of Stoic pretenses to equanimity, Fielding, like other admirers of Cicero and Horace, nevertheless endows some of his good characters with such well-accepted Stoic traits as benevolence and fortitude. Although he always insists that benevolence, to be effective, needs to be tempered with prudence, he obviously sympathizes more with the naiveté of Mr. Allworthy in _Tom Jones_ or of Heartfree in _Jonathan Wild_ than with the cynical worldly wisdom of Bliful or Jonathan Wild; and he does not ridicule Mr. Allworthy's contention that charity is "an indispensable duty, enjoined both by the Christian law and by the law of nature itself" or even his statement that it is one duty that can almost be said to be its own reward (II. v). In an essay in _The Champion_ (Thursday, January 3, 1739-40) Fielding says that he does not know a better definition of virtue than that it is a delight in doing good. Although he likes to point out that the worldly reward for benevolence is likely to be poverty and contempt, he does not dispute the old teaching that the real reward for virtue is a quiet mind. The virtuous Heartfree never for long loses his inner peace, even when he is unjustly thrown into jail and condemned to the gallows. In _Amelia_ Fielding in his own voice reminds the reader "that however few of the other good things of life are thy lot, the best of all things, which is innocence, is always within thy power; and though Fortune may make thee often unhappy, she can never make thee completely and irreparably miserable without thy own consent" (VIII.iii, end). Although Fielding carefully qualifies his argument here, since there is a difference in connotation between saying with the Stoics that a wise (i.e., virtuous) man is a happy (i.e., tranquil) man and saying that fortune cannot make us "completely and irreparably miserable" without our own consent, and although he obviously equates the word "unhappy" with misfortune, nevertheless he is at the same time

linking himself with the tradition of Boethius and with the old
argument that good fortune is not essential to peace of mind.
The other side of the picture is represented by the wicked Mrs.
Ellison in _Amelia_ and by Jonathan Wild (in _Jonathan Wild_), both
of whom lack peace of mind. "In the bosom [of the unmasked]
Mrs. Ellison all was storm and tempest; anger, revenge, fear,
and pride, like so many raging furies" (VIII.iii, end). Jonathan Wild, who was great but not good and who understood all
the arts of climbing on the wheel of fortune, was happy in the
sense that he was materially successful, but psychologically
"he was under a continual alarm of frights, and fears, and
jealousies. He thought every man he beheld wore a knife for
his throat, and a pair of scissors for his purse" (III.13 end).
Characters like Heartfree and Amelia who are not successful in
the worldly sense have frequent occasion to demonstrate the
virtue of fortitude. Amelia, who heroically endures the inces-
sant troubles caused by her imprudent husband, is as much of a
Christian-Stoic saint as Richardson's Clarissa. And since
equanimity (as opposed to depression or elation) is the desired
earthly goal of Stoics, Epicureans, and Christians alike,
Fielding has both the worthy Dr. Harrison and Amelia's husband,
Booth, remind her, when fortune in the end at last seems to
smile, that the proper balance is the important thing, that
true fortitude includes the ability to accept good luck as well
as bad luck with an even temper (XII.viii). This is the same
lesson that sixteenth- and seventeentn-century moralists had
been fond of preaching (see above, e.g., pp. 111, 225-26).

As we saw earlier, those of Fielding's characters who
achieve a certain measure of wisdom (along with good fortune)
choose to live the Horatian retired life. Some, like Mr. Allworthy and Dr. Harrison, are wise men who stand on the sidelines representing a standard against which the frequently erring protagonists can be measured. Others, like Mr. Wilson in
_Joseph Andrews_ and the Man of the Hill in _Tom Jones_, are examples
of country mice who recount for us the unfortunate experiences
that have caused them to reject the exciting city. They belong
to the same family as Spenser's Meliboe. The Man of the Hill,
incidentally, is one more character who fortifies himself with
the lines from Horace (Satires, II.7.82 ff), so popular in the
seventeenth century (see above p. 237), that celebrate the well-
rounded man who is wholly contained in himself (VIII.xiii). In
his retirement he has occupied his time in reading the ancients
and expresses a middle-of-the-road attitude toward the old philosophers that is typical of many a Christian humanist and that
reminds us of Thomas More's remark that although these writers
"are not sufficient to be taken for our physicians, some good
drugs have they yet in their shops for which they may be suffered to dwell among our poticaries" (_Dialogue of Comfort_, p.
150). According to the Man of the Hill, the philosophy of the
ancients teaches us how to fortify our minds against the cap-
rices of fortune but the Scriptures give us the assurance of
another life. "Philosophy makes us wiser, but Christianity

makes us better men" (VIII.xiii).

This survey of some of the fortunes of Stoic ideas in Renaissance English literature has had the rather un-Stoic purpose of describing the way things have been instead of trying to prescribe the way they ought to be. For it would be idle to expect users of the word "Stoic" suddenly to reform their ways and to begin employing the term with scrupulous precision. My hope has merely been that readers will be alerted to the variety of possible meanings and combinations of ideas and to the vitality of these old doctrines, illogical though they may often seem.

Chapter VII. Notes

[1]The _Garden_ _and_ _the_ _City_, pp. 100-107. See also Rostvig, _Happy_ _Man_, II, iii. For an extended discussion of Stoicism in Pope, see Mack's introduction to the Twickenham edition of _An_ _Essay_ _on_ _Man_.

[2]_Five_ _Miscellaneous_ _Essays_ _by_ _Sir_ _William_ _Temple_, ed. Monk, p. xxiii.

[3]See Rostvig, II, 174-76.

[4]Quotations are from _Complete_ _Works_ _of_ _Henry_ _Fielding_, ed. Henley. References to _Joseph_ _Andrews_, _Jonathan_ _Wild_, _Tom_ _Jones_, and _Amelia_ are to book and chapter number.

[5]Ed. Herbert Davis (Oxford: Basil Blackwell, 1959). References are to book and chapter number.

[6]_Four_ _Essays_ _on_ "_Gulliver's_ _Travels_," p. 107 ff.

[7]See, e.g., Bonamy Dobree, _English_ _Literature_ _in_ _the_ _Early_ _Eighteenth_ _Century_, pp. 248-59.

[8]_Clarissa_ (Everyman 882).

List of Works Cited

Adams, Robert P. The Better Part of Valor: More, Erasmus,
Colet, and Vives on Humanism, War, and Peace, 1496-1535.
Seattle: U of Washington P, 1962.

---. "Designs by More and Erasmus for a New Social Order."
Studies in Philology 42 (1945): 131-45.

---. "The Philosophic Unity of More's Utopia." Studies in Philology 38 (1941): 45-65.

Adler, Mortimer J. The Idea of Freedom: A Dialectical Examination of the Conceptions of Freedom. New York: Doubleday,
1958.

Alfred. King Alfred's Version of the Consolations of Boethius
Done into Modern English. Trans. Walter John Sedgefield.
Oxford: Oxford UP, 1900.

Allen, Don Cameron. Doubt's Boundless Sea: Skepticism and
Faith in the Renaissance. Baltimore: Johns Hopkins UP,
1964.

---. Image and Meaning: Metaphoric Traditions in Renaissance
Poetry. Baltimore: Johns Hopkins UP, 1960.

---. Mysteriously Meant: The Rediscovery of Pagan Symbolism
and Allegorical Interpretation in the Renaissance. Baltimore: Johns Hopkins UP, 1970.

---. "The Rehabilitation of Epicurus and His Theory of Pleasure
in the Early Renaissance." Studies in Philology 41 (1944):
1-15.

---. The Star-Crossed Renaissance. Durham, North Carolina:
Duke UP, 1941.

Allen, Peter R. "Utopia and European Humanism: The Function of
the Prefatory Letters and Verses." Studies in the Renaissance 10 (1963): 91-107.

Anderson, Fulton H. Francis Bacon: His Career and His Thought.
Los Angeles: U of Southern California P, 1962.

Aquinas, Saint Thomas. The Summa Theologica. Trans. Fathers
of the English Dominican Province. Rev. Daniel J. Sulli-
van. Great Books of the Western World. Chicago: Ency.
Brit., 1952.

Aristotle. "Ethica Nicomachea," Trans. W. D. Ross. The Works.
Ed. W. D. Ross. 11 vols. 1925. Oxford UP, 1940. Vol 9.

---. "Politica." Trans. Benjamin Jowett. Works. Ed. W. D.
Ross. 11 vols. 1925. Oxford: Oxford UP, 1961. Vol. 10.

Armstrong, A. H. "Later Platonism and Its Influence." Classical Influences on European Culture A.D. 500-1500. Ed. R.
R. Bolgar. Cambridge: Cambridge UP, 1971. 197-201.

Armstrong, Robert L. "Cambridge Platonists and Locke on Innate Ideas." Journal of the History of Ideas 30 (1969): 187-202.

Arnold, E. Vernon. Roman Stoicism. 1911. New York: Humanities Press, 1958.

Ascham, Roger. The Schoolmaster. Ed. Lawrence V. Ryan. Ithaca: Cornell UP, 1967.

Atkins, J. W. H. English Literary Criticism: The Medieval Phase. Cambridge: Cambridge UP, 1943.

---. English Literary Criticism: The Renascence. London: Methuen, 1947.

Augustine, Saint. The City of God against the Pagans. Trans. George E. McCracken et al. Loeb Classical Library. Cambridge, Massachusetts: Harvard UP, 1957.

Ault, Norman. Elizabethan Lyrics from the Original Texts. London: Longmans, Green, 1928.

Ayres, Philip J. "Marston's Antonio's Revenge: The Morality of the Revenging Hero." Studies in English Literature, 1500-1900 12 (1972): 359-74.

Bacon, Francis. The Advancement of Learning. Ed. G. W. Kitchin. Everyman's Library 719. 1915. London: Dent, 1934.

---. The Essayes or Counsels Civil and Moral. Everyman's Library 10. 1906. London: Dent, 1932.

---. The Works. Ed. James Spedding. 7 vols. London, 1858-74. Vol. 3.

Bacquet, Paul. "L'imitation de Sénèque dans 'Gorboduc' de Sackville et Norton," Les Tragédies de Sénèque et le Théâtre de la Renaissance. Ed. Jean Jacquot and Marcel Oddon. Paris: Editions du Centre National de la Recherche Scientifique, 1964. 154-74.

Baker, Herschel. The Dignity of Man. Cambridge, Massachusetts: Harvard UP, 1947.

---. The Wars of Truth. Cambridge, Massachusetts: Harvard UP, 1952.

Bald, R. C. "'Thou Nature art my goddess': Edmund and Renaissance Free-thought." Joseph Quincy Adams Memorial Studies. Ed. J. G. McManaway et al. Washington, D. C.: 1948. 337-50.

Baldwin, William. The Sayings of the Wise: A Book of Moral Wisdom Gathered from the Ancient Philosophers (1555). London, 1907.

Baron, Hans. "Marvell's 'An Horatian Ode' and Machiavelli." Journal of the History of Ideas 21 (1960): 450-1.

Battenhouse, Roy W.  "Chapman and the Nature of Man."  ELH 12 (1945): 87-107.

---. Marlowe's Tamburlaine: A Study in Renaissance Moral Philosophy. Nashville: Vanderbilt UP, 1941.

Baugh, Albert C.  "The Middle English Period (1100-1500)." A Literary History of England.  Ed. Albert C. Baugh. New York: Appleton, 1948.  109-312.

Bement, Peter.  "The Stoicism of Chapman's Clermont D'Ambois." Studies in English Literature, 1500-1900 12 (1972): 345-57.

Bennett, H. S. Chaucer and the Fifteenth Century.  Oxford: Oxford UP, 1948.

Berman, Ronald.  "Nature in Venice Preserv'd."  ELH 36 (1969): 529-43.

Bhattacharya, Sachchidananda.  A Dictionary of Indian History. New York: George Braziller, 1967.

The New English Bible.  2nd Ed.  Oxford and Cambridge: Oxford and Cambridge U Presses, 1970.

Boas, George.  Essays on Primitivism and Related Ideas in the Middle Ages.  Baltimore: Johns Hopkins UP, 1948.

---. Rationalism in Greek Philosophy.  Baltimore: Johns Hopkins UP, 1961.

Boethius.  The Consolation of Philosophy.  Trans. W. V. Cooper. Ed. Irwin Edman.  Modern Library.  New York:  Random, 1943.

---. The Consolation of Philosophy.  Trans. Richard Green. Indianapolis: Bobbs, 1962.

Bogard, Travis.  The Tragic Satire of John Webster.  Berkeley: U of California P, 1955.

Bolgar, R. R.  The Classical Heritage and Its Beneficiaries. Cambridge: Cambridge UP, 1954.

Bowers, Fredson Thayer.  Elizabethan Revenge Tragedy 1587-1642. Princeton: Princeton UP, 1940.

Bowra, Cecil Maurice.  From Virgil to Milton.  London:  Macmillan, 1963.

Bradbrook, Muriel C.  Themes and Conventions of Elizabethan Tragedy.  Cambridge: Cambridge UP, 1935.

Bradley, A. C. Shakespearean Tragedy.  1905.  New York: Fawcett World Library, 1968.

Bredvold, Louis I.  "The Naturalism of Donne in Relation to Some Renaissance Traditions."  Journal of English and Germanic Philology 22 (1923): 471-502.

Breton, Nicholas.  The Works in Verse and Prose.  Ed. Alexander

Grosart. 2 vols. Chertsey Worthies' Library. 1879. New York: AMS Press, 1966. Vol. 1.

Brinton, Crane. A History of Western Morals. New York: Harcourt, 1959.

Brodeur, Arthur Gilchrist. The Art of "Beowulf." Berkeley: U of California P, 1959.

Browne, G. F. King Alfred's Books. London: Macmillan, 1920.

Browne, Sir Thomas. The Letters. Ed. Geoffrey Keynes. 1931. London: Faber and Faber, 1946.

Buckley, George T. Atheism in the English Renaissance. Chicago: U of Chicago P, 1932.

Bullough, Geoffrey. "Sénèque, Greville et le Jeune Shakespeare," Les Tragédies de Sénèque et le Théâtre de la Renaissance. Ed. Jean Jacquot and Marcel Oddon. Paris: Editions du Centre National de la Recherche Scientifique, 1964. 189-201.

Burnet, John, Trans. and ed. Early Greek Philosophy. 4th ed. New York: Macmillan, 1930.

Burton, Robert. The Anatomy of Melancholy. Ed. Floyd Dell and Paul Jordan-Smith. 1927. New York: Tudor, 1948.

Bush, Douglas. Mythology and the Renaissance Tradition in English Poetry. Cambridge, Massachusetts: Harvard UP, 1937.

---. The Renaissance and English Humanism. 1939. Toronto: U of Toronto P, 1956.

Bussell, F. W. Marcus Aurelius and the Later Stoics. Edinburgh: T. and T. Clark, 1910.

Campbell, Lily Bess. Shakespeare's Tragic Heroes: Slaves of Passion. 1930. New York: Barnes, 1952.

Campion, Thomas. The Works. Ed. Walter R. Davis. New York: Doubleday, 1967.

Caputi, Anthony, John Marston, Satirist. Ithaca: Cornell UP, 1961.

Carlyle, Robert Warrand and A. J. A History of Medieval Political Theory in the West. 6 vols. 1903-36. London: Blackwood, 1928. Vol. 5.

Case, Arthur E. Four Essays on "Gulliver's Travels." Princeton: Princeton UP, 1946.

Caspari, Fritz. Humanism and the Social Order in Tudor England. Chicago: U of Chicago P, 1954.

Cassirer, Ernst. The Myth of the State. New Haven: Yale UP, 1946.

Cast, David. "Aurispa, Petrarch, and Lucian: An Aspect of

Renaissance Translation." Renaissance Quarterly 27 (1974): 157-73.

Castiglione, Count Baldassare. The Book of the Courtier. Trans. Sir Thomas Hoby. Ed. Drayton Henderson. Everyman's Library 807. London: Dent, 1928.

Catlin, George. The Story of the Political Philosophers. New York: McGraw, 1939.

Chambers, R. W. "Beowulf and the 'Heroic Age' in England," Man's Unconquerable Mind. 1939. Philadelphia: Albert Saifer, 1953.

---. Thomas More. New York: Harcourt, 1935.

Chang, Joseph S. M. J. "'Of Mighty Opposites' Stoicism and Machiavellianism." Renaissance Drama 9 (1966): 37-57.

Chapman, George. The Plays and Poems. Ed. Thomas Marc Parrott. 4 vols. London: Routledge, 1910. Vol. 1.

---. The Poems. Ed. Phyllis Brooks Bartlett. New York: MLA, 1941.

Chaucer, Geoffrey, The Works. Ed. F. N. Robinson. 2nd ed. Cambridge, Massachusetts: Houghton, 1957.

Chew, Audrey. "Joseph Hall and Neo-Stoicism." PMLA 65 (1950): 1130-45.

Chew, Samuel C. The Pilgrimage of Life. New Haven: Yale UP, 1962.

Choyce Drollery. Ed. J. W. Ebsworth. Boston, Lincolnshire, 1876.

Cicero, Marcus Tullius. Academica. Trans. H. Rackham. Loeb Classical Library. 1933. Cambridge, Massachusetts: Harvard UP, 1956.

---. De Finibus Bonorum et Malorum. Trans. H. Rackham. Loeb. London: Heinemann, 1914.

---. De Natura Deorum. Trans. H. Rackham. Loeb. 1933. Cambridge, Massachusetts: Harvard UP, 1956.

---. De Officiis. Trans. Walter Miller. Loeb. London: Heinemann, 1928.

---. De Re Publica, De Legibus. Trans. Clinton Walker Keyes. Loeb. 1928. Cambridge, Massachusetts: Harvard UP, 1961.

---. De Senectute, De Amicitia, De Divinatione. Trans. William Armistead Falconer. Loeb. 1923. London: Heinemann: 1927.

---. Tusculan Disputations. Trans. J. E. King. Loeb. London: Heinemann, 1927.

Clark, Ira. "Samuel Daniel's 'Complaint of Rosamond.'" Renais-

290

sance Quarterly 23 (1970): 152-62.

Colie,Rosalie L. 'My Ecchoing Song': Andrew Marvell's Poetry of Criticism. Princeton: Princeton UP, 1970.

---. Paradoxia Epidemica: The Renaissance Tradition of Paradox. Princeton: Princeton UP, 1966.

Congreve, William. The Complete Plays. Ed. Herbert Davis. Chicago: U of Chicago P, 1967.

Cornwallis, Sir William the Younger. Essayes. Ed. Don Cameron Allen. Baltimore: Johns Hopkins UP, 1946.

Cowley, Abraham. Essays, Plays and Sundry Verses. Ed. A. R. Waller. Cambridge: Cambridge UP, 1906.

---. Poems. Ed. A. R. Waller. Cambridge: Cambridge UP, 1905.

Cox, Richard H. Locke on War and Peace. Oxford: Oxford UP, 1960.

Craig, Hardin. "The Shackling of Accidents." Philological Quarterly 19 (1940): 1-19.

Crane, Ronald S., ed. A Collection of English Poems 1660-1800. New York: Harper, 1932.

Croll, Morris W. Style, Rhetoric, and Rhythm. Ed. J. Max Patrick and Robert O. Evans with John M. Wallace and R. J. Schoeck. Princeton: Princeton UP, 1966.

Cross, J. E. "On the Genre of the Wanderer." Neophilologus 45 (1961): 63-75.

Culverwel, Nathaniel. An Elegant and Learned Discourse of the Light of Nature. Ed. Robert A. Greene and Hugh MacCallum. Toronto: U of Toronto P, 1971.

Cunliffe, John W. The Influence of Seneca on Elizabethan Tragedy. London: Macmillan, 1893.

Cunningham, J. V. Woe or Wonder: The Emotional Effect of Shakespearean Tragedy. 1951. Denver: Alan Swallow, 1964.

Curry, Walter Clyde. Chaucer and the Medieval Sciences. New York: Oxford UP, 1926.

---. "Destiny in Chaucer's Troilus." PMLA 45 (1930): 129-68.

Daiches, David. A Critical History of English Literature. 2 vols. New York: Ronald Press, 1960.

Daniel, Samuel. Poems and a Defence of Ryme. Ed. Arthur Colby Sprague. Cambridge, Massachusetts: Harvard UP, 1930.

Davies, Sir John. Orchestra. Ed. E. M. W. Tillyard. London: Chatto and Windus, 1945.

---. The Poems. Ed. Clare Macllelen Howard. New York: Columbia UP, 1941.

Deane, Herbert A. The Political and Social Ideas of St. Augustine. New York: Columbia UP, 1963.

Dekker, Thomas. The Dramatic Works. Ed. Fredson Bowers. Cambridge: Cambridge UP, 1953-. Vols 1 and 2.

---. The Non-Dramatic Works. Ed. Alexander B. Grosart. 5 vols. 1884-6. New York: Russell and Russell, 1963. Vol. 3.

Deloney, Thomas. The Novels. Ed. Merritt E. Lawlis. Bloomington: Indiana UP, 1961.

d'Entreves, A. P. Natural Law. London: Hutchinson's University Library, 1951.

de Santillana, Georgio. The Origins of Scientific Thought. Chicago: U of Chicago P, 1961.

Dobree, Bonamy. English Literature in the Early Eighteenth Century 1700-1740. Oxford: Oxford UP, 1959.

Dryden, John. The Best of Dryden. Ed. Louis I. Bredvold. New York: Nelson, 1933.

---. The Essays. Ed. W. P. Ker. 2 vols. 1900. New York: Russell and Russell, 1961. Vol. 1.

---. Four Tragedies. Ed. L. A. Beaurline and Fredson Bowers. Chicago: U of Chicago P, 1967.

---. The Poems and Fables. Ed. James Kinsley. London: Oxford UP, 1962.

---. Poetical Works. London: Routledge, 1867.

---. Poems 1685-1692. Ed. Earl Miner. The Works. Berkeley: U of California P, 1969. Vol. 3.

Dunbar, William. The Poems. Ed. W. Mackay Mackenzie. London: Faber and Faber, 1950.

Du Vair, Guillaume. The Moral Philosophie of the Stoicks. Englished by Thomas James (1598). Ed. Rudolf Kirk. New Brunswick: Rutgers UP, 1951.

Earle, John. Microcosmography or a Piece of the World Discovered in Essays and Characters. Ed. Harold Osborne. London: University-Tutorial P, 1933.

Edelstein, Ludwig. The Meaning of Stoicism. Cambridge, Massachusetts: Harvard UP, 1966.

---. "The Philosophical System of Posidonius," American Journal of Philology 57 (1936): 286-325.

Eliot, T. S. "Seneca in Elizabethan Translation." Selected Essays. 3rd ed. London: Faber and Faber, 1951.

Ellis-Fermor, Una M. The Jacobean Drama. London: Methuen, 1936.

Elton, William R. 'King Lear' and the Gods. San Marino, California: Huntington Library, 1966.

Elyot, Sir Thomas. The Boke Named the Gouernour. Ed. Foster
    Watson. Everyman's Library 227. London: Dent, 1907.

Encyclopedia Britannica. 1910 ed.

Erasmus, Desiderius. The Education of a Christian Prince.
    Trans. and ed. L. K. Born. New York: Columbia UP, 1936.

---. The Praise of Folly. Trans. Hoyt H. Hudson. 1941.
    Princeton: Princeton UP, 1947.

---. Proverbs or Adages Gathered out of the Chiliades & Eng-
    lished (1569) by Richard Taverner. Ed. De Witt T. Starnes.
    Gainesville, Florida: Scholars Facsimiles and Reprints,
    1956.

Evans, K. W. "Sejanus and the Ideal Prince Tradition." Stu-
    dies in English Literature, 1500-1900 11 (1971): 249-64.

Farnham, Willard. The Medieval Heritage of Elizabethan Trag-
    edy. Berkeley: U of California P, 1936.

Felltham, Owen. Resolves Divine Morall and Politicall. Temple
    Classics. London: Dent, 1904.

---. The Poems. Ed. Ted-Larry Pebworth and Claude J. Summers.
    SCN Editions and Studies. University Park, Pennsylvania:
    Pennsylvania State U, 1973.

Ferguson, Arthur B. "Reginald Pecock and the Renaissance Sense
    of History." Studies in the Renaissance 13 (1966): 147-
    65.

Ferguson, John. Moral Values in the Ancient World. London:
    Methuen, 1958.

Fielding, Henry. The Complete Works. Ed. William Ernest Hen-
    ley. 16 vols. 1902. New York: Barnes 1967.

Finkelpearl, Philip J. "Beaumont, Fletcher, and 'Beaumont and
    Fletcher': Some Distinctions." English Literary Renais-
    sance 1 (1971): 144-64.

---. John Marston of the Middle Temple: An Elizabethan Drama-
    tist in His Social Setting. Cambridge, Massachusetts:
    Harvard UP, 1969.

Finney, Gretchen L. "A World of Instruments." ELH 20 (1953):
    87-120.

Fisch, H. "The Limits of Hall's Senecanism." Proc. of the
    Leeds Philosophical Soc. 6 (1950): 453-63.

Fisher, John H. John Gower: Moral Philosopher and Friend of
    Chaucer. New York: New York UP, 1964.

Ford, John. Dramatic Works. Reprinted from the original quar-
    tos. Ed. Henry de Vocht. Louvain: Librairie Universi-
    taire, 1927.

Fraenkel, Eduard. Horace. Oxford: Oxford UP, 1957.

Friedman, Donald M. Marvell's Pastoral Art. Berkeley: U of
California P, 1970.

Gilson, Etienne. History of Christian Philosophy in the Middle
Ages. New York: Random, 1955.

Gower, John. English Works. Ed. G. C. Macaulay. 2 vols.
Early English Text Society es. 81-82 (1900-1901).

Grace, William J. "Milton, Salmasius, and the Natural Law."
Journal of the History of Ideas 24 (1963): 323-36

Grant, Michael. Roman Literature. Baltimore: Penguin, 1958 ed.

---, ed. Roman Readings. Baltimore: Penguin, 1958.

---. The World of Rome. New York: Praeger, 1960.

Greene, Robert. The Plays and Poems. Ed. J. Churton Collins.
2 vols. Oxford: Oxford UP, 1905. Vol. 2.

Greene, William Chase. Moira: Fate, Good, and Evil in Greek
Thought. Cambridge, Massachusetts: Harvard UP, 1948.

Greenfield, Stanley B. A Critical History of Old English Literature. New York: New York UP, 1965.

Greenlaw, Edwin. "The Captivity Episode in Sidney's Arcadia."
Manley Anniversary Studies. Chicago: U of Chicago P,
1925. 54-63.

Greville, Fulke, Lord Brooke. Poems and Dramas. Ed. Geoffrey
Bullough. New York: Oxford UP, 1945.

---. The Life of Sir Philip Sidney. Ed. Nowell C. Smith.
Oxford: Oxford UP, 1907.

---. The Works in Verse and Prose Complete. Ed. Alexander
Grosart. 4 vols. Fuller Worthies' Library. 1870. New
York: AMS Press, 1966. Vol. 3.

Grimal, Pierre. "Les Tragédies de Sénèque." Les Tragédies
de Sénèque et le Théâtre de la Renaissance. Ed. Jean
Jacquot and Marcel Oddon. Paris: Editions du Centre
National de la Recherche Scientifique, 1964. 1-10.

Hadas, Moses, ed. Essential Works of Stoicism. New York:
Bantam, 1965.

---, ed. and trans. The Stoic Philosophy of Seneca: Essays
and Letters. New York: Doubleday, 1958.

Halifax, George Savile, Marquis of. Works. Ed. Walter Raleigh.
1912. New York: Augustus M. Kelley, 1970.

Hall, Joseph. Heaven upon Earth and Characters of Vertues and
Vices. Ed. Rudolf Kirk. New Brunswick: Rutgers UP, 1948.

---. Works. Ed. Philip Wynter. 10 vols. Oxford: Oxford UP.
1863.

294

Hall, Vernon, Jr. "Julius Caesar: A Play without Political
  Bias." Studies in the English Renaissance Drama. Ed.
  Josephine Waters Bennett, Oscar Cargill, Vernon Hall, Jr.
  New York: New York UP, 1959.

Haller, William. The Rise of Puritanism. New York: Columbia
  UP, 1938.

Hamilton, Gary D. "Irony and Fortune in Sejanus." Studies in
  English Literature, 1500-1900 11 (1971): 265-81.

Harris, William O. Skelton's Magnyfycence and the Cardinal
  Virtue Tradition. Chapel Hill: U of North Carolina P.
  1965.

Hawes, Stephen. The Pastime of Pleasure. Ed. William Edward
  Mead. Early English Text Society os 173. London, 1928.

Haydn, Hiram. The Counter-Renaissance. 1950. Gloucester,
  Massachusetts: Peter Smith, 1966.

Hayes, Thomas W. "The Dialectic of History in Marvell's Horatian Ode." Clio 1, i (1971): 26-36.

Hebel, J. William, Hoyt H. Hudson, et al, eds. Poetry of the
  English Renaissance 1509-1660. New York: Appleton, 1953.

Heiserman, Arthur Ray. Skelton and Satire. Chicago: U of Chicago P, 1961.

Henderson, Sam H. "Neo-Stoic Influence on Elizabethan Formal
  Verse Satire." Studies in English Renaissance Literature.
  Ed. Waldo F. McNeir. Baton Rouge: Louisiana State U,
  1961. 56-86, 217-21.

Henryson, Robert. The Poems and Fables. Ed. H. Harvey Wood.
  1933. Edinburgh: Oliver and Boyd, 1958.

Herbert of Cherbury, Edward Lord. Autobiography. Ed. Sidney
  Lee. London: Routledge, 1886.

---. De Religione Laici. Ed. and trans. Harold R. Hutcheson.
  New Haven: Yale UP, 1944.

Herbert, George. The Works. Ed. F. E. Hutchinson. Oxford:
  Oxford UP, 1941.

Herndl, George C. The High Design: English Renaissance Tragedy and the Natural Law. Lexington: U of Kentucky P,
  1970.

Herrick, Robert. The Poetical Works. Ed. F. W. Moorman. 1921.
  London: Oxford UP, 1947.

Heywood, Thomas. A Woman Killed with Kindness. Ed. R. W. Van
  Fossen. The Revels Plays. Cambridge, Massachusetts:
  Harvard UP, 1961.

Hicks, Robert Drew. "Seneca." Encyclopedia Britannica. 1910
  ed.

---. "Stoics." Encyclopedia Britannica. 1910 ed.

Higgins, Michael. "The Development of the Senecal Man."
Review of English Studies 23 (1947): 24-33.

Highet, Gilbert. The Classical Tradition. Greek and Roman
Influences on Western Literature. New York: Oxford UP,
1949.

---. Juvenal the Satirist. Oxford: Oxford UP, 1955.

Hinman, Robert B. Abraham Cowley's World of Order. Cambridge,
Massachusetts: Harvard UP, 1960.

Hobbes, Thomas. Leviathan. Ed. Michael Oakeshott. Oxford:
Basil Blackwell, 1946.

Hoccleve, Thomas. The Regement of Princes. Ed. Frederick J.
Furnivall. Early English Text Society 72. London, 1897.

Holroyd, Michael. Lytton Strachey: A Critical Biography. 2
vols. New York: Holt, 1968.

Hooker, Richard. Works. Ed. John Keble. 3 vols. 1888. New
York: Burt Franklin, 1970.

Hoopes, Robert. Right Reason in the English Renaissance. Cambridge, Massachusetts: Harvard UP, 1962.

Horace. The Satires and Epistles. Trans. Smith Palmer Bovie.
Chicago: U of Chicago P, 1959.

Horowitz, Maryanne Cline. "Natural Law as the Foundation
for an Autonomous Ethic: Pierre Charron's De la Sagesse."
Studies in the Renaissance 21 (1974): 204-27.

Hughes, Merritt Y. "Virgilian Allegory and The Faerie Queene."
PMLA 44 (1929): 696-705.

Huizinga, Johan. The Waning of the Middle Ages. Trans. F.
Hopman. London: Edward Arnold, 1924.

Jacquot, Jean. George Chapman (1559-1643): Sa Vie, Sa Poesie,
Son Théâtre, Sa Pensée. Annales de L'Université de Lyon,
Lettres, 3^me Serie, Fasc. 19. Paris: Societé D'Edition
Les Belles Lettres, 1951.

---. "Religion et raison d'état dans l'oeuvre de Fulke Greville." Etudes Anglaises 5 (1952): 211-22.

---. "Sénèque, la Renaissance et nous." Les Tragédies de Sénèque et la Théâtre de la Renaissance. Ed. Jean Jacquot
and Marcel Oddon. Paris: Editions du Centre National de
la Recherche Scientifique, 1964. 271-307.

Jackson, W. T. H. The Literature of the Middle Ages. New
York: Columbia UP, 1960.

Jefferson, Bernard L. Chaucer and the Consolation of Philosophy of Boethius. Princeton: Princeton UP, 1917.

Johnson, Samuel. Works. Ed. G. Birkbeck Hill. 11 vols. 1825. New York: AMS Library, 1970. Vol. 7.

Jonson, Ben. Works. Ed. Charles H. Herford and Percy Simpson. 11 vols. Oxford: Oxford UP, 1925-52.

Kaske, R. E. "Sapientia et Fortitudo as the Controlling Theme of Beowulf." Studies in Philology 55 (1958): 423-56.

---. "The Sigemund-Heremod and Hama-Hygelac Passages in Beowulf." PMLA 74 (1959): 489-94.

Kastner, L. E. and H. B. Charlton, eds. The Poetical Works of Sir William Alexander, Earl of Stirling. Manchester: Manchester UP, 1921.

Kay, W. David. "The Christian Wisdom of Ben Jonson's 'On My First Sonne.'" Studies in English Literature, 1500-1900 11 (1971): 125-36.

Keeton, George W. Shakespeare's Legal and Political Background. London: Isaac Pitman, 1967.

Kemble, J. M., trans. The Poetry of the Codex Vercellensis. London: Aelfric Society, 1843.

Klaeber, Fr., ed. Beowulf and the Fight at Finnsburg. 3rd ed. Boston: D. C. Heath, 1941.

Knott, John R. "Milton's Heaven." PMLA 85 (1970): 487-95.

Kristeller, Paul Oskar. The Classics and Renaissance Thought. Cambridge, Massachusetts: Harvard UP, 1955.

---. "The Platonic Academy of Florence." Renaissance News 14 (1961): 147-59.

Kyd, Thomas. Works. Ed. Frederick S. Boas. Oxford: Oxford UP, 1901.

Lanson, Gustave and Paul Tuffrau. Manuel D'Histoire de la Littérature Française. 1931. Paris: Hachette, 1935.

Lapp, John. "Racine est-il Sénèquien?" Les Tragédies de Sénèque et le Théâtre de la Renaissance. Ed. Jean Jacquot and Marcel Oddon. Paris: Editions du Centre National de la Recherche Scientifique, 1964. 127-38.

Lathrop, Henry Burrowes. Translations from the Classics into English from Caxton to Chapman, 1477-1620. University of Wisconsin Studies in Language and Literature 35. Madison: U of Wisconsin P, 1933.

Lebègue, Raymond. "Christianisme et Libertinage en France." Les Tragédies de Sénèque et le Théâtre de la Renaissance. Ed. Jean Jacquot and Marcel Oddon. Paris: Editions du Centre National de la Recherche Scientifique, 1964. 87-91.

Leech, Clifford. "'The Atheist's Tragedy' as a Dramatic Comment on Chapman's Bussy Plays." Journal of English and Germanic Philology 52 (1953): 525-30.

Lemmi, Charles William. "The Symbolism of the Classical Episodes in The Faerie Queene." Philological Quarterly 8 (1929): 270-87.

Levi, Anthony, S. J. French Moralists: The Theory of the Passions 1585 to 1649. Oxford: Oxford UP, 1964.

Levitsky, Ruth M. "The Elements Were So Mix'd." PMLA 88 (1973): 240-45.

---. "Rightly to be Great." Shakespeare Studies 1. Ed. J. Leeds Barroll. Cincinnati: U of Cincinnati P, 1965.

Lewalski, Barbara Kiefer. "Milton: Political Beliefs and Polemical Methods, 1659-60." PMLA 74 (1959): 191-202.

Lewis, C. S. English Literature in the Sixteenth Century Excluding Drama. Oxford: Oxford UP, 1954.

Lipsius, Justus. Two Bookes of Constancie. Trans. Sir John Stradling. Ed. Rudolf Kirk. New Brunswick: Rutgers UP, 1939.

Locke, John. An Essay Concerning Human Understanding. Ed. John W. Yolton. 2 vols. Everyman's Library 332. London, 1961. Vol. 1. 9-43.

---. Two Tracts on Government. Ed. Philip Abrams. Cambridge: Cambridge UP, 1967.

---. Two Treatises of Government. Ed. Peter Laslett. New York: New American Library, 1965.

Lodge, Thomas. Rosalynde. Ed. W. W. Greg. 1907. Freeport, New York: Books for Libraries P, 1970.

Long, A. A. Hellenistic Philosophy: Stoics, Epicureans, Sceptics. New York: Scribner's 1974.

Lovejoy, Arthur O., George Boas et al. A Documentary History of Primitivism and Related Ideas in Antiquity. Baltimore: Johns Hopkins UP, 1935.

Lovejoy, Arthur O. "'Nature' as Norm in Tertullian." Essays in the History of Ideas. New York: George Braziller, 1955.

---. The Great Chain of Being. Cambridge, Massachusetts: Harvard UP, 1942.

Lucas, Frank Laurence. Seneca and Elizabethan Tragedy. Cambridge: Cambridge UP, 1922.

Lydgate, John. Fall of Princes. Ed. Henry Bergen. 4 vols. Early English Text Society es 121-24. London: Oxford UP, 1924.

Lyly, John. Works. Ed. R. Warwick Bond. 1902. 3 vols. Oxford: Oxford UP, 1967. Vol. 2.

Mack, Maynard, ed. An Essay on Man. By Alexander Pope. Vol. 3, part 1 of Poems. Twickenham Edition. New Haven: Yale UP,

1950.

---. The Garden and the City: Retirement and Politics in the
Later Poetry of Pope, 1731-1743. Toronto: U of Toronto P,
1969.

---. King Lear in Our Time. Berkeley: U of California P, 1965.

Maclean, Hugh N. "Fulke Greville: Kingship and Sovereignty."
Huntington Library Quarterly 16 (1953): 237-71.

---. "Fulke Greville on War." Huntington Library Quarterly
21 (1958): 95-109.

---. "Greville's 'Poetic,'" Studies in Philology 61 (1964):
170-91.

Madsen, William G. "The Idea of Nature in Milton's Poetry."
Three Studies in the Renaissance. New Haven: Yale UP,
1958. 185-283.

Major, John M. Sir Thomas Elyot and Renaissance Humanism.
Lincoln: U of Nebraska P, 1964.

Malone, Kemp, ed. Deor. Methuen's Old English Library. London,
1933.

---. "On Deor 14-17." Studies in Heroic Legend and in Current
Speech. Ed. Stefan Einarsson and Norman E. Eliason.
Copenhagen: Rosenkilde and Bagger, 1959. 142-57.

---, trans. Ten Old English Poems Put into Modern English
Alliterative Verse. Baltimore: Johns Hopkins UP, 1941.

---. "The Old English Period." A Literary History of England.
Ed. Albert C. Baugh. New York: Appleton. 1948. Bk. 1 pt.
1.

Manly, John Matthews, ed. Specimens of the Pre-Shaksperean
Drama. 2 vols. 1897. New York: Dover, 1967.

Marburg, Clara. Sir William Temple: A Seventeenth Century
"Libertin." New Haven: Yale UP, 1932.

Mark, Henry L. "The Good Life and the Aging Brain." The Johns
Hopkins Magazine 19 (1968): 21-25.

Marston, John. The Plays. Ed. H. Harvey Wood. 3 vols. Edinburgh: Oliver and Boyd, 1934.

---. The Scourge of Villanie (1599). Ed. G. B. Harrison.
The Bodley Head Quartos. London: John Lane, 1925.

Marvell, Andrew. The Poems and Letters. Ed. H. M. Margoliouth. 2 vols. Oxford: Oxford UP, 1927.

Mason, H. A. Humanism and Poetry in the Early Tudor Period.
London: Routledge, 1959.

Mates, Benson. Stoic Logic. Berkeley: U of California P, 1961.

Mayo, Thomas Franklin. Epicurus in England (1650-1725). Dallas:

Southwest P, 1934.

Mazzeo, Joseph A. "Cromwell as Machiavellian Prince in Marvell's 'An Horatian Ode.'" Journal of the History of Ideas 21 (1960): 1-17.

McEuen, Kathryn Anderson. Classical Influence upon the Tribe of Ben. Cedar Rapids, Iowa: Torch P, 1939.

McNeill, William H. The Rise of the West. Chicago: U of Chicago P, 1963.

Mendell, Clarence W. Our Seneca. New Haven: Yale UP, 1941.

Miller, Clarence H. "Some Medieval Elements and Structural Unity in Erasmus' The Praise of Folly." Renaissance Quarterly 27 (1974): 499-511.

Milton, John. The Works. Ed. Frank Allen Patterson. 18 vols. New York: Columbia UP, 1931.

Miner, Earl. "Patterns of Stoicism in Thought and Prose Styles, 1530-1700." PMLA 85 (1970): 1023-34.

Minor Poets of the Seventeenth Century. Ed. R. G. Howarth. Everyman's Library 873. London: Dent, 1931.

The Mirror for Magistrates. Ed. Lily B. Campbell. Cambridge: Cambridge UP, 1938.

Mommsen, Theodor. "St. Augustine and the Christian Idea of Progress." Medieval and Renaissance Studies. Ed. E. F. Rice, Jr. Ithaca: Cornell UP, 1959.

Montaigne, Michel de. The Essayes of Michael Lord of Montaigne. Trans. John Florio. Everyman's Library 440. 1910. London: Dent, 1928.

More, Thomas. Utopia and a Dialogue of Comfort. Ed. John Warrington. Everyman's Library 461. 1910. London: Dent, 1951.

---. Utopia. Ed. Edward Surtz, S. J. New Haven and London: Yale UP, 1964.

Morel, Jacques. "'Hercule sur l'OEta' et les Dramaturges Français." Les Tragédies de Sénèque et le Théâtre de la Renaissance. Ed. Jean Jacquot and Marcel Oddon. Paris: Editions du Centre National de la Recherche Scientifique, 1964. 93-111.

Muller, Herbert J. Freedom in the Ancient World. New York: Harper, 1961.

---. Freedom in the Western World. New York: Harper, 1963.

Murray, Gilbert. The Stoic Philosophy. Conway Memorial Lecture. London: Putnam, 1921.

Muscatine, Charles. Chaucer and the French Tradition: A Study in Style and Meaning. Berkeley: U of California P, 1957.

---. "Form, Texture, and Meaning in Chaucer's Knight's Tale."
PMLA 65 (1950): 911-29.

Musgrove, S. The Universe of Robert Herrick. Auckland University College Bulletin 38. English Series 4. Auckland:
The Pelorus Press, 1950.

Nash, Jerry C. "Rabelais and Stoic Portrayal." Studies in
the Renaissance 21 (1974): 63-82.

Neilson, W. A. and K. G. T. Webster, eds. Chief British Poets
of the Fourteenth and Fifteenth Centuries. Boston:
Houghton, 1916.

Nitze, William A. "Vertu as Patriotism in Corneille's Horace."
PMLA 67 (1952): 1167-72.

Norena, Carlos G. Juan Luis Vives. International Archives of
the History of Ideas 34. The Hague: Martinus Nijhoff,
1970.

Oates, Whitney J., ed. The Stoic and Epicurean Philosophers.
New York: Random, 1940.

Ong, Walter J., S. J. "Tudor Writings on Rhetoric." Studies
in the Renaissance 15 (1968): 39-69.

Ornstein, Robert. "The Atheist's Tragedy and Renaissance Naturalism," Studies in Philology 61 (1954): 194-207.

---. "Donne, Montaigne and Natural Law." Journal of English
and Germanic Philology 55 (1956): 213-29.

---. The Moral Vision of Jacobean Tragedy. Madison: U of Wisconsin P, 1960.

Otway, Thomas. The Works. Ed. J. C. Ghosh. 2 vols. Oxford:
Oxford UP, 1932. Vol. 2.

Owst, Gerald Robert. Literature and the Pulpit in Medieval
England. Cambridge: Cambridge UP, 1933.

Palmer, Ralph Graham. Seneca's De Remediis Fortuitorum and the
Elizabethans. Institute of Elizabethan Studies 1. Chicago: U of Chicago P, 1953.

The Paradise of Dainty Devices (1576-1606). Ed. Hyder Edward
Rollins. Cambridge, Massachusetts: Harvard UP, 1927.

Parnassus Biceps (1656). Ed. George Thorn-Drury. London,
1927.

Pastore-Stocchi, Manlio. "Un Chapitre D'Histoire Littéraire
aux XIVe et XVe Siècles. 'Seneca Poeta Tragicus.'"
Les Tragédies de Sénèque et le Théâtre de la Renaissance.
Ed. Jean Jacquot and Marcel Oddon. Paris: Editions du
Centre National de la Recherche Scientifique, 1964. 11-
36.

Patch, Howard R. The Goddess Fortuna in Mediaeval Literature.
Cambridge, Massachusetts: Harvard UP, 1927.

---. The Tradition of Boethius: A Study of His Importance in Medieval Culture. Oxford: Oxford UP, 1935.

Perkinson, Richard H. "Nature and the Tragic Hero in Chapman's Bussy Plays." Modern Language Quarterly 3 (1942): 263-85.

Perlette, John M. "Anthony Ascham's 'Of Marriage.'" English Literary Renaissance 3 (1973): 299.

Plato. Works. Trans. B. Jowett. 4 vols. 1871-92. New York: Dial Press, n. d. Vol. 3.

Plutarch. "On Tranquillity of Mind." Trans. W. C. Helmbold. Moralia. Loeb Classical Library. 15 vols. 1939. Cambridge, Massachusetts: Harvard UP, 1962. Vol. 6.

---. "Consolation to His Wife." Trans. Philip H. De Lacy and Benedict Einarson. Moralia. Loeb. 15 vols. 1939. Cambridge, Massachusetts: Harvard UP, 1959. Vol. 7.

Presson, Robert K. "Boethius, King Lear, and 'Maystresse Philosophie.'" Journal of English and Germanic Philology 64 (1965): 406-24.

---. "Wrestling with this World: A View of George Chapman." PMLA 84 (1969), 44-50.

Raab, Felix. The English Face of Machiavelli: A Changing Interpretation 1500-1700. London: Routledge and Kegan Paul, 1964.

Raitiere, Martin N. "More's Utopia and The City of God." Studies in the Renaissance 20 (1973): 144-68.

Ralegh, Sir Walter. Works. 8 vols. Oxford: Oxford UP, 1829. Vol. 2.

Rand, Edward Kennard. Founders of the Middle Ages. Cambridge, Massachusetts: Harvard UP, 1928.

Rebholz, Ronald A. The Life of Fulke Greville First Lord Brooke. London: Oxford UP, 1971.

Rebhorn, Wayne A. "The Metamorphoses of Moria: Structure and Meaning in The Praise of Folly." PMLA 89 (1974): 463-76.

Rees, Ennis. The Tragedies of George Chapman: Renaissance Ethics in Action. Cambridge, Massachusetts: Harvard UP. 1954.

Rees, Joan. Fulke Greville, Lord Brooke, 1554-1628: A Critical Biography. Berkeley: U of California P, 1971.

Reese, Max M. The Cease of Majesty: A Study of Shakespeare's History Plays. New York: St. Martin's, 1961.

Ribner, Irving. Jacobean Tragedy: The Quest for Moral Order. New York: Barnes, 1962.

Richardson, Samuel. Clarissa. 4 vols. Everyman's Library 882.

London: Dent, 1932.

Rochester, John Wilmot, Earl of. The Complete Poems. Ed. David M. Vieth. New Haven: Yale UP, 1968.

Roper, Alan H. "Boethius and the Three Fates of Beowulf." Philological Quarterly 41 (1962): 386-400.

Rostvig, Maren-Sofie. The Happy Man: Studies in the Metamorphoses of a Classical Ideal. 2 vols. Oslo Studies in English. Oslo: Akademisk Forlag, 1954 and 1958.

Sabine, George Holland. A History of Political Theory. New York: Holt, 1937.

Saltonstall, Wye. Picturae Loquentes. Luttrell Reprints 1. Oxford: Oxford UP, 1946.

Sams, Henry W. "Anti-Stoicism in Seventeenth and Early Eighteenth-Century England." Studies in Philology 41 (1944), 65-78.

Saunders, Jason Lewis. Justus Lipsius: The Philosophy of Renaissance Stoicism. New York: Liberal Arts P, 1955.

Schoeck, R. J. "Recent Scholarship in the History of Law." Renaissance Quarterly 20 (1967): 279-91.

Schoell, Franck L. Etudes sur L'Humanisme Continental en Angleterre à la Fin de la Renaissance. Paris: Champion, 1926.

Schofield, William Henry. English Literature from the Norman Conquest to Chaucer. London: Macmillan, 1925.

Schwartz, Elias. "Seneca, Homer, and Chapman's Bussy D'Ambois." Journal of English and Germanic Philology 56 (1957): 163-76.

---. "Chapman's Renaissance Man: Byron Reconsidered." Journal of English and Germanic Philology 58 (1959): 613-26.

Secular Lyrics of the XIVth and XVth Centuries. Ed. Rossell Hope Robbins. Oxford: Oxford UP, 1952.

Seebohm, Frederic. The Oxford Reformers. 2nd ed. London: Longmans, Green, 1869.

Selden, John. Table Talk. Ed. Samuel Harvey Reynolds. Oxford: Oxford UP, 1892.

Seliger, M. "Locke's Natural Law and the Foundation of Politics." Journal of the History of Ideas 24 (1963): 337-54.

Seneca, Lucius Annaeus. Epistulae Morales. Trans. Richard M. Gummere. Loeb Classical Library. 3 vols. London: Heinemann, 1917.

---. Moral Essays. Trans. John W. Basore. Loeb. 3 vols. 1928. Cambridge, Massachusetts: Harvard UP, 1958. 3 vols.

---. <u>Tragedies</u>. Trans. Frank Justus Miller and Ella Isabel Harris. <u>The Complete Roman Drama</u>. Ed. George Eckel Duckworth. 2 vols. New York: Random, 1942. Vol. 2.

Shadwell, Thomas. <u>The Complete Works</u>. Ed. Montague Summers. 5 vols. London: Fortune P, 1927. Vol. 4.

Shakespeare, William. <u>The Complete Works</u>. Ed. George Lyman Kittredge. Boston: Ginn, 1936.

Sidgwick, Henry. <u>Outlines of the History of Ethics</u>. 5th ed. London: Macmillan, 1922.

Sidney, Sir Philip. <u>Poems</u>. Ed. John Drinkwater. Muses Library. London: Routledge, 1910.

---. <u>The Complete Works</u>. Ed. Albert Feuillerat. 4 vols. 1912. Cambridge: Cambridge UP, 1939.

<u>Silver Poets of the Sixteenth Century</u>. Ed. Gerald Bullett. Everyman's Library 985. 1947. London: Dent, 1949.

Simmonds, James D. <u>Masques of God: Form and Theme in the Poetry of Henry Vaughan</u>. Pittsburgh: U of Pittsburgh P, 1972.

Sirluck, Ernest. "Introduction." <u>The Complete Prose Works of John Milton</u>. New Haven: Yale UP, 1959. Vol. 2.

Skelton, John. <u>The Complete Poems</u>. Ed. Philip Henderson. 2nd ed. London: Dent, 1948.

Sonnenschein, E. A. "Stoicism in English Literature." <u>Contemporary Review</u> 124 (1923): 355-65.

Sophocles. <u>Antigone</u>. Trans. R. C. Jebb. <u>The Complete Greek Drama</u>. Ed. Whitney J. Oates and Eugene O'Neill, Jr. 2 vols. New York: Random, 1938. Vol. 1.

Southwell, Robert. <u>The Poems</u>. Ed. James. H. McDonald and Nancy P. Brown. Oxford: Oxford UP, 1967.

Spaeth, J. Duncan, ed. and trans. <u>Old English Poetry</u>. Princeton: Princeton UP, 1927.

Spencer, Theodore. <u>Death and Elizabethan Tragedy</u>. 1936. New York: Pageant Books, 1960.

---. <u>Shakespeare and the Nature of Man</u>. New York: Macmillan, 1942.

Spenser, Edmund. <u>Poetical Works</u>. Ed. J. C. Smith and E. De Selincourt. 1912. London: Oxford UP, 1940.

Sprat, Thomas. <u>The History of the Royal Society of London (1667)</u>. Facsimile of first edition. Ed. Jackson I. Cope and Harold Whitmore Jones. St. Louis: Washington U, 1958.

Stewart, Hugh Fraser. <u>Boethius: An Essay</u>. Edinburgh: William Blackwood, 1891.

Stollman, Samuel S. "Milton's Samson and the Jewish Tradition."

Milton Studies 3 (1971), 185-200.

Strathmann, E. A.  Sir Walter Ralegh: A Study in Elizabethan Skepticism.  New York: Columbia UP, 1951.

Summers, Joseph H.  George Herbert: His Religion and Art.  Cambridge, Massachusetts: Harvard UP, 1968.

Surrey, Henry Howard, Earl of.  Poems.  Ed. Emrys Jones.  Oxford: Oxford UP, 1964.

Surtz, Edward L., S. J.  "The Defence of Pleasure in More's 'Utopia'".  Studies in Philology 46 (1949): 99-112.

---.  "Epicurus in Utopia."  ELH 16 (1949): 89-103.

---.  "Logic in Utopia."  Philological Quarterly 29 (1950): 389-401.

---.  The Praise of Pleasure: Philosophy, Education, and Communism in More's "Utopia."  Cambridge, Massachusetts: Harvard UP, 1957.

Sutherland, James.  English Literature of the Late Seventeenth Century.  Oxford: Oxford UP, 1969.

Sutherland, Raymond Carter.  "The Meaning of Eorlscipe in Beowulf."  PMLA 70 (1955): 1133-42.

Swift, Jonathan.  Gulliver's Travels.  Ed. Herbert Davis.  The Prose Works.  Oxford: Basil Blackwell, 1959.

Taylor, Jeremy.  The Whole Works.  Ed. Reginald Heber.  15 vols. 1822.  Rev. Charles Page Eden.  London, 1850.  Vol. 3.

Temple, Sir William.  The Early Essays and Romances with the Life and Character of Sir William Temple by his Sister Lady Giffard.  Ed. G. C. Moore Smith.  Oxford:  Oxford UP, 1930.

---.  Five Miscellaneous Essays.  Ed. Samuel Holt Monk.  Ann Arbor: U of Michigan P, 1963.

---.  The Works.  1814.  New York: Greenwood Press, 1968.

Thomson, Patricia.  Sir Thomas Wyatt and His Background.  Stanford: Stanford UP, 1964.

---.  "Sir Thomas Wyatt: Classical Philosophy and English Humanism."  Huntington Library Quarterly 25 (1961/62), 79-96.

---.  "Wyatt's Boethian Ballade."  Review of English Studies 15 (1964), 262-7.

Tierney, Brian.  "Natura id est Deus: A Case of Juristic Pantheism."  Journal of the History of Ideas 24 (1963), 307-22.

---.  Rev. of Les Juristes Suisses à Bologne by S. et S. Stelling-Michaud.  Renaissance News 14 (1961): 99-100.

Tillyard, E. M. W.  The Elizabethan World Picture. London:

Chatto and Windus, 1950.

Tottel's Miscellany (1557). Ed. Hyder Edward Rollins. Cambridge, Massachusetts: Harvard UP, 1928.

Tourneur, Cyril. The Atheist's Tragedy, or, The Honest Man's Revenge. Ed. Irving Ribner. Cambridge, Massachusetts: Harvard UP, 1964.

Ulreich, John C., Jr. "A Paradise Within: The Fortunate Fall in Paradise Lost." Journal of the History of Ideas 32 (1971): 351-66.

Underwood, Dale. Etherege and the Seventeenth-Century Comedy of Manners. New Haven: Yale UP, 1957.

Ure, Peter. "Fulke Greville's Dramatic Characters." Review of English Studies ns 1 (1950): 308-23.

---. "John Marston's Sophonisba: a Reconsideration." Durham U Journal 41 ns 10 (1949-50): 81-90.

Vaughan, Henry. The Complete Poetry. Ed. French Fogle. Anchor AC-7. Garden City, New York: Doubleday, 1964.

---. The Works. Ed. Leonard Cyril Martin. 2 vols. Oxford: Oxford UP, 1914.

Vickers, Brian. Francis Bacon and Renaissance Prose. New York: Cambridge UP, 1968.

Waith, Eugene M. The Herculean Hero in Marlowe, Chapman, Shakespeare and Dryden. New York: Columbia UP, 1962.

Wallace, John M. Destiny His Choice: The Loyalism of Andrew Marvell. New York: Cambridge UP, 1968.

Walton, Izaak. The Compleat Angler. Ed. Geoffrey Keynes. The Modern Library. New York: Random, 1939.

Webster, John. The Complete Works. Ed. F. L. Lucas. 4 vols. London: Chatto and Windus, 1927.

Wenley, R. M. Stoicism and Its Influence. Boston: Marshall Jones, 1924.

West, Michael. "Spenser and the Renaissance Ideal of Christian Heroism." PMLA 88 (1973): 1013-1032.

Whallon, William. "The Idea of God in Beowulf." PMLA 80 (1965): 19-23.

Whitehead, Alfred North. Science and the Modern World. New York: Macmillan, 1925.

Wieler, John William. George Chapman: The Effect of Stoicism upon His Tragedies. New York: Columbia UP, 1949.

Williams, Blanche Colton, ed. Gnomic Poetry in Anglo-Saxon. New York: Columbia UP, 1914.

Williamson, George. The Senecan Amble: A Study in Prose Form from Bacon To Collier. London: Faber and Faber, 1951.

Winterbottom, John A. "Stoicism in Dryden's Tragedies." Journal of English and Germanic Philology 61 (1962): 868-83.

Wood, Neal. "Some Common Aspects of the Thought of Seneca and Machiavelli." Renaissance Quarterly 21 (1968): 11-23.

Woodhouse, A. S. P. Puritanism and Liberty. London: Dent, 1950.

Wyatt, Thomas. Collected Poems. Ed. Kenneth Muir. Muses Library. London: Routledge and Kegan Paul, 1949.

Zanta, Léontine. La Renaissance du Stoïcisme au XVIe Siècle. Paris: Champion, 1914.

Zeller, E. The Stoics, Epicureans, and Sceptics. Trans. Oswald J. Reichel. London: Longmans, 1870.